The Demise
of the Library School

The Demise of the Library School

Personal Reflections on Professional Education in the Modern Corporate University

By Richard J. Cox

Library Juice Press
Duluth, Minnesota

Copyright Richard J. Cox, 2010

Published in 2010 by Library Juice Press
PO Box 3320
Duluth, MN 55803
http://libraryjuicepress.com

This book is printed on acid-free paper that meets all present ANSI standards for archival preservation.

Library of Congress Cataloging-in-Publication Data

Cox, Richard J.
 The demise of the library school : personal reflections on professional education in the modern corporate university / Richard J. Cox.
      p. cm.
 Summary: "A series of meditations on critical themes relating to the education of librarians, archivists, and other information professionals, playing off of other commentators analyzing the nature of higher education and its problems and aims"--Provided by publisher.
 Includes bibliographical references and index.
 ISBN 978-1-936117-18-5 (alk. paper)
1. Library education. 2. Library schools--Curricula. 3. Archives--Study and teaching (Higher) 4. Information science--Study and teaching. 5. Professional education. I. Title.
 Z668.C87 2010
 020.7--dc22

                                                            2010006381

Table of Contents

	Prologue	vii
1.	Setting the Scene	1
2.	Reading, Writing, and the Old Library School	25
3.	A Personal Interlude: Loving Books, Without Apology	55
4.	The Spectacle of the Corporate University	81
5.	Rethinking the Traditional School (and Values)	115
6.	Archival Studies: A Case Study	141
7.	Looking for Our Way (Reading and Writing) in Professional Schools	181
8.	Teaching in the Professional School in the Changing University	225
	Epilogue	265
	Works Cited	281
	Index	325
	About the Author	335

Prologue

Introduction. Librarians, later types of information professionals, and faculty in library and information science schools have written – since their origins in the late nineteenth century amid a growing sense of identity – critiques, complaints, and confessions about their education (its benefits and pitfalls). This genre of academic and professional writing, certainly not unique to library and information science, has concentrated on predictable issues such as the relationship between academic and practitioner expectations, the knowledge supporting particular fields and how that knowledge is generated, the implications of information technologies, and the changing identity of librarians and other information professionals.[1] Some commentators have focused on specific areas, such as cataloguing and classification, to consider the gaps occurring between what practitioners think they need taught to them and what educators are offering in the classroom.[2] Others have considered how these schools are using various competency statements compiled by professional associations for the design of their curriculum.[3] In more recent years, as issues such as political correctness, gender politics, and minority rights have emerged (among many complex and challenging issues), some faculty members have sought to add to the professional agenda courses on social responsibility and ethics.[4]

---

[1] Lawrence W.S. Auld, "Seven Imperatives for Library Education," *Library Journal* 115 (May 1990): 55-59; Andrew Dillon and April Norris, "Crying Wolf: An Examination and Reconsideration of the Perception of Crisis in LIS Education," *Journal of Education for Library and Information Science* 46, no. 4 (2005): 280-298; and R. P. Holley, "The Ivory Tower as Preparation for the Trenches," *College and Research Libraries News* 64, no. 3 (March 2003): 172-175 as windows into such matters.

[2] For example, Janet Swan Hill, "What Else Do You Need to Know? Practical Skills for Catalogers and Managers," *Cataloging and Classification Quarterly* 34 (2002): 245-261.

[3] June Lester and Connie Van Fleet, "Use of Professional Competencies and Standards Documents for Curriculum Planning in Schools of Library and Information Studies Education," *Journal of Education for Library and Information Science* 49 (2008): 43-69.

[4] J. V. Carmichael and Shontz, M.L. "A 'Despised' 'Semi-Profession': Perceptions of Curricular Content Relating to Gender and Social Issues Among 1993 MLIS/MLS Graduates," *Journal of Education for Library and Information Science* 38(2)

And we are not even getting started in considering the various problems, perils, possibilities, and promises posed by the professional schools for librarians, archivists, and other information experts commencing in the form of the library school that now seems to have existed so distant in the past. Many segments of the information professions have developed, through professional associations, their own individual certification programs (archivists represent just one example), sometimes with tenuous connections to the graduate programs offered by library, library and information science, and information schools. These changes have occurred in a little less than a generation. Issues such as intellectual property and digitization, one pushing the other, have threatened to overwhelm other topics in the education of information professionals, in seemingly contradictory ways just as the World Wide Web brings promises (usually overstated) of unprecedented access to banks of information (some of which were more like closed vaults, although now threatened to be closed again by corporate lawyers laboring for publishers and Google).

Information technology has been a major source of concern and change for library and information science schools, often pushing older curricular aspects to the side, moving up issues about computer competencies and literacy ahead of others, and placing such professional schools on the constantly slippery slope of hitting a moving target and fueling tensions between educators and practitioners in an area where resolution has never been achieved (the perennial gap between theory and practice).[5] Perhaps less successful have been the efforts to diversify, in terms of race and ethnicity, the faculty and curriculum of library and information science schools, although the intensity of activity here has increased.[6]

Spring 1997: 98-115; Suzanne Hildenbrand, "The Information Age Versus Gender Equity?: Technology and Values in Education for Library and Information Science," *Library Trends* 47, no. 4 (1999): 669-685.

[5] See, for example, Andrew Dillon and April Norris, "Crying Wolf: An Examination and Reconsideration of the Perception of Crisis in LIS Education," *Journal of Education for Library and Information Science* 46, no. 4 (Fall 2005): 280-298. Thanks to Tim Schlak for the reference.

[6] A sense of such issues can be gained from Denice Adkins, " Latino Librarians on Becoming LIS Educators: An Exploratory Investigation of the Barriers in Recruiting Latino Faculty," *Journal of Education for Library and Information Science*, 45 (Spring 2004): 149-161; Claudia J. Gollop, "Library and Information Science Education: Preparing Librarians for a Multicultural Society," *College and Research*

PROLOGUE

Everyone knows that an information professional's work is not static, but no one probably foresaw the speed of such change. It is a regular feature in professional journals for librarians, archivists, and other of their colleagues to write accounts about why their pre-professional education is inadequate for the era they now work in.[7] The emphasis is often on the practical, what has utility on the job, while what is lost is a broader historical sense of librarianship and the information professions (a gap that perhaps makes it impossible to ascertain fully what is right or wrong with such professional education). Christine Pawley notes that "LIS faculty whose research specialty is history seem to be a vanishing breed," and that "history seems in general to have been pushed to the margins of LIS scholarship."[8] Reasons for this include a simple disinterest by faculty, demands for other courses such as in information technology, the sense of needing to offer courses with practical implications, and limitations in the study of library and information science history. What is not a regular feature are assessments of the changes facing these professional schools themselves (there are complaints and charges, but this is different than assessments). In fact, what we have neglected are the implications of a major shift in the nature of the university for professional schools in library and information science.

Commentaries about the transformation of higher education into a corporate model have been offered for a long time, from both within and from without the university. There is a specific date when we can mark the shift to the corporate university. Stephen Shapin, in his major assessment of

---

Libraries 60, no. 4 (1999): 385-395; and Christine Pawley, "Unequal Legacies: Race and Multiculturalism in the LIS Curriculum," *Library Quarterly* 76 (April 2006): 149-168. I am indebted to Elisabeth Rodriquez for these citations.

[7] See, for example, Mark Dimunation, "Red Wine and White Carpets: What We Didn't Learn in Library School, or When the Dog and Pony Goes Bad," *RBM: A Journal of Rare Books, Manuscripts, and Cultural Heritage*, vol. 7, no. 1 (2006): 73-84. I am indebted to Kate Colligan for this reference.

[8] Christine Pawley, "History in the Library and Information Science Curriculum: Outline of a Debate," *Libraries & Culture* 40, no. 3 (Summer 2005): 223-224. For other essays with a similar perspective see Donald G. Davis, Jr., "Ebla to the Electronic Dream: The Role of Historical Perspectives in Professional Education," *Journal of Education for Library and Information Science* 39, no.3 (Summer 1998): 228-235 and Wayne A. Wiegand, "Tunnel Vision and Blind Spots: What the Past Tells Us About the Present; Reflections on the Twentieth-Century History of American Librarianship," *The Library Quarterly* 69, no.1 (January 1999): 1-32. I am thankful to Robert Riter for these references.

the nature of science as a vocation, mentions President Dwight Eisenhower's farewell address on January 17, 1961 where Eisenhower lamented the negative influences on the political system by the military-industrial complex, and also pointed out the potential for corrupting scientific research. Eisenhower stated, "The free university, historically the fountainhead of free ideas and scientific discovery, has experienced a revolution in the conduct of research. Partly because of the huge costs involved, a government contract becomes virtually a substitute for intellectual curiosity. For every old blackboard there are now hundreds of new electronic computers. The prospect of domination of the nation's scholars by Federal employment, project allocation, and the power of money is ever present – and is gravely to be regarded."[9] Predictions about the emergence of the modern corporate university, where higher education is run like a business, driven by the potential prominent sources of revenue (ranging from big government such as alluded to by Eisenhower to tuition paid by students or their sponsors), are not new. However, observers about the library school and its successors the library and information science school and more recently the iSchool (or information school) have tended to look at everything and in every direction except the transformation of the university, the home of these schools.

Purpose of This Volume. My intention with this volume is to try to place library and information science professional schools and their role and future in the debate about the modern corporate university. What I am offering is not a study but a series of personal observations reacting to the growing scholarly literature about higher education. About two decades ago, I began reading regularly books on the topic of higher education, its history, role in society, issues, challenges, and prospects in order to understand my own place and purpose in a professional school in a research university and working within a specialization within the information professions (archival studies). This was a personal quest to understand better my own role and responsibilities, partly motivated by a discussion with some colleagues about the seemingly endless stream of university memoranda sending contradictory (at least, this is what it appeared to look like to me) messages about faculty activities. As I expressed frustration with these messages, one of my colleagues indicated that it was up to me to figure out how to interpret them – that we were more like independent entrepreneurs than employees (whether this was true or not, it was enough to set me on a quest

---

[9] Stephen Shapin, *The Scientific Life: A Moral History of a Late Modern Vocation* (Chicago: University of Chicago Press, 2008), p. 81.

PROLOGUE	xi

to think through the nature of faculty work in a professional school). Ironically, this sense of faculty independence is precisely one of the issues the modern corporate university seems committed to change.

Through the years my personal library on higher education grew (who knew that this literature was both so broad and deep?). A few years ago (Fall 2006) I offered a doctoral seminar, under the guise of professional issues, on "Rethinking Professional Education." The aim of this seminar was to introduce, first, doctoral students to the nature, history, and purpose of higher education, with a focus on the American university system. The course had students consider the idea of the university, the role of faculty, the place of professional schools in higher education, the debate about the nature of the modern university, the responsibilities of faculty (scholarship, reading, teaching, writing, and publishing), and challenges to the university's historic mission as played out by new limitations on intellectual property and free speech. The second purpose was to assist doctoral students learn about critical issues confronting Schools of Library and Information Science, giving doctoral students a foundation for understanding both the nature of these schools as well as the research being conducted about the education of librarians, archivists, and other information professionals. After all, the majority of our doctoral students had in mind to be faculty members in such professional schools, so it seemed appropriate to get them thinking about the nature of these schools as soon as possible.

My initial offering of this seminar included a range of doctoral students, from first-year to those who had been in the program for several academic years. What surprised me were the comments made by experienced doctoral students that this was the first time they were hearing much about teaching, tenure, governance, academic freedom, and other issues related to being successful faculty members (and my sense is that this is not unique to my school). The following year, when I became chair of doctoral studies, I transformed this seminar into the framework for the required introductory seminar for doctoral studies; this necessitated adding material about specific elements of our doctoral program and allowed additional exploration about how a former library school, then library and information school, was morphing into an iSchool. Teaching this seminar has allowed me to explore more deeply the nature of professional education in the modern corporate university and much of what appears in this volume originally appeared as a blog entry or discussion board item in the seminar and has been modified due to conversation with my doctoral students (this explains why there is some repetition, but I have allowed this to remain because it generally builds around what I see as critically important issues and attitudes).

The Book's Structure. What follows is a series of what could be better called meditations than chapters on a series of critical themes relating to the education of librarians, archivists, and other information professionals, usually playing off of other commentators analyzing the nature of higher education and its problems and promises. As one of my doctoral students remarked, my chapters provide a forum for allowing many voices to be heard about the state of the modern university, and it is precisely my intention to do this, directing those voices at the professional school in the university. Originally this was an effort to immerse doctoral students, the future faculty members in library and information science schools and iSchools, into the cacophony of opinions about the strengths, weaknesses, challenges, and possibilities for these schools. The purpose of publishing this book is to persuade the faculty and administrators of library and information science schools that they also need to consider the growing commentaries on higher education as a source informing them about the possible future they face. I am sure that the leaders of the iSchool movement would suggest that this is precisely what they are doing; however, the iSchool movement has a long way to go in articulating its mission and approaches (a topic I return to in the epilogue).

Chapter one sets the scene for understanding the purpose of university, debates about this purpose (especially how the university provides some sort of public good), struggles to make the university meaningful, and the changing nature of the university. Much of my initial discussion, reflecting just a portion of the considerable university literature on this topic, considers the efforts to explain (or defend) the role of faculty and how well they are doing. The point is to begin considering how professional schools fit (or don't) in the university, especially as the university is transforming itself, laying a foundation for the following chapters.

The next chapter seeks to examine some of the prominent features, at least features we normally associate with these schools, of the old library school and its faculty – reading, writing, a faith in libraries and books, and our teaching about such matters. I hint at how new scholarship about books and printing (meaning both analog and digital forms of the book) and related issues ought to prompt us to rethink what we do about these topics in our schools (not abandon them, but embrace them with new vigor). The new interdisciplinary approaches to such topics may have a better home in the new iSchools, but that is still uncertain. And how we decide to use distance education approaches, how we view teaching, how well we deal with new accountability and assessment demands, and how

PROLOGUE   xiii

and for whom we write all may depend on how we view books in all their forms, real and yet to be imagined.

There are two chapters where I more directly present my most personal perspectives on critical aspects of the library and information science schools. Chapter three is my reflection on why prospective students for library schools and their successors bring with them strong interests in both books and reading (and by this I mean via the handling of books as artifacts). It is an interest I share, and one that I worry could be lost in the future education of information professionals. What evidence do I have for this? Partly, it is an observation that some of the most compelling assessments on books, their history, the reading of them, and how digital versions still build from the ordered assemblage of their printed versions are mostly coming from individuals outside of the library and information science community. Most important, perhaps, may be that the prediction of the death of the printed book is exaggerated, or at least premature. When looking at the pervasive influence of the World Wide Web and the growing community of e-book reading devices (such as the Kindle), I get nervous that we may stop examining the older printed book and allow it to be taken over as a subject of study by a mix of historians and antiquarians. Besides, I am sure that anyone examining my own book will discover that it is a book about books, as every book can be shown to be. Indeed, an additional glance will demonstrate that this is a book drawing on both print and digital sources, written by someone who on any given day could be found spending nearly equal amounts of time reading a book, browsing on the Web, scratching notes with a pen, or composing on a laptop. I am a transitional figure, floating in the great divide between print and the computer. And I am having fun, not suffering.

The other highly personal chapter concerns the education of archivists, and it is published in this volume as the sixth chapter; I also include this essay in this volume as a means of demonstrating from where I am coming when I write about professional education. In many ways, as will be obvious when reading this chapter, the status, both improved and still shaky in certain aspects, of archival graduate education reflects many of the same issues previously faced by librarians and other information professionals in their own schools. There are challenges of satisfying both a community of practitioners and the university administrators, debates about the education of practitioners that often stay inwardly focused within a particular community, stresses about the aim of such professional education, frustration with credentials rather than education, wrestling with how to view discussions about competencies and skills, and other such matters.

The major difference between graduate archival education programs and the former library schools, some now iSchools, may be that archival studies is still trying to be firmly established while the library schools (at least a significant portion) are now shifting from only professional schools to research centers; in other words, the problem with such education is that what it is connected to is still very much a moving target. In this sense, there are still many unresolved issues in the relationship between practitioners and educators and, in the archival community, even between different camps of educators (some emphasizing practical training and others trying to build research centers and cohorts of new doctoral students intended to become the next generation of faculty).

One of the chief aims of my extended essay is to focus on the implications of the changing university for the present and future state of what were at one time functioning library schools. This is the modern corporate university, considered in chapter four. The corporate university is challenging many of the traditional elements of the university, such as academic freedom, who owns the intellectual property produced by faculty, and how new educational delivery systems (best evident with distance education) may be transforming faculty responsibilities. Some of the excesses of the corporate university may be a response to what some have seen as academic excesses, most graphically displayed in the culture wars debates of the 1980s and 1990s. None of these are particularly new problems, but there seems to be something new about the issues generated by the corporate university. For the transforming library school, the primary issues relate to matters like the rewarding of credentials to fledging professionals and the responsibility of faculty to contribute to the knowledge needed by those professionals. For the university overall, one of the chief concerns is how it contributes to the public good, a matter that certainly relates to the library school in all its various permutations.

One of the persistent themes in the growing quantity of reflections on the state of higher education is the question of the role of the university in society, usually reflected in terms of values and a sense of the public good, a topic I explore in chapter five. In this chapter I consider the values of the library school and its successors within the context of discussion and debate about the values of the college and university. What emerges when we examine the library school is the issue of the importance of printed books, reflective reading, information access, the role of and reactions to information technologies, and how any of this can fit together within the curriculum of a library school, looking backward, or an iSchool, looking ahead. Not only do we need to educate our students about the uses of information technology, we need to prepare them to be able to analyze these technologies (in other words, generating a healthy skepticism). We can achieve this if we immerse our students into the history of information uses and technologies, matters that have generally been pushed to the side in order to accommodate more technology training (but it is education not training that is needed). Reflecting on these issues requires library and information science faculty to re-evaluate what their real values are – how they see themselves and their schools in both universities and society at large. Our task is not just to provide practical or vocational training; it is to push students to examine critical topics such as the ethics of information access and the public good of open access to information. iSchools, just as library schools, need a grand narrative that extends far beyond providing a ticket to a job.

Chapter seven is a reflection acknowledging that many faculty in professional schools are in search of their own professional and scholarly identity, seeking to connect not just with the professional community but the public that the profession supposedly serves and the university community that they work with and for. As a member of a library and information science school, this quest leads me to examine the tasks of both reading and writing. This chapter is more personal than I originally intended because I wish to emphasize that this is my own view; other faculty and practitioner graduates from the library schools and their successors may feel less of a need to worry about such matters or, if they do, they probably approach them in very different ways. Some faculty have re-oriented themselves to focus on teaching technology and other tools, while others have shifted to focus on research that earns them a place in the research university. This is also a highly personal chapter since I am discussing matters where I think I have myself failed. While I am an avid reader, commentator on scholarly and other volumes on a variety of professional topics, and frequently published author, I have failed, despite some modest efforts, to break outside of professional circles to participate in discussions in the public square. While I advocate the need for us to develop a much more focused vision or identity for our schools that have us participating in public discussions, I have not succeeded myself in doing this. I ruminate on the nature of reading, reflection, and writing, drawing inspiration and advice from commentators about such concerns who reside far outside of the library school. I hope it is not too late for myself to take on something of the role of a public scholar.

The final chapter, number eight, focuses more on the critical responsibility of teaching. Teaching potentially reclaims the value of a professional school, but only if it is linked to a serious commitment to scholarship and recognized as a form of scholarship (in much the same way that theory and practice have been seen as alternative approaches in the content of teaching). For far too long research has been represented as an alternative to teaching and vice versa, but it is my opinion that the two must be inseparably connected. It is the fashion at this time to glory in the availability of sophisticated educational technologies and disparage the old face-to-face lecture or seminar methods. Yet, it is obvious that as teaching is being re-invented, that this is not always for the best. In many schools the requirements to deliver courses using the Internet for both on-campus and distance programs dramatically redistributes the time faculty must devote to course preparation and interaction with students; while some will argue that such preparation and interaction is the normal responsibility of a teacher, it is also the teacher's responsibility to be well-grounded in the knowledge of the topic being taught. Time spent building digital course shells, running elaborate discussion boards, answering e-mails, and being placed in a 24/7 availability mode is time taken away from reading to stay current with a field or in seeking to expand into other aspects of a field or in conducting research to advance a profession's knowledge. Keeping this balance has become more problematic in the emerging corporate university, where so much of what we do is measured in dollars – and it is difficult to generate healthy revenue in both teaching and researching at the same time. It is doubly problematic for library and information science schools where reading and writing, as elements of critical thinking, were not only practiced by faculty but also taught to students seeking to enter the information professions. It is because of such contradictory messages from universities to professional schools that many faculty struggle to discern what their primary responsibilities are and become uneasy about the prospects for staying (one reason why there is a lot of personal reflection about my belonging in a professional school in this chapter).

We need not only to teach our students but to teach ourselves, that is, discover our mission, and others in the university. And, if we truly believe in our mission, we need to engage the public as well. Since we have a serious need for new faculty, in nearly all major core and specialized areas of library and information science, we also must grapple with the kinds of issues reflected in this chapter and the others if we hope to attract the kinds of individuals who can succeed in these professional schools. They need to bring imagination, energy, and vision to these schools, especially if we hope to build new or rebuild old professional schools, and we need to provide realistic parameters for what these faculty must do. We cannot present

PROLOGUE   xvii

dozens of different conflicting agendas or avoid articulating any agenda at all (except for a corporate, financial bottom line).

In a brief epilogue I wrap up a few miscellaneous strands and consider some recent debates about the value of the American Library Association accreditation of MLIS degree programs, acrimonious debates between educators and practitioners about the nature of library and information science education, and, the possible prospects for the nascent iSchool movement. Some of these debates commenced long before the corporate university emerged, but it is clear that this model of higher education complicates such issues even more and may be a deciding factor in where we wind up. Whether this is good or bad is uncertain at this time.

What Are the Values We Should Protect? Woven through these chapters is my concern that the next evolutionary stage of the library and information science school could bring with it losses in some important features of the older school. William Chace provides a companion lament in his consideration of the deterioration of English departments: "What are the causes for this decline? There are several, but at the root is the failure of departments of English across the country to champion, with passion, the books they teach and to make a strong case to undergraduates that the knowledge of those books and the tradition in which they exist is a human good in and of itself. What departments have done instead is dismember the curriculum, drift away from the notion that historical chronology is important, and substitute for the books themselves a scattered array of secondary considerations (identity studies, abstruse theory, sexuality, film and popular culture). In so doing, they have distanced themselves from the young people interested in good books."[10] In one obvious sense, we could place the same emphasis on the loss of the book in the traditional library curriculum. However, we perhaps need to rethink what we believe are the core values of the old library school, removing these from the sometimes vitriolic debates about the value of library and information science education for the institutions in the field (I will return to this in my epilogue).

Trying to characterize all of the older or traditional values in library schools, many of which remained or were revised in the next generation of library and information schools, is a nearly impossible task. To make an attempt to develop a comprehensive catalog would be a significant historical project, and that is not my intent here. In this book I have written

---

[10] William M. Chace, "The Decline of the English Department," *American Scholar* 78 (Autumn 2009): 33.

extensively about a few of these values, such as reading and the centrality of books, because they are of interest to me as well as many of the individuals applying to the MLIS programs. However, it is relatively easy to extrapolate from even these few areas to identify other critical values supported by the older versions of these professional schools.

It should be no surprise that the mission of the historic library school was in equipping individuals to become librarians and to support the library profession; after all, fifty to a hundred years ago, the library community constituted the information profession. Individuals were being trained to work in libraries and these institutions were real physical places functioning to support real communities. The focus was on providing real services, from everything from after-school programs to literacy services, mostly oriented to assisting the residents of the immediate community with meeting practical information needs. Reviewing the curriculum of these schools would find an emphasis on information artifacts, that is, physical print materials, supported with courses on cataloguing and classification, managing libraries, with a strong commitment to libraries as a public good and a broad social agenda of free (or nearly free) access to information and notions of securing access to the right or important information sources (a part of the library school and library profession agenda that has taken on various guises, such as reading quality literature, at different times with accompanying debates and controversies). The schools were dedicated to providing the credential to become a practicing librarian, buttressed by the ultimate emergence of the American Library Association Committee on Accreditation and its standards and guidelines and the fact that most faculty in these schools possessed a strong affinity to professional practice (usually because they themselves had some degree of professional experience as librarians).

As library schools became library and information science schools in the 1970s and after, many of these values remained in modified form. The expansion of some of these schools into information science occurred by the adding of new programs and new degrees, with little modification to the MLIS programs but lots of changes to the overall mission of these professional schools. The emergence of the library and information science paradigm began the transition of library schools from a single disciplinary approach to a more multi-disciplinary knowledge base and, in an even more transparent fashion, from an orientation to the library profession to a plethora of information professions including librarianship. These latter library and information science schools also moved from an interest in physical structures such as libraries to encompass both real places and cyberspace and physical as well as virtual artifacts, and because of an increasing stress on emerging information technologies enlarged their sense of time to include looking ahead at the implications of these technologies for librarians and other information professionals. To a certain extent access to information expanded to include, although not always comfortably, both free and for fee access and the concept of literacy expanded to include both information and computer literacy. In these schools, students arrive with a greater range of interests, including concerns about how to use the portable data assistants and social computing experiences they are far more accustomed to using than many of the faculty (I cautiously joined Facebook, I hate text messaging, and I am skeptical about most claims for future digital information technologies). A host of other changes occurred in the evolution of these professional schools, including the expansion of the notion of core course content (from cataloguing and classification to the organization of information), offering courses with slightly different orientations such as moving from administering institutions like libraries to managing information (sometimes not always connected to organizations), and from arguing about the public good benefits of libraries to preparing individuals to operate in a rapidly changing Information Age. Supporting these changes is a more diverse mix of faculty, some researchers and some practitioners, with varying degrees of interest in teaching (although teaching remains the core responsibility for most faculty, as is the case for professional schools). How these differences relate to the emergence of the iSchool movement is something I consider briefly in the epilogue.

What This Book Is Not About. As the above suggests, I am painting in broad strokes a personal picture of professional schools in the changing American university, intending to suggest topics for continued discussion. This is not a comprehensive portrait; that is a task for someone else. What follows are merely my own reflections in what I have observed thus far, raising a small set of issues that I hope will be considered as the traditional library school seems to fade into the distance.

The first matter I should clarify is that this is not a book about my own school. Of course, conversations and debates with my colleagues at the University of Pittsburgh have spurred me to wrestle with the nature of library, library and information science, and archival education, but I am not offering anything that is intended to be a criticism of my own home or any of my fellow faculty members. For this reason, I am not naming any names, so that when the few who read this book do so that they keep their focus on me as the author and not blame anyone else. When Lucinda Roy wrote her book about the unfortunate shootings at Virginia Tech, she observed that she thought that she would have to leave her academic home.[11] I don't believe I have stated anything here that will create such a problem for me. We are engaged in some exciting ventures at the University of Pittsburgh School of Information Sciences, and I intend to end my career here.

This is not a book about undergraduate education. The majority of commentaries on higher education focus on undergraduate education, and I have done as best as I can to extrapolate from them the relevant discourse for graduate and professional education. That there are differences can be seen in Charles Muscatine's recent book on undergraduate education, arguing for reforms in the curriculum to provide a greater emphasis on teaching, more interaction between students and faculty, and the offering of small seminars.[12] There is considerable merit in his recommendations, but some of them do not translate well to graduate education (although some could argue that they do, given the incessant debate in the information professions about the relationship between theory and practice, skills and competencies, and other such matters). Muscatine is relentless in his criticism about the focus on research, lamenting how this detracts from teaching and produces a lot of poor published research. However, his argument that it is the rare professor who can do well in both research and teaching cuts against my personal belief that teaching and research are mutually essential for there to be a quality in either one of these two faculty responsibilities. It is more difficult to argue, when considering professional schools such as in library and information science, that teaching ought to be elevated above all else (although many practitioners would argue just that). To do so would undermine these schools in the research university, and it may explain why the iSchool movement has taken hold.

It is also not my intent to downplay the seriousness of real financial and other practical issues facing higher education. There have been some fine assessments of such problems with useful recommendations for resolution. While faculty members, such as myself, may react negatively to the new corporate mentality of the university, we also must admit that problems such as deteriorating physical plants, declining salaries, poor market conditions, rising tuition, increasing class sizes, and other such challenges require a new commitment to planning approaches and accountability

---

[11] Lucinda Roy, *No Right to Remain Silent: The Tragedy at Virginia Tech* (New York: Harmony Books, 2009).
[12] Charles Muscatine, *Fixing College Education: A New Curriculum for the Twenty-first Century* (Charlottesville: University of Virginia Press, 2009).

structures.[13] While I worry about the implications of the new climate of accountability and assessment on the historically important roles and responsibilities of faculty, I also understand that we must engage in such activities in order to ensure that we use our limited resources in a wise way. However, one of our most precious resources is time, and how we will achieve a balance between one version of assessments after another and the time we also have for teaching and research troubles me.

There are other perspectives of mine I should clear up at the outset. For example, there are a number of criticisms I offer about the embracing of distance education by library schools and their successors. Let me clarify that I am not opposed to distance education and its educational (and other) potential positive attributes. However, no matter how many wonderful things can be claimed if we utilize such technologies, there usually are few discussions of the potential negative implications.[14] We can reach more potential students, but what are the impacts on these larger class sizes on the responsibilities of each individual faculty member? How does the nature of the technologies change what is taught? And, if more time commitments are made on faculty to stay current with educational technologies, what happens to the need for them to be able to perform research and have time for reflection so that they are both offering current knowledge to their students and contributing to a profession's knowledge?

Some may wonder, and justly criticize, what I have written here. This is not a research study. I tend to think of it as a commentary, mostly on what others have said about the nature of the modern university and what it is morphing into. Some might see this as a memoir, since I have made ample description of my own career in a professional school. Indeed, academic memoirs have grown in number, and they have become a topic of academic study themselves. Cynthia Franklin sees memoirs as a means by which academics have chosen to speak beyond their scholarship and beyond the theoretical parameters of that scholarship to reach a broader audience and to reflect on their own vocations.[15] Maybe that is what I am doing.

Conclusion. Parts of this book have appeared in other published forms, but since they have been so changed in their use in this volume I am not

---

[13] See, for example, James C. Garland, *Saving Alma Mater: A Rescue Plan for America's Public Universities* (Chicago: University of Chicago Press, 2009). Garland, now retired, was president of the Miami University of Ohio.
[14] See, for example, Curtis J. Bonk, *The World Is Open: How Web Technology Is Revolutionizing Education* (San Francisco: Jossey-Bass, 2009).
[15] Cynthia G. Franklin, *Academic Lives, Cultural Theory, and the University Today* (Athens: University of Georgia Press, 2009).

listing these earlier essays or blog postings. When it seems relevant, I have made reference to an earlier version and listed all of the various essays in my List of Works Cited at the end. These earlier publications were part of my feeling my way along with some thoughts about professional education. What is in this volume is also certainly not a final work. In my final efforts of writing this book, I resolved more than a few times just to give up and abandon the project. However, I believe there are some ideas here that others may connect with or gain something useful from, so I offer it with apologies for being long-winded or for offering any offense to others who have worked hard to establish excellence in the education of librarians, archivists, and other information professionals.

Richard J. Cox
Pittsburgh, Pennsylvania
January 2010

Chapter One

Setting the Scene

Introduction. The prospects of library schools – the old moniker for what are now termed library and information science schools or information schools (iSchools for short) – continue to generate discussion among their deans, faculty and graduates. Much of the discussion has not changed for decades, reflecting disharmony between faculty and practitioners about what is or is not being taught.[16] The various factors beating against the securities and perceptions of the old style library school with a focus on libraries as places holding physical artifacts have led some commentators to look for broader explanations (such as postmodernism) for the travails of the educational programs.[17]

Such tensions, endemic to all professions, are unlikely to dissipate. What has changed is how we identify these schools, some jettisoning library from their titles and adopting information or information science as their core focus, a trend starting when a cluster of these schools closed.[18] One

---

[16] For a brief historical assessment, reflecting the persistence of particular themes of the debates about the relevance of library schools to supporting its own professional community in the United States, see A. Bohannen, "Library Education: Struggling to Meet the Needs of the Profession," *Journal of Academic Librarianship* 17, no. 4 (1991): 216-219.

[17] These factors include, among other things, the rise of new information technologies, the commodification of information or knowledge, and social agendas constructed around ideas of public knowledge; see Dave Muddiman, "Towards a Postmodern Context for Information and Library Education," *Education for Information* 17, no.1 (March 1999): 1-19.

[18] The critical study, generating lots of commentary, was the study by Marion Paris on four American library schools failing in the late 1970s and 1980s. Paris stretches on politics, and squabbles within the schools and between the schools and university administrations, the inabilities of library school leaders and educators to explain themselves. Paris ends her article with a forecast: "Library education programs that survive and grow will share at least four attributes: strong, imaginative, forward-looking leadership; sound teaching that will inspire the next generation to be better than the present one; a timely and relevant research agenda; and a strong mission. University administrators will continue to need to be shown why education for the information professions is important to society and likely to

might hope that the energy emanating from such debates would strengthen the schools, but such discussions are hard and not always helpful because emotions run high and many unsubstantiated claims are made. Criticism, from both within and outside of the schools, is sometimes seen as a threat to the core values of our society, encompassing such heated topics as the future of the printed book, reading, and literacy. Just as often, what drives the criticism are larger issues about the nature of professional education and the role of the university and its now entrenched corporate model.

For a long time (more than two decades and counting), most of the attention has been focused on the literal closings of library schools, although now the issue seems to be about whether these schools will morph into something quite different (such as schools of information or information science, as some have already done).[19] In fact, the reason that I

---

become more so in the future. For if library educators cannot explain what it is that they do, and why, someone else may tell them. And it may be that they will be told to do nothing at all." Marion Paris, "Why Library Schools Fail." *Library Journal*, October 1, 1990, pp. 38-42 (quotation p. 42). Her full study is *Library School Closings: Four Case Studies* (Metuchen, NJ: Scarecrow Press, 1988). The actual and threatened closings of these schools resulted in a number of suggested strategies for making these schools more relevant within their own universities including embracing information science, understanding the need for enhanced technical preparation, producing quality research, de-emphasizing vocational training, understanding the differences between education and training, involving practitioners in the schools, transforming the image of the schools, and other related issues. See Abraham Bookstein, "Library Education, Yesterday, and Today: Library Education in the University Setting," *Library Quarterly* 56 (October 1986): 360-369; R. W. Budd, "A New Library School of Thought," *Library Journal* 117 (May 1, 1992): 44-48; L-M Cheng, "Uncovering Some Problems in the Library and Information Science Education by Following the Footstep of History," *Journal of Educational Media & Library Sciences* 31, no. 2 (1994): 195-217; K. De La Pena-McCook and June Lester, "Keeping the Library in Library Education," *American Libraries* 29 (March 1998): 59, 61, 63; William R. Eshelman, "The Erosion of Library Education," *Library Journal* 108 (July 1983): 1309-1312; F. W. Lancaster, "Implications for Library and Information Science Education," *Library Trends* 32 (Winter 1984): 337-348; L. Ostler and T. Dahlin, "Old Wine into New Bottles: Responses to New Approaches in Library Education," *Library Acquisitions: Practice and Theory* 22 (Spring 1998): 41-43; Samuel Rothstein, "Why People Really Hate Library Schools: The 97-Year-Old Mystery Solved at Last," *Library Journal* 110, no. 6 (April 1985): 41-48; Herbert S. White, "Education vs. Training: A Problem of Definition," *Journal of Academic Librarianship* 10, no. 4 (1984): 198ff.

[19] The more recent discussions about the issues of library education largely stem from ALA President Michael Gorman's criticism of what he perceives to be the

am considering the end of the library school is not because these schools literally will end, but that what will remain may be unrecognizable as professional schools educating librarians. Many explanations have been offered for why such schools are closed, and these assessments are not particularly new, with complaints about professional schools ignoring classical education foundations extending back to the mid-nineteenth century and worries about creeping specializations in the university appearing in the early twentieth century. Even after all this time, there seems to be little consensus about the schools, and, as a result, these tensions and threats are real, focusing on matters like the loss of "library" in their titles, a topic so super-charged that many will ignore anything written about "library" schools.[20] Often, with such name changes, the wrong issues are considered and important matters get ignored.

Additional questions have been raised because there are fewer deans being appointed who have some academic affiliation or experience with libraries, revealing multifarious opinions about the value of such degrees or what may or may not be happening in other graduate programs in the university (all while ignoring the qualities of the people offered deanships or the fact that these schools do more than educate librarians). Whether or not one has a background or experience in libraries or library education is not the primary issue; besides, we can discern the same controversies when scholars are appointed to head libraries and business leaders to head museums (both fairly regular events in these changing and challenging times).

And so it goes with library schools. Do they have a future in the university? My guess is that library schools have a questionable future, but

---

chasm between that education and the needs of the field. See Michael Gorman's "What Ails Library Education?" *The Journal of Academic Librarianship*, 30 (March 2004): 99-101 and "Whither Library Education?" *New Library World* 105, nos. 9/10 (2004): 376–380.

[20] Librarians and others have been reiterating many of the same complaints or concerns for library education – such as the clerical nature of such education or the qualification of faculty in the schools – for more than a century; for example, see A. Bohannen, "Library Education: Struggling to Meet the Needs of the Profession," *Journal of Academic Librarianship* 17, no. 4 (1991): 216-219; L-M Cheng, "Uncovering Some Problems in the Library and Information Science Education by Following the Footstep of History," *Journal of Educational Media & Library Sciences* 31, no. 2 (1994): 195-217; Andrew Dillon and April Norris, "Crying Wolf: An Examination and Reconsideration of the Perception of Crisis in LIS Education," *Journal of Education for Library and Information Science* 46, no. 4 (2005): 280-298.

this problematic prognosis has as much to do with trends that have been perpetuated both by people who want these schools to survive and the changing nature of higher education. I am not particularly optimistic about the university in general, as higher education institutions race after money, banter about with corporate language, and try to be relevant to society in practical ways suggesting little more than vocational training. While there are growing choruses of protest about such trends, the nature of the university continues to move steadily along the path to becoming just another business, where profits become the measure for success, capitalistic ventures the main activities, and basic job skills replace any sense of a well-rounded education. Yet, something will be built on the foundations (optimistic) or ruins (pessimistic) of the old library schools.

The pre-eminent issues facing library schools can be summarized rather easily, although how or whether we deal with them is no easy process, intertwined as they are with matters afflicting the university, as well as what and how we define the general public good. First, these schools may be trying to do too many things with too few faculty and resources. Second, these schools are partially the victim of the corporatization of the university. And, third, these schools have lost, perhaps completely, a sense of what traditionally attracted students to library schools. Affecting all of these matters is that we may have lost an effective voice in the university and public forum, and regaining it by redefining these schools into something completely different may or may not be the best means of regaining our voice (especially in such difficult economic times).

The mixed messages, academic-speak, and constantly morphing priorities bombarding graduate and undergraduate programs in every university has many library schools hopping about as well. The issues I have enumerated are different from the ones usually featured in discussions and debates about library schools. Predictions about the demise of the library school are usually countered by statements about thriving student numbers, the amounts of research and other grants acquired, and respect about the school held by university administrators – all important, but not always the most critical concerns (unless survival is the *only* issue). There is often no vision of a public good expressed in the discussions, just signs of library schools adopting and adapting the current academic buzzwords of the new corporate university. We need to rethink what we are doing, and, as well, be clearer about how there is value in many aspects of the historic roles of professional schools educating individuals to be librarians, archivists, and other information professionals.

A Little Cosmos of Learning: The Idea of the University. Why does anyone choose to pursue an undergraduate or graduate degree? Why do some want to prepare for a career as a member of a faculty? While many people opt to go after such education because of familial pressure, the lure of higher salaries or a particular kind of lifestyle, acquiring credentials to practice a profession or even because of a sense of a response to a vocational calling, the place to start in answering such questions should be with considering the mission of the university and its historical place in society. Indeed, from the emergence of the modern university in the nineteenth century, individuals associated with this peculiar institution have tried to describe and define its main purposes and values. From John Henry Newman's pithily titled, *The Idea of the University*, published in 1859 and recounting his experiences with leading the Catholic University of Ireland (today the University College Dublin),[21] to Jaroslav Pelikan's re-examination of Newman's university idea a century and a half later, scholars, faculty, and administrators have sought to explain the purpose of the university, its role in society, the relationship of teaching and research, the perceived crises in higher education, troublesome matters such as the role of athletics, and the university's function as a means for preserving knowledge.[22] Many other observers have tried to understand what the university represents or what it could be. Garry Wills' account of Thomas Jefferson and the founding of the University of Virginia in the early nineteenth-century evaluates Jefferson's campus design and how it reflected his concept of a university. In looking across the campus, Wills muses, "In the shapes of the buildings, interconnected but highly individual, a little cosmos of learning took shape, a musical dance of forms, a microcosm of his beloved Newtonian scheme of things."[23] But one wonders if such clear and orderly notions about higher education still ring true today (if it hasn't been replaced by the corporate university with the campus as factory, financial institution, or stock market).

Are students flooding into professional schools, long a fixture of the modern university, with a longing for learning, or are they just after a credential? How can we instill in these students the desire to learn not just

---

[21] Yale University Press issued an excellent edition of Newman's book in 1996 edited by Frank M. Turner and with a number of interpretative essays by other commentators.
[22] Jaroslav Pelikan, *The Idea of the University: A Reexamination* (New Haven: Yale University Press, 1992).
[23] Garry Wills, *Mr. Jefferson's University* (Washington, D.C.: National Geographic, 2002), p. 8.

to practice a craft, the hunger to learn over a lifetime not just to earn a living? Has the idea of the modern university changed so much that corporate values and bottom line student numbers and dollars dominate everything? Do such agendas weaken or rejuvenate professional schools such as the type I am discussing in this volume? Such questions propelled me into intensive reading and thinking about the university because I realized that enough weird stuff happens in the academy that reading what others – other professors, presidents and other administrators, former students, and those from outside just taking a shot at explaining or exhorting the university's purpose – have to say could enhance my understanding. Even those seriously studying the history of the university, such as William Clark, remind us that what we now accept readily as the university's most recent version (although perhaps the corporate model may be the next version of this venerable institution) emerging in the Enlightenment is also the result of adopting new managerial controls, notions of academic production, and contending with market forces and government regulation.[24] Clark Kerr's classic explanation of the evolution of the institution into the "multiversity" a half-century ago, cited ever since by anyone studying the university, also explains why we have seen so many attempts, from insiders such as students to chancellors and presidents and outsiders such as journalists and politicians, to sort out the complexities shaping higher education: "The university is so many things to so many different people that it must, of necessity, be partially at war with itself."[25] Such conflict is evident in any discourse about higher education, including professional schools such as the ones described here.

Good for What? Over the thousand plus years of the university, there have been many opinions expressed about the idea of the university, providing both personal and useful observations. Long-time academics such as Jacques Barzun[26] and many university presidents such as William M.

---

[24] William Clark, *Academic Charisma and the Origins of the Research University* (Chicago: University of Chicago Press, 2006).
[25] Clark Kerr, *The Uses of the University* (Cambridge: Harvard University Press, 1963), pp. 8-9.
[26] Jacques Barzun, *The American University: How It Runs, Where It Is Going*, 2nd. ed. (Chicago: University of Chicago Press, 1999; org. pub., 1968). Individuals interested in Barzun's ideas about higher education, teaching, and scholarship might also find useful his *A Jacques Barzun Reader: Selections from His Works*, ed. Michael Murray (New York: HarperCollins, 2002).

Chace,[27] A. Bartlett Giametti,[28] Frank H. T. Rhodes,[29] and Harold T. Shapiro[30] offer astute assessments (and sometimes defenses of their administrations) of higher education considering the nature of the university, its history, faculty, students, administrators and their governance roles, supporters of higher education, the financial challenges of keeping the university functioning, teaching, research and the production of knowledge, the impact of information technologies, the uses of a liberal education, the public utility of the university, and the ethical issues affecting scientific and other research. George Dennis O'Brien argues that the university is not an idea but an institution, facing real challenges and having real solutions to them, and getting to the heart of the issue so many seek to address: "Learning in any field, however arcane, is a good-in-itself, but when one creates an institution of learning with facilities and fees, good-in-itself has to answer this question: good for what?"[31]

Former Harvard University president Derek Bok produced two of the best books about the purpose of the university (and Bok has continued to write with verve, insight, and conviction about the challenges facing higher education) that are particularly relevant when considering professional schools within the academy. Bok's *Beyond the Ivory Tower: Social Responsibilities of the Modern University* is true to its title, seeking to reconsider basic academic values, evaluating academic efforts to confront social problems, and examining how the university tries to connect to society. The essays revolve around Bok's conviction that the "function of the university is to engage in teaching and research of the highest attainable quality."[32] His later *Higher Learning* is his exploration of the difficult task of figuring out how to teach students in a major research university, and Bok includes an interesting chapter on the state of professional schools in the university. As

---

[27] William M. Chace, *100 Semesters: My Adventures As Student, Professor, and University President, And What I Learned Along the Way* (Princeton: Princeton University Press, 2006).
[28] A. Bartlett Giametti, *A Free and Ordered Space: The Real World of the University* (New York: W. W. Norton and Co., 1990).
[29] Frank H. T. Rhodes, *The Creation of the Future: The Role of the American University* (Ithaca: Cornell University Press, 2001).
[30] Harold T. Shapiro, *A Larger Sense of Purpose: Higher Education and Society* (Princeton: Princeton University Press, 2005).
[31] George Dennis O'Brien, *All the Essential Half-Truths About Higher Education* (Chicago: University of Chicago Press, 2000), p. 18.
[32] Derek Bok, *Beyond the Ivory Tower: Social Responsibilities of the Modern University* (Cambridge: Harvard University Press, 1982), p. 35.

Bok argues, "Universities should do their best to improve the quality of their programs not only because students and society have to cope with pressing problems but also because education is important for its own sake."³³ These, and other expressions of ideas about the university, also relate to the professional schools in their midst, although one sometimes wonders about how often the faculty and administrators of these schools seek to relate their programs to these broader questions about universities in our society (except when they are threatened with closure in times of economic stress and restructuring).

Not Always At Our Best: Remembering the University. Anyone who has worked in the university as a faculty member or an administrator has wrestled with the meaning and purpose of higher education. Many former college and university presidents have opted to offer their insights about higher education not in the form of learned essays about the topic but as memoirs about their experiences. Gretchen von Loewe Kreuter recounts her experiences as an interim president at a troubled small college in the Midwest. The end result is both illuminating and bitter at times. Kreuter, in considering problems in meeting with faculty, observes: "In general, faculty members are not at their best in groups," and she laments that we are not prepared to be faculty in graduate seminars where the "universally understood purpose is to seem brilliant yourself and to humiliate your peers."³⁴ Jill Ker Conway's engrossing three volume autobiography, following from her childhood in Australia through her education and ultimately to her position as president of Smith College,³⁵ leads her to conclude that a "president's relationship to a faculty involves more double binds than a bad marriage on the brink of collapse," with the "result ... that most presidents are scapegoats for the inevitable disappointment of scholarly life, and they listen to more complaining than affirmation."³⁶ Conway's insight probably explains why so many retired presidents gather together their essays written while in office, smooth them into a coherent observation, and then offer them to the world. It is their final defense for what they have done or tried to do.

---

³³ Derek Bok, *Higher Learning* (Cambridge: Harvard University Press, 1986), p. 6.
³⁴ Gretchen von Loewe Kreuter, *Forgotten Promise: Race and Gender Wars on a Small College Campus* (New York: Alfred A. Knopf, 1996), p. 59.
³⁵ Jill Ker Conway, *The Road from Coorain* (New York: Vintage Books, 1990); *True North: A Memoir* (New York: Alfred A. Knopf, 1994); and *A Woman's Education: The Road from Coorain Leads to Smith College* (New York: Vintage Books, 2001).
³⁶ Conway, *A Woman's Education*, p. 65.

While we might read into these memoirs something of the personal insecurity of these educational leaders, it is also important to understand that this might be the result of the uncertainties of how to evaluate the effectiveness of such education. Every year parents and high school students flock to read the latest guides to the best schools or peruse the latest rankings in different fields (often with different aims), and these guides and rankings, no matter how unscientific they may be attest to a concern for understanding how effective such education can or ought to be. Loren Pope's guide stresses the value of teaching and mentoring, student-teacher interaction, values, and a variety of other aspects seemingly forgotten in many colleges and universities today.[37] Professional schools, such as those in library and information science, have mostly fixated on the *U.S. News & World Report* rating system that generates controversy and dismay, but one that quite naturally is used by the schools receiving high rankings. From time to time revelations about efforts by various schools to manipulate the rankings, a kind of teaching to score well on the examination rather to help students learn, suggests how insecure we can be about the purpose of higher education.[38] The question that remains unanswered for LIS schools is just what might constitute the distinctive elements or characteristics for an alternative rating system for its own purposes. While the American Library Association provides rich detail about many aspects of these schools in its annual reports, we lack the kind of inspirational attributes posed by Pope and watch in dismay how easily and quickly the schools will adopt for marketing purposes the *U.S. News & World Report* rankings, no matter how unreliable they may be. Such actions affirm that higher education is just another business.

Historical analyses of the university suggest, of course, that the economic features of the university are important, and, in addition, common sense dictates that we accept that administrative factors such as

---

[37] Loren Pope, *Colleges That Change Lives: 40 Schools That Will Change the Way You Think About Colleges* (New York: Penguin Books, 2006; rev. ed.).
[38] Such a revelation occurred in 2009, when it was reported how Clemson University was seeking to improve its ranking in the *U.S. News and World Report*. Martin Van Der Werf, "Researcher Offers Unusually Candid Description of University's Efforts to Rise in Rankings," *Chronicle of Higher Education*, June 3, 2009, http://chronicle.com/daily/2009/06/19270n.htm. From time to time there have been efforts among various groups of colleges and rankings to not cooperate with this ranking; see Eric Hoover, "Letter Circulating Among College Presidents Asks Them Not to Participate in Rankings Survey," *Chronicle of Higher Education*, April 9, 2007, http://chronicle.com/daily/2007/04/2007040902n.htm.

finances and marketing are critical for success. Colleges and universities, like any institutional form, were not immediate successes, and they have gone through many changes and faced many challenges about what should be taught in the university, the tensions between the liberal arts curriculum and professional training, government influence on the nature of higher education, the role of private foundations, the nature of what faculty do, and the perceptions of higher education through American culture such as films and popular magazines.[39] The historical perspective is difficult to find within the professional schools, such as those in library and information science. Some decades ago, courses on the history of libraries, library and information science, and books and printing were pushed to the side to make room for courses on information technologies and other technical matters. Even now, with a remarkable resurgence of scholarship on topics like the history of information science, computing, and reading, these topics have managed only to re-establish themselves in a few schools of library and information science. What is being lost in this? For one, we do not help our students to be able to take the long view, to understand how a particular information technology emerged or how it came to be used. For another, we become more susceptible to believing all the hyperbole thrown out about the power of information and the information professions. We lose sight of the fact that every era was an information age and that while ours is unique in its computational power, it is not special for its reliance on information. Our perspective is always on the present, and we forget that current debates and problems for such schools may not be new at all.

Looking for Purpose (or Something). There are many personal narratives about the promises in and problems confronting higher education, revealing many approaches to understanding the evolution of the university. Some have examined the religious origins of colleges and universities, and then the shift away from religion as a concern of these institutions[40] or how they sought to reconcile religion and science when morality seemed a more important aspect of higher education.[41] Others have examined how specific disciplines – such as English, philosophy, economics, and political science,

---

[39] John R. Thelin, *A History of American Higher Education* (Baltimore: Johns Hopkins University Press, 2004). An example of an excellent institutional study is Hugh Hawkins, *Pioneer: A History of the Johns Hopkins University, 1874-1889* (Ithaca, NY: Cornell University Press, 1960).
[40] George Marsden, *The Soul of the American University: From Protestant Establishment to Established Nonbelief* (New York: Oxford University Press, 1994).
[41] Julie A. Reuben, *The Making of the Modern University: Intellectual Transformation and the Marginalization of Morality* (Chicago: University of Chicago Press, 1996).

have changed or not changed in the modern American university[42] or how the notion of intellectuals in American life has shifted "from a civic foundation to a professional and academic one" in the university, especially with the emergence of new graduate and professional programs in the sciences, social science, history, and literary studies (one of many laments about the demise of the public intellectual)[43] that ought to give pause to those in professional schools, such as ones educating librarians, whose objectives naturally embrace concerns of public policy and a societal good.

Those probing into the history of the university often are searching for the key to establishing a new coherent purpose of higher education that they fear has been lost. Harry R. Lewis, a computer science professor at Harvard University, gets to the heart of such concerns when he writes, "Within academe it is hard to inspire support for a core for a simple reason. We have not come to agreement – indeed we have had little discussion – about the purpose of higher education. In the absence of any big concept about what college is supposed to do for students, both students and faculty members prefer the freedom of choice that comes with the elective curriculum. We would each rather do our own thing than embrace our collective responsibility for the common good. But the argument that students have nothing in common is false, and the conclusion that a college education should have no core is wrong."[44] It is possible that one of the critical issues for the old library school is the loss of a core, as the focus seems to have shifted from the library and librarian to a vast array of venues and information professions.[45]

While Lewis is considering undergraduate education, we can still wonder just how the notion of a core curriculum in LIS programs reflects or doesn't reflect a common purpose for the education of librarians, archivists, and other information professionals. For many decades we have had the accreditation standards of the American Library Association to

---

[42] Thomas Bender and Carl E. Schorske, eds., *American Academic Culture in Transformation: Fifty Years, Four Disciplines* (Princeton, NJ: Princeton University Press, 1997).

[43] Thomas Bender, *Intellect and Public Life: Essays on the Social History of Academic Intellectuals in the United States* (Baltimore: Johns Hopkins University Press, 1993), p. xiv.

[44] Harry R. Lewis, "A Core Curriculum for Tomorrow's Citizens," *Chronicle of Higher Education, The Chronicle Review* (September 7, 2007), p. B20.

[45] Blaise Cronin, "Holding the Center while Prospecting at the Periphery: Domain Identity and Coherence in North American Information Studies Education," *Education for Information*, 20 (2002): 3–10.

provide some sort of coherent statement about such a purpose, but these standards have not covered every program within these schools. Indeed, these schools are more complex than ever, educating individuals to work as information professionals where educational standards are less formalized (archivists) and considering new aims for preparing the next generation of information professionals, such as reflected in the iSchool movement. Some may argue that there is no present stability in the idea of LIS schools, some perceiving this as just a reflection of the information professions and others as a problem needing to be resolved. What did Melvil Dewey have in mind when he launched the first library school?

The Faculty. Some might say that the history of the university is really about, or should be about, the history of faculty. What do faculty in a university do? Do they teach a little, but mostly engage in important research and scholarship? Do they have bosses, in the sense that most people in corporations and other institutions do? Or, are faculty members more like independent entrepreneurs? Many outsiders such as policymakers and media pundits, as well as parents often paying the bills, have questioned just what is happening with the modern university. Friends and foes alike want to know more about what is being taught, how efficiently the university is being run, why costs seem to be out of control, and just how practical or useful is the research being done by universities and their faculties.

Even after centuries of development and more than a century of the modern university, the nature, activities, and roles of the academic faculty are debated and changing. Charles Bernstein writes, "The academic profession is not a unified body but a composite of many dissimilar individuals and groups pursuing projects ranging from the valiantly idiosyncratic to the proscriptively conventional... . [M]ost of the popular generalizations about what professors do or do not do are unsupported by facts."[46]

Bernstein's comment is appropriate for considering the typical school of information sciences. Given the diversity of academic specializations represented by faculty members in an IS school, it is not surprising to discover that there are many different ideas about information nor does everyone consider themselves scientists either. There is not one information science but many sciences; not one, but many, information professions. How do we define such a school in a way that both the public and

---

[46] Charles Bernstein, "A Blow is Like An Instrument," *Daedalus* 126 (Fall 1997), p. 181.

university administrators can grasp what it is about or what it should be doing?

The stability of faculty is more uncertain than at any other time in the history of the university, complicating the IS schools also in extreme flux (continuing their move from library schools to schools of information). Faculty salaries are falling behind inflation, they are now seen to be the employees of an industry of vital importance in the economy, and part-time faculty are on the rise in both size and importance. Some of these changes might suggest potential for the future of faculty in LIS programs, as student enrollment has moved from the liberal arts into the professions. According to some, the quality of the lives of faculty is being diminished, as working hours increase, and there is worry that the quality of individuals attracted to academic posts may be on the decline.[47] Maybe this is not so great a time to build new schools (or, perhaps, this is the perfect time to establish new programs and reinvent old ones).

Intellectual Matters. Many have written about the role of the faculty, and some have considered the academic's place in the larger scheme of the life of the mind, a topic Jacques Barzun discoursed about a half century ago: "Though millions have literacy and hundreds of thousands had 'education,' plus the rudiments of a profession, it becomes harder and harder to find the few tens of thousands who are willing, let alone eager, to attend to intellectual matters."[48] Professional schools are interesting intersections between the public and the academy, and, sometimes, it seems hard to find the nature of any intellectual matter in schools focused on credentials, skills, and attitudes – training, if you will – more than education. However, many of these schools also host doctoral programs, and one must wonder what the connection is between the holders of terminal masters – the MLIS degree – and doctoral programs? Could not the doctoral programs be the intellectual core of the library and information science programs?

Probing, in often-indelicate fashion, into the nature of the role of the faculty in the university and other levels of higher education, can result in cynical and controversial perspectives. For a particularly offbeat and acerbic perspective on the state of the professoriate and the university, Cary Nelson

---

[47] Scott Jaschik, "The Evolving (Eroding?) Faculty Job," *Inside Higher Education*, May 1, 2006 at http://insidehighered.com/news/2006/05/01/faculty, reporting on a book by Jack H. Schuster and Martin Finkelstein, *The American Faculty: The Restructuring of Academic Work and Careers* (Baltimore: Johns Hopkins University Press, 2006).

[48] Jacques Barzun, *The House of Intellect* (New York: HarperCollins, 2002; org. pub. 1959), p. 13.

and Stephen Watt reflect about academic keywords.[49] Their volume is a nice balance to the many handbooks that have been produced to aid faculty and administrators working in the university, such as the one co-edited by A. Leigh DeNeef and Craufurd D. Goodwin; the volume includes essays and other resources on the nature of higher education, issues confronting the modern university, academic employment, teaching and advising, research funding, publishing and research, and academic administration.[50] These volumes over time provide a nice historical record of how academics perceive their own role in higher education. Are there separate handbooks for library and information science faculty? I do not personally know of any, although the literature on LIS education is extensive. If we want to represent a dean of an LIS, IS, or iSchool would it be in an office filled with books or one filled with computers of various sizes and purposes? Or, would we find both in the background? And what would this say about the mooring of such graduate programs, if it suggests anything?

There are a growing number of assessments appearing about the plight of other professional schools that might help. I occasionally read about journalists and their employing publications because, first, the media is a barometer of what is happening with information in the digital age and, second, their products, newspapers and news magazines, have long been important documents that librarians and archivists administer. Neil Henry, a former news reporter and now journalism professor, has given us a surprisingly compelling study of journalism and the professional schools supporting this field. Henry worries about whether the weakening of journalism is a troubling sign of what is happening with our society, "in which there are ever fewer arbiters who are trusted and recognized by a consensus of citizens,"[51] even in a field plagued by matters such as plagiarism, fabrication, and ethical miscues. What caught my attention, however, is how Henry depicts the role of journalists in our society as experts who "regard serving the public trust as central to their purpose, and they believe in questioning and, if necessary, challenging power and vested interests to protect that trust. They question the powerful on the behalf of the ordinary citizen and regard corporate and political elites as subjects to be watched closely, not as figures to be fawned over. Journalists are

---

[49] Cary Nelson and Stephen Watt, *Academic Keywords: A Devil's Dictionary for Higher Education* (New York: Routledge, 1999).
[50] A. Leigh DeNeef and Craufurd D. Goodwin, eds., *The Academic's Handbook*, 2nd. Ed. (Durham: Duke University Press, 1995).
[51] Neil Henry, *American Carnival: Journalism Under Siege in an Age of New Media* (Berkeley: University of California Press, 2007), p. 11.

professionals with ethical and moral standards who inform the people in a democracy about the community and the world so that we all may become knowledgeable enough to make decisions about the best ways to improve our lives."[52] Later, Henry writes, "journalism ... means bearing witness and telling the truth."[53] How does Henry's characterization of journalists differ from how we think of the role of the university professor, including those in professional schools, especially those so central to the modern information age?

Better Than Real Life. Given that so many academics, including a large number of faculty members who teach creative writing and literary studies, make their livings by writing, it should not be surprising that there are many academic novels. What better way to gain a sense of the role of the faculty than to read about it in glorious prose, providing every luscious detail one could wish for in what faculty members do (or, maybe, wished they did!). Every academic can name a few of his or her favorites, but Elaine Showalter provides an excellent analysis of such writing over the past half-century, arguing that "reading academic novels from 1950 to the present gives a good overview of the way the academy and its scribes have moved from hope to endurance to anticipation to cynicism and around to hope again."[54] These novels provide interesting, often hilarious, insights into the life of the university professor. We all want to write a piece of fiction just to get some of our frustrations out of our system!

These fictional accounts represent a range of offbeat, as well as insightful, ideas about the university. Many academics have written novels, mysteries, and short stories about the nature and culture of higher education. There are probably very few academics who have not read or who do not have their own personal favorites. I have several favorites, including Jane Smiley's *Moo* (about a small Midwestern university faculty intrigue);[55] Alexander McCall Smith's three short academic novels about the adventures of Professor Moritz-Maria von Igelfeld, a seldom-read linguist always in search of acclaim and respect;[56] David Lodge's set of novels about

---

[52] Henry, *American Carnival*, p. 58.
[53] Henry, *American Carnival*, p. 210.
[54] Elaine Showalter, *Faculty Towers: The Academic Novel and Its Discontents* (Philadelphia: University of Pennsylvania Press, 2005), p. 13.
[55] Jane Smiley, *Moo* (New York: Fawcett Columbine, 1995).
[56] Alexander McCall Smith, *Portuguese Irregular Verbs* (New York: Anchor Books, 2003); *The Finer Points of Sausage Dogs* (New York: Anchor Books, 2003); and *At the Villa of Reduced Circumstances* (New York: Anchor Books, 2003).

the academy with dead-on descriptions of academic conferences;[57] Kingsley Amis's *Lucky Jim*, following the trials and tribulations of a professor in an English university;[58] and Richard Russo, *Straight Man*, chronicling the career of a harried chairman of an English department in an impoverished college in Pennsylvania.[59] If you wonder what any of these novels have to do with life in the real university or in a professional school just consider that these fictional renderings depict extra-marital affairs, faculty meetings, grant writing hi-jinx, political in-fighting at professional conferences,[60] and the travails of publishing, sabbaticals, and tenure. A few idle moments at a faculty meeting often lead to a mental outline of a novel set in an old library school beset by the challenges of new information technologies.

Perhaps academic work is just ripe for fictional accounts because it is such a wonderfully peculiar dimension of a way to make a living. Because of this, I always set aside a little time to read new explorations about the nature of work, both to understand my own sense of work and its meaning in the university and to muse over just what my students are facing in their own future endeavors. The travel writer and social commentator Alain de Botton has written an engaging inquiry into work. De Botton provides insights into the routines of work, encompassing even the mundane activities of the academic world. "To see ourselves as the centre of the universe and the present time as the summit of history," de Botton muses, "to view our upcoming meetings as being of overwhelming significance, to neglect the lessons of cemeteries, to read only sparingly, to neglect the pressures of deadlines, to snap at colleagues, to make our way through conference agendas marked '11:00 a.m. to 11:15 a.m.: coffee break,' to behave heedlessly and greedily and then to combust in battle – maybe all of this, in the end, is working wisdom."[61] It all sounds like a typical academic's day of

---

[57] David Lodge, *The British Museum Is Falling Down* (New York: Holt Rinehart and Winston, 1965); *Changing Places: A Tale of Two Campuses* (New York: Penguin Books, 1978); and *Nice Work* (New York: Penguin Books, 1990).

[58] Kingsley Amis, *Lucky Jim* (New York: Penguin Books, 1992; org. published 1954).

[59] Richard Russo, *Straight Man* (New York: Vintage Books, 1998).

[60] Academic conferences are particularly prone to satirizing. In a comic, fictional send-up of academic meetings in literary and cultural studies, David Damrosch, *Meetings of the Mind* (Princeton: Princeton University Press, 2000) provides insights into why fiction writers have so much good material to work with when setting their works on college and university campuses.

[61] Alain de Botton, *The Pleasures and Sorrows of Work* (New York: Pantheon Books, 2009), pp. 124, 126.

faculty meetings, encounters with students, and the filling in of forms (and why we may want to spice it up in a fictional account).

Another book on the nature of work gets closer to us because it is written by an academically trained individual who, in part, is reflecting on work as defined in our knowledge era. Matthew B. Crawford has a Ph.D. in political philosophy, prepared for an academic career, and gave it all up in order to run a motorcycle repair shop. I guess it is not altogether surprising that he has written a book on manual work and its value in our society. Crawford critiques the notion of knowledge work, in part because he finds "manual work more engaging *intellectually*," and his book is his effort to "understand why this should be so."[62] Crawford explores the notion of what a "good job" entails, and he puts some of this into a historical perspective (for example): "White-collar professions, too, are subject to routinization and degradation, proceeding by the same logic that hit manual fabrication a hundred years ago: the cognitive elements of the job are appropriated from professionals, instantiated in a system or process, and then handed back to a new class of workers – clerks – who replace the professionals."[63] So, as you might imagine, Crawford has a lot of uncomfortable things to say about our ideas of the information society, the knowledge era, and computer literacy. He wonders if it isn't the case that "college habituates young people to accept as the normal course of things a mismatch between form and content, official representations and reality."[64] Crawford hasn't inspired me to take up tools and build something – I am a total failure at this, but he has made me reflect a little more on the relationship between the theory and practice aspects of what we deal with in our classrooms. And, as well, he makes me understand better why some academics decide to vent their frustrations in the form of fictional musings about the academy.

Over the Edge. Reflecting on the role of faculty is not always an easy task. The academic lifestyle can be both a great blessing and a great curse. Many talented men and women have failed in their efforts to secure a regular faculty position or to achieve tenure. Don J. Snyder's bitter memoir about his failure to achieve tenure in an English department and his subsequent happiness in abandoning academe in his appropriately titled *The Cliff*

---

[62] Michael B. Crawford, *Shop Class as Soulcraft: An Inquiry into the Value of Work* (New York: Penguin Press, 2009), p. 5.
[63] Crawford, *Shop Class as Soulcraft*, p. 44.
[64] Crawford, *Shop Class as Soulcraft*, p. 147.

Walk,⁶⁵ a book every academic administrator or mentor of junior faculty or advisor to doctoral students ought to read, is but one example. For a much more upbeat memoir about success in university life, James Lang comments on learning how to teach, write, provide service, and evaluate and mentor students, with some hilarious insights.⁶⁶ Though we lack such candor in written accounts about library schools and their successors, anyone associated with such schools will recognize the features. The struggles of faculty in such professional schools are not all that different from their colleagues in other parts of the university (except maybe the focus on more blatant vocational aims places these schools closer to the emerging corporate model of higher education and the financial bottom line).

Some have sought to understand how faculty members produce knowledge through their symbolic capital (consisting of their research, teaching, and service). David Downing, drawing on various models of professionalization and economic theories, considers the "key contemporary problems" facing faculty and their universities – labor issues, disciplinarity, epistemological challenges, and theory construction and refinement – with particular focus on English departments (Downing's home).⁶⁷ Others, such as law professor Deborah L. Rhode, describe the full range of functions faculty have (or assume they have) a responsibility to perform. Rhode considers the university's mission and the role of faculty in producing scholarship, teaching, administration, and engaging the public – all while considering the many complaints leveled against the modern university.⁶⁸ Lewis A. Coser's classic study *Men of Ideas*, originally published in 1965, also provides plenty of contrast between the public and academic intellectual, their role in society, and how they function in various institutions, including the university. Coser is also sensitive to some of the seeming contradictions for the scholar working within the university, noting, for example, "The very effort among academic men to prevent the academy from becoming too highly bureaucraticized leads them to engage in activities that necessarily distract them from those scholarly tasks that the

---

⁶⁵ Don J. Snyder, *The Cliff Walk: A Memoir of a Job Lost and a Life Found* (Boston: Little Brown and Co., 1997).
⁶⁶ James Lang, *Life on the Tenure Track: Lessons from the First Year* (Baltimore: Johns Hopkins University Press, 2005).
⁶⁷ David B. Downing, *The Knowledge Contract: Politics and Paradigms in the Academic Workplace* (Lincoln: University of Nebraska Press, 2005), p. 11.
⁶⁸ Deborah Rhode, *In Pursuit of Knowledge: Scholars, Status, and Academic Culture* (Stanford, CA: Stanford Law and Politics, Stanford University Press, 2006).

academy is supposed to foster and protect."⁶⁹ More recently, we learn how various academic groups – how anthropologists, historians, economists, political scientists, literary scholars, and philosophers think and interact with each other.⁷⁰

Has there been much in the way of self-reflection among the faculty of LIS schools? The answer is yes, but such analysis seems to have settled on the place of these schools within the university or the nature of the curriculum rather than on the issues of the role of faculty. Considering how LIS faculty view themselves and how this view has changed over the past century would be a good topic for additional research, and it could add much to the understanding of our profession and the education supporting it.

What Professors Say and Do. The role of faculty is becoming more complex, as seen by the discussion about the Academic Bill of Rights and its leading advocate David Horowitz, affecting public perceptions enough that the American Association of University Professors released a statement of "Freedom in the Classroom." There is concern that professors have censored themselves in the classroom, answering four common charges posed by Horowitz and his supporters that professors indoctrinate students, that they fail to provide balance in their instruction, that they are hostile to students who disagree with them, and that they introduce irrelevant political ideas in classroom lectures – or as Horowitz believes, just good, old "institutionally supported indoctrination."⁷¹ Countering such charges is made even more difficult by the nearly impossible task faculty now face in keeping up with email, blogs, text messages and all the other stuff that electronic information technologies present to them.⁷² While library school faculty members seemingly have been immune to charges about politicizing their classrooms (at least we do not hear much about

---

⁶⁹ Lewis A. Coser, *Men of Ideas: A Sociologist's View* (New York: Simon and Schuster, 1997), p. 283.
⁷⁰ See Michèle Lamont, *How Professors Think: Inside the Curious World of Academic Judgment* (Cambridge: Harvard University Press, 2009), an interesting study in the process of peer review of a variety of academic disciplines by funding agencies, seeking to inform academics about how such evaluation works and to assist them to get outside of the "disciplinary tunnel vision that afflicts so many" (p. 12).
⁷¹ Scott Jaschik, "Reframing the Debate About What Professors Say," *Inside Higher Education*, (September 11, 2007), http://insidehighered.com/news/2007/09/11/aaup, accessed September 11, 2007.
⁷² Piper Fogg, "When Your In Box Is Always Full," *Chronicle of Higher Education*, June 6, 2008, available at http://chronicle.com/weekly/v54/i39/39b01901.htm.

such matters), they certainly have not been immune to the additional tasks posed by the new technologies.

We can wonder how these new and emerging technologies can be harnessed for teaching in better and more effective ways. Clay Shirky provides a readable account of the impact of information technologies on supporting new ways for people to work together. Shirky, a faculty member at New York University's Interactive Telecommunications Program, considers how Flickr, blogs, MySpace, Wikis, flash mobs, and open source software enable groups to form, organizations to manage differently, amateurs to challenge professionals, and actions to be carried out collectively. Shirky also considers both the positive and negative implications of the new and emerging technologies.[73] There is no reason to think that we cannot employ these technologies in the classroom and our teaching.

The various technologies exaggerate various legal, political, and ethical challenges librarians and other information professionals might face in the real world. One can ask whether there have been any of these problems with teaching in a professional school, such as one in library and information science, where faculty members regularly (and expectedly) deal with matters such as censorship and freedom of information. Given the targeting of libraries in the USA Patriot Act and other activities in the post-9/11 debates about national security and the war on terrorism, one could expect this to be a regular classroom topic and finding some mythical "neutral ideal" into courses[74] might be impossible. Isn't this the case with faculty teaching students on the graduate level in a school of information sciences? It is, unless we become fixated on teaching skills, techniques, and attitudes that place blinders on students.

Maybe such issues are more the concern of undergraduate education. Rudolph H. Weingartner, a former dean at the University of Pittsburgh, provides a clue about this when he concedes a "liberal education does not aim at preparing students for their first jobs," that it is "preprofessional" and "pre-life." Weingartner notes how many criticize liberal education, assuming that "human beings are prepared by nature to understand the world, to keep pace with social and technological change, to make wise decisions about their own futures and the futures of others, to lead

---

[73] Clay Shirky, *Here Comes Everybody: The Power of Organizing Without Organizations* (New York: Penguin Press, 2008).
[74] Jaschik, "Reframing the Debate."

CHAPTER ONE 21

satisfying lives."[75] It is probably because of the challenges of educating individuals in this way that the issues that Horowitz and his supporters assail emerge in the undergraduate classroom. At the graduate level, in a professional school, rightly or wrongly we assume that students have gone through this earlier educational process (although I admit I am often disappointed by the preparation that many of the students have for completing graduate work). When we introduce students to the promises and perils of the information age, we find that they often have difficulty in understanding the messier aspects of information work. Michael Bérubé, the Paterno Family Professor in Literature at Pennsylvania State University, considers the classroom to be an "extraordinary and potentially volatile space." Bérubé argues, "This is so common and ordinary a feature of college classrooms that it should need no defense. Quite literally, it should go without saying that college classrooms are places where students and professors can pursue illuminating analogies, develop trains of thought, play devil's advocate, and make connections between past and present."[76] I love the classroom.

Perhaps if professors in professional schools do not feel such tensions (if they are, they aren't talking), it is because they are teaching the wrong way. Although we are trying to educate students about a lot of tools and techniques, we also ought to be pushing the same students to understand the ethical, moral, and other challenges these tools and techniques bring with them. Sometimes, I wonder if we are doing this (although sometimes others from the outside do it for us, even in funny and off-beat ways).

My own school has been educating individuals to function as librarians for well over a century. The Library and Information Science program is internationally recognized for preparing public, school, children's and youth services, medical, academic, digital, and special librarians, as well as archivists and preservation administrators. Some of these positions are quite new in their origins. Now our graduates might work as a Webmaster or an Electronic Records Specialist, jobs the first graduates in 1901 could never have imagined. We also have graduates of our program teaching in countries around the world as well. Don Borchert, in a humorous book, provides a sense of these challenges: "Libraries are a footnote to our civilization, an outpost to those unfamiliar with the concept, and a cheap,

---

[75] Rudolph H. Weingartner, "On the Practicality of a Liberal Education," *Liberal Education* (Summer 2007).
[76] Michael Bérubé, "Freedom to Teach," *Inside Higher Education* (September 11, 2007), http://insidehighered.com/views/2007/09/11/berube, accessed September 11, 2007.

habit-forming narcotic to the regular patron. Walk into a public library and it is usually as calm and inviting as a warm bath. It is clean, well kept, and quiet enough to do the Sunday crossword puzzle (the one you brought with you from home, not the one torn surreptitiously out of the library's copy of the paper while no one was looking…). The staff is invariably professional, courteous, and unobtrusive. They are almost always educated – not just disillusioned college grads who could find nothing in their own field but majors in Library Science, a degree as arcane as alchemy or predicting the future by reading the entails of a recently slaughtered lamb."[77] An assessment like this ought to force us right back to the drawing board to reflect on what we are doing in our professional schools.

Conclusion. In conclusion to this initial chapter, let me repeat what I stated earlier: the reason that I am considering the end of the library school is not because these schools literally will end, but that what will remain may be unrecognizable as professional schools educating librarians. I am not personally concerned about whether we have schools called library or information schools (although many in the field are concerned, incensed even, by the name changes). What I am worried about is whether some of the important things that the old library schools did might be lost in the trendy new information schools. I believe the latter have a lot of potential to offer, but I also worry that they might ignore much that the former were focused on, especially as the new pressures generated by the notion of the corporate university intensify. I worry that the reasons many students come to the schools might be unsupported and that important tasks such as encouraging reading, supporting literacy, understanding the printed book, staffing libraries, and disseminating knowledge might be buried under other tasks as the schools hire fewer faculty with experience or interest in traditional institutions such as libraries or archives. While the old form was plagued by a burden with credentialism and overly concerned with an accreditation system that seems more concerned with the lowest common denominator rather than innovation or the generation of knowledge, the library school still offers many important services to a larger public good in society. Gary Olson and Jonathan Grudin, in their description of the iSchool movement, provide a telling comment about what is going on; affirming that library science continues to have an important role in the new schools, they state, "They were producing librarians but failed to meet the

---

[77] Don Borchert, *Free for All: Oddballs, Geeks, and Gangstas in the Public Library* (New York: Virgin Books, 2007). The discovery of this book came just before our December 2007 graduation ceremony, and I used it in my brief remarks.

academic standards of leading research universities."[78] Anyone who knows anything about these schools might quibble somewhat with such an assessment, but most will acknowledge that this is generally an accurate statement (and that the concern about research, especially in educating students to understand research methods, is not particularly new).[79] It is one worth ruminating about in considering professional schools in the modern university.

---

[78] Gary M. Olson and Jonathan Grudin, "The Information School Phenomenon," *Interactions* 16 (March/April 2009): 15-19 (quotation pp. 15-16).
[79] See, for example, Peter Hernon and Candy Schwartz, "Regaining 'the Foundation of Understanding': the Role of LIS Education." *Library & Information Science Research* 17, no. 1 (1995): 1-3 and "The Desire is Present, but is the Expertise?" *Library and Information Science Research* 23, no. 3 (Autumn 2001): 209.

Chapter Two

Reading, Writing, and the Old Library School

Introduction: Why Read? Higher education has become dependent on the World Wide Web and, as one result, the art and understanding of the value of reading seems to have fallen by the wayside. Faculty members browse through the Web looking for materials to use in lectures or to adopt as inexpensive, convenient readings for students. Students search quickly and often sloppily for materials to use in papers or PowerPoint presentations. And, because of such activities, reflection and learning are adversely affected. Some, especially those in library and information science schools, defend the move from books and reading as due to the decline of the importance of print, the creation of a new virtual library, and the demands of teaching practical skills to individuals who will function as information professionals. Yet, reflective reading is critical to any individual who strives to be a scholar and to function as an academic. Mark Edmundson, an English professor at the University of Virginia, even argues that reading just makes life more enjoyable (even if students and faculty often complain about the burdens of heavy reading demands – not me, I love it). His argument about the importance of a liberal arts education challenges faculty and students in a professional school, but one might ask whether such a perspective is not also critical for students preparing to work in libraries, archives, and other information centers. Reading is not just about training or entertainment, it is essential to developing a well-rounded life.[80]

Since nearly every writer attributes part of their success to reading and writing and publishing as crucial to an academic's success,[81] faculty should be readers (of every kind). Francine Prose states, "Like most, maybe all, writers, I learned to write by writing and, by example, from books."[82] Given the connection between writing and the love of reading, it is no surprise that some have complained about the negative, seemingly paradoxical,

---

[80] Mark Edmundson, *Why Read?* (New York: Bloomsbury, 2004).
[81] J. Peder Zane, ed., *Remarkable Reads: 34 Writers and Their Adventures in Reading* (New York: W. W. Norton, 2004), p. 7.
[82] Francine Prose, *Reading Like a Writer: A Guide for People Who Love Books and for Those Who Want to Write Them* (New York: HarperCollins, 2006), p. 2.

impact of graduate study on their writing. Prose comments, "The only time my passion for reading steered me in the wrong direction was when I let it persuade me to go to graduate school. There, I soon realized that my love for books was unshared by many of my classmates and professors." Prose was plagued by "warring camps of deconstructionists, Marxists, feminists, and so forth, all battling for the right to tell students that they were reading 'texts' in which ideas and politics trumped what the writer had actually written."[83] There are so many others who have lamented the negative influences of the academy on writing that this is not something anyone should ignore, and graduate students need to be cautious as they seek how to produce academic text as they are sometimes influenced by their academic advisors and student colleagues to write for other academics and specialists and not for the educated public.[84]

Reading, and its supposed demise, has drawn considerable heat from a variety of commentators; many of the critics of higher education, for example, have seen reading as a litmus test for the condition of our universities. The classic writing in this vein, although much contested, is Sven Birkerts, *The Gutenberg Elegies*, where he argues that we must "ask how modifications in our way of reading may impinge upon our mental life. For how we receive information bears vitally on the ways we experience and interpret reality" (and given the multitude of changing means by which we receive information, library and information science faculty might be rearranging their reality on a regular basis).[85]

The writings by public scholars such as Birkerts get to the heart of certain aspects of what library schools have traditionally focused on and that has become the topic of so much public and professional debate (even if the schools seem to stay out of the debate). There is a sense of a faith in writing, books, and libraries that seems to many to have been swept aside. There is also a pleasure to be found in reading, one that can be seen indirectly in Michael Pollan's account of his building of a personal study

---

[83] Prose, *Reading Like a Writer*, p. 68.
[84] Jill Ker Conway, in William Zinsser, ed., *Inventing the Truth: The Art and Craft of Memoir*, rev. ed. (Boston: Houghton Mifflin Co., 1998), p. 44.
[85] Sven Birkerts, *The Gutenberg Elegies: The Fate of Reading in an Electronic Age* (Boston: Faber and Faber, 1994), p. 72. See also Sven Birkerts, *Reading Life: Books for the Ages* (Saint Paul, Minnesota: Graywolf Press, 2007); Andrew Delbanco, *Required Reading: Why Our American Classics Matter Now* (New York: Farrar, Straus, and Giroux, 1997); Wendy Lesser, *Nothing Remains the Same: Rereading and Remembering* (Boston: Houghton Mifflin, 2002); and Anne Fadiman, *Rereadings: Seventeen Writers Revisit Books They Love* (New York: Farrar, Straus and Giroux, 2005).

and library,⁸⁶ and more directly in Alberto Manguel's writings.⁸⁷ Manguel believes that books resist categorization and organization, but, instead, "refuse to sit quietly on shelves," is but one of many reasons that faculty, especially in professional schools equipping future librarians and information professionals, need to look beyond the technical and acquire a love of reading (and I will reflect more extensively on Manguel in the next chapter).

Where is the Joy of Reading? Fears that librarians and society alike may be neglecting the value of the traditional book and the benefits of reading such sources have, at various times, exploded into vociferous and high-profile debate. Nicholson Baker's diatribe on the removal of books from libraries in favor of computer terminals and what he sees as poor methods for preservation (microfilm and digitization) of printed texts not too many years ago led to considerable media scrutiny.⁸⁸ Baker's book has a number of companion works milder in their criticism and more balanced in their perspective, including the writings of Nicholas A. Basbanes.⁸⁹ Yet, we understand that the way in which society values books and libraries also makes them targets, well documented by a growing number of scholars and commentators.⁹⁰ These books raise many questions about how the continuously-evolving schools of library and information science need to maintain some focus on books and printing, if for no other reason other than society acknowledges their importance as cultural and community icons (will this stay a focus in iSchools?).

There has been a resurgence of scholarly and research interest in the future of the book, reading, and libraries. Karin Littau considers a "great

---

⁸⁶ Michael Pollan, *A Place of My Own: The Education of an Amateur Builder* (New York: Random House, 1997).

⁸⁷ Alberto Manguel, *A History of Reading* (New York: Viking, 1996); *A Reading Diary: A Passionate Reader's Reflections on a Year of Books* (New York: Farrar, Strauss, and Giroux, 2004); and *Into the Looking-Glass Wood: Essays on Books, Reading, and the World* (San Diego: Harcourt, Inc, 1998).

⁸⁸ Nicholson Baker, *Double Fold: Libraries and the Assault on Paper* (New York: Random House, 2001).

⁸⁹ Nicholas A. Basbanes, *Every Book Its Reader: The Power of the Printed Word to Stir the World* (New York: Harper Collins, 2005) and *A Splendor of Letters: The Permanence of Books in an Impermanent World* (New York: HarperCollins, 2003).

⁹⁰ James Raven, ed., *Lost Libraries: The Destruction of Great Book Collections since Antiquity* (New York: Palgrave Macmillan, 2004); Rebecca Knuth, *Libricide: The Regime-Sponsored Destruction of Books and Libraries in the Twentieth Century* (Westport, Conn.: Praeger, 2003); and Jonathan Rose, ed., *The Holocaust and the Book: Destruction and Preservation* (Amherst: University of Massachusetts Press, 2001).

many theories of reading," such as its history, material conditions, physiology, fictional renderings, literary criticism, and reading and sexual politics.[91] Littau reflects how we generally see two books, one material and the other ideational, and that this marks the "dividing line between two fields of study: cultural history and literary theory,"[92] causing one to wonder just how library schools consider such matters, if they do at all (at least if they do across the board). If there is evidence about how much of this scholarship occurs outside of library science schools,[93] there are also some important contributions coming from individuals associated with these schools (although not as many as we might want or wish for).[94]

The new scholarship on the history of the book, printing, and publishing has come from literary and cultural studies scholars considering how people, communities, and society interacts with texts over time (certainly a topic that ought to fit well with how the new iSchools are describing their mission – but only time will confirm this). However, just as library and information science faculty need to be cautious in being too technical in their approach to reading, immersing it too deeply in notions of information retrieval and Web surfing, these other disciplines sometimes seem to have lost sight of reasons why people read for enjoyment and meaning rather than just information seeking. Denis Donoghue examines how literary theory, among other things, has overwhelmed a broader sense of the nature and value of reading.[95] Robert Alter provides an even harsher portrait of the contrast between literary theorists and those initially attracted to the study of literature because of a joy in reading (perhaps suggesting some of the same challenges the new iSchools may face with students who are attracted to these professional schools because they want to be a

---

[91] Karin Littau, *Theories of Reading: Books, Bodies, and Bibliomania* (Cambridge: Polity Press, 2006), p. 10.
[92] Littau, *Theories of Reading*, p. 1.
[93] Geoffrey Nunberg, ed., *The Future of the Book* (Berkeley: University of California Press, 1996); R. Howard Bloch and Carla Hesse, eds., *Future Libraries* (Berkeley: University of California Press, 1995); and David D. Hall, *Cultures of Print: Essays in the History of the Book* (Amherst: University of Massachusetts Press, 1996), as examples.
[94] Frederick G. Kilgour, *The Evolution of the Book* (New York: Oxford University Press, 1998) and Redmond Kathleen Molz and Phyllis Dain, *Civic Space/Cyberspace: The American Public Library in the Information Age* (Cambridge: MIT Press, 1999).
[95] Denis Donoghue, *The Practice of Reading* (New Haven: Yale University Press, 1998).

librarian and love books).[96] The most common statement made by applicants to the typical MLIS program concerns their love of books; is this evident in our curriculum?

The Printed Book and Reading. Reflecting on reading is invaluable for reconsidering publishing, a topic of significance for academics that, for better or worse, are successful based on their ability to publish peer-reviewed research studies in professional and scholarly journals, monographs, and professional venues. There are two excellent insider accounts of the constantly shifting tide of publishing books that every academic ought to read, especially those in library schools and their successors. Jason Epstein, known for founding Anchor Books and creating the Library of America series, provides an optimistic view of the publishing industry, embracing the Internet and online publishing.[97] André Schiffrin, equally well known for his work at Random House and his founding of The New Press, provides a more cynical view.[98] While neither Epstein or Schiffrin have much to say about the education or practices of librarians, others writing about publishing do, such as Lindsay Waters's extended essay on the fate of university presses, negatively commenting about the impact of university library practice in curtailing the purchases of printed books in favor of new information technologies.[99] If nothing else, here is an issue worthy of study and debate in the new library schools, whatever they may be called.

Other scholarship on aspects of book publishing, such as the matter of the small bookstore and its future in face of the chain bookstores (or now, perhaps, online bookstores), suggest other connections between libraries and publishers. Sociologist Laura Miller's study of the capitalism of bookselling suggests a lot about customers' expectations of booksellers, and how booksellers have tried to diversify their appeal by transforming their stores into entertainment and social or community centers, efforts "to make the bookstore into more than just a place that houses books."[100] We have

---

[96] Robert Alter, *The Pleasures of Reading in an Ideological Age* (New York: W. W. Norton and Co., 1996).
[97] Jason Epstein, *Book Business: Publishing Past Present and Future* (New York: W. W. Norton, 2002).
[98] André Schiffrin, The *Business of Books: How International Conglomerates Took Over Publishing and Changed the Way We Read* (New York: Verso, 2000).
[99] Lindsay Waters, *Enemies of Promise: Publishing, Perishing, and the Eclipse of Scholarship* (Chicago: Prickly Paradigm Press, 2004).
[100] Laura Miller, *Reluctant Capitalists: Bookselling and the Culture of Consumption* (Chicago: University of Chicago Press, 2006), p. 125.

seen the same trends by libraries, mimicking the physical setup of bookstores and also providing coffee shops, and we have seen such issues enter into library school courses.

For faculty involved in educating future librarians and information professionals, the topic of reading also ought to suggest not just considering new digital processes but the impact of printing on society. Elizabeth L. Eisenstein's magisterial *The Printing Press as an Agent of Change* is not only considered one of the most important books published in the twentieth century, but it has been the starting point for nearly everyone analyzing the potential implications of a move from a print to a digital era. Eisenstein sees printing as leading to revolutions in science, religion, and commerce.[101] Some scholars, most notably Adrian Johns, discern a much more complicated picture of printing's influence on society events by focusing on one nation, England, and the various technicians, merchants, guilds, and authors who were involved in the emergent publishing industry.[102] No matter the continuing debates about the influence of printing, we still must acknowledge that it made possible and necessary a number of scholarly printing attributes, such as the footnote (a device often perplexing students but which some of us love, cherish, and use too much).[103]

There are many different scholarly perspectives on the meaning of printing for society and the nature and importance of reading. The advent of printing was far more complex than how the advocates of a sweeping revolution often describe it. Print did not stabilize text as rapidly as has been suggested, David McKitterick argues in his major study on the subject, seeing "that innovations in printing were gradual: that both in its technical achievements and in the social (including religious and political) consequences it was not invariably appropriate to speak of rapid

---

[101] Elizabeth L. Eisenstein, *The Printing Press as an Agent of Change: Communications and Cultural Transformations in Early-Modern Europe* (New York: Cambridge University Press, 1979). An abridged version of Eisenstein's massive work is available as *The Printing Press in Early-Modern Europe* (Cambridge: Cambridge University Press, 1993), although it lacks the richness of her full work.

[102] Adrian Johns, *The Nature of the Book: Print and Knowledge in the Making* (Chicago: University of Chicago Press, 1998). For a convenient means of seeing the different perspectives of these two scholars, see Adrian Johns, "How to Acknowledge a Revolution," *American Historical Review* 107 (February 2002): 106-125 and Elizabeth L. Eisenstein, "An Unacknowledged Revolution Revisited," *American Historical Review* 107 (February 2002): 87-105, her response.

[103] Anthony Grafton, *The Footnote: A Curious History* (Cambridge: Harvard University Press, 1997).

transformation."[104] Instead, he postulates, society, including both authors and printers, were able to live with a more uncertain notion of what was read on the printed page, where "Instability is characteristic of each stage in the production of a book even after it has left the author's hands. At least for the first three-and-a-half centuries after Gutenberg, printing itself was defined and (frequently) understood not just as offering a standardization impossible in a manuscript environment, but also as a medium endlessly subject to invention and compromise."[105] McKitterick urges us to reconsider how we perceive such major technologies and their roles, that it is not the technology driving change but that the technology is the result of a much more complex set of historical, social, political, economic, as well as technical, elements. Read from the vantage of the library school emerging into schools of information sciences or "iSchools," there is much food for thought in McKitterick's work as we peer into our own future. As David Friedman, messing around with the potential of future technologies, states, the "future is radically uncertain. In interesting ways."[106] Indeed.

We must remember that we always can see something of the future by looking into the past. English professor H. J. Jackson considers the relationship between when books became more commonly available and ownership brought with it a desire to annotate books, usually with ownership marks (Jackson contends that nearly all marginalia was an effort to claim ownership of a book by personalizing it as both an object and the ideas or information contained in it).[107] Her work is an effort both to contribute to the history of the book and printing (she discusses how early printers often added manuscript notes to aid readers, the industry of publishing guides to instruct readers how to mark up their books, and printing marks intended to assist public readings of books) and the burgeoning field of scholarship on reading. Jackson considers marginalia as a permanent record of the reading experience, noting, among other things,

---

[104] David McKitterick, *Print, Manuscript and the Search for Order 1450-1830* (New York: Cambridge University Press, 2003), p. 4.
[105] McKitterick, *Print, Manuscript and the Search for Order 1450-1830*, pp. 216-217.
[106] David D. Friedman, *Future Imperfect: Technology and Freedom in an Uncertain World* (New York: Cambridge University Press, 2008), p. 4. He discusses, among other things, intellectual property, personal privacy, transparency and its mixed blessings, e-business. open space and scholarship, computer crime, biotechnology, and virtual reality. He is deliberately provocative, and he often presents extreme opposite possibilities of various scenarios.
[107] H. J. Jackson, *Marginalia: Readers Writing in Books* (New Haven: Yale University Press, 2001), p. 81.

how readers addressed their scribbling to later readers and transforming marginalia, which seems to be a solitary pastime into a "semipublic occasion."[108] Marginalia, often ignored, is useful for understanding the reception of literature, giving eyewitness recollections about the reading of a particular book, presenting proof that a book was actually read, and documenting the history of reading.[109] It is why, for many, whatever future the digital book has depends on its ability to incorporate the features offered by the printed book (as well as new features only available in the e-book), and why schools committed to understanding the connection of information, technology, and people ought to be researching and teaching such matters.

Whatever else the faculty members of a school of library and information sciences may become invested in, in terms of teaching and scholarship, they must remember that reading, particularly reading books, transforms lives (some of us have even heard students say they have been changed by the books assigned to them – how wonderful). And we have considerable testimony to this fact in essay collections[110] and memoirs and collected reviews of literary editors and columnists adding to our understanding of reading's significance.[111] From my vantage LIS faculty always need to keep in mind the pleasure and significance of reading books, since books continue to be of interest to both our students and society

---

[108] Jackson, *Marginalia*. p. 95.

[109] Other interesting scholarly studies of reading include William J. Gilmore, *Reading Becomes a Necessity of Life: Material and Cultural Life in Rural New England, 1780-1835* (Knoxville: University of Tennessee Press, 1989), with ample references to the emergence of early libraries and the role of booksellers, and Ronald J. Zboray, *A Fictive People: Antebellum Economic Development and the American Reading Public* (New York: Oxford University Press, 1993), expanding on the Gilmore study.

[110] Diane Osen, ed., *The Book That Changed My Life: Interviews with National Book Award Winners and Finalists* (New York: The Modern Library, 2002).

[111] Such as Lynne Sharon Schwartz, *Ruined by Reading: A Life in Books* (Boston: Beacon Press, 1996), who captures the sense of the magic in reading, and Anne Fadiman, *Ex Libris: Confessions of a Common Reader* (New York: Farrar, Straus, and Giroux, 1998), contrasting the act of reading and writing on a computer with that of older technologies. Other examples include Maureen Corrigan, *Leave Me Alone, I'm Reading: Finding and Losing Myself in Books* (New York: Random House, 2005); and Michael Dirda, *Book by Book: Notes on Reading and Life* (New York: Henry Holt and Co., 2005), *An Open Book: Coming of Age in the Heartland* (New York: W. W. Norton and Co., 2003), and *Readings: Essays and Literary Entertainments* (Bloomington: Indiana University Press, 2000).

(now, if we can just inspire students to read books assigned to them in their courses!).

Teaching Sinking Knowledge. Teaching is often taken for granted, as a task anyone can do, secondary to or supported solely by a research agenda. Yet, teaching is a complicated, time-consuming responsibility where there have been more failures than successes and, just to make it all that greater of a challenge, where one often has little sense of whether they have succeeded or failed. Ken Bain's study of one hundred college teachers deemed to be successful provides a window into what characteristics enable a faculty member to engage students, capture their interests, and actually help them to learn. Bain, a historian of American foreign policy, helps anyone to understand why university teaching is not something to be seen as a burden or dismissed too lightly but rather that it is at the heart of the academic's work and calling.[112] It is both sobering and enlightening to think about this when many of us know that poor teaching does not stop tenure or promotion but that poor research nearly always will.

There are many excellent discussions about teaching. Sam Pickering, an English professor at the University of Connecticut and better known as the inspiration for the film *Dead Poet's Society*, provides entertaining, disturbing, and provocative essays about the nature of teaching, viewing teaching as more art and calling rather than a process which can be measured and engineered as some of technology or science. Consider one of Pickering's insights: "Knowledge like a corpse in a river sinks, then later and unexpectedly rises to the surface."[113] Another classic discourse on teaching as art and calling is that by James M. Banner, Jr., and Harold C. Cannon, where they, most appropriately for the new iSchools, "distinguish knowledge from information."[114] Many others – English professor Jay Parini,[115] historian Peter Filene,[116] and educator Thomas Hatch all provide

---

[112] Ken Bain, *What the Best College Teachers Do* (Cambridge: Harvard University Press, 2004).
[113] Sam Pickering, *Letters to a Teacher* (New York: Grove Press, 2004).
[114] For Banner and Cannon, "Information is to knowledge what sound is to music, the unorganized material out of which the structured result is composed. We do not ask teachers to convey information; we seek information from newspapers, the stock market ticker tape, or price tags on items in a store. Instead, we ask teachers to transmit knowledge, that which is organized and formally known about a subject – facts, findings, explanations, hypotheses, and theories accepted for their proven accuracy, significance, beauty, utility, or power." James M. Banner, Jr., and Harold C. Cannon, *The Elements of Teaching* (New Haven: Yale University Press, 1997), p. 9.
[115] Jay Parini, *The Art of Teaching* (New York: Oxford University Press, 2005).

useful comments about teaching done at the college or university level. Hatch's comment that "what teachers have to do is akin to playing twenty (or thirty or forty) games of chess all at once" ought to make one want to glance at this brief book (if not run away to a deserted island for a break from the classroom, realizing how bad we often are at playing one game of chess).[117]

I'm the Teacher! First-hand accounts of teaching, describing challenges and joys, can be very useful for the academic, especially since most of the emphasis on preparing to be a university faculty member is spent mastering knowledge and demonstrating the ability to conduct research and publish. Patrick Allitt, a historian at Emory University, leads us through one course with humor and charm.[118] Michael Bérubé provides a close telling of teaching in an English department, in order "to offer curious readers a look into the classroom dynamics of undergraduate courses in contemporary literature and culture, since these are some of the most widely derided and maligned courses in the literature of conservative complaint."[119] Chris Anderson, another English professor, provides a different perspective about personal faith issues and their role in teaching (and the difficulties in teaching about them).[120] Such observers are grappling with personal perspectives, objectivity, and honesty in the classroom, sometimes gummed up in concerns about teaching values. These and other commentators would tell anyone that of course values are being discussed in the classroom. Others have been writing of such matters for a very long time. Jacques Barzun, drawing on more than a half century of teaching at all levels, makes many astute observations about the challenges of teaching; for example, observing college students, Barzun concludes they "want education for their souls, training for life, organized social and artistic activities, psychiatric help, and career planning and placement"[121] (I think

---

[116] Peter Filene, *The Joy of Teaching: A Practical Guide for New College Instructors* (Chapel Hill: University of North Carolina Press, 2005).

[117] Thomas Hatch, *Into the Classroom: Developing the Scholarship of Teaching and Learning* (San Francisco: Jossey-Bass, 2006), p. 5.

[118] Patrick Allitt, *I'm the Teacher, You're the Student: A Semester in the University Classroom* (Philadelphia: University of Pennsylvania Press, 2005).

[119] Michael Bérubé, *What's Liberal About the Liberal Arts? Classroom Politics and 'Bias' in Higher Education* (New York: W. W. Norton and Co., 2006), p. 20.

[120] Chris Anderson, *Teaching as Believing: Faith in the University* (Waco, Texas: Baylor University Press, 2004).

[121] Jacques Barzun, *Begin Here: The Forgotten Conditions of Teaching and Learning* (Chicago: University of Chicago Press, 1992), p. 157.

some of these students have recently been in my office). And sometimes they want this in one course. Neil Postman's two interesting contributions to this, also discuss the objectives of teaching as being equipping students to think and to build a framework for continuous learning.[122] But as will be seen, the pressures of the corporate university work against such grand plans.

Teaching, long considered more art than science, has stimulated strenuous debate (partly because it is constantly changing with all kinds of gee-whiz technologies, such as talking pens on tablet PCs, blogs, and wikis).[123] Some aspects of teaching, such as distance education, have been controversial, leading to angry polemics[124] (and I will discuss the implications of such education systems for library and information science later in this volume). Some have placed this new educational delivery approach in the context of the many changes being wrought by information technology. For some, issues such as distance education have led to reflection on the meaning and purpose of teaching. Classicist James J. O'Donnell suggests that the "real roles of the professor in an information-rich world will be not to provide information but to advise, guide, and encourage students wading through the deep waters of the information flood. Professors in this environment will thrive as mentors, tutors, backseat drivers and coaches."[125] O'Donnell sounds an alarm about refreshing our thinking about the nature of teaching and higher education, writing, "If we continue to provide only for those who come to us, and only for those who submit to our four-year credentialing disciplines, we may reasonably expect that other paths will be found to do some of our traditional business. We must use our imagination to remake ourselves as a larger, virtual presence in our society."[126] Library schools seem to have tackled this challenge, but perhaps at the loss of some other important

---

[122] Neil Postman, with Charles Weingartner, *Teaching as a Subversive Activity* (New York: Dell Publishing Co., Inc., 1969) and *Teaching as a Conserving Activity* (New York: Dell Publishing Co., Inc., 1979).

[123] Jeffrey R. Young, "Film School: To Spice Up Course Work, Professors Make Their Own Videos," *Chronicle of Higher Education*, volume 54, Issue 34, Page A13, available at http://chronicle.com/free/v54/i34/34a01301.htm?utm_source=at&utm_medium=en

[124] David F. Noble, *Digital Diploma Mills: The Automation of Higher Education* (New York: Monthly Review Press, 2001).

[125] James J. O'Donnell, *Avatars of the Word: From Papyrus to Cyberspace* (Cambridge, MA: Harvard University Press, 1998), p. 156.

[126] O'Donnell, *Avatars of the Word*, p. 177.

features of real graduate education. O'Donnell even reimagines the classroom: "The best classroom is one in which the student begins to think, speak, write, and act in new ways made possible by that classroom."[127] Have these schools also embraced this? Not always, I think.

Many academics have contributed lengthy discourses on the challenges of teaching, advising, and mentoring students. Jane Tompkins, an English professor, gives a remarkably candid assessment of herself as teacher and the problems of being in higher education. She seeks a "holistic" approach to working with students, or, as she characteristically explains: "There's too much emphasis on matters related exclusively to the head and not enough attention given to nurturing the attitudes and faculties that make of knowledge something useful and good."[128] What do we make of such concerns when we become involved with education, especially as we believe that distance education is the classroom of the future or the benchmark for what we think education is?

The debate about distance education mostly concerns the delivery of teaching, rather than its substance. We know the world is changing, and we know that includes the university. We need to consider the implications of everything we do. As we move into new methods of educating and training professionals, especially as we move past the early stages of distance education, university faculty need to be prepared to evaluate what we are doing. Reports about the uneven success of distance education ought to be embraced as a call to reconsider how we can improve this educational delivery mechanism.[129] Library and information science schools were among the first to embrace distance education approaches, perceiving them to be ways to reach students and build enrollments,[130] reaching audiences who may not be able to be on-campus,[131] often declaring online and on-campus education to provide few differences in their approaches (and

---

[127] O'Donnell, *Avatars of the Word*, p. 185.
[128] Jane Tompkins, *A Life in School: What the Teacher Learned* (Cambridge, MA: Perseus Books, 1996), p. 206.
[129] Reports about distance education are discussed by David Shieh, "Professors Regard Online Instruction as Less Effective Than Classroom Learning," *Chronicle of Higher Education*, February 10, 2009, available at http://chronicle.com/free/2009/02/11232n.htm.
[130] D. D. Barron, "Distance Education and the Closing of the American Library School," *Library Quarterly* 61 (July 1991): 273-282.
[131] R. Chepesiuk, "Learning Without Walls," *American Libraries* 29 (October 1998): 63-67.

maybe their outcomes),[132] and gaining experience and offering testimonies about such digitally-based teaching.[133] What these faculty members have been slow to do, unfortunately, is to gather up research about the effectiveness of such educational approaches, except to gather some fairly simplistic commentary from experienced online students that what they did was beneficial.[134] When more careful analysis is done, some critical issues emerge, such as the balance between the ease of scheduling flexibility versus greater burdens on faculty and loss of the more spontaneous interaction between on-campus students.[135] However, all such matters may be just side issues, since distance education has been persistently identified as one of the hallmarks of the financial bottom-line corporate university.

New information technologies have the potential for transforming teaching, and this certainly includes what has been assembled to support distance education. Julie Frechette, associate professor of communication and the director of the Center for Community Media at Worcester State College, concludes her essay about the use of technology in teaching this way: "As with other digital developments, faculty continue to grapple with these questions as pedagogical paradigms for effective learning are rapidly changing. Fortunately, clichés of the professor as preoccupied with research over teaching, the political over the personal, literature over television, print over digital media, high art over popular culture, and conferencing over social networking have increasingly been challenged through profound socio-cultural changes, many of which have undoubtedly been promulgated by new technologies and a new generation of learners. If social networking, 3D simulations, blogs and Web pages are means to enhancing the student-teacher relationship, then perhaps we should be less hesitant about using

---

[132] James S. Healy, "Distance Library Education," *Library Trends* (39), no. 4 (Spring 1991): 424-440.
[133] N. Oder, "LIS Distance Ed Moves Ahead," *Library Journal* 126 (1 October 2001): 54-56.
[134] Rae-Ann Montague and Marina Pluzhenskaia. "Web-based Information Science Education (WISE): Collaboration to Explore and Expand Quality in LIS Online Education," *Journal of Education for Library and Information Science* 48, no. 1 (2007): 36-51.
[135] Ruth V. Small, A Comparison of the Resident and Distance Learning Experience in Library and Information Science," *Journal of Education for Library and Information Science* (40), no. 1 (1999): 27-47.

them as we strive to find powerful and creative means to improve the learning experience."[136] Good points.

Colleges and universities have long been hot beds of debate about what should and should not be taught. The so-called culture wars in higher education in the 1980s and 1990s is the most recent and perhaps best known of these debates. Outsider commentaries, ones that often fanned the flames of controversy, can be seen in a number of books. James Atlas called attention to the controversy over the concepts of great books, a literary canon, and other issues stimulating debate within universities and media coverage and political heat from the outside.[137] Benjamin R. Barber considered many of the aspects generating public debate about what is taught in both K-12 and the university, examining the political crises and controversies about education, including debates about canons, democratic values, political correctness, postmodernism, and radical political perspectives.[138] English professor Gerald Graff wrote the most balanced assessment of teaching during the height of debate about the culture wars, stating, "conflict has to mean paralysis only as long as we fail to take positive advantage of it."[139] Graff points out that one major source of the contentious debates about the nature of university education stems from its "deeply contradictory mission": "The university is expected to preserve, transmit, and honor our traditions, yet at the same time it is supposed to produce new knowledge, which means questioning received ideas and perpetually revising traditional ways of thinking."[140] Library schools, given their historic mission, ought to have been caught right in the middle of such issues, but they seemed remarkably quiet during these stormy years.

Teaching, Accounts, and Accountability. There are new means by which to evaluate the nature of the kinds of graduate education we are offering to those preparing for professional degrees. English professor Richard Lanham, reflecting on the emergence of online education, argues that "we might think of this online/campus comparison as an 'audit' of the current campus in terms of the attention economy" (by attention economy Lanham

---

[136] Julie Frechette, "Crossing the (Digital) Line," *Inside Higher Education*, May 16, 2008, available at http://insidehighered.com/views/2008/05/16/frechette.
[137] James Atlas, *Battle of the Books: The Curriculum Debate in America* (New York: W.W. Norton and Co., 1992).
[138] Benjamin R. Barber, *An Aristocracy of Everyone: The Politics of Education and the Future of America* (New York: Ballantine Books, 1992).
[139] Gerald Graff, *Beyond the Culture Wars: How Teaching the Conflicts Can Revitalize American Education* (New York: W.W. Norton and Co., 1992), p. 5.
[140] Graff, *Beyond the Culture Wars*, p. 7.

means that it is not information that is the main coin of the realm in our present era but our ability to attend to the vast information reservoir and make sense of it). Lanham suggests we have never been able to make such an accounting of higher education before because "there was no other way of doing business, no new ground from which to view the old." Lanham poses a set of interesting "assumptions" about higher education needing to be evaluated, including the need for on-campus teaching, full-time faculty, tenure, faculty motives and work habits, the implications of new educational technologies, and the economic circumstances of the university. As Lanham concludes, "The Internet constitutes a pure economics of attention. The virtual university, the university conducted electronically, is the university in a pure economics of attention. That is why it constitutes so valuable an auditor. How the university fits and fares in this economic expressive space, in this new rhetoric, provides a litmus test of what it has been, its strengths, its weaknesses, and what is to become of it."[141] Only time will tell if he is correct about this. And, it might be added, library schools have a long way to go in operating with such accountability (but so do all professional schools), even if some of the points made by Lanham echo the rhetoric used by these schools in their embracing of distance education.

It is difficult to answer the question of what it means to be educated. There are very few critical analyses of this, other than speculations on the purpose of the university. Others, teaching at lower levels, have tried to grapple with this matter, and they are worth a read, such as Alfie Kohn's work.[142] One of the more interesting attempts to address this in higher education is Derek Bok's *Our Underachieving Colleges*. Bok, reviewing the many complaints leveled against the university, argues that these complaints can't be lightly dismissed, although he reminds us just how difficult it can be to present a concise or unified view about the purpose of higher education: "anyone seeking a common purpose must go all the way back to a time before the Civil War, when colleges united around a classical curriculum aimed at mental discipline and character building."[143] We should note that this long predates the origins of library schools.

---

[141] Richard Lanham, *The Economics of Attention: Style and Substance in the Age of Information* (Chicago: University of Chicago Press, 2006), chapter 7.
[142] Alfie Kohn, *What Does It Mean to Be Well Educated? And More Essays on Standards, Grading, and Other Follies* (Boston: Beacon Press, 2004).
[143] Derek Bok, *Our Underachieving Colleges: A Candid Look at How Students Learn and Why They Should Be Learning More* (Princeton: Princeton University Press, 2006), p. 24.

Bok discusses the shift to vocationalism, the role of teaching writing and speaking, the challenges posed by trying to teach students to think, the issues of focusing on building character or making good citizens, the concern about diversity among students and faculty, the meaning of the global society, and a variety of other compelling and contentious issues. In his book, Bok does focus on one testy problem, the preparation of academics to be teachers. He considers that doctoral programs do not focus on teaching, remarking "In the eyes of most faculty members in research universities, teaching is an art that is either too simple to require formal preparation, too personal to be taught to others, or too innate to be conveyed to anyone lacking the necessary gift. Lacking formal preparation, graduate students have learned to teach by modeling themselves after they admire who have taught them. This tradition introduces a profoundly conservative bias into faculty behavior that acts as an anchor to deter major changes in established forms of instruction and educational practice."[144] This problem certainly has affected professional schools as well, perhaps even more so since these schools rely so heavily on practitioners as adjuncts.

Bok notes that academics seem to do just fine with keeping up with the content of their own fields, but not with teaching approaches. Bok argues, "Until Ph.D. programs include a serious preparation for teaching and convey a deeper understanding of the complexities of student learning, faculties will not only have little inclination to change their ways, they will not even perceive much need to do so."[145] Are library schools doing any better here? In my opinion, LIS doctoral students need to avail themselves of every opportunity they can to learn something about teaching. They should read about the art and science of teaching. They should find a mentor to work with in order to learn more about teaching. And they should make special note of every good and bad aspect of teaching they observe, resolving to build on the good and not do the bad.

This has become especially important in our so-called information age. Matthew Kay, discussing teaching 13 year olds armed with laptops and

---

[144] Bok, *Our Underachieving Colleges*, pp. 314-315.
[145] Bok, *Our Underachieving Colleges*, p. 324. Bok stresses that doctoral programs should provide some focus on teaching: "The content involved need not consist merely of practical training in pedagogy but could include readings and discussions on the history and purposes of the curriculum, the state of research on teaching methods and student learning, and the implications of this research for organizing courses, choosing instructional strategies, and assessing student work" (pp. 340-341).

other technology, at the Science Leadership Academy, suggests that "it is more crucial that they learn how to sift thoughtfully through increasing amounts of information.... . The issue now is distinguishing between rich resources and the online collection of surface facts, misinformation, and inexcusable lies that masquerade as the truth. It will be hard for our students to be thoughtful citizens without this ability to discern the useful from the irrelevant."[146] Although this focuses on middle schoolers, the point can be extended to students entering into professional schools who seem to be arriving with less and less well-developed skills in research or in analyzing the information they do find.

We need to remind ourselves that technology is just a tool or, as John Palfrey reminds us, "We need to teach students and faculty how to make use of both rivers and oceans of information."[147] Technology often tends to divert our attention from other issues that ought to carry more weight.

Truths R Us. University professors love to lay claim to academic freedom, and, it is, of course, an important issue. The American Association of University Professors is a group that has been especially committed to making sure that professors do not use their classrooms to indoctrinate and disrespect students and to defend faculty falsely accused of doing so. One critic of the AAUP's latest efforts, Peter Wood (executive director of the National Association of Scholars), believes that the group cares far more about faculty than the students.[148] However, given the nature and mission of LIS schools, I wonder just why it appears that we hear so little about such matters of academic freedom in the classroom in these schools. Considering what we teach and what our students are preparing to do, one might guess that the old library school and its successors could be a beehive of controversy. Generally, however, they are pretty quiet. Why is that?

---

[146] Matthew Kay, "Putting Technology in Its Place," *New York Times*, October 11, 2008, available at http://lessonplans.blogs.nytimes.com/2008/10/11/putting-technology-in-its-place/?th&emc=th

[147] From an interview of John Palfrey by Andy Guess, in "Understanding Students Who Were 'Born Digital,'" *Inside Higher Education*, October 2, 2008, http://insidehighered.com/news/2008/10/02/digital. Palfrey is co-author, with Urs Gasser, of *Born Digital: Understanding the First Generation of Digital Natives* (New York: Basic Books, 2008).

[148] Peter Wood, "Truths R Us," *Inside Higher Education*, September 21, 2007, available at http://insidehighered.com/views/2007/09/21/wood, accessed September 21, 2007.

Academic freedom is a much-discussed topic, often used to suggest that faculty can do just about anything they want. Matthew W. Finkin and Robert C. Post examine this area of academic life, drawing on the important 1915 and 1940 statements by the American Association of University Professors and numerous case studies, freedom in the areas of research and publication, the classroom, intramural speech, and extramural speech. As they conclude, "Academic freedom is not the freedom to speak or to teach just as one wishes. It is the freedom to pursue the scholarly profession, inside and outside the classroom, according to the norms and standards of the profession."[149] Finkin and Post argue that the notion of academic freedom is the result of a covenant between the university and the general public, and that it is a critical one for supporting the "social good of advancing knowledge."[150] They try to demonstrate the intricacies of supporting academic freedom, such as noting that "no university currently deals with its faculty as if academic freedom of research and publication were an individual right to be fully free from all institutional restraint. Universities instead hire, promote, grant tenure to, and support faculty on the basis of criteria of academic merit that purport to apply professional standards. Individual faculty have no right of immunity from such judgments."[151] As they deal with the various dimensions of academic freedom, they occasionally discuss aspects of higher education that seem to be susceptible to much misinterpretation; here is an example: "It is important ... to distinguish between respect for person and respect for ideas. Faculty must respect students as persons, but they needn't respect ideas, even ideas held by students. In higher education no idea is immune from potentially scathing criticism."[152] While others have been rightly concerned about the growing relationship of corporations with universities as the gravest threat on the academy's future, with particular worries about the exaggeration of such problems by the rise of new electronic communications, with "novel threats to the privacy, integrity and autonomy of campus exchanges,"[153] one might just as rightly conclude that most of the problems stem from more mundane misunderstandings about the role

---

[149] Matthew W. Finkin and Robert C. Post, *For the Common Good: Principles of American Academic Freedom* (New Haven: Yale University Press, 2009), p. 149.
[150] Finkin and Post, *For the Common Good*, p. 44.
[151] Finkin and Post, *For the Common Good*, p. 58-59.
[152] Finkin and Post, *For the Common Good*, p. 105.
[153] Interview by Scott Jaschik with Robert M. O'Neil, author of *Academic Freedom in the Wired World: Political Extremism, Corporate Power, and the University* (Cambridge: Harvard University Press, 2008), *Inside Higher Education*, March 6, 2008.

of both the university and its faculty in society. Professional schools and their faculties are not immune from such matters.

The Other Side of Reading: Writing. Such public misunderstandings may result from the fact that academics haven't always been able to communicate to the public about themselves and their lives (faculty in professional schools seem to fixate on practitioners in their field). More than ever, the academic life is the writing life. Professors daily write memoranda, reports, grant proposals, study papers, and position papers, as well as scholarly and professional essays and books. One's success in the university depends on the quality and quantity of writing. Frank Cioffi, who has taught writing at a number of colleges, offers a "manifesto for the protection, for the nurturance, of this endangered species" – the "written argument, which logically explains and defends a controversial idea." He describes the process of writing essays, identifying and targeting audiences, planning the writing project, developing a thesis for the essay or monograph, being creative in the research paper or essay, and the importance of style, all focused on the "academic argument," the prevalent form of nonfiction writing.[154] Unlike other advice books on writing, Cioffi's stresses the importance of imagination, including drawing on personal insight and feelings, to write lively and persuasive essays. Given the general sterility of writing in the information professions, looking for inspiration anywhere to improve one's writing is an important activity. And, for anyone contemplating an academic vocation, reflecting on his or her own commitment to writing is an essential task.

One of the pre-eminent issues in academic writing has been that of audience. In a classic attack on the loss of academics who write for a broader public audience, Russell Jacoby summed up the situation like this: "Younger intellectuals no longer need or want a larger public; they are almost exclusively professors. Campuses are their home; colleagues their audience; monographs and specialized journals their media. Unlike past intellectuals they situate themselves within fields and disciplines – for good reason. Their jobs, advancement, and salaries depend on the evaluation of specialists, and this dependence affects the issues broached and the language employed."[155] Jacoby's book is still generating commentary, both

---

[154] Frank Cioffi, *The Imaginative Argument: A Practical Manifesto for Writers* (Princeton: Princeton University Press, 2005).
[155] Russell Jacoby, *The Last Intellectuals: American Culture in the Age of Academe* (New York: Farrar, Straus and Giroux, 1987), p. 6.

positive and negative.[156] No matter. How many faculty in LIS or iSchools can be considered having an audience including the public? Not very many.

A full generation later Richard A. Posner provides another perspective on public intellectuals, this time critiquing the tendency of academics to write outside their own expertise on other matters of public import.[157] Despite a clumsy research methodology and some overblown rhetoric, the Posner book still makes some powerful points about the need for more academics to expand their audiences beyond a small handful of academic colleagues. In both the Jacoby and Posner tomes, the nature of the writing style is a serious issue in how academics seek to reach their audiences. More than a few academics have defended, of course, their style of writing and their audiences, deriding a soft concept of the notion of a public intellectual. Michael Warner, for example, comments, "If one were really to argue that everyone should write clearly and that everyone should take political positions publicly, one would be arguing in effect *against* the idea of a public intellectual as a special role."[158] Obviously, such debates and discussions are an inherent part of the self-reflection about the university and the role of its faculty. Given the nature of the topics and issues reflected in LIS and iSchools, ranging from matters of public policy to the concerns with information literacy, we should expect to see more writing (both research and policy position statements) for the public than we do.

Mastering the Essay: A Beginning. Graduate students and faculty alike must master the art of writing the academic essay, and there have been important primers written about the art of the essay, considering composing a thesis, the use and citing of evidence, the structure of the essay, and the importance of style.[159] There are always certain aspects of academic writing

---

[156] Scott McLemee argues that Jacoby was offering more an analysis of the conditions necessary for supporting public intellectuals (those who seek a discourse with society in a clear fashion about important issues) rather than a critique of the university environment and what it might had contributed to the demise of such scholars. Scott McLemee, "After the Last Intellectual," *BookForum* 14 (September/October/November 2007): 15, 17, 59.

[157] Richard A. Posner, *Public Intellectuals: A Study of Decline* (Cambridge: Harvard University Press, 2001).

[158] Michael Warner in Jonathan Culler and Kevin Lamb, eds., *Just Being Difficult? Academic Writing in the Public Arena* (Stanford, CA: Stanford University Press, 2003), p. 119.

[159] Scott F. Crider, *The Office of Assertion: An Art of Rhetoric for the Academic Essay* (Wilmington, Del.: ISI Books, 2005) and Jacques Barzun, *Simple and Direct: A Rhetoric for Writers*, rev.ed. (Chicago: University of Chicago Press, 1985).

generating new challenges, such as incorporating numbers and statistics into an essay or monograph. Jane E. Miller, for example, argues, "Writing about numbers is a complex process: it involves finding pertinent numbers, identifying patterns, calculating comparisons, organizing ideas, designing tables or charts, and finally, writing prose... ."[160] Of course, just seeking to produce clear, concise, understandable language can be a challenge, as Richard Mitchell pokes fun at in his book on undergraduate writing.[161] (Of course, I am trying to violate every basic, commonsense principle in writing in this book).

Academics, as they advise doctoral and other students, often tend to reduce scholarly writing to formulaic practices, perhaps one reason why there is so much bad academic writing and why so few university and college professors ever reach a broader reading audience. For advice on quality writing, students or professors ought not to be so timid in reading about the experiences of well-known and accomplished writers of both fiction and non-fiction. And there is a lot of good counsel to be had from such sources. Anne Lamott's *Bird by Bird* is one of the best of such writing guides. Drawing from her personal experience, Lamott's book is the classic, inspirational guide for those thinking of trying writing or who are looking for advice about it. In a witty and lively fashion, the author discusses all facets of writing, from planning a project to dealing with multiple rejections of finished pieces. Lamott provides a lot of excellent advice about the practical aspects of writing, including having others read drafts to working with editors and publishers. As she strongly asserts, writing is not a magical process, but it is hard work, marked by trial and error, discouragement, and, often, unexpected results[162] (I will comment on Lamott again). Too often doctoral students and working academics are focused on the mechanics of research, rather than the art of writing the research in a manner that enables it to be read and comprehended. Many recommend taking writing classes, and Nancy Bunge's set of interviews with successful writers and proven teachers of writing provides a number of insights into the learning curve of writing.[163]

---

[160] Jane E. Miller, *The Chicago Guide to Writing About Numbers* (Chicago: University of Chicago Press, 2004), p. 7.
[161] Richard Mitchell, *The Leaning Tower of Babel and Other Affronts by the Underground Grammarian* (New York: Simon and Schuster, 1984).
[162] Anne Lamott, *Bird by Bird: Some Instructions on Writing and Life* (New York: Anchor Books, 1995; org. pub. 1994).
[163] Nancy Bunge, *Master Class: Lessons from Leading Writers* (Iowa City: University of Iowa Press, 2005).

Everyone associated with the academy understands that faculty members are apprenticed in the craft of writing. But there are also many personal memoirs by writers that can be read with profit by academics. These authors ruminate about the act of writing, the relationship between reading and writing, life experiences and writing, the nature of writing and receiving criticism, and the forces compelling one to write, bringing a passion to writing that can be lost in the publish or perish environment of the academy. Joyce Carol Oates muses, "I've never thought of writing as the mere arrangement of words on the page but the attempted embodiment of a vision; a complex of emotions; raw experience."[164] It is easy for academics to lose such vision and passion, or to wonder if they ever possessed such attributes. Yet, it is even easier for academics to lose their way if they lack passion for or commitment to a life necessitating dedication to research and composition about their research.

Successful writers who publish about their vocation have much to offer academics (if we will take the time to read what they have to say). Nearly every such memoir offers something of value.[165] Roy Peter Clark views writing as "less as a special talent and more as a purposeful craft," and he offers his tips as a set of tools for this purpose.[166] Many writers, such as Bret Lott, argue to indulge the creative side of writing nonfiction, and there is ample enough need for good writing in that area.[167] Peter Turchi, using the map as a metaphor for the craft of writing and the process of developing a view of the world and one's place in it, suggests, "A prerequisite for finding our way through any story or novel is to be lost: the journey can't begin until we've been set down in a place somehow

---

[164] Joyce Carol Oates, *The Faith of a Writer: Life, Craft, Art* (New York: HarperCollins, 2003), p. 30.

[165] See, for example, Richard Rhodes, *How to Write: Advice and Reflections* (New York: HarperCollins Publishers, 1995); Ray Bradbury, *Zen in the Art of Writing* (Santa Barbara, Calif.: Joshua Odell Editions, 1996); Annie Dillard, *The Writing Life* (New York: HarperPerennial, 1990); Bonnie Friedman, *Writing Past Dark: Envy, Fear, Distractions and Other Dilemmas in the Writer's Life* (New York: HarperPerennial, 1993); Stephen King, *On Writing: A Memoir of the Craft* (New York: Pocket Books, 2000); Wendy Lesser, *The Amateur: An Independent Life of Letters* (New York: Vintage Books, 1999); and Norman Mailer, *The Spooky Art: Thoughts on Writing* (New York: Random House, 2003).

[166] Roy Peter Clark, *Writing Tools: 50 Essential Strategies for Every Writer* (New York: Little, Brown and Co., 2006), p. 4.

[167] Bret Lott, *Before We Get Started: A Practical Memoir of the Writer's Life* (New York: Ballatine Books, 2005).

unfamiliar."[168] The graduate student beginning dissertation work or the scholar starting any research project can relate to this initial feeling of being lost, and, sometimes, all they need do is to look inward at their experiences. Margaret Atwood stresses how fiction writers learn their trade by reading and observation, based mostly on her personal experiences; perhaps, doctoral students and academics need to pay far more attention to these and other influences on their work.[169] Bell hooks reviews her development and experiences as a writer, with some candid comments about the academic and writing: "The only reason I went to graduate school and acquired a Ph.D. in American literature was so that I could support myself as a writer. Everyone knew that academics writing books were lucky to find a publisher and a few readers. In those days no one that I knew saw writing as a way to make a living."[170] Fiction and creative writers are generally most useful for comments on style, creativity, the task of writing, working with agents, getting published, and other aspects of the writing life, and, fortunately there are convenient compilation of writers discussing the act of writing and publishing.[171] None of these are attributes faculty in professional schools ought to neglect, in their own work and that of their students.

The Sound of Writing. Developing appropriate writing styles for particular venues of scholarly and professional publishing is a skill all academics and aspiring academics must master. Ben Yagoda provides some useful advice, comparing writing styles to fingerprints in their distinctiveness, suggesting the mimicking of writing styles. Yagoda, a journalism professor, helps in teaching a writer not only the rudiments of style, but he considers how styles need to change and adapt from one's beginning stages to their more developed and mature writing phases.[172] Graduate students and scholars

---

[168] Peter Turchi, *Maps of the Imagination: The Writer as Cartographer* (San Antonio, Texas: Trinity University Press, 2004), p. 113.

[169] Margaret Atwood, *Negotiating with the Dead: A Writer on Writing* (Cambridge: Cambridge University Press, 2002). See also Ellen Gilchrist, *The Writing Life* (Jackson, Miss.: University Press of Mississippi, 2005).

[170] bell hooks, *Remembered Rapture: The Writer at Work* (New York: Henry Holt and Co., 1999), p. 155.

[171] Marie Arana, ed., *The Writing Life: Writers on How They Think and Work: A Collection from the Washington Post Book World* (New York: Public Affairs, 2003) and Kevin Smokler, ed., *Bookmark Now: Writing in Unreaderly Times* (New York: Basic Books, 2005) are good examples.

[172] Ben Yagoda, *The Sound on the Page: Style and Voice in Writing* (New York: HarperResource, 2004).

need to go through a similar process, learning the styles of their field and the journals they publish in. Others provide similar advice. Noah Lukeman offers this, "The *art* of writing cannot be taught, but the *craft* of writing can. No one can teach you how to tap inspiration, how to gain vision and sensibility, but you can be taught to write lucidity, to present what you say in the most articulate and forceful way. Vision itself is useless without the technical means to record it."[173] Lukeman understands the challenges of academic and scholarly writing, noting that the "academic style is an issue in and of itself. It is perhaps the most commonly encountered form of stylistic error, for professors (and graduate students – frequently with theses) often try to break into mainstream publishing. Style is inevitably their obstacle." He adds that "their prose is unnecessarily convoluted" and "their foremost concerns are accuracy and thoroughness, whereas the foremost concern of a trade writer is keeping the reader engrossed."[174] Ok, I confess and offer this work as evidence of my transgressions.

Nearly every book offering writing advice focuses on the barriers to writing. Advice such as take a class, just do it, and read other writers is legion. Neurologist Alice W. Flaherty provides clinical perspectives on the relationship between writing and emotion underlying the reasons how and why we write.[175] This is not a book intended to help someone transform him or herself into an accomplished writer, but it is an interesting discourse that helps us understand more about what is involved. Academics, at least those hoping to have long and successful careers in the university or college, can't afford to fight such problems. Two newer books on academic writing provide considerable amounts of useful tips about how to avoid such pitfalls. W. Brad Johnson and Carol A. Mullen offer 65 points about how to be successful academic writers, providing straightforward and commonsensical advice on building positive habits for writing, setting boundaries to be able to manage it, finding and working with mentors, and developing relationships with publishers. For example, they argue that "if you want to become a prolific academic, then weave the act of writing into the fabric of your identity and the mosaic of your daily life."[176] Paul J. Silvia covers much of the same ground, suggesting that writing (and writing well)

---

[173] Noah Lukeman, *The First Five Pages: A Writer's Guide to Staying Out of the Rejection Pile* (New York: Fireside Book, Simon & Schuster, 2000), p. 15.
[174] Lukeman, *The First Five Pages*, p. 68.
[175] Alice W. Flaherty, *The Midnight Disease: The Desire to Write, Writer's Block, and the Creative Brain* (Boston: Houghton Mifflin Co., 2004).
[176] W. Brad Johnson and Carol A. Mullen, *Write to the Top! How to Become a Prolific Academic* (New York: Palgrave Macmillan, 2007), p. 5.

is an activity that one learns to do. Silvia provides very commonsensical advice such as, "writing begins and ends with words. To write well, you need to choose good words" or, "To write a lot, you must make a schedule and stick to it. That's how you write a book. Don't wait for the summer, and don't wait for a sabbatical."[177]

I tell my own students, in similar fashion, to aim for a regimen of writing everyday; it is the only way to get longer projects done. It is not too far from learning to write stories. Just like any writer, academics, whether publishing scientific research results or composing a biography, are telling stories. Tom Hallman provides a glimpse into the power of stories: "I don't have a master's degree from Columbia, I never did an internship at the *Washington Post*, and I was fired from my first job as a copy editor in New York: I'm an extremely average reporter. Extremely average reporters can win Pulitzers if they know how to tell stories."[178] This is certainly one I will use with my own students, if for no other reason than I believe that our schools educating individuals for different varieties of information professionals in what so many claim to be a new and distinct form of information era are also identifying and generating all kinds of interesting stories.

The notion of storytelling connects to a more fundamental aspect of writing. One aspect of writing that is so often forgotten or minimized, at least in academic writing, is the connection of writing with living. Pushed on this topic, most academics spin some variation of the "publish or perish" syndrome, a characteristic of the university that has led to a lot of poor and generally meaningless writing and publishing (except as a means to get tenure). One ought to read Thomas Merton – the monk, essayist, poet, novelist, and mystic – to get a feel of the inner person that often drives individuals to write, even if they never publish.[179] What Merton offers might not transform the university professor in his or her approach to writing, but it will at least stimulate some different thinking about their objectives in writing and publishing. The effort is well worth it.

Most fiction writers have grappled with such fundamental questions. Sara Paretsky, the author of the popular V I Warshawski novels, and well

---

[177] Paul J. Silvia, *How to Write a Lot: A Practical Guide to Productive Academic Writing* (Washington, D.C.: American Psychological Association, 2007), pp. 61, 115.
[178] Tom Hallman in Mark Kramer and Wendy Call, eds., *Telling True Stories: A Nonfiction Writers' Guide from the Nieman Foundation at Harvard University* (New York: Plume, 2007), p. 212.
[179] Robert Inchausti, ed., *Echoing Silence: Thomas Merton on the Vocation of Writing* (Boston: New Seeds, 2007).

known to avid readers of mysteries, reaffirms the need for writers to speak out plainly and bluntly through their writing, asserting, "Every writer's difficult journey is a movement from silence to speech" and urging writers not to "be silenced, either by pernicious laws, or by mob screaming." [180] If a writer such as Paretsky sees such challenges for a writer, how should academics, especially in the information professions, see barriers today in their own mission and work? Clearly, the same challenges are pernicious threats to them as well, affecting what they choose to research and publish.

The Faculty and Publishing. Every doctoral student, successful ones at least, will write a dissertation. The quality of the dissertation, not only its ability to demonstrate research competence, but its relevance to the profession and its potential for publication, will make or break a fledgling academic career. Since graduate schools and advisors spend little energy in explaining what to do with a dissertation once it is done, William Germano offers advice on figuring out the marketplace, identifying what a broader readership means and revising for it, working with an editor and publisher, helping the beginning scholar understand why the dissertation is not yet a book, determining whether a dissertation should be expanded into a book, the basic common weaknesses to revising dissertations into books (audience, voice, structure, length), and planning and carrying out the revision.[181]

Germano offers this general advice and commentary about the nature of scholarly writing and publishing: "Scholars who write and publish are probably happier than those who don't. This is a completely impressionistic take, I admit, and there are doubtless deeply depressed academics who nonetheless publish furiously. But like physical exercise, writing is the tiring thing that gives you more energy after you've done it. Writing is a risk, and risk is exciting, and excitement is something you will fight to sustain in your professional life as you age and your students don't." One's commitment to writing for publication is something that anyone contemplating an academic career should consider as carefully as possible, because it is a "lifelong occupation," requires practice, and must be a kind of "devotional exercise."

---

[180] Sara Paretsky, *Writing in an Age of Silence* (New York: Verso, 2007), pp. 111, 134.
[181] William Germano, *From Dissertation to Book* (Chicago: University of Chicago Press, 2005). Other useful guides for dissertation work include Beth Luey, ed., *Revising Your Dissertation: Advice from Leading Editors* (Berkeley, CA: University of California Press, 2004); Joan Bolker, *Writing Your Dissertation in Fifteen Minutes a Day: A Guide to Starting, Revising, and Finishing Your Doctoral Thesis* (New York: Henry Holt and Co., 1998); and Eviatar Zerubavel, *The Clockwork Muse: A Practical Guide to Writing Theses, Dissertations, and Books* (Cambridge: Harvard University Press, 1999).

Writing, good or bad, also defines you: "What you write is a part of who you are, and in that sense every volume of your writing is a piece of autobiography." We should never see a doctoral student walking about without a laptop or a Moleskine book or, better yet, both!

Above all, in order to be successful at publishing, or any other aspect of the academic life, one must manage their most precious commodity – time. David Perlmutter argues that managing time requires commitment, the establishment of a comfortable work environment, reasonable goals, and planning.[182] Are there particular challenges for faculty in professional schools? Peter Levine reminds us, "Academics are strongly influenced by policies regarding funding, hiring, promotion, and tenure. Often universities that compete internationally for academic prominence do not reward applied research – let alone service – despite rhetoric to the contrary."[183] Levine adds, "Fortunately, universities do reward scholars who break new ground in their disciplines by working with communities. Thus is a strategy of using community engagement to achieve genuine scholarly insight is better suited to the existing academic marketplace than a strategy based on 'service.'"[184] Faculty in professional schools in research universities can also be successful, and, as an added bonus, they can mentor their successors in how to do it as well.

Beyond the Dissertation. Many think that one of the obstacles to academics getting published and contributing to public knowledge is the dissertation process and product itself. William M. Chace writes, "In most cases, after dissertations are finished, only those who have written them and the professors required to inspect them have read them." A few become scholarly monographs, Chace observes, but "Most others disappear into an archive at the university where they were written and where they find oblivion."[185] My sense is that this is the fate of far too many dissertations

---

[182] David Perlmutter, "Do You Really Not Have the Time?," *Chronicle of Higher Education*, August 22, 2008, available at http://chronicle.com/jobs/news/2008/08/2008082201c.htm. David D. Perlmutter is a professor in the William Allen White School of Journalism and Mass Communications at the University of Kansas.
[183] Peter Levine in Charlotte Hess and Elinor Ostrom, *Understanding Knowledge as a Commons: From Theory to Practice* (Cambridge, MA: MIT Press, 2007), p. 261.
[184] Levine, p. 263.
[185] William M. Chace, *100 Semesters: My Adventures As Student, Professor, and University President, And What I Learned Along the Way* (Princeton: Princeton University Press, 2006), pp. 113-114.

done in LIS programs, although it can certainly be prevented if a little care is taken.

Beyond the dissertation and its published offspring, there are useful guides for scholarly publishing. William Germano, an experienced editor and administrator in both university and trade presses, offers useful advice about how to prepare a scholarly work for publication. He discusses the nature of publishing and range of functions of publishers, how to approach publishers, writing the manuscript, identifying a potential publisher, preparing and submitting a book proposal, the role of editors, the reviewing process, the nature and mechanics of a contract, intellectual property challenges, delivering the manuscript, and the production process.[186] Others, writing such advice, have generally focused on the same litany of topics.[187] Understanding the rudiments of publishing is not only essential for getting published, it ought to be a topic faculty in library and information science programs research and teach about; the nature of the book, and the predictions about its demise (at least in printed form), is a critical theme in the nature of our presented information age.

Successful publishing is much more complicated than just finding one's voice or audience, with many barriers to book publishing often presenting themselves in the constantly shifting trends in academic publishing (a topic that ought to be prominent in the courses in library and information science schools). Lindsay Waters describes the decline in university press publishing of many types of scholarly monographs (with a focus on the humanities), attributing some of the problems to the shifts by university libraries from print acquisition to digital initiatives. Waters's extended essay is a stimulating and disturbing read, and one that every academic and academic-to-be ought to read and reflect on.[188] Getting published also depends, as well, on the quality of the research that an academic has done, whether they are seeking to contribute a highly esoteric research study to a particular field's scholarly literature or they are trying to

---

[186] William Germano, *Getting It Published: A Guide for Scholars and Anyone Else Serious About Serious Books* (Chicago: University of Chicago Press, 2001).

[187] See, for example, Walter W. Powell, *Getting into Print: The Decision-Making Process in Scholarly Publishing* (Chicago: University of Chicago Press, 1985) and Franklin H. Silverman, *Publishing for Tenure and Beyond* (Westport, Conn.: Praeger, 1999).

[188] Lindsay Waters, *Enemies of Promise: Publishing, Perishing, and the Eclipse of Scholarship* (Chicago: Prickly Paradigm Press, 2004). Some academics seek to write textbooks or professional reference works that become standards in their fields, described by Franklin H. Silverman in *Authoring Books and Materials for Students, Academics, and Professionals* (Westport, Conn.: Praeger, 1998).

reach a broader public by making their research less jargon-laden and more accessible to a lay audience. Faculty in the library and information science field have the opportunity to do both well, given the field's interest in topics such as information seeking behavior and the history and nature of publishing – subjects that many outside the discipline are concerned about, although like many other disciplines, LIS faculty have not done very well in contributing to a public scholarship, and there are many excellent guides to the purpose and practice of research that help to clarify the nature of this function of the university professor.[189]

Conclusion. Reading, writing, and teaching using these skills remains part of the old library school regimen (or so it seems). Now both students and their teachers surf for information more than read and reflect. This may be partly due to the fact that many of our students are arriving lacking these basic skills or, at least, having any interest in learning to use them. Therese Huston, exploring the challenges of college and university faculty being required to teach topics they don't know, also offers lots of useful advice about teaching strategies, interacting with students (especially the differences in attitudes and aims between faculty and students), and the assessment of teaching – generally revealing that it is easy to lose sight of the fact that our students (even at the graduate level) don't share our love of learning or our passion for our specialized expertise.[190] Perhaps, we have jettisoned some of the notions supporting the old library school not just because of crowding new technical specialties into its curriculum, but because we believe we need to offer new and trendier specializations and themes in order to attract new varieties of students (but I doubt this,

---

[189] See, for example, Wayne C. Booth, Gregory G. Colomb, and Joseph M. Williams, *The Craft of Research*, second ed. (Chicago: University of Chicago Press, 2003). Doctoral students who go into academic positions, and who take a shot at academic careers, will want to stock up on the various guides to writing offered through the University of Chicago Press. For example, Charles Lipson, *Cite Right: A Quick Guide to Citation Styles – MLA, APA, Chicago, the Sciences, Professions, and More* (Chicago: University of Chicago Press, 2006) is, perhaps, the most handy guide to unraveling citation style challenges.

[190] Therese Huston, *Teaching What You Don't Know* (Cambridge, MA: Harvard University Press, 2009). This is not a topic I had thought much about until reading her book. "Teaching what you don't know is an increasingly common reality for a majority of academics," she writes. "The only instructors who may be exempt from the pressure to teach beyond their area of expertise are senior tenured faculty members at research universities and some part-time adjunct faculty" (p. 9).

because I think that most students still come to our schools because of deep seated interests in books and reading).

Chapter Three

A Personal Interlude: Loving Books, Without Apology

Introduction: Books, Libraries, and Librarians. While I was writing an earlier version of this chapter, originally planned as a brief essay, a vigorous discussion erupted on JESSE, the unofficial listserv for the Association for Library and Information Science Education, with contributors debating about the relationship between libraries and information science, library and information science schools versus iSchools, the kinds of individuals who hold or should hold faculty positions, and the nature of education preparing the next generation of faculty. As these things usually go, the debate was both interesting and frustrating. There was the usual defense of libraries and the customary assertion of the need to introduce students to the theories and methodologies of information science. Of course, nothing was resolved. As a lurker to this debate, I worried about the impact on those who tried to follow it, especially as some current doctoral students did post to the list, most often asking questions or seeking advice. I worried about whether some of these individuals might change their minds about academic research and teaching careers, in a field desperately needing a fresh supply of replacements for an aging professoriate.

I also reflected on how this discussion has little to do with the reality of what goes on in my world. As I read the personal statement portion of the applications to our MLIS program, I cannot but help notice how many profess that a *love* of reading and books, often connected to childhood experiences of parents reading to them, is what motivates them to submit their application. It is hard to find evidence in the JESSE discussion, however, that books have much of a place in library and information science education. It reminds one of the many books and articles written about the wars fought in literature departments, whereby students attracted to study there discover that an affection for reading, an interest in the classics, and a concern to study the important writers often are out of place. Critical theory, postmodernism, cultural studies, and other philosophical and theoretical models reign supreme, at least as far as the rhetoric goes. One could surmise that the study of books in LIS programs also has weakened significantly in the digital era. Some critics believe that multiple aspects of information technology have pushed out any emphasis on traditional libraries or printed books, pointing to the loss of the word "library" in the names of most former LIS schools and the rise of the "iSchool" movement in more recent years.

Turning Back the Clock at Spruce Head. Not so long ago we could easily find evidence of an interest in books, reading, and other traditional skills and activities without much difficulty. In a visit to a wonderful, congested little bookstore in Spruce Head, Maine (Lobster Cove Bookshop), perched picturesquely on the coast there, I picked up a pile of books written by librarians about their craft and their education. Ruth Hill Viguers, writing in the mid-1960s, suggests, "Nothing builds up respect for the librarian among teachers, parents, or young people as do a wide knowledge of books, enthusiasm for them, and ability to communicate that enthusiasm."[191] She describes the words in books as possessing "lasting power," requiring library educators and librarians alike to "know books" and "read widely."[192] Just as a reality check, let me also state that Viguers wrote nearly half-a-century ago that, "Few children today have parents who take the trouble to see that they have the best book experiences"[193]; my current reading of MLIS applications suggests otherwise, and I suspect that this was not so much of a problem then (maybe just another example of over-stating the case to make another point).

Writing about the same time, another children's librarian and educator, Frances Clarke Sayers, had similar thoughts about the role and nature of librarianship: "We have been called many things in our time – gentle and genteel; modest and mousy; learned and lame; dedicated and dowdy; unprepossessing and underpaid. I hope for the day when we shall be called the belligerent profession; a profession that is informed, illuminated, radiated by a fierce and beautiful love of books – a love so overwhelming that it engulfs community after community and makes the culture of our time distinctive, individual, creative, and truly of the spirit."[194] Today, we hear less about books or reading, and more about information or knowledge, acquired by harnessing computer literacy or technological proficiency. Just a generation or two ago, information and knowledge was the result of reading, as Sayers suggests: "A love of reading encompasses the whole of life: information, knowledge, insight and understanding,

---

[191] Ruth Hill Viguers, *Margin for Surprise: About Books, Children, and Librarians* (Boston: Little, Brown, and Co., 1964), p. 76.
[192] Viguers, *Margin for Surprise*, p. 77.
[193] Viguers, *Margin for Surprise*, p. 73.
[194] Frances Clarke Sayers, *Summoned by Books: Essays and Speeches*, compiled by Marjeanne Jensen Blinn (New York: Viking Press, 1965), p. 28.

pleasure; the power to think, to select, to act, to create – all of these are inherent in a love of reading."[195]

My selection of excerpts of two insiders about the nature of books and reading in LIS education and work is completely subjective, the result of just some incidental discoveries at a used bookshop. My efforts to peruse the writings of scholars and public intellectuals about books and reading is more deliberate, and it is in such efforts that I discovered some years ago Alberto Manguel.

Looking from the Outside In: Alberto Manguel and Printed Books. From time to time, outsiders to the LIS field come along and write about books or libraries in a way reminiscent of how librarians and educators in the field once seemed to feel about books, and, as well, it is often these books that land in bookshops (chain and independent) and draw public attention (in other words, there are a lot of people who still buy and read print books). Alberto Manguel is one of these individuals; best characterized as a public scholar, Manguel has written a series of provocative works on reading, visual images, and books, including at least one brief novel playing with the nature of reading and writing.[196] First coming on the scene as the editor of literary and other anthologies, Manguel has subsequently become known for his entertaining and informative analyses of our connection to literary and visual texts. He is truly an international scholar – born in Argentina, working in Canada, and now also living part-time in France.

Manguel is probably best known among librarians for his *A History of Reading*, published in 1996 and subsequently appearing on many syllabi in LIS programs. While the reader gains a good sense of how the act of reading has changed through time, the book is a highly personalized account of reading – or, as one reviewer has described it, the book is "an autobiography of a great reader."[197] In this book, the importance, and pleasure, of reading shine through. We read about the necessity of reading in the construction of self, how re-readings of books bring new insights, reading as a form of initiation rite into society, and how books and readers often merge into one entity. For avid readers entering LIS schools, assigning this book to them is like offering them dessert.

---

[195] Sayers, *Summoned by Books*, p. 43.
[196] For some of these works, not cited below, see Alberto Manguel, *Reading Pictures: A History of Love and Hate* (New York: Bloomsbury, 2001); *Stevenson Under the Palm Trees* (Canongate, 2004); *With Borges* (London: Telegram Books, 2006); and *Homer's The Iliad and The Odyssey: A Biography* (New York: Atlantic Monthly, 2007).
[197] Seth Lerer, "Histories of Reading," *Raritan* 20, 1 (Summer 2007): 108-127 (quotation p. 122).

Manguel spun-off several other books closely related to his musings in the history of reading. In his *Into the Looking-Glass Wood: Essays on Books, Reading, and the World*, Manguel gathers together previously published essays, all, in one way or another, affirming what he announces on the first page, "For me, words on a page give the world coherence."[198] Later, Manguel provides a deeper view of his own reading practice in his *A Reading Diary* (where he recounts his rereading of his own favorite books)[199], followed by a reflection on humanity's need to tell stories in his *The City of Words*: "Under certain conditions, stories can assist us. Sometimes they can heal us, illuminate us, and show us the way. Above all, they can remind us of our condition, break through the superficial appearance of things, and make us aware of the underlying currents and depths."[200] Funny, this is not how I usually hear people discuss the World Wide Web, where the emphasis is on information and its potential power and influence, but it does remind me of many conversations with students about how they came to be a student in a school like ours.

It is in his newest book, *The Library at Night*, where Manguel lets his most profound feelings for books shine through. Early in the book, Manguel indicates that he opted not to write another history of libraries, "but merely to give an account of [his] astonishment" about what libraries represent.[201] The result is a magical, highly personal, tour about the library as myth, order, space, power, shadow, shape, change, workshop, mind, island, survival, oblivion, imagination, identity, and home. This covers essentially every manner in which individuals have reflected on books and libraries, from the ancient world to the present. Manguel freely ranges over libraries drawing on his eclectic reading, personal experience, others' experiences, and diverse scholarship. In some ways this is a book to be read leisurely and reflectively, akin to reading someone's commonplace book of collected observations on the nature of libraries, printed books, and the World Wide Web as the potential new universal library. It is not intended to be viewed as a comprehensive scholarly analysis; in fact, Manguel often manages both to delight and disgust, captivate and antagonize, his readers.

---

[198] Alberto Manguel, *Into the Looking-Glass Wood: Essays on Books, Reading, and the World* (San Diego: Harcourt, Inc., 1998), p. 3.
[199] Alberto Manguel, *A Reading Diary: A Passionate Reader's Reflections on a Year of Books* (New York: Farrar, Straus and Giroux, 2004).
[200] Alberto Manguel, *The City of Words* (Toronto: House of Anansi Press, Inc., 2007), pp. 9-10.
[201] Alberto Manguel, *The Library at Night* (New Haven: Yale University Press, 2008), p. 4.

Manguel's observations about libraries will resonate with others who love libraries and the books in them. He captures how libraries reflect the world, imposing order even if libraries often form, unform, and form again in chaotic fashion.[202] He assiduously notes how libraries construct societal memory: "To hold and transmit memory, to learn through the experience of others, to share knowledge of the world and of ourselves, are some of the powers (and dangers) that books confer upon us, and the reasons why we both treasure and fear them."[203] Over the past century we have watched libraries and archives being destroyed because they represent symbolic identity and community memory. Destroy them, and you destroy a people's identity.

Most importantly, Manguel's beautiful and lyrical writing suggests the personal importance of libraries and contents. Examining his own library, Manguel reflects, "My books hold between their covers every story I've ever known and still remember, or have now forgotten, or may one day read; they fill the space around me with ancient and new voices."[204] It is precisely how I feel about my own library. Considering the demise of the ancient Library of Alexandria, he suggests, poetically, that the "Library that wanted to be the storehouse for the memory of the world was not able to secure for us the memory of itself."[205] With Manguel we have an effective representative of libraries to the public. Anyone familiar with the scholarship on libraries will find something to quibble about in this set of reflections about books, reading, and the nature of libraries (for me, I disagree with the manner in which he assesses Nicholson Baker's *Double Fold* diatribe about the issues of library preservation). However, I am here to praise Alberto Manguel for writing a beautiful extended essay on the value of libraries and what they contain, an essay that all book lovers and readers can relate to, as well as the scholars and other specialists on books and their history and technologies.

The beauty of Manguel's reflections will not be lost on many, perhaps most, students entering MLIS programs and embarking on careers as librarians or, perhaps, even as information professionals (the later being those who see their work extending beyond the walls of libraries and the bookshelves – and books – lining them). They will agree with Manguel's conviction that the "existence of any library ... allows readers a sense of what their craft is truly about, a craft that struggles against the stringencies

---

[202] Manguel, *The Library at Night*, pp. 47, 165.
[203] Manguel, *The Library at Night*, p. 266.
[204] Manguel, *The Library at Night*, p. 14.
[205] Manguel, *The Library at Night*, p. 27.

of time by bringing fragments of the past into their present."[206] They will recognize why he talks about the sense of order that any library brings with it to the information their books hold. Most especially they will understand why he writes about the space of a book's pages, creating "its own reading space, its own physical landscape in which the texture of the paper, the color of the ink, the view of the whole ensemble acquire in the reader's hands specific meanings, that lend tone and context to the words."[207] Our new students will associate with Manguel's notion that "compared to a book that betrays its age in its physical aspect, a text called up on the screen has no history,"[208] a debatable, but intriguing, point worth debate in the classroom.

Some of my colleagues who read this might scoff or, worse, think that I have lost my mind. I don't want to argue that we should turn back the clock, toss out technology courses, put library back into the name of all schools, or turn our backs toward the emergence of the idea of the iSchool that seeks to unite the former LIS schools with other schools with an interest in the issues and challenges of the Information or Digital Age. In my own personal library of six thousand or so printed books, the computer – with its access to my own university's fabulous collection of digital resources and the window into the riches (and, yes, dross) of the World Wide Web – is essential. The glow of the computer screen at night is not reflecting the light of burning books and decaying, forgotten libraries; rather it is enhancing Manguel's claim that "libraries, in their very being, not only assert but also question the authority of power,"[209] a reason why libraries – and archives and museums also holding books of various sorts – are so often targeted in war, civil unrest, and by despotic regimes.

Our new students bring with them a sense of the value of books and libraries because so many come to us because they long ago fell in love with reading. Manguel worries that "reading often requires slowness, depth and context" that might be lost in the browsing and surfing on the Web.[210] Our job as the educators and first mentors of new librarians and other information professionals includes, of course, instilling in these students an appreciation of the nature of information and evidence, history and culture, and literature and art that is also found in new and emerging digital sources dispersed across our society. However, this is something that should come

---

[206] Manguel, *The Library at Night*, p. 30.
[207] Manguel, *The Library at Night*, pp. 74-75.
[208] Manguel, *The Library at Night*, p. 225.
[209] Manguel, *The Library at Night*, p. 123.
[210] Manguel, *The Library at Night*, p. 79.

not with our dampening their enthusiasm for books and reading, as some others have already identified, seeing that there is actually a connection between reading and the rise of e-books (in other words, not seeing e-books or the loss, perhaps, of the printed book as just threats).[211]

Manguel's sense of the value of books and their reading partly developed because he was one of many individuals who read to the Argentinean scholar and writer Jorge Luis Borges when he had become blind, an individual whose world revolved around books.[212] While I cannot say I have ever read an application to our program by someone with quite a pedigree like Manguel's, I would hope that we honor the same expressions of conviction that we see in the personal statements of our potential students and transform such interests into the richer and deeper notions that twenty-first century librarians and other information professionals need to possess. Even if a new student brings the sense of the bookman that writer Larry McMurty has – "A bookman's love of books is a love of *books*, not merely of the information in them"[213] – I hope we have something profound to offer this individual as well.

Why bother with Manguel in educating the next generation of librarians, now usually referred to as information professionals? First, I would argue that his voice is as legitimate as any other in the great debate about the future of the book and the utility of the book, printed or digital. Second, it is obvious that Manguel touches on aspects of this debate that many in LIS schools look away from, namely the beauty, utility, and tactile values of the printed book, as well as the proved success of the printed book as a conveyor of information, evidence, and scholarship.

Shifting Debates. Librarians, archivists, and other information professionals have long heard predictions of the demise of the printed book and maybe even the book itself. Such predictions have appeared routinely in the scholarly, professional, and popular literature for several decades, but they have been increasing in frequency. Every day, someone writes a prediction about the demise of the printed book. Books, since their inception, have generated lots of attention. And, even today in their supposed twilight years, many different views about books and their role in society appear to challenge us to rethink what they mean to us. Roger Mummert writes about the emergence of new courses about the history of books and printing for undergraduates, noting, "Courses on the history of

---

[211] Tom Peters, "The Future of Reading," *Library Journal*, November 1, 2009, available at http://www.libraryjournal.com/article/CA6703852.html.
[212] Alberto Manguel, *With Borges* (London: Telegram Books, 2006), p. 31.
[213] Larry McMurty, *Books: A Memoir* (New York: Simon and Schuster, 2008), p. 38.

the book itself have grown along with the ascendancy of electronic information. Students today often blindly grant authority to the online world. Curators want to reconnect them with original sources and teach them to question those sources."[214]

Maybe there is hope for the printed book. In late March 2009, the University of Michigan Press announced that it was moving from mostly print to mostly digital or print-on-demand editions, with the declining economics of traditional publishing and the lure of being able to publish more scholarly studies being cited as the reasons for this new approach.[215] Earlier, other university presses announced their plans to make books available through the Kindle.[216] For some, such an announcement sends a chill through their spine, spelling the end of the beauty and utility of printed books, the kinds of comforts so ably described by Manguel in his writings. Concerns with university presses may be the reason why we are seeing histories of these presses.[217] At the least, we may be seeing such efforts by both university presses and libraries as an effort to ensure that their digitization efforts are secure as for-profit entities, such as Microsoft, drop out of the game,[218] as well as the need for university presses to be more entrepreneurial in order to gain new kinds of readers who want to read digitally.[219] Now, every time the Association of American University Presses meets, their deliberations will revolve around the business of academic publishing, their mission, and what they should do with the issue of digital publishing.[220] And faculty in the old library schools will follow the arguments, as will their colleagues in the new fangled iSchools; let's hope,

---

[214] Roger Mummert, "Handle This Book! Curators Put Rare Texts in 18-Year-Old Hands," *New York Times*, November 2, 2008, in the special education supplement, p. 30.

[215] Scott Jaschik, "Farewell to the Printed Monograph," *Inside Higher Education*, March 23 2009, http://www.insidehighered.com/news/2009/03/23/michigan, accessed March 23, 2009.

[216] Scott Jaschik, "University Presses Start to Sell Via Kindle," *Inside Higher Education*, June 24, 2008, http://insidehighered.com/news/2008/06/24/kindle.

[217] Such as Nicholas A. Basbanes, *A World of Letters: Yale University Press, 1908-2008* (New Haven: Yale University Press, 2008).

[218] Andy Guess, "Post-Microsoft, Libraries Mull Digitization," *Inside Higher Education*, May 30, 2008, http://insidehighered.com/news/2008/05/30/microsoft.

[219] "Ideas to Shake Up Publishing," *Inside Higher Education*, July 26, 2007, available at http://insidehighered.com/news/2007/07/26/ithaka.

[220] See, for example, Jennifer Howard's report on the 2007 annual meeting of the Association, "Changes and Challenges in Publishing World Dominate Talk at University-Press Association's Meeting," *Chronicle of Higher Education*, June 18, 2007.

even if they look at these issues in different ways, that they talk to each other.

Some years ago, I contended that the growing literature on all sides of the debate about the viability of the printed book was good for didactic purposes and cited some of the leading representatives of the various perspectives.[221] Indeed, we continue to argue about the value of the physical book, although the substance of the argument has shifted to considering new digital readers, such as the Kindle, and their advantages or disadvantages over the experience of reading traditional printed books.[222] Sven Birkerts remains "uneasy" about such devices because he sees in the "turning of literal pages—pages bound in literal books—a compelling larger value," worrying that we will lose a "certain kind of cultural understanding."[223] Birkerts resorts to intense sentimentality, the kind of emotional attachment that the information scientist eschews, writing, "I'm not blind to the unwieldiness of the book, or to the cumbersome systems we must maintain to accommodate it—the vast libraries and complicated filing systems. But these structures evolved over centuries *in ways that map our collective endeavor to understand and express our world.* The book is part of a system. And that system stands for the labor and taxonomy of human understanding, and to touch a book is to touch that system, however lightly." It is hard to imagine (although, I guess, not impossible) anyone writing that about a computer (although those who have Apples speak in such terms).

Birkerts makes a number of other important points about what the Kindle may or may not represent. He argues that the "Kindle still lives within the context of print," a concept that has been "reinforced by our libraries and bookstores, by the obvious physical adjacency of certain texts, the fact of which telegraphs the cumulative time-bound nature of the enterprise." He worries about "an info-culture of the near future composed entirely of free-floating items of information and expression, all awaiting

---

[221] Richard J. Cox, "Debating the Future of the Book," *American Libraries* 28 (February 1997): 52-55.

[222] Although the argument often continues to focus on whether libraries as places or even librarianship in general will survive, such as what happened at the 2009 EDUCAUSE conference; see Steve Kolowich, "Bookless Libraries?" *Inside Higher Education,* November 6, 2009, available at http://www.insidehighered.com/news/2009/11/06/library.

[223] This and subsequent references are to Sven Birkerts, "Resisting the Kindle," *Atlantic Online* (March 2, 2009), http://www.theatlantic.com/doc/200903u/amazon-kindle, accessed March 2, 2009.

their access call." What we may gain in access we may lose in terms of context, how a text "moved through the culture." Birkerts is not worrying about whether people will stop reading or not, but that "as Wikipedia is to information, so will the Kindle become to literature and the humanities: a one-stop outlet, a speedy and irresistibly efficient leveler of context."

The Kindle may be inconsequential in comparison with Google and its efforts to digitize the world's printed books. Every day, we read news articles and press releases (often it is difficult to tell them apart) about how every document, book, article, work of art, and piece of ephemera will be digitized and placed on the Web. In some ways, this is only a continuation of a historic quest to build a universal library or archive. Google, and its aim to digitize all of the world's books, has drawn considerable commentary, most of it, at least by the public and the media, quite positive. The saga is a "seductive" one for archivists and librarians, as Ian Wilson, the head of Canada's National Archives and Library, writes in an introduction to Jean-Noël Jeanneney's book about Google: Google's offer is "seductive to chronically underfunded libraries and archives, the custodians of our societies' cumulative documentary heritage. The potential to open the extensive, sometimes fragile holdings of these institutions for education, research, and other public uses is powerful and realizes a central goal of generations of both librarians and archivists."[224] Wilson, reflecting on Jeanneney's text, wonders if Google and such objectives are a good match.

Google's book project forces us to reflect on the contrast between the long-term cultural mission of librarians and archivists with the short-term business aims of Google. Commentators like Jeanneney don't worry about the future of the role of librarians or libraries,[225] but this may depend on how well they can resolve the implications posed by the work of Google. What are the various challenging issues we face with Google's digital book project? For now, Google is not charging for access, but the company makes no guarantee that it will not add a commercial aspect to this at some time in the future. Google also has nearly caved into pressure from certain governments, such as China, to allow censoring by restricting access to certain web sites; will it also censor who has access to the digitized books? Google has no sense about the issues of preservation. Nor has Google really developed any logical concepts about the selection of books to be digitized. Some have even noted that some of Google's scanning work

---

[224] Ian Wilson in Jean-Noël Jeanneney, *Google and the Myth of Universal Knowledge: A View from Europe*, trans. Teresa Lavender Fagan (Chicago: University of Chicago Press, 2007), p. viii.
[225] Jeanneney, *Google and the Myth of Universal Knowledge*, pp. 23, 72.

seems sloppy, where some digitized pages "are either skewed, blurred, swooshed, folded back, misplaced, or just plain missing."[226] The greatest problem about any of this, however, may be that Google is one of those highly volatile dot.com enterprises. If we depend on this company for digitizing massive quantities of books, what might happen when the company collapses or is bought out?

From such commercial and societal changes there emerges a new mandate for professionals such as archivists and librarians. Jeanneney argues that we must educate people to have the appropriate "intellectual tools" to master the Internet. Adults, he muses, "will find our digitized collections indispensable instruments for maintaining perspective in the face of the bombardment of new information, which they themselves must place in context, classify, and weigh. Unless a culture organizes that information, society is condemned to accept the mere dissemination of information, harmful to intellectual clarity and to a rich and harmonious public life."[227] Faculty in library and information science schools have sometimes opted to assume that this means giving students more technology courses rather than courses enabling students to understand the evolution of the book (from manuscript to print to digital). And with such notions, we return to the importance of the work of librarians and archivists and, perhaps, the continuing value of the printed book.

Scholars who have studied and written about the long history of text clearly see that understanding the e-book requires placing it into its historical context. English professor Peter L. Shillingsburg reminds us that we are "but 15-20 years into an era whose counterpart introduced a 500-year reign,"[228] still seeing continuing advantages printed books have over digital texts and even that the understanding of an e-book is possible because we possess a perception of a book because of its printed predecessor. This scholar argues, quite effectively, that we can only comprehend a text by seeing that it is "significantly affected by its constituting context and medium. As students of texts, we care about provenance, contexts, histories, bibliography, and the accuracy of texts because all these affect how we read and how we understand the text."[229]

---

[226] Ronald G. Musto, "Google Books Mutilates the Printed Past," *The Chronicle Review*, 55, June 12, 2009, p. B4,
http://chronicle.com/weekly/v55/i39/39b00401.htm.
[227] Jeanneney, *Google and the Myth of Universal Knowledge*, p. 87.
[228] Peter L. Shillingsburg, *From Gutenberg to Google: Electronic Representations of Literary Texts* (Cambridge: Cambridge University Press, 2006), p. 4.
[229] Shillingsburg, *From Gutenberg to Google*, p. 140.

Whether we buy into the more pessimistic assessments of the impact of the rise of the digital book on the quality of life is beside the point; the real issue is that this new technological form changes how, what, and why we read. Or, as someone like Manguel might perceive this, whether we can love the virtual book like we love the physical version.

We can put this, if we want, in a broader view about the history of book destruction. Fernando Báez, director of Venezuela's National Library, gives us a sweeping history of book destruction noting that although books have been destroyed for over 5000 years, "we barely have any idea why."[230] Báez admits that it is "impossible to document precisely" all the destructions of "libraries, book collections, and publishing houses."[231] Báez partly attributes humankind's destruction of these cultural materials to "behavior originating in the depths of personality, in a search for the restitution of an archetype of equilibrium, power, or transcendence... . The destructive ritual, like the constructive ritual applied to the building of temples, houses, or any work, fixes patterns that return the individual to the community, to shelter, or to the vertigo of purity."[232] He enumerates reasons why books are important to society and individuals, and concludes that "books are not destroyed as physical objects but as links to memory, that is, as one of the axes of identity of a person or a community,"[233] while acknowledging that there is no one reason why books are destroyed (suggesting why he provides description after description of the instances in the history of book destruction – it is in the reading of the litany of such events that the reader begins to understand both how important books are and why they and the repositories holding them are regularly and dramatically attacked). He provides one overarching theme about "bibliocaust," namely that the destruction of books is an "attempt to annihilate a memory considered to be a direct or indirect threat to another memory thought superior."[234] In adopting this perspective, Báez eliminates the idea that book burning and library destruction is the work of ignorant and uneducated people and adeptly places this activity as part of a human impulse closely associated with the urge to save, commemorate, learn, and remember. The push to end printed books, in favor of digital books, may fit in here somewhere.

---

[230] Fernando Báez, *A Universal History of the Destruction of Books: From Ancient Sumer to Modern Iraq*, translated by Alfred MacAdam (New York: Atlas and Co., 2008), p. 6.
[231] Báez, *A Universal History of the Destruction of Books*, p. 173.
[232] Báez, *A Universal History of the Destruction of Books*, p. 9.
[233] Báez, *A Universal History of the Destruction of Books*, p. 12.
[234] Báez, *A Universal History of the Destruction of Books*, p. 14.

Whatever one thinks about the value of printed books, a recent report reveals that scholars are far more dependent on digital resources. As Jennifer Howard summarizes the report, it concludes that "scholars still value libraries as buyers and archivers of scholarship, and many still use them as gateways to scholarly information. However, it also confirms that researchers increasingly find what they need through Google Scholar and other online resources, a trend the report's authors anticipate will accelerate as more and more knowledge goes digital."[235] However, this does not consider the value that scholars place on their libraries of printed books, carefully annotated and arranged over years of work and reflection. There may be some special promise in the new technologies of printing books. Clive Thompson believes that "Books are the last bastion of the old business model—the only major medium that still hasn't embraced the digital age." He thinks we need to stop worrying about publishing and refocus on reading's future. He wants to "release" books from their captive nature in paper and ink, allowing annotations, links, and other markups. Thompson continues, "I'm not suggesting that books need always be social. One of the chief pleasures of a book is mental solitude, that deep, quiet focus on an author's thoughts—and your own. That's not going away. But books have been held hostage offline for far too long. Taking them digital will unlock their real hidden value: the readers."[236]

The Ruined Remains. Book lovers have long marveled at their ability to track down or, in a serendipitous fashion, discover printed treasures, rarities, and just plain useful books. Printed books have a way of surviving long beyond their primary purpose, reappearing in yard sales, second-hand bookstores, library sales, and flea markets. Kevin J. Hayes, considering Patrick Henry and his reading, suggests, "books often functioned as social capital. The acts of loaning and borrowing books greatly strengthened bonds between friends – assuming, of course, that they returned the books they borrowed."[237] Some might argue that access to the World Wide Web has subsumed this function, but I doubt that those who continue to buy printed books and build personal libraries would agree with such an assessment. Studies are appearing charting the decline of independent

---

[235] Jennifer Howard, "Scholars' View of Libraries as Portals Shows Marked Decline," *Chronicle of Higher Education*, August 26, 2008, http://chronicle.com/daily/2008/08/4351n.htm.
[236] Clive Thompson, "The Future of Reading." *WIRED* June 2009 p. 50 http://www.wired.com/techbiz/people/magazine/17-06/st_thompson.
[237] Kevin J. Hayes, *The Mind of a Patriot: Patrick Henry and the World of Ideas* (Charlottesville: University of Virginia Press, 2008), p. 7.

bookstores but, perhaps, also even the chain bookshop in the face of new ways of marketing books as digital objects or hawking traditional printed ones over the Internet.[238] What can we expect with e-books and digital surrogates?

While no one will argue very strenuously about the necessity of digitization as a means of enhancing access to our documentary heritage, some will still worry about whether digitization is a safer, more reliable approach for administering the documents of our past. Two commentators on the challenges of digital preservation provide some sense of the understanding of these issues: "In the past, ephemera such as playbills, advertisements, menus, theater tickets, broadsheets, etc. have survived, albeit sometimes rather haphazardly, and are now collected, stored, conserved and valued as vital witnesses to political, economic, social and private aspects of the past. Today, these artifacts appear on the web for a matter of days, to disappear from view as if they had never existed."[239] More importantly, however, are the limitations of a digital version of real objects versus the necessity of digitizing: "Creating surrogates can never replicate or preserve everything about an original object, but creating no surrogates could mean that everything is lost in the case of fragile or compromised originals: brittle books printed on acid-based paper, older newspapers, ancient and medieval books and manuscripts, crumbling sculptures, ruined buildings, photographs on glass plates, explosive nitrate film stock."[240] If we worry about what the digitization of something like a manuscript or book takes away from the artifact, should we also not worry about replacing a printed corpus of books with the virtual world of e-books?

Some of the most strident commentators on the notion of the Web as a replacement for the library or the Web site for the printed book have exaggerated this. In this vein, Mark Herring argues, on the one hand, that "We have known about the inability of Web-based information to be preserved in anything approaching perdurability, and we have our rush to digitize everything,"[241] and on the other, after weighing a lot of evidence, asking a fundamental question about the role and the future of libraries,

---

[238] See, for example, Laura Miller, *Reluctant Capitalists: Bookselling and the Culture of Consumption* (Chicago: University of Chicago Press, 2006).

[239] Marilyn Deegan and Simon Tanner, eds., *Digital Preservation* (London: Facet Publishing, 2006), pp. 4-5.

[240] Deegan and Tanner, *Digital Preservation*, p. 10.

[241] Mark Y. Herring, *Fool's Gold: Why the Internet Is No Substitute for a Library* (Jefferson, North Carolina: McFarland & Co., Inc., 2007), p. 164.

suggesting that "requiring libraries to be as lean and as nondescript as the Web solves nothing. Rather than bemoaning the cost of libraries... , we should be celebrating the value they add to the research environment. After all, it was they that enabled our intellectual history from the beginning. Are we positively certain it is now time to replace them with so weak an ersatz as the Web?"[242] Herring is not alone. "Preserving the scholarly record is more difficult in a digital world than a print one," Christine Borgman believes, "due to the rapid evolution of technology, changes in intellectual property regulations, and new business models for publishing."[243] Preserving research is also difficult because so much of the new forms of scholarship are occurring outside of the parameters of libraries and publishers, the players most responsible for the archiving of the scholarship.

We also might wonder what the potential loss of the library as a place (whether because we stop going there or because they actually disappear) might do to society and its inhabitants. Writer Sara Paretsky states, "When I enter a library, when I enter the world of books, I feel the ghosts of the past on my shoulders, urging me to courage."[244] Can we feel the same when we open up our laptops? Perhaps. But maybe we need to learn to look at this in a different way. Jeff Gomez, for example, believes that the shift to the e-book will help to keep a greater variety of books in print and to broaden the scope of titles being published (while also thinking that the printed book will be around for a very long time). Gomez argues, instead, that "What should be remembered at all times is that the words compiled into books have a much larger purpose than to collect dust on shelves. It is ideas that matter and should be unleashed, not constrained by print."[245] Gomez never discounts the lure of book collecting or disparages those who prefer to read books that are physical artifacts (although he does point out that the range of titles available in print is being transformed so that there will be a more modest range of titles available). Gomez also sidesteps the issue of a decline in reading, noting that with blogs, e-publications, and other digital outlets, that there is more to read than ever before. He does suggest, however, that the decline in certain kinds of print-related jobs, such as book reviewing, may have led to some of the exaggerated tones set in the debate about the

---

[242] Herring, *Fool's Gold*, p. 128.
[243] Christine Borgman, *Scholarship in the Digital Age: Information, Infrastructure, and the Internet* (Cambridge, MA: MIT Press, 2007), p. 48.
[244] Sara Paretsky, *Writing in an Age of Silence* (New York: Verso, 2007), p. 138.
[245] Jeff Gomez, *Print is Dead: Books in Our Digital Age* (New York: MacMillan, 2008), p. 47.

future of the book. Others, such as Christine Borgman, believe there is plenty of life left in printed books, taking the long view: "Publishing printed books will remain a viable market, perhaps forever, for certain kinds of content."[246]

Borgman has some colleagues agreeing with her. Anthony Grafton believes print has a future. Grafton indicates that the promise of a universal library or archives will not be easily achieved, a "patchwork of different interfaces and databases, some open to anyone with a computer and WiFi, others closed to those who lack access or money."[247] Ultimately, Grafton believes that the various problems and challenges will be worked out, but in the meantime, with the vast variety of print and digital venues, he believes that traditional libraries and archives will continue to play an important role: "For now, and for the foreseeable future, if you want to piece together the richest possible mosaic of documents and texts and images, you will have to do it in those crowded public rooms where sunlight gleams on varnished tables, as it has for more than a century, and knowledge is still embodied in millions of dusty, crumbling, smelly, irreplaceable manuscripts and books."[248] What does any of this mean for the shift from the traditional library school to the iSchool?

Picking Through the Debris. Book collecting has long been a passion for individuals, but it may be an activity accelerating in importance as the printed book is predicted to be on its last legs. Larry McMurty, for example, gives us a rambling memoir of book collecting and bookselling. McMurty, best known for his *Lonesome Dove* and screenwriting for films such as *The Last Picture Show*, describes how he was first introduced to books as a youth, started collecting books, became a bookstore owner, and has always been more of a bookman (or reader) than a writer. One learns more about McMurty and his perspective on his craft as a writer than they learn about book collecting and selling, especially how more comfortable he is with the latter activities than the former. McMurty laments that "eventually all novelists, if they persist too long, get worse ... . Writing great fiction involves some combination of energy and imagination that cannot be energized or realized forever. Strong talents can simply exhaust their gift, and they do."[249] McMurty tries to tell us that book selling is very different, "being based on acquired knowledge" and, hence, being "progressive."

---

[246] Borgman, *Scholarship in the Digital Age*, p. 113.
[247] Anthony Grafton, *Worlds Made by Words: Scholarship and Community in the Modern West* (Cambridge: Harvard University Press, 2009), p. 309.
[248] Grafton, *Worlds Made by Words*, p. 329.
[249] Larry McMurty, *Books: A Memoir* (New York: Simon and Schuster, 2008), p. 115.

"The longer they deal and the more they know, the better books they handle."[250] For him, despite the predictions, bookselling is not a dying profession.

Mostly what one walks away with from this book is how much McMurty seems to not like writing, while how much he loves books and their collecting. And here we get the obligatory comments about the value of books, the importance of reading, and how the Internet is not a replacement for books or libraries. While real lovers of books will certainly enjoy McMurty's lingering descriptions of great deals he has made and famous books he has had pass through his hands, it might be his observations about the place of the book in our culture that one will most recall: "Today the sight that discourages book people most is to walk into a public library and see computers where books used to be. In many cases not even the librarians want books to be there. What consumers want now is information, and information increasingly comes from computers."[251] Our students may be having the same reaction when they come to our schools, finding computing where they expected to find some emphasis still on books. Those of us in schools supposedly educating future librarians certainly share some blame for this, but there are some who love *both* books and computers (like me). It is also what attracts many to come to schools like mine, where we then do everything but consider the importance of the book and print in our society. I expect to see citations to and quotations from McMurty's book in future applications to our program.

Collecting tells us a lot about an individual, but also a lot about the society that individual lives in. William Davies King suggests something of this, writing, "Collecting is a constant reassertion of the power to own, an exercise in controlling otherness, and finally a kind of monument building to insure survival after death. For this reason, you can often read the collector in his or her collection, if not in the objects themselves, then in the business of acquiring, maintaining, and displaying them. To collect is to write a life."[252] For me, collecting books (I don't acquire rare books, but books in my own areas of expertise) is to write in a literal sense. King goes one step farther in considering the psyche of collecting, reflecting, "The lessons of the collections is that collecting is not all pathology. Indeed, collecting can come very close to what is involved in the making of art."[253]

---

[250] McMurty, *Books*, p. 115.
[251] McMurty, *Books*, p. 221.
[252] William Davies King, *Collections of Nothing* (Chicago: University of Chicago Press, 2008), p. 38.
[253] King, *Collections of Nothing*, p. 126.

However, King also reveals that the writing of his book is part of his personal process in grappling with the rather compulsive and sometimes-strange fixation he has with collecting. He describes eight years of psychotherapy, his failed marriage, and an affair with a student, his own misgivings about his career and life, and how all of his personal torments and tribulations are wrapped up in his personal collecting activities. King writes, "My refuge from the present, as from the past, is collecting."[254] Indeed, nearly all book collecting may be an effort to escape from the digital tsunami threatening both reading and the printed book.

Many believe that Google and its immense digitization agenda will create more ruined libraries. Robert Darnton, being the historian of the eighteenth-century that he is, starts his analysis of the Google digitization copyright deal with the promises of that earlier era's Republic of Letters, where people could become citizens by engaging in reading and writing, and where he wants "to invoke the Enlightenment in an argument for openness in general and for open access in particular."[255] Initially, Darnton tackles some of the more inane features of recent copyright legislation. Darnton provides some history of libraries and scholarly publishing, and disciplines as well, to note how complex the world has gotten and how different it is from just a couple of centuries. Darnton believes that the library is still at the center of the university (and the universe), but that it exists now because of its ability to utilize cyberspace via its networks. And he believes that some of the old disciplinary and other barriers to learning have collapsed, where the Republic of Letters can now support both professional scholars and a host of amateurs: "The democratization of knowledge now seems to be at our fingertips. We can make the Enlightenment ideal come to life in reality."[256]

This scholar provides a more positive analysis of the widespread book digitization efforts, without predicting the end of the printed book, Darnton reminds us that there is a "fundamental contradiction" in this Googlization of the world's libraries: "Yet if we permit the commercialization of the content of our libraries, there is no getting around a fundamental contradiction. To digitize collections and sell the product in ways that fail to guarantee wide access would be to repeat the mistake that

---

[254] King, *Collections of Nothing*, p. 149.
[255] Robert Darnton, "Google and the Future of Books," *The New York Review of Books* 56, no. 2 (February 12, 2009): 9-11 (quotation p. 9). Darnton recently pulled together his essays on books in his *The Case for Books: Past, Present, and Future* (New York: Public Affairs, 2009).
[256] Darnton, "Google and the Future of Books," p. 10.

was made when publishers exploited the market for scholarly journals, but on a much greater scale, for it would turn the Internet into an instrument for privatizing knowledge that belongs in the public sphere."[257] This does not deter Darnton from grasping the more positive benefits from the digitization of all this stuff, although he states that in order to digitize we must also democratize: "We must open access to our cultural heritage. How? By rewriting the rules of the game, by subordinating private interests to the public good, and by taking inspiration from the early republic in order to create a Digital Republic of Learning."[258] What worries Darnton, instead, is that we are allowing the lawsuit against Google to settle an important issue of public policy, noting that it is already too late to do much more than worry about the future, contending that the "settlement creates a fundamental change in the digital world by consolidating power in the hands of one company. Apart from Wikipedia, Google already controls the means of access to information online for most Americans, whether they want to find out about people, goods, places, or almost anything."[259] He is worried, and we all should be worried as well. Darnton believes that "if we get the balance wrong at this moment, private interests may outweigh the public good for the foreseeable future, and the Enlightenment dream may be as elusive as ever."[260] Too bad, I liked the dream. And for Darnton, the dream requires that we maintain and support both traditional and virtual libraries.[261] It is why we must be very careful, as traditional library schools slowly fade into either LIS or iSchools, to consider what we don't teach or research in the latter iterations of the old professional school.[262]

Maybe It Doesn't Make Much Difference. It may be that the power of books has less to do with their form than with their purpose. Books, along with movies and television shows, provide stories and "human beings need stories," writes Paul Auster. "They need them almost as desperately as they need food, and however the stories might be presented – whether on a printed page or a television screen – it would be impossible to imagine life

---

[257] Darnton, "Google and the Future of Books," p. 10.
[258] Darnton, "Google and the Future of Books," p. 10.
[259] Darnton, "Google and the Future of Books," p. 11.
[260] Darnton, "Google and the Future of Books," p. 11.
[261] See his Robert Darnton, "The Library in Your Future," *New York Review of Books* 55 (June 12, 2008): 72-73, 76, 78-80.
[262] Darnton's essay on bibliography as an area of study and the nature of the history of books, both topics that once were well-established in the traditional library school, are reminders of what might be lost; Darnton, *The Case for Books*.

without them."²⁶³ Considering something like the power of stories might make more sense than reflecting on the power of technology. Writer Jonathan Franzen, for example, suggests, "One of the great irritations of modern technology is that when some new development has made my life palpably worse and is continuing to find new and different ways to bedevil it, I'm still allowed to complain for only a year or two before the peddlers of coolness start telling me to get over it already Grampaw–this is just the way life is now."²⁶⁴ Other much older writers, such as Ray Bradbury, also profess a love for books and libraries; Bradbury sees the Internet as "distracting." "It's meaningless; it's not real. It's in the air somewhere," quips Bradbury.²⁶⁵

The real issue may be that the predictions about the end of the printed book simply accelerate unrealistically the timetable for such a change. *Newsweek*'s technology writer, Steven Levy, when asked about the future of the book, and printing, and reading, answers this way:

> I think about that a lot. I think that, as wonderful as the form of the book is, it's ridiculous to think that we're not going to come up with some electronic device that is able to replicate 99% of the good stuff about a physical book along with all the extra virtues you could have, like electronic storage. It's going to happen. I don't know whether it's going to happen in five years or ten years or thirty years. But it's got to happen, and you're going to have something which is flexible and as readable – and pleasurable as a physical book. And they'll have all the stuff that comes with being digital – searchability, connectivity, you name it. And that's going to be a huge change, and eventually it will change the way writers work and what they write, just as the printed book made the novel possible. So I think that, in the short term, yeah, you find me still writing books and hoping that people will still buy the books. And I think they will buy books, if not necessarily mine. But in the long term all publishing has got to be electronic, and I think that's going to change a lot of things. Some of those changes will be things that we'll miss, but I think that if you take a broad view of history, everything will work out just fine. You know, it's sad in a sense that we

---

²⁶³ Paul Auster in Toni Morrison, ed., *Burn This Book: PEN Writers Speak Out on the Power of the Word* (New York: HarperCollins, 2009), p. 69.
²⁶⁴ Jonathan Franzen, "I Just Called to Say I Love You," *Technology Review* 111 (September/October 2008): 88-95, also available at http://www.technologyreview.com/Infotech/21173/page1/.
²⁶⁵ Jennifer Steinhauer, "In His Own Words," *New York Times*, 20 January 2009, available at http://www.nytimes.com/2009/06/20/us/20ventura.html?_r=1&th&emc=th.

don't have the oral tradition, that we don't sit and tell long stories over bonfires. We've moved on to something else. Maybe it's time to return.[266]

Some even suggest that as individuals come accustomed to using electronic resources that their interest in more traditional print materials will increase.[267]

Others take an even more positive view, based on the long view. At the moment, many are arguing that e-book devices such as the Sony Reader and Kindle are not developed far enough to support higher education in both teaching and research. Matthew Battles, for example, is sanguine about e-book readers such as the Kindle, since the "culture of letters has *always* been subject to disruption and transformation. Indeed, since the advent of print, technologies of the book have changed dramatically, and with them the book's place in society. The world of letters not only transcends these technological changes—it thrives because of them."[268] Battles makes his case by examining the history of the book and the technologies supporting it:

> Technologies shift—and with those shifts come changes in our consciousness. We read differently now than did the contemporaries of Johannes Gutenberg or Jane Austen. By the nineteenth century, books were no longer individually crafted works of art, but products of industry – no longer richly bound and ornately hand-decorated, but serviceably assembled using interchangeable parts. Yet despite these far-reaching shifts, the sequences of words themselves have been handed down more or less intact from age to age. Changes in their outward form—from scribal artifact to assembly-line product to networked device – have historically been the means by which books, and the knowledge and culture they transmit, become more widely and equitably distributed, enriching human society. Vellum has yielded to linen and wood-pulp, which in turn are yielding to pixels; and hand-lettering has yielded to the printing press, which in turn is yielding to

---

[266] Stephen Levy interview, *Ubiquity*, Volume 8, Issue 39 (October 2, 2007 – October 8, 2007, http://www.acm.org/ubiquity/interviews/v8i39_levy.html.
[267] Edward Tenner, "The Prestigious Inconvenience of Print," *Chronicle of Higher Education*, December 15, 2006, http://chronicle.com/weekly/v53/i27/27b00701.htm.
[268] Matthew Battles, "In Defense of the Kindle," *Atlantic*, March 5, 2009, http://www.theatlantic.com/doc/200903u/amazon-kindle-2.

code. Human civilization is a thing of innovation and metamorphosis, not stasis. Now as ever, we get the books our times demand.[269]

And so it goes, with the debate continuing.[270]

At the moment, the concern about e-books seems more fanciful than fact-based, constituting less than three percent of total book sales, although growing quickly.[271] And there are always good signs in all this, even as we hear daily rumors about publishers struggling or going out of business. Laura Vanderkam reports from an National Endowment for the Arts (NEA) survey that the "percentage of Americans who read a novel, short story, poem or play in the past year rose from 46.7% in 2002 to 50.2% in

---

[269] Battles, "In Defense of the Kindle."

[270] As the debate about the nature of reading, writing, and publishing continues, some more scholarly and better researched tomes are appearing. See, for example, Dennis Baron, *A Better Pencil: Readers, Writers, and the Digital Revolution* (New York: Oxford University Press, 2009). Predictions of how the continuing development of computing technologies is changing the manner in which we read, write, and learn continue to pour out from every possible arena. English professor Dennis Baron gives us a sensible examination of writing and reading practices in the context of the history of communication technology. "Computers and the internet are neither the best developments in the history of writing nor the worst," Baron contends. "They are simply the latest in a series of innovations in how we do things with words" (p. xv). He discusses writing as a technology; how each new writing technology has been greeted with suspicion (and how technologies are not neutral); and considers the impact of the technologies of the pencil, handwriting, writing on clay, and word processing. Baron is especially intrigued by issues such as concerns about learning how to trust texts, a matter that is not unique to our era as so many have suggested. The primacy of print didn't happen overnight, but it emerged very gradually, and, moreover, digital text will not be the last means of representing information. Baron is, in fact, optimistic as he looks backward to assess the future of reading and writing. Writing on the screen deepens and broadens writing, he believes, and there are more writers and readers than ever before, embracing the virtual word. Such optimism extends from his way of seeing technology: "By definition it is artificial, a device fashioned for a purpose. Pens are no more natural than keyboards, penmanship no better at reflecting the human spirit than digitized text. But for those of us who have gotten used to keying in our words, working with pens and pencils has already begun to seem less natural, less automatic, less of a direct connection from mind to text, than going online" (p. 66). Some day, keying in words may seem less natural as well.

[271] Motoko Rich, "Book Fair Buzz Is Not Contained Between 2 Covers," *New York Times*, June 1, 2009.

2008."[272] Nevertheless, commentators such as Nicholas Clee expound, "Perhaps the digital revolution will decentralize publishing and bookselling, as Gutenberg's movable type did in the 15th century. Publishing, printing and bookselling may come together again. Will the bookshop of the future consist of a few hundred bestsellers and a print-on-demand machine?"[273] Others agree. It may be that the possibilities of digital publishing will allow some new economic models for publishing books, especially as the general economic woes continue (and encourage more publishing experimentation with on-demand publishing and reprinting).[274]

University press directors, such as University of Michigan Press director Phil Pochoda, who are leading the charge into digital publishing, also recognize the long-term love affair with books. Pochoda refers to academics as "people of the book, specifically, the printed book." They "often do their research largely through and about books, and generally present the results of their research in carefully formulated and formatted books. They teach about and from books; they encase themselves within walled environments of books both in their professional settings as well as in their domicile; books tend to be strewn haphazardly but consistently on any available horizontal surface throughout their domain, resembling the way that dogs mark their terrain with urine." Considering humanists, Pochoda understands that the "circulation of physical books helps define the professional and personal, formal and informal, networks of many academics; books are routinely presented to friends and family, deans and colleagues, for reasons that are both social and professional; they are among the primary signifiers of identity both of the benefactor and the recipient." Pochoda nicely summarizes my own world, when noting that, "there is world-changing value in the miraculous searchability, accessibility and connectivity that the digital world offers to scholars and scholarship worldwide."[275] I would contend that you can only fully understand this if you place the digital world into its historical context.

---

[272] Laura Vanderkam, "Books from, and for The People," *USA Today*, March 12, 2009, p. 9A.
[273] Nicholas Clee, "The Decline and Fall of Books," *Times Online*, May 7, 2009.
[274] Scott McLemee, "Print or Byte?" *Inside Higher Education*, April 6, 2009, available at http://www.insidehighered.com/layout/set/print/views/mclemee/mclemee237.
[275] Paul Pochoda, "University Press 2.0," University of Michigan Press Blog, May 27, 2009, http://www.typepad.com/services/trackback/6a00e552560e8d8834 011570a9a24a9.

Others counter such notions of a complete shift from print to digital by noting the advantages that scholarly books possess, primarily, that they "remain the most effective technology for organizing and presenting sustained arguments at a relatively general level of discourse and in familiar rhetorical forms — narrative, thematic, philosophical, and polemical — thereby helping to enrich and unify otherwise disparate intellectual conversations." Peter J. Dougherty, the director of the Princeton University Press, thinks that publishers, especially university presses, need to re-invent themselves as stimulants for new forms of scholarship. He believes that "books remain valuable precisely because they are distinct from the other, more transitory, forms of scholarly communication. But university presses have to grasp the stinging nettle, jump-start a serious discussion about content, get strategic, invent projects. If university presses attempt to be more creative by introducing new subjects into our existing lists, the resultant hybrid vigor, to borrow a phrase from the biologists, will put us on a stronger course and renew the place of books in the world of ideas. For in the future, as in the past, we will be judged by the character of our content."[276] In the future, library schools and their successors will be judged by how well they deal with such matters.

Conclusion. My main aim in this chapter is to reveal both something about myself, as well as to explore the interesting debates concerning a topic that ought to be basic in the education of librarians and other information professionals. I love printed books, and this book is based on a wide range of reading on matters relating to my work in educating students to become archivists and university faculty in whatever form the old library school will assume in the future. Moreover, I love reading books, inscribing marginal comments in them on successive readings, revisiting them for preparing course lectures, and loaning them to students. A careful inspection of my citations will reveal that I also read the professional and scholarly literature as well as many online venues, but I must acknowledge that nothing quite compares to the sustained, orderly, and in-depth argument found in a book.

Books as conveyors of information and receptacles of knowledge are topics worthy of both traditional library and newer information schools. There is honest debate about whether this is a relevant issue for teaching future information professionals, although it is fairly clear that it has been pushed aside in favor of focusing on new technological tools. This must be

---

[276] Peter J. Dougherty, "A Manifesto for Scholarly Publishing," *The Chronicle Review*, 55, June 12, 2009, p. B10, http://chronicle.com/weekly/v55/i39/39b01001.htm.

a disappointment to many of our students, given their initial interests in our schools. However, it is also clear that the pressures on our schools by the new corporate university agenda may be the more critical challenge facing us these days.

Chapter Four

The Spectacle of the Corporate University

Introduction: Losing our Souls. Historically, the library and archives professions have advocated for free and open access to information. On one hand, university faculty, including those at library and information science schools, have become accustomed to ready access to information, much of it free to them and certainly representing a much greater pool of information than the normal citizen can peruse. On the other hand, universities have become the site of speech codes and other restrictions, intended to encourage diversity but often hindering speech, civil liberties, and other traditional academic freedoms. Even when speech codes are not present, universities, as part of their increasing concern about their corporate interests, are generating more restrictions about intellectual property.[277]

Academic freedom has become an especially contentious and tentative issue since the terrorist attacks of September 11, 2001 and the new intensity in national security.[278] Martha C. Nussbaum, admittedly writing both before the events of 9/11 and after, sees that higher education is in good shape as well as critical to producing good citizens who see and understand the world around them. As she reflects, "If we cannot teach our students everything they will need to know to be good citizens, we may at least teach them what they do not know and how they may inquire," arguing that education in the university is much more than just preparing to practice a profession or pursue a career.[279] Political correctness in the university, especially controversies concerning matters of affirmative action, deconstruction, feminism, gay and lesbian studies, and multiculturalism,

---

[277] Donald Alexander Downs, *Restoring Free Speech and Liberty on Campus* (Oakland, CA: The Independent Institute and Cambridge University Press, 2005); Robert M. O'Neil, *Free Speech in the College Community* (Bloomington: Indiana University Press, 1997).

[278] Beshara Doumani, ed., *Academic Freedom After September 11* (New York: Zone Books, 2006).

[279] Martha C. Nussbaum, *Cultivating Humanity: A Classical Defense of Reform in Liberal Education* (Cambridge: Harvard University Press, 1997), p. 295.

generated deep public distrust of the university long before the events of 9/11.[280]

Despite challenges to free speech in the academy, many write critiques of higher education freely and frequently. Most of the analyses of the corporate model of the university written by faculty members and university administrators extend beyond just the financial issues related to higher education. Former Harvard dean Harry R. Lewis examines the struggles Harvard College dealt with during his years as its dean: "The problems are how and what we teach, how and why we assign grades to students, how we do or do not help students develop a sense of responsibility for themselves, and how money affects students generally and college athletes in particular."[281] Such candid views may not be new in higher education, but the intensity of the responses to such views by advocates of the corporate model is, perhaps, something different.

Intellectual property, as just one example, has become one of the great contested issues for librarians, archivists, and other information professionals. It is ironic that one of the hottest parts of the battlefields is right in the university itself. As faculty in these schools strive to introduce students to the parameters and perils of intellectual property issues, they may as well discuss their own work, labor that their university may claim it owns. What happens to lectures posted on the Web, distance education courses offered online, faculty work-for-hire, and the notion about whether academic work is something that should be owned at all?[282] As library and information science schools embrace new educational delivery tools and expand their course offerings so that they need to hire armies of adjuncts, the issues of intellectual property become more complicated; even though these schools offer courses on such issues, it is not always the case that they have resolved these matters in their own practical management.

Culture Wars and Academic Freedom. Some disciplines, such as literary studies, have been the lightning rod for distress about the state of the contemporary university, especially at the height of the so-called culture wars in the 1980s and 1990s.[283] English professor Jeffrey Hart contends the

---

[280] Jeffrey Williams, ed., *PC Wars: Politics and Theory in the Academy* (New York: Routledge, 1995).

[281] Harry R. Lewis, *Excellence Without a Soul: How a Great University Forgot Education* (New York: Public Affairs, 2006), p. 1.

[282] Corynne McSherry, *Who Owns Academic Work? Battling for Control of Intellectual Property* (Cambridge: Harvard University Press, 2001).

[283] Edith Kurzweil and William Phillips, eds., *Our Country, Our Culture: The Politics of Political Correctness* (Boston: Partisan Review Press, 1994).

"goal of liberal education" is the "knowledge of the great narrative and other possible narratives, and the ability to locate new things in relation to the overall design, and the ability to locate other civilizations and other cultures to it."[284] Being able to accomplish this depends on our having access to the critical books that are the "bearers of essential civilizational knowledge," but Hart argues that many of these texts have disappeared from study in university classrooms.[285] Another literary scholar, Marjorie Garber, counters the common criticisms made against the role of the academy, most often seen in literary studies and humanities, concerning the demise of the amateur scholar (replaced by the professional academic), the need for every scholarly pursuit to be interdisciplinary, and the challenges of understanding academic jargon. Garber writes, for example, about the interdisciplinary dream: "I think we need to take cognizance of this tendency in academic and intellectual life to imagine that the truth, or the most revealing methods, or the paradigm with the answer, is just over the road apiece – in your neighbor's yard or department or academic journals rather than your own."[286] We are always, however, on the road trying to get there (or somewhere).

For whatever reason the humanities, especially English and history, generate the most reflection about the nature and purpose of higher education, probably because these fields host the most dramatic and disruptive internal debates about their own place in the university and the universe. Many of these debates are an extension or byproduct of the culture wars splitting American society and that was particularly pernicious in the academy.[287] Despite concerns voiced by critics of higher education, others from within the university have tended to soften such concerns. Stanley Fish debunks the idea of political agendas dictating a field like literary studies, suggesting that if one wants to affect political change, trying to do so from the platform of an academic discipline seems to be just

---

[284] Jeffrey Hart, *Smiling Through the Cultural Catastrophe: Toward the Revival of Higher Education* (New Haven: Yale University Press, 2001), p. x.
[285] Hart, *Smiling Through the Cultural Catastrophe*, p. xii.
[286] Marjorie Garber, *Academic Instincts* (Princeton: Princeton University Press, 2003), p. 67.
[287] James Davison Hunter, *Culture Wars: The Struggle to Define America* (New York: Basic Books, 1991); James L. Nolan, Jr., ed., *The American Culture Wars: Current Contests and Future Prospects* (Charlottesville: University Press of Virginia, 1996); and Russell Jacoby, *Dogmatic Wisdom: How the Culture Wars Divert Education and Distract America* (New York: Anchor Books, 1994).

foolishness.[288] Likewise, Gregory S. Jay provides an even-handed assessment of the problems with virulent forms of multiculturalism and other literary theories, providing a historical understanding of such debates and re-asserting the responsibility of academics for quality research and teaching.[289] Robert Scholes tracks the emergence of English as a central discipline in the university starting in the late nineteenth century and then considers the factors leading to its decline, mostly focusing on changes within the discipline itself where a sense of its purpose was lost.[290]

Why is it, since LIS schools are so focused on texts and information, that we have seen so little evidence of these debates there? Is it because these professional schools have been consumed more by debates about credentials, accreditation, mundane matters such as the naming of their schools, and technocratic concerns that push them to look inward rather than engaging in public issues? Chris Hedges provides a clue about what might have happened, writing, "The new classes of expert professionals have been trained to focus on narrow, specialized knowledge independent of social ideas or conceptions of the common good. A doctor, lawyer, or engineer may become wealthy, but the real meaning of their work is that they sustain health, justice, good government, or safety. The flight from the humanities has become a flight from conscience. It has created an elite class of experts who seldom look beyond their tasks and disciplines to put what they do in a wider, social context. And by absenting themselves from the moral and social questions raised by the humanities, they have opted to serve a corporate structure that has destroyed the culture around them."[291] Efforts to move toward the iSchool model include trying to address broader audiences, but only time will allow us to assess how serious this may be.

---

[288] Stanley Fish, *Professional Correctness: Literary Studies and Political Change* (Oxford: Clarendon Press, 1995).

[289] Gregory S. Jay, *American Literature and the Culture Wars* (Ithaca: Cornell University Press, 1997).

[290] Robert Scholes, *The Rise and Fall of English: Reconstructing English as a Discipline* (New Haven: Yale University Press, 1998).

[291] Chris Hedges, *Empire of Illusion: The End of Literacy and the Triumph of Spectacle* (New York: Nation Books, 2009), pp. 110-111. Ironically, Hedges notes that tens of millions of Americans are functionally illiterate or read at levels that are such low levels as to make it difficult to hold jobs or advance themselves (p. 44), while library schools or iSchools promise to provide systems to enable access to ever increasing amounts of information that still must be read.

Clueless in Academe. Many forces challenge the nature of civil discourse and free speech in higher education. Multiculturalism has been a potent source for both discontent and discovery in the university for the past quarter of a century or more. Henry Louis Gates, Jr,, considering African-American studies issues at the height of the American culture wars, understands that education does not occur in a "vacuum,"[292] noting that education has always been political. Rather than merely dismissing the concept of a literary canon, Gates suggests we need to understand where such an idea has come from, lamenting what he sees as the unnecessary fragmentation of disciplines and perspectives, especially at a time when we need to challenge students to comprehend the substance of differences and similarities between various groups. Has such fragmentation occurred in LIS schools?

Many observers, both inside and outside of the academy, have contributed to such debates. Distinguished sociologist Nathan Glazer sees multiculturalism as "just the latest in this sequence of terms describing how American society, particularly American education, should respond to its diversity."[293] Glazer, acknowledging that we cannot avoid conflict and debate in both society and the university, believes "we all now accept a greater degree of attention to minorities and women and their role in American history and social studies and literature classes in schools."[294] Arthur M. Schlesinger, Jr., reminds us that debates about the substance of what is taught have always been present, while suggesting that the past is what it is and that it is dangerous to try to transform it into some kind of "filiopietistic commemoration."[295] Historian David A. Hollinger considers the limitations of multiculturalism, especially in its inability to resolve conflicts and the challenges even in defining it; Hollinger argues that we need to accept, among other things, "multiple identities" and "constructed character of ethno-racial groups."[296] Mary Lefkowitz challenges the notion

---

[292] Henry Louis Gates, Jr,, *Loose Canons: Notes on the Culture Wars* (New York: Oxford University Press, 1992), p. xv.
[293] Nathan Glazer, *We Are All Multiculturalists Now* (Cambridge: Harvard University Press, 1997), p. 8.
[294] Glazer, *We Are All Multiculturalists Now*, p. 14.
[295] Arthur M. Schlesinger, Jr., *The Disuniting of America: Reflections on a Multicultural Society* (New York: W. W. Norton & Co., 1992), p. 99.
[296] David A. Hollinger, *Postethnic America: Beyond Multiculturalism* (New York: Basic Books, 1995), p. 116.

of Afrocentrism.[297] For every view such as these, it is easy to find many more that are more conservative or liberal, sympathetic or critical.[298]

One might argue, of course, that academic entities are prone to such conflict, a trait deftly described by some insiders. English professor Hazard Adams, reflecting on his experience as an academic administrator, suggests, "Universities organize in ways that would horrify any businessman, but this in itself often makes university work more interesting for the worker, if the unexpected and preposterous can be regarded as diversion."[299] John M. Ellis considers the rise of fashionable theories, the rejection of traditional values and perspectives, and the loss of interest in or love for literature, concluding (among other things) that there has been a "startling decline in the intellectual quality of work in the humanities and a descent to intellectual triviality and irrelevance that amounts to a betrayal of the university as an institution."[300] Gerald Graff, another English professor, follows on the path cleared by Ellis. Graff makes many useful observations about the changing and often still uncertain condition of the university, such as his assessment of how universities see human knowledge: "About a century ago, universities imagined the world of knowledge as a kind of immense pyramid that was built by a process in which each scholarly specialist added a small brick or two to the growing edifice of objective truth. With the collapse of this positivistic view of knowledge in the early twentieth century, scholars and educators have increasingly come to see the world of knowledge as resembling a dynamic conversation rather than as an accumulation of discrete bricks of fact. Yet we still are left with a curriculum composed of separate bricks, which we call courses."[301]

How do we examine LIS education in light of such issues; have these schools been immune to such matters? Do we feel comfortable in teaching controversial issues in our classrooms? Daniel Schwarz reminds us, "In our age of PowerPoints, listservs, and computer Blackboards, let us not forget

---

[297] Mary Lefkowitz, *Not Out of Africa: How Afrocentrism Became an Excuse to Teach Myth as History* (New York: New Republic Book, Basic Books, 1996).

[298] See the range of essays in Robert Royal, ed., *Reinventing the American People: Unity and Diversity Today* (Washington, D.C.: Ethics and Public Policy Center, published by William B. Eerdmans Pub Co., 1995), p. 17.

[299] Hazard Adams, *The Academic Tribes*, 2nd ed (Urbana: University of Illinois, 1988), p. 21.

[300] John M. Ellis, *Literature Lost: Social Agendas and the Corruption of the Humanities* (New Haven: Yale University Press, 1997), p. 228.

[301] Gerald Graff, *Clueless in Academia: How Schooling Obscures the Life of the Mind* (New Haven: Yale University Press, 2003), p. 63.

that great teaching derives from a human voice and personality talking passionately and clearly about a subject that she or he knows a great deal about and wants to share with others... . We need to cultivate intellectual curiosity – one of the great gifts teachers can share with our students... ."[302] Some might argue, I know I would, that some of the uncomfortable issues such as debating the canon or arguing about multiculturalism derive from pursuing that intellectual curiosity. However, in library schools and their successors sometimes it seems that PowerPoints, listservs, and computer Blackboards represent the intellectual content.

History on Trial. Whatever preconceptions one brings to the waging of the culture wars in the university, there are both positive and negative consequences one sees in the conflict. Historians, aiming to interpret the past (always a potentially contentious objective), have also written interesting assessments of the role of the university. What Graff does for English, Lawrence Levine does for history. Levine answers the critics of the university as the source of all problems in American society, especially the manner in which the American past and its interpretation by historians, history museum curators, historic site administrators, and public intellectuals was then under scrutiny. The "problem is that the charges against the university are so hyperbolic, so angry, so conspiracy-minded, and so one-sided they can find almost nothing positive to say." But Levine counters, "there *is* fragmentation in the United States; there *is* distrust; there *is* deep anger – and much of this is reflected in and acted out in universities, but none of it is *caused* by universities or by professors or by young people."[303] What we see here, of course, is that the anger is on *both* sides of these debates.

Others perceive positive elements that might emerge from even the most vicious debates: "The culture wars, though unnerving and nasty," write Gary B. Nash, Charlotte Crabtree, and Ross E. Dunn, "offer the public a grand opportunity to talk with historians and history teachers about how history is written, how research has changed in recent decades, and how arguments about the past illustrate a democracy at work."[304] Likewise, historian Peter N. Stearns counters the critics of higher education who see everything that is wrong stemming from what is happening in the

---

[302] Daniel R. Schwarz, *In Defense of Reading: Teaching Literature in the Twenty-First Century* (West Sussex, UK: Wiley-Blackwell, 2008), p. 127.
[303] Lawrence Levine, *The Opening of the American Mind: Canons, Culture, and History* (Boston: Beacon Press, 1996), p. 31.
[304] Gary B. Nash, Charlotte Crabtree, and Ross E. Dunn, *History on Trial: Culture Wars and the Teaching of the Past* (New York: Alfred A. Knopf, 1997), p. 7.

classroom.[305] Stearns argues that teaching the humanities, especially history, ought to be focused on understanding the past, not on memorizing for tests or supporting some kind of misguided patriotism. He states that the emphasis ought not to be on some canon of approved works, a false orthodoxy, but about equipping students to sort through facts (often best displayed in case studies and problems) to derive meaning, build interpretations, and add to knowledge.

The process of debate, exploring a topic from all perspectives, is what ought to be important. There needs to be room for disagreement. The problem with the culture war notion is that all too often the debate is buried under nasty words and a sense that the other perspective is always wrong. Again, that these debates have been somewhat absent in LIS programs suggests not a reason for why we should be thankful, but more a reason for concern. It is healthy to air out real differences of opinion about substantial issues, and issues such as intellectual property, literacy, information access, privacy, and other matters ought to be heating up the classroom in library schools, both the new and old version.

Too Many Priorities? Library schools (old and new) have small faculties, most laboring with a half- to a full-dozen tenure stream or tenured faculty. For most universities and larger colleges, our schools are like fly specks on a circus tent. Yet, in the two decades I have been engaged with such a school, I have witnessed these small faculties not only try to sustain their masters degree and doctoral programs, but add new masters degrees, establish undergraduate information science programs, and create distance education offerings. There are perfectly valid reasons for each of these endeavors and there have been some successes, yet when examined together they seem overwhelming in scope and far too ambitious. What is driving these heroic efforts are the deans and faculties of the schools themselves, usually trying to prove to their parent academic units that they are relevant and useful (and who wouldn't do this?), even if reflecting their own doubts about their missions as the nature of the library and information professions change and the trends of the Digital Era spur on additional questions and challenges. Uncertain about what might win them favor, these schools seem to go in many different directions at once.

While there is nothing wrong with the primary aim of gaining favor and support (who, after all, does not wish for a visionary and energetic dean to lead their school?), the price can be enormous. Teaching loads increase,

---

[305] Peter N. Stearns, *Meaning Over Memory: Recasting the Teaching of Culture and History* (Chapel Hill: University of North Carolina Press, 1993), p. 7.

meetings proliferate, and the hours spent with teaching increase at the expense of nearly every other activity, most preciously time for reading, reflecting, and researching (the kinds of activities that attracted many to the academy in the first place). It is a common observation from within higher education that the "traditional triad of faculty obligations—teaching, scholarship, and service—have not altered at all" while many other responsibilities have become the norm for faculty.[306] However, more often than not, the energy of the library schools' faculties and administrators is ultimately devoted to generating revenue and defended, often strenuously, as just common business sense. David Kirp, in his book about the marketing of higher education, wisely argues that money has always been a concern in universities, but that "what *is* new, and troubling, is the new power that money directly exerts over so many aspects of higher education." Kirp sees that higher education can never be just like the corporation or government, because the core of the academic community is "teaching, learning, and research."[307] Such an assessment would be true for the library school as well. Indeed, it is easy to understand that the addition of many professional schools starting in the late nineteenth century were as much about generating external financial support as about dealing with real professional and social challenges. Maybe nothing is new.

We can consider one of these new initiatives, namely, distance education, as an example of the price exacted on ambition and success. Distance programs can be delivered effectively as real education, offering the opportunity to reach new audiences. One could also make the argument that the traditional methods of classroom instruction, now swamped by PowerPoint slides and other tools, are not without flaws. Many have also speculated about the effectiveness of the traditional lecture and seminar, long since past as innovative educational methods. Nevertheless, there are more disturbing aspects to distance education than merely pedagogical concerns, theories, and applications.

Like all educational systems, delivering distance education depends on other elements being in place. First, distance education needs to operate within priorities formulated by each library school, more than only generating revenue. Second, there needs to be an infrastructure allowing

---

[306] David Evans, "Redefining Faculty Roles," *Chronicle of Higher Education*, September 14, 2009, available at http://chronicle.com/blogPost/Redefining-Faculty-Roles/8016/?sid=at&utm_source=at&utm_medium=en, accessed September 14, 2009.
[307] David Kirp, *Shakespeare, Einstein, and the Bottom Line: The Marketing of Higher Education* (Cambridge: Harvard University Press, 2003), pp. 3, 113.

faculty and students to interact effectively within the online environment. In many schools, hampered by limited resources and over-burdened by good intentions, neither element is in place, and educational objectives may be replaced with business goals. Eric Gould's tempered assessment of the university in its new corporate culture argues that the notion of a more expensive "high quality liberal education" is being lost to "relatively cheap, on-line vocational learning or conventional degrees with clearer signs of high returns upon graduation... ."[308] Obviously, such problems are far larger and go much deeper than what one observes in the traditional library schools, and, for some, these problems only generate long-standing and weary debates about education in the field extending back to the days of Melvil Dewey.

Some will object that a library school is supposed to provide vocational education (training), but that is always too simplistic a view. A. Bartlett Giametti believed that even professional education needed within it a "liberal temper; that is, technical or professional study ought to be animated by a love of learning... ."[309] This is precisely what can be lost as library schools switch to the information sciences and both continuing education and professional education continue to be the "celebrated cash cows of academe."[310] The sirens of distance education may be particularly seductive for library schools, and the rocky shoals particularly destructive, as there is already a deeply entrenched vocational emphasis. Personally, I have been regularly engaged in debates with some current students arguing for more application, more hands-on approaches, and far less theoretical discussions, lectures, and readings. At times, the tension in such schools between theory and practice is thick, and not only between the professoriate and students but also between faculty factions, but it is a century long (and more) debate.

Distance education challenges because it connects directly into the historic debates about practice and theory. Given that teaching in an online environment requires considerable additional time by the instructor for both preparing and teaching, especially with its 24/7 online environment creating student expectations that can be a burden even for the most committed teacher, it makes sense that any school offering such a program would have its larger priorities clearly defined. Knowing how to balance time and other resources between teaching, researching, supporting the

---

[308] Eric Gould, *The University in a Corporate Culture* (New Haven: Yale University Press, 2003), p. 53.
[309] A. Bartlett Giametti, *A Free and Ordered Space: The Real World of the University* (New York: W. W. Norton and Co., 1990), p. 120.
[310] Gould, *The University in a Corporate Culture*, p. 71.

doctoral program, and providing service to a variety of professional communities requires this. It may seem impossible for a small faculty to be fully engaged in an on campus program, distance education operation, research and writing, keeping current with professional and scholarly literature, and nurturing doctoral students. Yet, that is exactly the decision some library schools have made, arguing vociferously that they need to be doing everything. In a sense, then, distance education threatens to turn professional schools into teaching factories, weakening an already weakened professional school in the modern university, but perhaps appealing to many who desire for a practical vocational orientation in their university experience. We might be making easy short-term gains that lessen the profile of a professional school in the university as its intellectual and scholarly base evaporates; no matter what stance we take on the issue of evaluating the effectiveness of distance education or its allure for reaching new students, the chief criterion for gauging a program usually seems to be the *number* of students (by which I mean tuition revenue) in the virtual classrooms. It is what Cornell West calls the "market-driven technocratic culture" permeating higher education, "with the narrow pursuit of academic trophies and the business of generating income from grants and business partnerships taking precedence over the fundamental responsibility of nurturing young minds."[311] West's own controversial reputation and celebrity status might make some look askance at his criticism, but in this instance we need to consider the substance not the source. West's criticism is a valid one.

When I published an essay on the above issues, especially on the matter of distance education, I had just become Chair of the Library and Information Science program; it was a coincidence, since the essay had been written and accepted for publication nearly a year before.[312] The students in our distance program were upset by my remarks and wrote a letter to the dean, suggesting, among other things, "If Dr. Cox were to teach a course in the FastTrack program he would find that we are a passionate, diverse, hard-working and vocal group of students who are grateful for the opportunity to earn a Master's degree from such a reputable school. He would know that we entered this program expecting to earn, not simply purchase, our degrees." Since this time, I have taught online (in fact, I actually had taught a decade before two synchronous distance education

---

[311] Cornell West, *Democracy Matters: Winning the Fight Against Imperialism* (New York: Penguin Press, 2004), p. 186.
[312] The essay in question was "Why Survival Is Not Enough," *American Libraries*, June/July 2006, pp. 42-45.

courses) in our program, and I do not believe that my views have changed very much. While I continue to believe that distance education can be a valuable program, I also remain convinced that it can generate many problems for both faculty and students if not planned and executed well. In a response to these particular students, I also noted that my essay, like this book, was concerned with the general state of LIS education, not just distance education.

The Allure of Money. Many professional schools, including library schools, have bought in, completely, to the university's money making potential, but at some cost to program integrity. Educator Alfie Kohn writes, "If you're in a sailboat without a map or a destination, you can get up to a good speed, but only in the direction that the prevailing winds are blowing."[313] Kohn's comment is important. Some library schools have lost their own moorings. Long oriented to their own professional community and craft, these schools often did not build records of scholarship or a recognizable academic profile within their own universities. Many of these schools have mixed track records in securing research grants, partly because they lack faculty doing research and are more engaged in professional service (this has changed for a few, but mostly for those expanding their vision far beyond libraries). As the universities shifted towards the corporate model, these schools sought ways of justifying their existence, usually by establishing undergraduate programs, distance education programs, and any other mechanism by which they could create new revenue streams. Along with their success have come other problems. Faculty sit through meeting after meeting, seeking to manage a multitude of programs, providing real-life versions of novelist Richard Russo's fictional academic mulling over faculty meetings: "How many good books have gone unread, essays unwritten, research discontinued, in order to make room for brain-scalding meetings like this one?"[314] While some will contest this bleak assessment, many others only need to reflect on recent faculty meetings to gather evidence supporting such a perspective. And even if a case can be made for the fact that some of this may extend from systematic problems in library education and the broader profession that date back decades before the advent of distance education, the use of new technologies, financial incentives offered by universities, and the alluring easy measure of student body counts all exaggerate the nature of the problems.

---

[313] Alfie Kohn, *What Does It Mean to Be Well Educated: And More Essays on Standards, Grading, and Other Follies* (Boston: Beacon Press, 2004), p. xiii.
[314] Richard Russo, *Straight Man* (New York: Vintage Books, 1998), p. 281.

It gets worse. The problem of supporting on-campus, distance, undergraduate and graduate programs does not just affect one's time for other academic duties. Professional schools, just like other sectors of the modern university, are in danger of seeing the role of faculty deteriorate because they are more dependent on adjuncts, academic labor fitting well into the corporate model because of it's cost-efficient method of teaching. Henry Giroux again writes, "As power shifts away from the faculty to the managerial sectors of the university, adjunct faculty increase in number while effectively being removed from the faculty governance process. In short, the hiring of part-time faculty to minimize costs simultaneously maximizes managerial control over faculty and the educational process itself. As their ranks are depleted, full-time faculty live under the constant threat of either being given heavier workloads or simply having their tenure contracts eliminated or drastically redefined through 'post-tenure reviews.'"[315] Whatever the extent of this may be in reality, few will argue that it is not a concern.

This is especially a danger in professional schools such as library schools, where historically the regular faculty have been small, the ties to practitioners in the field are strong, and students often clamor for courses taught by individuals who "do" stuff rather than professors who are oriented to research and building professional and other knowledge. Professional schools have relied on adjuncts from their beginning, but they may be becoming more so as their programs proliferate, weakening themselves. Adjuncts are generally not involved in the school's intellectual and academic life, but they are sometimes guns for hire, without the time or luxury to participate much more fully in the life of the school than through what they do in their own classrooms. As a result, library schools develop a curriculum in which only part of the regular faculty are invested and that can easily spin away from any core knowledge focus, as they seek to satisfy nearly every professional constituency able to ante up the requisite funds for courses and programs. Of course, the focus on finances is not a new problem; in fact, most of the issues associated with the modern university are not new.[316] Yet, there is something new about the modern corporate university.

---

[315] Henry Giroux, "Neoliberalism, Corporate Culture, and the Promise of Higher Education: The University as a Public Sphere," *Harvard Educational Review* 72 (Winter 2002): 444.

[316] Harry R. Lewis, *Excellence Without a Soul: How a Great University Forgot Education* [New York: Public Affairs, 2006], p. 18.

The Corporate University. English professor, Phyllis Rose, reflecting on her life as an academic, laments the onslaught of poststructuralist criticism, and the loss of interest in reading, the value of literature, and the demise of any common core holding her colleagues together. She also wonders about the impact of information technology: "The average student arrives fitted out with computer, television, stereo, and cell phone... . These aren't students. They are self-contained information-processing systems, with the line between information and entertainment sometimes thin."[317] Like many other recent commentators about modern higher education, Rose attributes this not to the general progress in information technology but to the shift in American education in recent decades to a "consumer item" where universities "need to make students and their parents happy with their own experience and convinced that the money they have spent is well spent."[318]

There is a thunderous avalanche of writings about the transformation of the university into a corporate entity, with a focus on generating revenue, where research is geared to saleable products, students are customers, and intellectual curiosity or dissent is not deemed to be in the best interests of the new educational corporations.[319] There are individuals who are

---

[317] Phyllis Rose, "The Coming of the French: My Life as an English Professor," *American Scholar* 74 (Winter 2005): 67.
[318] Rose, "The Coming of the French," pp. 67-68.
[319] For a few of these recent writings, see Stanley Aronowitz, *The Knowledge Factory: Dismantling the Corporate University and Creating True Higher Learning* (Boston: Beacon Press, 2000); Derek Bok, *Universities in the Marketplace: The Commercialization of Higher Education* (Princeton: Princeton University Press, 2003); David L. Kirp, *Shakespeare, Einstein, and the Bottom Line: The Marketing of Higher Education* (Cambridge, MA: Harvard University Press, 2003); and Donald G. Stein, ed., *Buying In or Selling Out? The Commercialism of the American Research University* (New Brunswick, NJ: Rutgers University Press, 2004). The most important assessment of the nature of the corporate university may be Gaye Tuchman, *Wannabe U: Inside the Corporate University* (Chicago: University of Chicago Press, 2009). Tuchman, a well-known sociologist, studies her own institution, the University of Connecticut, although she writes about the institution in anonymous fashion and continues to not confirm that it is UConn. She charts how we have shifted from the university as a public good in the mid-twentieth university to the university as business. Many of the criticisms are familiar – universities are training not educating; accountability, auditing, and reporting have now overwhelmed both faculty and administrators as productivity measures but measures that often do not support fundamental activities such as teaching and research; the university is not a social institution, now it is an industry; branding and marketing consume ever greater amounts of resources (time and money); credentials are the products being sold; decisions are

CHAPTER FOUR

functioning much like their predecessors of a generation or two ago, spending their time reading, engaged in some form of scholarship, teaching, and mentoring students; the problem is, of course, it is just as likely that these are a dying breed, literally the last generation of faculty tenured under older principles and values. It is not my intent to summon up great hordes of statistics or facts to support this bleak scenario, but I do want to provide some impressionistic comments about what has happened.

One of my former doctoral students recounted to me being informed by his dean that he should never worry about the students or teaching, instead focusing on his personal research and grants. The university lost a good teacher as he became disenchanted with the academic life (although ultimately he returned in a non-tenure position). My former student terms this as a moral or ethical issue. These students had paid lots of money, he reflected, and he was repeatedly reminded that he could neglect the students. You become available to your research and collaborators, not your students. You conduct research that attracts large quantities of dollars but not necessarily students, because the subject of the research might not have much to do with what you teach or what your students expect you to teach. The prospects for a synergy between what you research and what you teach are negligible since students have been taken out of the picture. For that matter, the prospects for how your research adds to your expertise may be weak since the aim of such research is often funding, fame, and fashion rather than your teaching.

The ancient tension between theory and practice exists in all professions, but it is intensified in professional schools, where many disciplines collide with the university's demands. In such schools the strain materializes as friction between that of graduate education and vocational training, especially because both educators and most practitioners (whether they are lawyers, physicians, or librarians and archivists) recognize that the knowledge supporting their fields derives from some combination of theory, methodology, and practice. Looking at knowledge in this manner not only implies the need for cooperation between those in the academy and those in the field, but it also encompasses a respect for the educational process that now might be endangered. Tossed aside in the corporate university is a tolerance for asking questions about such matters. Alfie Kohn, considering this influence, writes, "Qualities such as a love of

---

made to get higher rankings, even if it is understood that such rankings are flawed – but Tuchman offers remarkably rich detail and research to back her criticism. This is a book drawing both praise and criticism, the best kind – one that stimulates debate about where higher education is heading.

learning for its own sake, a penchant for asking challenging questions, or a commitment to democratic participation in decision making would be seen as nice but irrelevant – or perhaps even as impediments to the efficient realization of corporate goals."[320] Faculty, in their new role as corporate staff, are pressured to produce results, meaning quantifiable ones such as dollars and enrolled students, not to engage in reflection and knowledge generation. And this works against the purpose of the university. As one writer reflects, "Debate, not censure, is the university's hallmark."[321]

More and more academics are speaking up about what the corporate university is doing to them. Stanley Fish considers the notion of the humanities and their values in the university and their long decline, starting, apparently, in 1891 when Andrew Carnegie congratulated some business school graduates for being "fully occupied in obtaining a knowledge of shorthand and typewriting" rather than wasting time "upon dead languages." Now we have a decline in tenured and tenure track faculty as we shift to the notion of the for-profit university. Fish states, "The for-profit university is the logical end of a shift from a model of education centered in an individual professor who delivers insight and inspiration to a model that begins and ends with the imperative to deliver the information and skills necessary to gain employment." This cheapens the notion of the professoriate, Fish claiming, "In this latter model, the mode of delivery – a disc, a computer screen, a video hook-up – doesn't matter so long as delivery occurs. Insofar as there are real-life faculty in the picture, their credentials and publications (if they have any) are beside the point, for they are just 'delivery people.'"[322] All of this suggests that information technology is replacing the humanities as the core of the university curriculum, or, as Ted Roberts adds, "If success in the 21st century is being defined by collaborative training that combines computer science/engineering skills with social sciences, languages, psychology and other disciplines, then IT is emerging as the 'new' liberal arts."[323] To some extent, this happened to library schools, as IT courses squeezed out courses on the history of books and printing.

---

[320] Kohn, *What Does It Mean to Be Well Educated*, pp. 22-23.
[321] Eric Lott, *The Disappearing Liberal Intellectual* (New York: Basic Books, 2006), p. 131.
[322] Stanley Fish, "The Last Professor," *New York Times*, January 18, 2009. The book reviewed is Frank Donoghue, *The Last Professors: The Corporate University and the Fate of the Humanities* (New York: Fordham University Press, 2008).
[323] Ted Roberts, "The "New" Liberal Arts," *Pittsburgh Post-Gazette*, June 24, 2008, http://www.post-gazette.com/pg/08176/892059-28.stm.

CHAPTER FOUR

University, Inc. Opinions about the corporate university have come from every quarter within the university and drawn the attention of outside commentators as well. Journalists and free-lance writers have had a field day lambasting what has seemed to be happening in the academy, leading to tomes which are not always fully accurate and often exaggerated, but, nevertheless, providing some astute critiques of the modern university.[324] Whether balanced or not, fair or unfair, such assessments must be read, reflected on, and responded to by those from within the academic ranks. Anyone contemplating a career as an academic needs to consider the implications of what the university may be becoming, especially if that career may be planned for residing in a professional school, where the attention to delivering goods that attract tuition-paying students seems particularly intense.

A considerable amount of the evaluation of the corporate university has been generated from within. Bill Readings laments about the university becoming a "transnational bureaucratic corporation."[325] Typical of Readings, he worries about the loss of a search for knowledge to be replaced by the "processing of information: something should be known, yet it becomes less and less urgent that we know what it is that should be known."[326] How does that resonate with a school of information sciences? Sociologist Stanley Aronowitz offers a biting criticism of this problem, lamenting that higher education has shifted to be more about credentials than about learning, less about vocational calling and more about jobs, a focus on training rather than educating, and greater interest in generating revenue than in fulfilling a societal mission.[327] Reflect on the credentialism in any professional school, even for just a moment, and we discover the need for analyzing the full implications of such a perspective.

Sometimes such analysis can seem bitter. Henry and Susan Searls Giroux provide an analysis of the implications of the corporate university, considering the decline of the idea of the university as a public good, where "critical education, public morality, and civic responsibility as a condition for creating thoughtful and engaged citizens is sacrificed all too willingly to the interest of finance capital, corporate greed, and the logic of

---

[324] Journalist Jennifer Washburn's *University, Inc.: The Corporate Corruption of American Higher* Education (New York: Basic Books, 2005) is an example.
[325] Bill Readings, *The University in Ruins* (Cambridge: Harvard University Press, 1996), p. 3.
[326] Readings, *The University in Ruins*, p. 86.
[327] Stanley Aronowitz, *The Knowledge Factory: Dismantling the Corporate University and Creating True Higher Learning* (Boston: Beacon Press, 2000).

profitmaking."[328] In one of their more telling observations, the Giroux's argue that the "corporate model fails to recognize that the public mission of higher education implies that knowledge has a critical function; that intellectual inquiry that is unpopular or debunking should be safeguarded and treated as an important social asset; and that faculty in higher education are more than merely functionaries of the corporate order."[329] How do we apply such concerns to the typical professional school?

Everything is open, in this corporate model, to being reduced to professional education. In an issue of the *Atlantic*, someone, identified only as Professor X and as an "adjunct instructor of English," comments on the process of teaching basic writing skills and the desire by the public to get a professional education (and the desire by the university to make money offering it). Professor X notes that adult education is a "substantial profit center for many colleges. Like factory owners, school administrators are delighted with this idea of mounting a second shift of learning in their classrooms, in the evenings, when the full-time students are busy with such regular extracurricular pursuits of higher education as reading Facebook and playing beer pong." This individual notes, "There is a sense that the American workforce needs to be more professional at every level. Many jobs that never before required college now call for at least some post-secondary course work."[330] Professional schools may have been ahead of their time.

Knowledge and Money. There have been efforts to provide balanced perspectives about the contentious issue concerning the corporate university. English professor Eric Gould presents a sympathetic portrait, arguing that the emergence of the modern American university occurred in a capitalist society and the more recent problems accompanying the corporate university are not new. Gould describes the "interplay between educational ideals and market forces in defining the modern American university."[331] As Gould notes, "Being not-for-profit does not mean that universities are altruistic; it simply means that trustees cannot personally

---

[328] Henry A. Giroux and Susan Searls Giroux, *Take Back Higher Education: Race, Youth, and the Crisis of Democracy in the Post-Civil Rights Era* (New York: Palgrave Macmillan, 2004), p. 66.
[329] Giroux, *Take Back Higher Education*, p. 265. *Take Back Higher Education* builds on themes and issues introduced by Henry A. Giroux in his *The Abandoned Generation: Democracy Beyond the Culture of Fear* (New York: Palgrave Macmillan, 2003).
[330] Professor X, "In the Basement of the Ivory Tower," *Atlantic*, June 2008, available at http://www.theatlantic.com/doc/200806/college.
[331] Eric Gould, *The University in a Corporate Culture*, p. x.

profit from a university's commerce. The university is very much a for-profit institution in actuality, and all aspects of its business are driven by this aim."[332]

Others have adopted a different tone when discussing what the modern university is becoming. James Engell and Anthony Dangerfield believe that money has always been an important factor in the development and functions of higher education. However, they also think that money has become too much of the driving force (although they believe that there are many choices yet to be made that can correct the circumstances higher education currently faces).[333] An earlier account of the new challenges facing the university is by Christopher J. Lucas, an education professor, who argues that the critics of higher education tend to over generalize in their critiques; Lucas offers suggestions for refocusing the academy on teaching, developing coherent curriculum, and being more accountable to society.[334] Roger L. Geiger believes that the university now, more than ever, depends on the marketplace for resources needed for its own survival (it cannot expect the state to bail it out). Geiger describes the nature of these higher costs, the emergence of financial aid as the norm, the increasing financial burden on students and their parents, and the increasing reliance on tuition. While the main attribute of the university continues to be the "possession of expert, specialized, theoretical knowledge" held by its faculty and professional staff, there continues to be a tension between the institution and its research and the growing commercialism of knowledge.[335] Steven Brint provides an interesting group of essays about changes and challenges in demographics, economic, technology, knowledge, and governance in the university.[336] And the list of such studies goes on. The issue in all these studies is how the individual, desiring to be or already a faculty member, decides to deal with these kinds of issues. Maybe they just tell us that the "real" university is a bit harder to deal with, or maybe that there really was never a golden age. The value of these publications is that they make us re-evaluate our own motives and objectives for joining the

---

[332] Gould, *The University in a Corporate Culture*, p. 22.
[333] James Engell and Anthony Dangerfield, *Saving Higher Education in the Age of Money* (Charlottesville: University of Virginia Press, 2005).
[334] Christopher J. Lucas, *Crisis in the Academy: Rethinking Higher Education in America* (New York: St. Martin's Press, 1996).
[335] Roger L. Geiger, *Knowledge and Money: Research Universities and the Paradox of the Marketplace* (Stanford: Stanford University Press, 2004), p. 7.
[336] Steven Brint, ed., *The Future of the City of Intellect: The Changing American University* (Stanford, CA: Stanford University Press, 2002).

academy, perhaps making us ask ourselves how we serve our professions, contribute to the public good, add to knowledge, and educate the next generation of citizens.

It is easy, considering the state of the modern university, to assume a pessimistic, fatalistic tone or to strike back and compose a jeremiad about the university's condition. This is particularly easy to do with the market factors and economics of the university. Frank Newman, Laura Courturier, and Jamie Scurry consider carefully how the market is threatening to change the nature of higher education, wrestling especially with what market forces do to the notion of a public good and placing the various debates into a broader historical context (before 1940 teaching was the primary responsibility of faculty, but after the end of the Second World War research and grants had become their main activity). These authors sound a warning: "For higher education to become simply another self-focused, revenue-oriented sector of society would be a tragedy of massive proportions. The task, then, is to rebuild the compact, renew the understanding between higher education and the public, and renew and strengthen the commitment to the public purposes of higher education."[337] It is not difficult to reflect on such a warning in a professional school, where faculty and administrators are seeking to deliver quality education but also needing to keep one eye on the revenue they generate.

Steal This Professional School. Branding has become a standard feature of the corporate university.[338] Sheila Slaughter and Larry Leslie, both professors of higher education, consider how the changing nature of the university and its place in the global marketplace are transforming how faculty work, how they are seen, and how they perceive themselves. They conclude that some faculty will teach more, others less, and the emphasis

---

[337] Frank Newman, Laura Courturier, and Jamie Scurry, *The Future of Higher Education: Rhetoric, Reality, and the Risks of the Market* (San Francisco, CA: Jossey-Bass, 2004), p. 215. See also Donald G. Stein, ed., *Buying In or Selling Out? The Commercialization of the American Research University* (New Brunswick, NJ: Rutgers University Press, 2004), considering athletics, commercial ventures with corporations, the patenting and licensing of academic discoveries, technology transfer concerns, industrial licensing, intellectual property, and so forth, all reflecting a wide range of perspectives about such matters. All of these problems can be found everywhere in the university, including in professional schools.

[338] James B. Twitchell, *Branded Nation: The Marketing of Megachurch, College, Inc., and Museumworld* (New York: Simon & Schuster, 2004).

CHAPTER FOUR 101

on revenue generation will affect all dimensions of the role of faculty.[339] Others, such as Robert Zemsky, Gregory R. Wegner, and William F. Massy believe that there must be a different kind of approach to embracing the notion of a market. Zemsky, Wegner, and Massy state, "to thrive, universities must be different, more creative, less rhetorical in their pursuit of excellence. They require leaders who want their institutions – as institutions – to become market enterprises that are ready, willing, and able to play public roles."[340] Let's figure out how to get the edge on our competitors.

What about education? Some observers sense a general decline in the quality of higher education, such as Richard H. Hersh and John Merrow, editing a volume that they think is a "unique" commentary on higher education because of the variety of perspectives represented, including "journalists, a pollster, a novelist, social scientists, college presidents, professors, and foundation officers."[341] There has been considerable focus on the growing use of graduate students and adjunct teachers to teach university courses, and the essays found in the volume edited by Benjamin Johnson, Patrick Kavanagh, and Kevin Mattson, consider the problems associated with this trend as one more piece of evidence of the negative influence of the so-called corporate university model.[342] However, try to run an interesting, varied, and quality program without such assets!

Sadly, the criticism about the influence of corporate goals and objectives has extended to education's lower levels. Larry Cuban asserts that the corporate model has thrown education of our younger citizens off-track, turning schools to focus on matters like standardized tests and measures or skills rather than learning.[343] Yet, there are considerable reasons why university faculty and administrators should consider the implications of business approaches in education. In an interesting and provocative

---

[339] Sheila Slaughter and Larry Leslie, *Academic Capitalism: Politics, Policies, and the Entrepreneurial University* (Baltimore: Johns Hopkins University, 1997).
[340] Robert Zemsky, Gregory R. Wegner, and William F. Massy, *Remaking the American University: Market-Smart and Mission-Centered* (New Brunswick, N.J.: Rutgers University Press, 2005), p. 9.
[341] Richard H. Hersh and John Merrow, eds., *Declining by Degrees: Higher Education and Risk* (New York: Palgrave Macmillan, 2005), p. 1.
[342] Benjamin Johnson, Patrick Kavanagh, and Kevin Mattson, eds., *Steal This University: The Rise of the Corporate University and the Academic Labor Movement* (New York: Routledge, 2003).
[343] Larry Cuban, *The Blackboard and the Bottom Line: Why Schools Can't Be Businesses* (Cambridge: Harvard University Press, 2004).

book, Richard S. Ruch examines what "traditional non-profit colleges and universities" can learn from the development of for-profit entities such as the University of Phoenix. Ruch contends that these traditional schools can learn about how to respond to market forces, adapting the organizational structure (including the idea of branding), redefining the notion of shared governance so that academic institutions can be more "timely and responsive," and developing a stronger customer orientation.[344] Ruch, drawing on his personal experience in working for for-profit educational operations, contends that what threatens higher education is not the competition for students but the radical change in education represented by the for-profit entities. There are a lot of problems in what the for-profits represent, such as the diminution of the concept of a higher public good in favor of the financial bottom line, but there are interesting ideas and approaches in the book worth consideration by any college or university. No wonder so many in professional schools, counting students and measuring revenues, have trouble sleeping at night. If we focus on such matters, we forget some of the matters that drew us to become part of the university in the first place. If we don't consider such issues, we lose the opportunity to work here at all.

What is the Purpose of the Corporate University? I have become weary with the discussions about success in higher education, often couched in terms of survival. What about making a difference? What about contributing to human knowledge? What about helping individuals determine what they want to do with their lives? Donald Kennedy dares to discuss faculty as being "moral teachers," setting "examples for the next generation of explorers."[345] Admittedly, the high-octane research discourses would seem to connect with the knowledge issue, but not really, at least not as discussed in the typical professional school. But is this an example for the next generation of educators? The driving forces behind these discussions often seem to be more about funding than they are about contributing to knowledge. And how can we be surprised about this tension or challenge? Mihaly Csikszentmihalyi provides this insight: "Today, business leaders cannot begin to foster a climate of positive order if their sole concern is making a profit. They must also have a vision that gives life meaning, which offers people hope for their own future and those of their children. We have learned how to develop five-minute and even one-minute managers.

---

[344] Richard S. Ruch, *Higher Ed, Inc.: The Rise of the For-Profit University* (Baltimore: Johns Hopkins University Press, 2001), pp. 148-149.
[345] Donald Kennedy, *Academic Duty* (Cambridge: Harvard University Press, 1997), p. 184.

But we would do better to ask ourselves what it takes to be an executive who helps build a better future. More than anything else, we need *hundred-year managers* at the helm of corporations."³⁴⁶ Jesus drove the moneychangers out of the temple. Who will do this for us?

I have had countless discussions about such matters, and I have heard colleagues declare that we cannot really discuss quality education, because we have to focus on generating revenue in order to survive. Fortunately, there were no students present at such discussions. The shock and outrage might have been too great. What is the point of existing if we are not educating individuals or contributing to a body of scholarship and knowledge with some modicum of benefit for society? You can be seen as uncooperative, as not being a leader, and, worse, as not fulfilling basic obligations, that the number one priority must always be revenue. There is another way to look at what is happening in higher education and the professional schools situated there. Bill Readings, in his analysis of the decline of the modern university, essentially argues, among many things, that administration has trumped the other essential functions of the university.³⁴⁷ In some professional schools, where research was already weak, it has been more tempting for faculty either to become absorbed by administrative matters or to allow other administrators merely to become the dominate force in their schools. Indeed, this may even be committed in the guise of being more *professional.* Even non-profits outside of the university are adopting a business mentality, leading the authors of one study to somewhat glibly state, "sometimes, the pursuit of profit directly conflicts with the pursuit of social good."³⁴⁸

In the university, and especially in the professional school, expressing love for learning becomes more difficult as larger classrooms are created, meeting financial analysts' expectations but muffling those who want to learn. None of this is very good for either the library school or university host since, as Jacques Barzun suggested a half-century ago, the "fundamental work" of the university is "scholarship." He continues, "In the laboratory this is called pure science; in the study and classroom, it is research and teaching. For teaching no less than research demands original

---

³⁴⁶ Mihaly Csikszentmihalyi, *Good Business: Leadership, Flow, and the Making of Meaning* (New York: Viking, 2003), pp. 11-12.
³⁴⁷ Bill Readings, *The University in Ruins* (Cambridge: Harvard University Press, 1996), p. 125.
³⁴⁸ William Foster and Jeffrey Bradach, "Should Nonprofits Seek Profits?" *Harvard Business Review* 83 (February 2005): 99.

thought, and addressing students is equally a form of publication."[349] The same synergy between scholarship and teaching must exist in the library school (or any professional school), because there these schools are also striving to convey knowledge to students. The press of other priorities, the chase for revenue, and the new passion for distance education are pulling the faculty of these schools away from research, reading, and reflection that the university academic must be committed to or risk intellectual atrophy and obsolescence.

Distance Education and the Corporate University. Issues of money generated by the corporate university model bring us back to distance education. While faculty may express concerns about the educational quality of such an effort, the focus can fixate on gaining the requisite financial and administrative support. This can lead to the wide path heading to hell, while trying to demonstrate to the university administrators that we are both creative and responsive to the needs of the university to generate revenue from any possible source.

Distance education can be delivered effectively, providing real education, offering the opportunity to reach audiences beyond those normally found on campus. One can also make the argument that the traditional methods of classroom instruction, now seeming to be almost completely overtaken by the use of PowerPoint slides, wasn't without its own flaws and problems.[350] However, delivering distance education depends on having two basic elements in place. One, distance education needs to be placed in a set of educational priorities extending beyond generating revenue, especially since an online 24/7 environment requires additional time by the instructor for both preparing and teaching. Two, there needs to be an adequate infrastructure allowing faculty to teach effectively within the online environment and students, as well, to learn. As it turns out, neither element is often in place.

How does the faculty balance its time and other resources between teaching, researching, and supporting the graduate programs and their professional communities, with the additional burden of an online degree program? When we think rationally, we recognize how difficult it can be to

---

[349] *A Jacques Barzun Reader: Selections from His Works*, ed. Michael Murray (New York: HarperCollins/Perennial Classics, 2002), p. 424. (Barzun originally wrote this in 1954).

[350] For some interesting discussions about PowerPoint and education, see Clifford Stoll, *High-Tech Heretic: Reflections of a Computer Contrarian* (New York: Anchor, 2000) and Edward R. Tufte, *The Cognitive Power of PowerPoint* (Cheshire, Conn.: Graphics Press, September 2003).

be fully engaged in an on campus program, distance education operation, their own research and writing, keeping current with their professional and scholarly literature, and nurturing doctoral students. Yet, that seems to be exactly the decision we often make, with some arguing vociferously that we need to be doing everything (although a careful checking of academic resumes might lead one to some interesting conclusions about how effectively distance education proponents are in supporting a fuller range of academic expectations). In a sense, then, distance education threatens to turn professional schools into teaching factories, weakening an already weakened professional school in the modern university, and we should be careful about just what we are committing ourselves to do. We might be adopting easy short-term gains that weaken professional schools in the university, and it is doubtful that a university would not close such a school if its intellectual and scholarly base evaporated over time.

Perhaps distance education can be accommodated if a school can provide adequate infrastructure support for the faculty teaching in this manner. Some professional schools have done this, usually in the form of educational technologists whose support free faculty to design courses, shape content, and teach. In some places, however, the faculty member assumes responsibility for everything, offering little more than a set of notes, a list of readings (some instructors rely on available online resources), the opportunity for a class chatroom, and access to the instructor. That access varies from excessive amounts of the instructor's time to nearly complete ignoring by the professor of the student.

Despite some serious issues plaguing distance education programs, they are often heralded as wonderful successes. One can ask on what basis such a success was determined. I have seen demographic profiles of the students and heard general platitudes about how students learn in different ways, but in many places we have not seen course evaluations by the students, gained any real information about how these students are faring in the job market, considered whether these students received an adequate education, or discussed more serious issues concerning the distance education program and its implications for the schools.

In my experience, despite whatever platitudes have been sounded about the educational technology, the chief criterion for gauging a program like this has been the number of students (by which I mean tuition revenue) in the virtual classrooms. To be honest, this may be not unlike other platitudes hoisted about in higher education. For example, every university states that teaching is the pre-eminent concern. Yet, everyone in a university understands that a great teacher with no research publications or research dollars will not be tenured. Indeed, one way of looking at distance education in a professional school is to understand that many professional schools lack faculty with great research reputations because of their generally applied orientation to their field, and they must compensate for this weakness by building other justifications for why their school is important. Distance education, with its ability to generate extraordinary revenue, is very tempting. Professional schools have also expanded out into undergraduate programs for much the same reasons, namely, that they can demonstrate how they are generating revenue for the university.

The Continuously Changing University. All of the research and writing about the corporate university suggests that academic life is constantly changing. The public continues to hold stereotypes of the university that indicates that being an academic is a good way to enjoy a quiet and long life. However, there is change occurring in every nook and cranny in the university, and some of it has little to do with money issues or business concerns. Higher education reporter Andy Guess describes new efforts by Harvard University in its Introduction to Computer Science course to deal with office hours for students (an experiment in virtual office hours). Teaching Fellows are using "real-time, online help sessions" based on "free, Java-based software." The virtual office hours are like a "traditional chat room, but with a window that can show what the instructor is seeing on his or her own computer." As Guess learns, "The idea isn't to revolutionize education, necessarily, but to make it easier for some students to get the help they need." Traditional regular office hours will continue, but what is interesting is whether such approaches can be carried over to other kinds of classes and disciplines. How we will balance online approaches with those relating to personal interactions. Diana G. Oblinger, a vice president for Educause, is reported as saying, "Although students may make significant use of online communication, it may not be what they want at this level, in this subject, or at this time in their educational career. They want the convenience of doing things online, but don't want to sacrifice the personal connections."[351] And it is precisely such matters that we will have to continue to evaluate in the emerging future university, and the answers may be difficult to develop or accept.

Sometimes those writing memoirs can point at particular aspects of change that have contributed to the transformation in perspectives and

---

[351] Andy Guess, "Office Hours: Coming to a Computer Near You," *Inside Higher Education*, September 18, 2007, http://insidehighered.com/news/2007/09/18/officehours, accessed September 18, 2007.

attitudes about higher education. Rudolph Weingartner, reflecting on sixty years as university faculty member and administrator, asserts, "Tuition and other college-related costs have gone up so fantastically, that those who have to pay this freight — the parents, note, not the students themselves — feel they have to get their money's worth. The easiest way to interpret that desire is to ask that the institution prepare their kids for a decent job they will get when they graduate. Not many parents think of a lifetime of jobs, unless they think profession: law, medicine, engineering. When that is envisaged from the beginning, that liberal education doesn't seem so bad, since, if properly configured, it prepares for professional school." But he disagrees: "The issue is not first job; the issue is a long trajectory of jobs."[352]

Customers and Credentials. There are visible symptoms, just like for any disease, in the encroaching corporatization of the university. Faculty can sit through endless meetings never focusing on the *quality* of education being offered. They can be transfixed by the number of students or the amount of revenue they generate or the amount of outside grant funds that can be secured. Research is often defined as money raised, and scholarship, unless money results, seems out of the purview of what goes on in the library school. None of this is meant to suggest that professional schools or any university unit should ignore commonsense business practices. However, it is one thing to be fiscally responsible and quite another to allow the financial bottom line become the primary focus or measure for all that happens within these schools.

Admittedly, library schools, their faculty, and their administrators did not create the corporate university. There are many forces pushing and pulling on every university unit. Donald Kennedy contends there is a problem with public misunderstanding of the university's mission: "Whereas those within the system generally believe that their mission is to produce graduates who can think well and work effectively, and reflect upon their culture and upon the material world, much of the world outside sees higher education as a credentialing device: a way of estimating, for employment or other purposes, the comparative worth of individuals."[353] This can be greatly exaggerated within professional schools. The library school is pushed by librarians expecting certain skills, pulled by those who want information technologists and influenced by the considerable Information Age hype; credentials do seem to be the product for sale. A

---

[352] Quoted in Andy Guess, "Looking Back on 60 Years in Academe," *Inside Higher Education*, October 3, 2007, available at http://insidehighered.com/news/2007/10/03/weingartner, accessed October 3, 2007.

[353] Kennedy, *Academic Duty*, p. 7.

great portion of the individuals coming to library schools want licenses to practice, and those hiring them want even more, usually individuals fully equipped to practice (rather than individuals still needing considerable seasoning through experience and testing of the knowledge they were introduced to in their graduate programs). Thus, it is easy to slip into promises about credentials or licenses to practice as a come on for prospective students. When a faculty member is seeking to help a student to learn something, it can be weary to only be asked questions about employment prospects, salary possibilities, and other such concerns.

This stress on credentials is a dangerous business, robbing professional schools of the ability to educate and to contribute to the knowledge that is a considerable public good. Jane Jacobs identifies higher education as one of the "five pillars of our culture" (along with community and family, science and science-technology, taxes and governmental powers, and the self-policing by the learned professions).[354] Not all is well with these bulwarks of modern life, as "credentialing, not educating, has become the primary business of North American universities."[355] Library schools have easily fallen prey to credentialing, partly because it is valuable for attracting students and having a steady supply of students seems to be the most visible and readily attainable mark of a successful program within the corporate university. Acquiring grants, research and otherwise, looms high on the list of signifiers of a successful unit within the corporate university as well. Packing in classrooms, especially if these students can be taught by less expensive adjuncts, is another mark of success for the corporate university.

There is a pact made with the devil in such activities, bringing indicators of even tougher times ahead for library schools. Jacobs describes a conference held in 2002 where "three of America's most prestigious universities" held a three-day seminar for the leaders of the main multinational corporations about the recent scandals in the accounting profession. Jacobs expected that these universities would communicate to the corporate leaders not to engage in such questionable practices, but instead the message was for these corporations not to be candid, not to offer any information unless forced to do so.[356] Given the subsequent, post 9/11 rise in national security centers in universities and the federal money dangled out there for academics by the federal government, one expects more such troubles ahead. The university has become too much a part of

---

[354] Jane Jacobs, *Dark Age Ahead* (New York: Random House, 2004), p. 24.
[355] Jacobs, *Dark Age Ahead*, p. 44.
[356] Jacobs, *Dark Age Ahead*, pp. 135-136.

the real world, rather than a critic and commentator on it. For schools educating individuals to work as librarians, archivists, and other information professions, there is much that is contrary in catering to corporate or government interests, especially when so many information professionals and their associations have worked against government secrecy and corporate shenanigans.[357]

Some of these problems have been accentuated by the recent economic collapse. Ralph Hexter, president of Hampshire College, worries about our "short-sightedness — focus on short-term goals and gains — and near-sightedness — seeking to maximize one vector without regard for context in which that vector has value to begin with." He discusses how higher education has, perhaps, missed the boat in educating students rather than simply perpetuating a race for high grades and credentials: "The system we use to grade students doesn't just mirror this scale of values. It blesses and promotes it... . Most colleges and universities do not question what students and their parents want of them: Enough seats in the 'right' majors so they can get their passport to a professional school. How? By wracking up the same string of A's during their undergraduate years as they did before. Little time for experimentation, for taking risks — where the only 'loss' might be a less than perfect transcript. If they don't get into the right graduate or professional program they might not get the credential that is the ticket to a job where they can reap larger profits more quickly than those who went before them, in the same fields. Because, the assumption is, those fields will always be profitable." Hexter counters this by doing away with grades at his institution, with a focus on individualized educational plans and portfolios.[358] I need to search for something like this. I am tired of students pre-occupied with grades and credentials who miss the point that they are here to learn something. Radical experimentation is in order.

There are, however, other ways of detecting the problems with seeing students as customers in a corporate university model. Many universities are establishing information competency programs. Why? Andy Guess, observing this trend, writes, "The problem is near-universal for professors who discover, upon assigning research projects, that superficial searches on the Internet and facts gleaned from Wikipedia are the extent — or a significant portion — of far too many of their students' investigations. It's

---

[357] See, for example, Herbert N. Foerstel, *Refuge of a Scoundrel: The Patriot Act in Libraries* (Westport, Conn.: Libraries Unlimited, 2004).
[358] Ralph Hexter, "The Economic Collapse and Educational Values," *Inside Higher Education*, December 18, 2008, http://www.insidehighered.com/views/2008/12/18/hexter.

not necessarily an issue of laziness, perhaps, but one of exposure to a set of research practices and a mindset that encourages critical thinking about competing online sources. Just because students walk in the door as 'digital natives,' the common observation goes, doesn't mean they're equipped to handle the heavy lifting of digital databases and proprietary search engines that comprise the bulk of modern, online research techniques."[359] As you can imagine, this can be particularly frustrating in a library school or its successor.

Wikipedia itself has provoked many to call for new roles in training students how to use such sources. Mark Wilson, a geology professor, argues, "It is time for the academic world to recognize Wikipedia for what it has become: a global library open to anyone with an Internet connection and a pressing curiosity. The vision of its founders, Jimmy Wales and Larry Sanger, has become reality, and the librarians were right: the world has not been the same since. If the Web is the greatest information delivery device ever, and Wikipedia is the largest coherent store of information and ideas, then we as teachers and scholars should have been on this train years ago for the benefit of our students, our professions, and that mystical pool of human knowledge." Wilson issues a call for "academics with research specialties" to "enroll as identifiable editors of Wikipedia," in order to "add our authority and hard-won knowledge to this growing universal library."[360] If such assessments can be made by someone in geology, why not by professors in library and information science?

The problem of how we view students is of a scale that social commentators outside of the university are noticing it. Nicholas Carr, for example, wonders if our immersion in networked communications isn't transforming the way we read or even how and what we can read. He argues that it is clear that we are reading more than ever, but he draws in some anecdotal and historical evidence to suggest that this is having an impact on our ability to read longer texts and to focus on certain other kinds of documents: "Never has a communication system played so many roles in our lives – or exerted such broad influence over our thoughts – as the Internet does today. Yet, for all that's been written about the Net, there's been little consideration of how, exactly, it's reprogramming us. The

---

[359] Andy Guess, "Research Methods 'Beyond Google," *Inside Higher Education*, 17 June 2008, http://insidehighered.com/news/2008/06/17/institute.
[360] Mark Wilson, "Professors Should Embrace Wikipedia," *Inside Higher Education*, April 1, 2008, at http://insidehighered.com/views/2008/04/01/wilson.

Net's intellectual ethic remains obscure."³⁶¹ Along with such societal changes come different aims for and expectations of students, who may be seen as just a different category of Web surfer (but one that is paying).

This corporate university model brings with it a shift in the culture of students, as Susan Blum detects in her book on plagiarism.³⁶² Blum demonstrates that plagiarism is a confusing topic, far more complicated than it first seems. I had expected to find a book mostly about student writing, but what I discovered was a book exploring the nature of teaching and the expectations students bring with them into college (and by extension, graduate school). Blum gives us a vivid glimpse into the world of students, considering some matters with direct implications for what we do in an iSchool. Drawing on extensive interviews with students, she notes, "Students even justify cheating, at least in the abstract, out of 'need.' If education is regarded by students at elite universities as putting in a certain effort to attain the desired end – a good grade, a degree, fun – then knowing how to achieve that goal is a measure of their competence."³⁶³ While I have not had direct experience with students plagiarizing, I have had considerable experience with students who seem to think that any aspect of required work (especially reading and class participation) is a burden. And Blum addresses these issues as well: "I have read hundreds of student evaluations of teachers when hiring new colleagues. Some questionnaires ask how much time the students spent on the class. The average seemed to be about four hours per week per class, even at first-rate universities. Sometimes students responding that they worked as little as three to four hours complained that the course had too intense a workload or had too much reading for them to finish."³⁶⁴ While this is an observation about undergraduate students, I think it applies just as much to many students at the graduate level, especially in professional schools where an emphasis on credentials seems more intense than in other university programs.

I admit that it is hard to understand why so many students seem uninterested in learning, even resistant to it. Blum offers this explanation: "Education specialists distinguish *intrinsic motivations* for learning (a love of knowledge for its own sake, or a need for knowledge in application) from

---

³⁶¹ Nicholas Carr, "Is Google Making Us Stupid?" *Atlantic* 302 (July/August 2008): 60.
³⁶² Susan D. Blum, *My Word! Plagiarism and College Culture* (Ithaca: Cornell University Press, 2009).
³⁶³ Blum, *My Word!*, p. 81.
³⁶⁴ Blum, *My Word!*, p. 118.

extrinsic motivations (good grades, teachers' or parents' praise, a diploma, a job). Students who value the work of learning for its own sake are less likely to cut corners, to rush or cheat, because they savor the experience itself."[365] The nature of professional schools puts such notions to the test because many students come there for particular credentials and exposure to practical knowledge, but my sense is that the university, in its rapidly evolving corporate mode, is becoming more like professional schools. Where once commentators on higher education often discussed professional schools as square pegs in round holes, now it seems unnecessary to characterize the relationship in this fashion.

Blum also has a lot to say about teaching and its evaluation. It might seem silly to worry about such issues in an environment where even the mechanics of teaching evaluations are problematic, but I think Blum's observation clearly demonstrates why teaching evaluations have to include far more than students' immediate reactions to their classroom experiences and how they view education. She connects such matters to why plagiarism occurs: "In these circumstances plagiarism might strike many students as a logical option: for those who are focused entirely on external goals such as high grades, a degree, or admission to the next level of education; for those who are in college to have fun; for those whose notion of education involves checking item off a list rather than reveling in a process of discovery; for those who are busy with other activities and obligations; for those who lack the ability to earn their rewards to which they feel they have a right."[366] My sense is that such issues are going to get worse in our current problematic economic situation. Blum notes that students coming into the university have often been long accustomed to getting high grades, and they become averse to taking any risks in learning because they are under great pressure to find jobs down the road. This is getting even worse as we watch the economy tank and good jobs become scarcer.

Conclusion: The Corporate Library School? Library schools, eager to prove themselves by acquiring financial resources or high profile projects, certainly are prone to engage in a money race. The legacy of jettisoning courses on traditional subjects, such as the history of the book, for new courses on technology or knowledge management, may catch up with these schools, as they add to courses and programs in national security and other areas to attract government and corporate support (this is not to say that such endeavors are not important, but it is the effort to establish such

---

[365] Blum, *My Word!*, p. 125.
[366] Blum, *My Word!*, p. 140.

programs to deal with immediate crises that suggest that these may not be long-term priorities). While the printed book and its culture has been with us for five hundred years, embattled or embraced by society, issues such as national security ebb and flow extremely quickly; could we imagine anything more prone to disappear in a few years than all the centers on national security or anything more blatantly created just to secure government funding? Indeed, the long-term shifting of library schools to schools of library and information sciences and then to schools of information studies or just schools of information has already built a solid foundation for these schools to engage in the money race, creating a culture of shifting priorities to acquire soft money.

The corporate university model also weakens, potentially at least, professional schools' faculty governance. In some places, elaborate strategic planning processes have been instituted. A school supporting diverse disciplines rather than a single information profession is stymied when university administrators complain that its plan lacks focus or clarity. Constantly being asked for a clearer picture, rather than understanding there are many information professions and many definitions of information, is a legacy of the diversification of library schools into information science and information schools. But this is not the most serious problem. As such plans are formulated, the voices of those who critique them are ignored. Lewis Lapham refers to this as the problem of adopting the idea of "military rules of engagement" where "democratic self-government" is viewed as "obnoxious, tiresome, inefficient, loud, disrespectful, and unsafe."[367] Whatever it is called, more and more power has been put in the hands of academic administrators and taken from faculty, primarily because their schools are under pressure to generate revenue, a task many faculty will gladly let others do (so that they can do the things they want to do, such as research and teaching).

Some might argue that there is nothing new with the idea of the corporate university, or the problems associated with it, since the university has always been part of the real world. Even the historic classical education emphasizing ancient languages, rhetoric, and philosophy were deemed to have practical benefit to those working in mercantile houses, the church, and government. Still, there is something intriguing and useful about having a group of people assembled who tinker with ideas and create knowledge. Otherwise, we transform the university into something no nobler than credentialing people to secure jobs. Learning is more than employment

---

[367] Lewis Lapham, "Crowd Control," *Harper's* 309 (October 2004): 9.

protection and benefits. The older idea of the university was that learning (not awarded credentials) prepared you for the real world, an idea needing resuscitation in the modern university. And it is an idea that apparently does not sit well with library schools striving to prove themselves relevant to the new university, as witnessed by their nearly universal embrace of distance education venues in order to market and extend their programs and grow their enrollment. No one will candidly state, of course, that such efforts are mostly about money, but as PowerPoint slides, posting of lecture notes, and virtual student discussion threaten to dumb down courses, what else ought we to conclude?

Chasing after revenue weakens the attention of these schools to other problems. Henry Giroux tells the story of two high school graduates who created a website offering to be living advertisements for any company who would fund their way through college. A financial institution agreed to do just that, and the media covered the story about the entrepreneurial skills of the young men with little criticism. As Giroux related, "nothing was said about spiraling tuition costs coupled with evaporating financial aid" or that what the students might be doing was "incompatible with the role the university should play as a site of critical thinking, democratic leadership, and public engagement."[368] I suspect some former library schools would embrace these students as exemplars of the kind of imaginative entrepreneurial souls they want in their classrooms. But of course most of these schools have tried to deal with their higher tuitions by morphing themselves into venues training individuals to work in places other than libraries or archives, where salaries and status can be marginal no matter how important the functions are that they provide for society. These schools are entrepreneurial enterprises and their faculties are entrepreneurs, since there is a buying in to all the hype surrounding the present Information Age. Traditional responsibilities, such as teaching and advising, are lamentable because they are expensive with little immediate financial return on the investment.

---

[368] Giroux, "Neoliberalism, Corporate Culture, and the Promise of Higher Education," pp. 426-27.

Chapter Five

Rethinking the Traditional School (and Values)

Introduction: What About Traditional Values? As the reader of this volume can tell, I have become weary with discussions about the *mere* survival of library schools. What about making a difference? What about contributing to human knowledge? What about helping individuals come to grips with what they want to do with their lives? What about the historic roles of the university as contributor to a public good? Given the debates and controversies about access to information, censorship, privacy, accountability of public officials and corporate leaders, intellectual property, and a host of other issues involving to some degree or another the notions of information and evidence, it is surprising that what were library schools and now are information schools have been mostly immersed in issues such as building student enrollments, distance education, and revenue.

It is ironic, for example, that schools, originally founded to prepare individuals to work in libraries (where books are presumably available), have generally turned away from studying books (with some exceptions). Of course, students in library school learn at least partially by reading books (and they learn by reading many other publications and doing other things as well). Even with the competition of e-books and e-journals, and most certainly the challenges posed by the World Wide Web, students in this kind of professional school need to learn about printed books, the five hundred year information revolution showing little sign of slowing down or losing its significance and certainly still accounting for a major portion of what libraries administer. The technology of book publishing and the economics of printing have been transformed, but the mechanism of reading persists much as it has since Augustine discovered his mentor silently perusing a book. The scholarly interest in reading, from various disciplines in the humanities, has been matched by popular interest in the nature of reading and the proliferation of book groups, ranging from an eloquent call for library schools to offer more on the history of reading to the very popular

Booklust publications (the latter immortalized by the author being the model for the librarian action figure).[369]

Everyone is susceptible to being blinded by the bright promises of technology. Technology, supported by design and engineering, can be mesmerizing. Examining a mid-nineteenth century cast iron bridge, perfectly blending form and function, can generate a sensation like gawking at an Old Masters painting in a museum; discarded as bridges needed to accommodate heavier traffic patterns, now we work to save these artistic expressions of Victorian engineering. The sweeping lines of a 1930s Art Deco toaster contribute to making us forget about its utilitarian uses and to appreciate it as an art object; some people go to specialty kitchen shops to pay twenty times the price of an ordinary (but functional) toaster to acquire a handmade reproduction of these appliances consigned to the rubbish heap by our mothers and grandmothers. After a generation of pressing fingers down on the keyboards of personal computers, many now also use beautifully designed fountain pens that feel comfortable in the hand and glide smoothly over paper, putting us back in touch with the sensation of writing; old fountain pens are desirable collectibles and dealers like Levenger's have built a customer base by offering products stressing writing's pleasures.

Such liaisons with technology are very different from the countless diatribes about the sterility and stresses of an increasing reliance on computer technology calling to us in the bookstores and libraries, once we navigate beyond the shelves of "idiots" and "dummies" guides about how to harness this technology. As long as people have had to contend with technological changes, there have been laments about the perils of making these transitions (think about the shifts in sound recording from LP's, through 8 tracks and cassettes, to compact disks).[370] In my own specialization, archival studies, we understand that every stage of writing and recordkeeping involved technical innovations. Clay tablets required one kind of technology, papyrus and parchment other forms, as did the hardware and software in our modern word processors. At every stage of a technology shift, some lamented what was lost, others made promises for

---

[369] Wayne A. Wiegand, "Out of Sight, Out of Mind: Why Don't We Have Any Schools of Library and Reading Studies?" *Journal of Education for Library and Information Science* 38 (Fall 1997): 314-326 and Nancy Pearl, *Booklust: Recommended Reading for Every Mood, Moment, and Reason* (Seattle, WA: Sasquatch Books, 2003) and spin-off publications.

[370] David Morton, *Off the Record: The Technology and Culture of Sound Recording in America* (New Brunswick, N.J.: Rutgers University Press, 2000).

CHAPTER FIVE   117

what would be gained, and others predicted the demise of civilization. Today, computers are blamed for most of society's problems (poor education, pornography, long work hours, the demise of social skills, and terrorism), and similar attributions were made in the past about much more primitive technologies. Naysayers have been around for a long time, such as scribes complaining about movable type printing five hundred years ago, one of the most dramatic technology changes in human history. Now, we take courses in calligraphy, study the illuminated page for clues about the design of Web pages, and mimic scribal hands in our printing fonts; the good qualities of technology stay with us.[371]

Seduced by Technology. I think about the ramifications of technology because of where I teach (a professional school focused on the information sciences), what I teach (archival studies), and the immense hype about the Information Age swirling about us every day (except when I stay at home, sealed off in my study with antique mission furniture, eighteenth century prints of writing tables, and reproduction medieval wax document seals). As a child I was fascinated by history, leading in the early 1970s to a career as an archivist. In the late 1980s I joined the faculty at the University of Pittsburgh School of Information Sciences (except in those days we used "library" in our name as well) to develop a graduate program in archival studies, picking up a doctorate in library and information science along the way. For nearly two decades, I have worked with information scientists employing scientific and technical approaches in their research, problem solving, and teaching. Over the past few years I have found myself wandering in a strange land, sometimes the lone humanist among technocrats, often offering minority opinions about curriculum design, course delivery, and entrance and graduation requirements. This has led me both to wonder what is wrong with professional schools and what is wrong with me. More reflection has brought me to the conclusion that the problems I am experiencing are not unique to my circumstances, but they are endemic to higher education, society, and its institutions.

I must also confess to being seduced by technology. When my daughter started college six years ago, we bought her an Apple Ibook computer, recommended for her Integrated Arts program at Penn State. I was intrigued by the computer's sleek design and silky feel, attractive interface, and general ease of use. I read about the reliability of Apple computers, but

---

[371] For a technologist who appreciates older technologies such as calligraphy, see David M. Levy, *Scrolling Forward: Making Sense of Documents in the Digital Age* (New York: Arcade Publishing, 2001).

then I began to be drawn to the advertising hype as well, about how Apple users were part of a kind of computer counterculture and just plain smarter. Not long after, an Apple store opened within ten minutes of my house, and my life changed. As you walked into the store, you were drawn to its gleaming white interior, the quotations of famous literary figures and philosophers about the nature of knowledge, the engaging display of computers, Ipods, speakers, and digital cameras, the enthusiastic Apple devotees and salespeople (so well-matched in their enthusiasm that it was hard to tell the difference between them), the "Genius" bar where you could go to work on serious technical issues, and the "lab" in the back where you could take classes about everything from the most basic pointers to producing a multi-media presentation. I converted and used an Apple Ibook G4 and proudly display an Apple logo sticker on my car's back windshield (now I use a MacBook). Somehow, I do feel smarter and more confident with my laptop with the glowing Apple logo on the back, and I feel camaraderie with other Apple users when I run into them at the neighborhood coffee shop, airport terminals, and bookstores. In some ways, I have the same feelings about my Apple as I do for my personal library of six thousand books; both reflect my identity and give me a sense of security, even though I know the books will be around long after my computer is abandoned for the next generation of technology. I confess that I am just as easily seduced by technology as the next person, even though I am a confirmed skeptic about its promises in our world.

We must recognize that the wise use of certain information technologies can enhance the educational process, and that many of our students are accustomed to and expect to be using modern information technologies; how do we integrate information technology into our teaching? Moreover, how do we educate students (and ourselves) to be able to evaluate critically the information technologies so that these technologies can be used appropriately, ethically, and wisely for the public good? I argue that the root cause of such problems is not merely technology (I am not a technological determinist or technophobe), but that they stem from problems such as eroding interest in the excitement of intellectual engagement, a loss of interest in educating and settling for training, and a belief in our mission to be change agents to contribute to the public good. The nature and value of technology as applied to education is only as good as our values; information technologies are only "tools" to be used or abused by us.

A school of information sciences, one might surmise, could be a good place for someone to learn about the role of information technology in society. Yet, that is not always the case. Postman, in his prognosis for the future of education, provides a fairly accurate description of what one might discover in such a school: "One would expect then that technology education would be a familiar subject in American schools. But it is not. Technology may have entered the schools, but *not* technology education." By this, he means that students do not learn about matters like the origins of the alphabet or the social consequences of the printing press; indeed, following his point, schools of information science crowded out courses like those on printing history for those on technical applications. Yes, learn to use the tools, but not to understand their fuller consequences. What should technology education be about? It should be "about how the meanings of information and education change as new technologies intrude upon a culture, how the meanings of truth, law, and intelligence differ among oral cultures, writing cultures, printing cultures, electronic cultures. Technology education is not a technical subject. It is a branch of the humanities."[372] In professional schools, however, it is the technical aspects that one would find most prevalent, whereby students are exposed to the "hows" and not the "whys" concerning information technology.

Technology in Professional Schools. Many commentators on the state of higher education are concerned with what is being taught about technology. University press administrator Lindsay Waters laments that the commercialized university has little tolerance for those who espouse humanistic pursuits, favoring instead "narrow-minded professionalism" that hates ideas.[373] Professional schools are technical schools, however, and they have little time or tolerance for such matters as the meaning and culture of technology. Moreover, faculty can easily engage in discussions about professionalism because they are equipping individuals to function in a particular field and because the students require being socialized to the field. Students also arrive expecting this kind of socialization, although their expectations can develop quickly into a demand for learning basic skills rather than learning the requisite knowledge of the discipline.

An information ecology is defined as a "system of people, practices, values, and technologies in a particular local environment. In information ecologies, the spotlight is not on technology, but on human activities that

---

[372] Neil Postman, *The End of Education: Redefining the Value of School* (New York: Alfred A. Knopf, 1995), pp. 189, 191.
[373] Lindsay Waters, *Enemies of Promise: Publishing, Perishing, and the Eclipse of Scholarship* (Chicago: Prickly Paradigm Press, 2004), pp. 15 and 67.

are served by technologies."[374] The fervor by which the high-tech industry markets its own products leads to extraordinary claims about the miraculous powers of its tools. Humans, and the factors they add to the information technologies, often seem beside the point. Even in a professional school educating information specialists, the sense of such an ecology can be difficult to maintain, possibly because of the peculiar place of this professional school in the university. As a way of ensuring some prominence, we need to remind ourselves that the university is, as well, an entity in a marvelous new information age. Drawing on the writings of many pundits, we claim that we are in THE information age, partly for persuading the university that we are an important player, one that the university needs to support. This is a kind of academic inferiority complex, where we are unsure about relating to other historic roles of the university. This may be quite natural, the typical plight of the professional school seeking its place in the university. But, for sure, it brings serious problems. It creates some irony in everything we do, causing us to ignore the advice we offer our students and to make unjustified claims. It causes us to ignore the human aspect, sometimes including ourselves, of the information era we claim to be in.

One of the persistent problems in reading and teaching about information technologies is the lack of historical context about the technologies. Many students do not remember when the PC did not exist or have grown to maturity along with the Internet; in a few more years, we will have students who think the World Wide Web has been here forever. It is more difficult to understand those who write about the modern technologies. Of course, there are fine histories of these technologies,[375] but these works are not the ones most often discussed in the public forum or, I fear, in our classrooms. Instead, much of the discussion stems from the "information pundits," individuals who from varying perspectives either damn technology as the source of all evils or praise it as the solution for all problems. Both views are missing the social, political, economic, and other contexts often best captured through the lens of history.

There has been a large-scale abandonment of a historical or contextual perspective in many professional schools. Given the choice between

---

[374] Bonnie A. Nardi and Vicki L. O'Day, *Information Ecologies: Using Technology with Heart* (MIT Press, 1999), p. 49.
[375] Such as Martin Campbell-Kelly and William Aspray, *Computer: A History of the Information Machine* (New York: Basic Books, 1996) and Paul N. Edwards, *The Closed World: Computers and the Politics of Discourse in Cold War America* (Cambridge: MIT Press, 1996).

teaching the history of the book or computer rather than the technologies, the former is sometimes dismissed as being "soft" and the latter embraced as "hard" skills that our students must possess. Neil Postman, a quarter of a century ago, understood the seriousness of making wrong choices. He lamented that we had "lost the arts of preservation," reminding us that "schools are, in fact, always given a measure of responsibility to serve as a society's memory bank, even in quiet times" – and that they weren't doing so well.[376] Without such a base, we can be "overwhelmed by philosophers, priests, conquerors, or even explorers," he argued.[377] For Postman, history is critical to *every* curriculum, at any level, since "every subject [should be] taught *as* history," enabling students "to understand, as they presently do not, that knowledge is not a fixed thing but a stage of human development, with a past and a future."[378] This suggests, of course, one way of educating our students, by getting them to see the bigger societal and historical picture (In library and information science education, there have been critics arguing for just such a larger picture).[379]

Internet Inertia. We can see problems with the lack of historical understanding in the predictions about the end of the printed book. Jacob Epstein thinks that the "Internet, with its unmediated and instantaneous transactions, its indifference to time and distance, and its negligible cost per unit of transmission, abhors middlemen," predicting the ultimate marginalizing of print books as books are delivered electronically directly to readers.[380] This suggests a new world of communication possibilities, a gold mine for those interested in the information professions. Epstein's comments caused me to wonder why communication can seem so poor among a faculty supposedly teaching about the use of information technologies to foster communication, understanding, and knowledge. Do we fear committing to writing, going on record, or being misinterpreted? Jeffrey Rosen, in his analysis of the decline of privacy, notes that "when intimate information is removed from its original context and revealed to strangers, we are vulnerable to being misjudged on the basis of our most

---

[376] Neil Postman, *Teaching As A Conserving Activity* (New York: Delta Book, 1979), p. 21.
[377] Postman, *Teaching As A Conserving Activity*, pp. 31-32.
[378] Postman, *Teaching As A Conserving Activity*, p. 138.
[379] See, for example, Wayne A. Wiegand, "Critiquing the Curriculum: The Entrenched LIS Agenda Needs to Change to Reflect the Most Critical Functions of the Library," *American Libraries* (January 2005): 58, 60-61.
[380] Jason Epstein, "The Coming Revolution," *The New York Review of Books* 47 (November 2, 2000): 4-5 (quotation, p. 5).

embarrassing and therefore most memorable, tastes and preferences."[381] It is why privacy is needed. Electronic mail messages are especially susceptible to misinterpretation. As Rosen explains, "Because e-mail messages are often dashed off quickly and sent immediately, without the opportunity for second thoughts that ordinary mail provides, they may, when wrenched out of context, provide an inaccurate window on someone's emotions at any particular moment."[382] Faculty colleagues at a school of information sciences are particularly sensitive to this, although one would expect that since the faculty members were educating students about harnessing information technology that they would draw on the technology for their own use.

Some of these challenges, even the mundane ones in seeking to invest faculty in using the technologies available to them, may be the result of the changing nature of the modern university. It is difficult to hold onto any sense of traditional values witnessed in the creation of library schools because of the university's strengthening relationship with businesses and government. Derek Bok's compelling assessment of the more sinister corporate influences on the modern university provides a clear sense of higher education captivated by bottom-line revenue, not an educational mission. Bok sees a university culture with problems mirroring the worst of corporate culture, arguing, "to keep profit-seeking within reasonable bounds, a university must have a clear sense of the values needed to pursue its goals with a high degree of quality and integrity. When the values become blurred and begin to lose their hold, the urge to make money quickly spreads throughout the institution."[383] This is nothing new. Nearly a half century ago, Jacques Barzun, in his classic assessment of the state of the modern university, lamented that one of the pressing problems was that the "government expects to buy research and ideas in the same way as it buys soap and chairs," providing a nice marker for when these problems may have started.[384] What are we selling?

Money and Influence – or Killing the Spirit. Students may, in their own way, contribute to this money quest. In discussing the mythical ideas of American capitalism, sociologist Richard Hughes notes that it is

---

[381] Jeffrey Rosen, *The Unwanted Gaze: The Destruction of Privacy in America* (New York: Random House, 2000), p. 9.

[382] Rosen, *Unwanted Gaze*, p. 75.

[383] Derek Bok, *Universities in the Marketplace: The Commercialization of Higher Education* (Princeton: Princeton University Press, 2003), p. 6.

[384] Jacques Barzun, *The House of Intellect* (New York: Perennial Classics, 2002; org. pub. 1959), p. 212.

"significant... that Americans commonly define the American dream, not in terms of inward peace and contentment but rather in terms of what one owns." Extending this notion, Hughes comments: "It is little wonder, then, that upon entering America's universities, relatively few students ask the question of vocation ... or the question of outreach ... . Instead, most students enter the university with one question that towers above all other questions: 'What can I choose for my major that will guarantee wealth, possessions, and economic security?' From this perspective, only a fool or a saint would major in religion, philosophy, history, or literary studies."[385] The critical issue is what are the values guiding library schools and their successors? And, obviously, this question must be asked by the faculty and deans of the schools since students often have their sights on the credential and the skills supposedly coming with it. Escalating tuitions, mounting student debt, and other similar factors compel students to have such practical perspectives.

By traditional values, what do I mean? Are we discussing the various statements, such as the American Library Association's Library Bill of Rights, professional ethics codes, and historic statements by library education pioneers? Certainly, these reflect some guiding values associated with the formation and history of library schools, especially since these codes are merely advisory, resulting in rehashes of platitudes and values commonly accepted by practitioners in the various fields making up the information professions. However, I mean a more straightforward issue, the reason most people come to these schools in the first place. As I converse with students or read their applications, I understand that many come to these schools because of a love of books, reading, and scholarship associated with the word, including interests encompassing the World Wide Web and digital publications. Some are surprised when they find that the faculty of these schools believe the book is dead, technical skills the focus of the courses, and reading is more an exercise akin to surfing the World Wide Web.

Are we dousing students' interests and motivations they have as they matriculate into library schools? As some of these schools have transformed themselves into high-tech centers interested in information, downplaying or eliminating courses stressing the history of the book, libraries, and related scholarship, is it not possible that we are dampening the enthusiasm students bring with them? We are not the only ones worried

---

[385] Richard T. Hughes, *Myths America Lives By* (Urbana: University of Illinois Press, 2004), p. 149.

about such concerns in the modern corporate university. Gerald Graff, in reviewing applications made for various doctoral programs, notes that these individuals often express their desire to get a PhD because they "love" their subject.[386] We can see the same love expressed by applicants to the former library schools, with statements about wanting to be librarians because their parents read to them, they love to read, they like to browse in bookstores, or they enjoy referring people to books for advice. Then they come to us to find out that we are not interested in books (in fact, we think they are dead), hear that surfing the Web is more important than reading, and learn that reflective reading is no longer critical or as important as grabbing bits of information to satisfy immediate needs. Indeed, sometimes the faculty members of these schools are so attuned to their students' expectations for vocational training that they shy away from orienting these students to the history, accumulated knowledge, and complexities of the nature of information and the diversity of the information professions. How much of this sort of problem is the result of the schools being focused on revenue, marketing and credentialing?

I am not arguing that learning about new information sources or technologies is unimportant or even at the core of what students in library and information science schools need to be taught, but I fear we have thrown out far more than just the baby with the bath water in the changes in these schools. In a recent academic year, when I taught a course on the history of the book and printing, I discovered a sense of deep longing by the students in the course for more intellectual challenges, more historical context, and more opportunities to pursue topics of interest to them that brought them here in the first place. I also learned of their deep frustration because they felt they were being taught how to use tools, to refine skills, but not being grounded in the field's more substantial knowledge. Writer and poet Linda Pastan reflected, "after I graduated my father insisted that I have some practical way of making my own living, so I got a master's degree in library science. That was about the most miserable year of my life."[387] When we lose people like Pastan, then we are doing something wrong, losing our way somewhere in cyberspace. Education is not intended to be miserable, but the waffling of these schools in what their mission is supposed to be has built a foundation for causing such misery.

---

[386] Gerald Graff, *Clueless in Academe: How Schooling Obscures the Life of the Mind* (New Haven: Yale University Press, 2003), p. 193.
[387] Linda Pastan, in Diane Osen, ed., *The Book That Changed My Life: Interviews with National Book Award Winners and Finalists* (New York: Modern Library, 2002), p. 148.

We also need to understand that such individuals, once dreaming of being librarians, may be found influencing others who have entertained such thoughts. Scott Douglas is alternately funny and scathing about the life of a public librarian (he is a librarian at the Anaheim Public Library in California).[388] He provides an insider's view of the hectic and often weird activities of someone working in a city library, on the front lines. And, although I could not bring myself to check, I am sure the book has rattled many librarians. I have a sense that the publisher worked with him to juice up the more ridiculous aspects at the expense of his obvious commitment to the public good of such institutions. His education as a librarian gets a pretty tough raking over the coals, although there is nothing particularly new in his comments on that score; we tend to be easy targets, especially since it is easy to play on the public perceptions of what a librarian needs to or should know. There are two reasons to read the book. First, perspective and new students will read it (I have this awful feeling it is sitting in the careers section at the bookstores). Second, there are many stories about work in public libraries that ring true about this sector of our field; if I had the equivalent for archives, I would use it in one of my courses (the closest I have is Nicholson Baker's *Double Fold* and he really didn't understand archives clearly enough – although I have used it more than once). We should embrace such stuff as a way of adding a little spice and controversy in our courses, and, if nothing else, to get some humor into our classes. Some, however, will worry that such publications will cut down on the number of students and the tuition generated from them. Too bad.

University Realities. The most important question may be how we each determine what our values are or should be. To ask the question out loud in the university is to invite someone else to hand you a list of values that you will be asked to accept as your own. Each person ruminating about values must start with their own, reflecting on what were the reasons originally motivating them to become a university faculty member. The reality is, of course, that the university has always been stuck in the middle of the world, where people have to make real things happen. Even classical education emphasizing ancient languages, rhetoric, and philosophy was deemed to have practical benefit to those who would work in mercantile houses, the church, and government. Still, there is something intriguing and useful about the idea of having a group of people assembled who can tinker with ideas, applied or even totally impractical except for being a reflection of

---

[388] Scott Douglas, *Quiet, Please: Dispatches from a Public Librarian* (Philadelphia: Da Capo Press, 2008).

knowledge. I have always been more of an individual who leans towards trying to make things that work, and it is a good commitment to have since I am in a professional school. But it is also better to have the freedom to tinker with stuff that might not have any short-term practical benefit. We need people who conceive of the long-term, try to see the big picture, who work always with an eye on the future. Otherwise, we transform the university into a place where workshops and institutes are taught with no aim in mind other than credentialing people to secure jobs. Learning is more than about employment protection and benefits.

The older university ideal was that it was a foundation of learning preparing you for life. It is an ideal that needs to be resuscitated in the modern university, but it is an ideal that is particularly hard to find support for in the corporate university. Two professors of education, for example, write, "We deplore the tendency toward 'narrow vocationalism,' both because it undermines genuine occupational preparation and because it impoverishes the intellectual and civic roles that higher education can play. But professionalism broadly understood provides its own avenues back to liberal education. Ethical issues, central to every profession, provide a hook for the deeper study of ethical and philosophical issues."[389] This suggests hope, because it places the ability to address such issues squarely back in the classroom and under the purview of the individual faculty member.

The most convenient means to discovering the essence of the realities facing higher education is to read any one of many commentaries on the state of the university by a former university president. Harold T. Shapiro, the former president of both the University of Michigan and Princeton University, provides some insight into such matters. Early in his book, Shapiro writes that the universities "serve society as both a responsive servant and a thoughtful critic. Thus, although the modern research university must serve society by providing the educational and other programs in high demand, the university must also raise questions that society does not want to ask and generate new ideas that help invent the future, at times even 'pushing' society toward it."[390] As one can easily surmise, this relationship between the university and any realistic sense of its connection to society suggests all kinds of difficult questions. For example, "Whether the public welfare is best served by a research agenda

---

[389] W. Norton Grubb and Marvin Lazerson, "Vocationalism in Higher Education: The Triumph of the Education Gospel," *The Journal of Higher Education* 76 (January-February 2005): 16.
[390] Harold T. Shapiro, *A Larger Sense of Purpose: Higher Education and Society* (Princeton: Princeton University Press, 2005), pp. 4-5.

shaped by contemporary market forces or by the scholarly priorities of a relatively independent professoriate is an open issue."[391] In some ways, the connection of the university to society can be seen in the existence of professional schools in higher education, a topic that has often generated more heat than light. Shapiro provides a refreshing view of this, arguing that the "rigid separation of professional from undergraduate and graduate education within the same institution (an American innovation) is a serious bureaucratic error. Yet by now it has become almost deified by a mistaken educational ideology. We should put aside the issue of whether or not to mix the so-called professional and academic, and focus intently on the most effective way of doing so."[392] To do so requires that both the university in general and any particular professional school have a clear sense of purpose and mission.

The Loss of a Message. As library schools have evolved into what they are now, a cacophony of different messages emerge about the information professions. Howard Gardner argues, "As a general rule, when one is addressing a diverse or heterogeneous audience, the story must be simple, easy to identify with, emotionally resonant, and evocative of positive experiences."[393] Matters are so complicated in the newer version of the library school that many faculty members have difficulty talking with each other let alone developing a coherent message others can follow or understand. This contributes to the tensions between academics and practitioners. It is also another reason why library schools and their successors struggle to explain themselves to university administrators. While it is relatively easy to explain what a history department or literature department is about (even with all the various conflicts present in those academic units), it is more difficult to explain what a library school, school of information sciences, or school of information is about.

Some have resorted to a focus on professionalism, but this generates problems as well. One critic of the university, Bill Readings, perceives that evidence of the decline of the university is its becoming obsessed with professionalism: "The University no longer has a hero for its grand narrative, and a retreat into 'professionalization' has been the consequence." In professional schools, this process might only be speeded up, especially where the schools have lost connection to their traditional constituencies as well as with the university as its own core values have eroded. Readings

---

[391] Shapiro, *A Larger Sense of Purpose*, p. 20.
[392] Shapiro, *A Larger Sense of Purpose*, p. 116.
[393] Howard Gardner, *Changing Minds: The Art and Science of Changing Our Own and Other People's Minds* (Boston: Harvard Business School Press, 2004), p. 82.

argues, "Professionalization deals with the loss of the subject-referent of the educational experience by integrating teaching and research as aspects of the general administration of a closed system: teaching is the administration of students by professors; research is the administration of professors by their peers; administration is the name given to the stratum of bureaucrats who administer the whole. In each case, administration involves the processing and evaluation of information according to criteria of excellence that are internal to the system: the value of research depends on what colleagues think of it; the value of teaching depends upon the grades professors give and the evaluations the students make; the value of administration depends upon the ranking of a University among its peers."[394] Professional schools often exhibit all of these symptoms, especially as they are immersed in fields where practitioners are worried or even antagonistic to the education of their peers in the university. Whatever the symptoms, the critical point is that they reflect a diminution from a higher mission of the university and professional school to educate and contribute to a repository of knowledge for a public good. Credentials, customers, revenue, and measures become the driving forces for evaluation, and professional schools are all the more susceptible to these forces.

What should be the university culture that library schools should exist in, relate to, and play off against? As Donald Kennedy asserts well, "The university is an institution that exists to advance the culture, both by acquiring new knowledge and by disseminating received knowledge in ways that inspire young people to use it – both creatively and constructively. In that way professors are agents for making society better than it was, generation by generation."[395] I am sure those chasing after corporate sponsorship of research, trying to cash in on new government initiatives on national security and other aspects of this post 9-11 world, building executive education programs, and constructing degrees online can point to some public good they are addressing. My concern is how many directions the old library school can be pulled and still have something meaningful to say. Neil Postman, discussing education before college, once commented, "For school to make sense, the young, their parents, and their teachers must have a god to serve, or even better, several gods." Postman was aiming at the need for a common, understandable meaning or purpose; "A god," Postman continues, "in the sense I am using the word, is the name of

---

[394] Bill Readings, *The University in Ruins* (Cambridge: Harvard University Press, 1996), p. 126.
[395] Donald Kennedy, *Academic Duty* (Cambridge: Harvard University Press, 1997), p. 68.

a great narrative, one that has sufficient credibility, complexity, and symbolic power to enable one to organize one's life around it."[396] Professional schools, except for getting students in and then out into jobs, often appear to lack any narrative that could be called *grand*. Chasing after money, trolling for students, and selling credentials do not seem to fit the bill.

If the university is lost to society, what other group or institution will assume its mission? Even in a professional school, sometimes looked askance at by other departments as being tainted by a vocational focus, faculty members are often the philosophers, the cynics, the questioners, and the visionaries of their professions. Without them, these vocations might only look as far ahead as what would be going on within their own four walls. And all – society, the disciplines, and the university— would suffer without such people. What a professional school should add to a university is a foot within the real world, a bridge between knowledge and its application to solving real problems and challenges. But it might be that professional schools have lost some of their edge because the rest of the university looks more like them. Now, professional schools are asked to count students as customers, make decisions enhancing revenues, and to take on work that generates additional funds. For sure, some of the work at solving practical problems continues, but the process of deciding what problems to consider is now heavily influenced by business factors. This means serious trouble for the future of library schools.

Citizens or Careerists. The world has seeped so much into the university that it is impossible to distinguish where one starts and the other ends. For a professional school that might not seem so bad, since supposedly we are in the business of educating (some would say training) people to go and practice a trade. Yet, a focus too much on this practical dimension of the graduate school, and we can hear any hope for innovation or creativity being sucked right out of it. We train students to be little more than cogs in the wheels of the institutions where they eventually secure positions. And that training will have lots of problems.

We might rationalize that we are a professional school where we are expected to turn out graduates with marketable skills. However, our graduates need to understand how to apply their skills in complex and challenging environments, and this is where the wisdom, knowledge, and cultural understanding come in. But, are we creating the suitable

---

[396] Neil Postman, *The End of Education: Redefining the Value of School* (New York: Alfred A. Knopf, 1995), pp. 4 and 6.

environment at our schools to allow education, not mere training, to occur? Are business plans, student head counts, revenues generated, customers (those people we used to refer to as "students") and other similar matters our only concerns? Education is, of course, also a public good, and its transformation into mostly a concern for credentials or profits is generating the basis for its failure as well. Martha C. Nussbaum notes, "Unlike all other nations, we ask a higher education to contribute a general preparation for citizenship, not just a specialized preparation for a career."[397] Even in our professional schools, we have to admit that we must not just teach about matters of technical and vocational education but address matters related to how technology is or should be used.

There are obvious ways of reflecting on core values. Are students "customers" or "consumers"? They may be customers in that they purchase something with the expectation of a product or outcome. They buy a course in order to learn something or to satisfy requirements for a degree. Certainly our students fall into that category. Universities are suffering from the wrong public persona. All of this is greatly exaggerated within the professional schools residing within universities. Faculty need to be more assertive in identifying what their reasons are for being in the university. Professional schools have bought in to the prevailing perspectives of the university engaged in trying to make money as much as in trying to educate or in striving to be the repository (or guardian) of human knowledge; some argue that universities have been taken over by vocational training, jettisoning higher ideals of learning.[398] Whatever the symptoms, the critical point is that these symptoms appear because the mission of the university and the professional school to educate and to contribute to public knowledge has been lost. Credentials, customers, revenue, measures, and other elements become the driving forces for evaluation, and professional schools are all the more susceptible to such forces. The irony is even greater in a school of information sciences. As Bill Readings argues, as knowledge in the university has been lost as a goal and replaced by the "processing of information," the university goes into a downward spiral: "something should be known, yet it becomes less and less urgent that we know what it is that should be known."[399] As the university spins into the ground, many

---

[397] Martha C. Nussbaum, *Cultivating Humanity: A Classical Defense of Reform in Liberal Education* (Cambridge: Harvard University Press, 1997), p. 294.
[398] See, for example, Christopher J. Lucas, *Crisis in the Academy: Rethinking Higher Education in America* (New York: St. Martin's Press, 1996).
[399] Readings, *The University in Ruins*, p. 86.

professional schools will be in the forward section, hitting the ground first and hardest. And few may be interested in erecting a memorial for us.

The emphasis on the entrepreneurial profiting does not mean that anyone or any group will do better. Physician Ronald Glasser wrote about how Americans are paying too much for health care for what they get, laying part of the blame on our treatment of it as a "commodity" rather than a "public good": "The evidence is clear that even when viewed through the reductive lens of purely economic self-interest, market-based, entrepreneurial medicine is a failure."[400] Education is, of course, also a public good, and its transformation into a concern for credentials or profits is generating the basis for its failure as well.

Overcoming Disharmony. One hears considerable discussion these days about disunity within the ranks of organizations, especially academic departments in universities. Most renowned are English departments which have been seemingly torn apart by scholars bent on over theorizing literature and texts versus those who claim to be interested in literature for its own merits. It seems that if you enjoy reading fiction of any kind, then English departments may be the last place for you to be, providing a delicious irony about the state of higher education. Professional schools may be the biggest nesting place for such incongruities, where the source of the dissension may be different, resulting from disparate academic backgrounds and professional orientations. In the typical former library school we have individuals with backgrounds in engineering, psychology, anthropology, information science, computer science, telecommunications, library science, the humanities, and the sciences. All are focused on some dimension of understanding information, but the faculty often cannot agree about information's definition (although there are now efforts within the iSchool community to develop more precise meanings).

Bringing a disharmonious faculty together to discuss a school's name, curricular issues, professional objectives and goals, budgets, or other such matters seems doomed from the start. But it is not always that way. One glance at the incredible array of writing about information, and it is not difficult to see why such diversity of viewpoint is important. It is, nevertheless, difficult to attract academic leadership that brings us together to resolve such differences of opinion and helps us, as an extra benefit, to chart the future. Most of the time the difficulties generated by the diversity are good practice for us, forcing us to become better and more articulate

---

[400] Ronald J. Glasser, "We Are Not Immune: Influenza, SARS, and the Collapse of Public Health," *Harper's* 309 (July 2004): 39.

advocates of our positions, but the exercise can be frustrating, making us look disorganized and unfocused in the academic community.

There are popular concepts of a customer that I suspect work against terming our students in this fashion. For businesses, customer relations mean the customer always being right, as well as the concept of giving them a dependable product with a short-term (one or two years) guarantee or a longer service contract than can be purchased. Does this kind of thinking really describe university students? For a professional school, such matters are particularly troublesome, as many of the fields they support have standardized or certification tests that it is tempting to focus on. Students generally know about these credentials, and many, even as they enter the school, believe that what they will be experiencing in the professional school is preparation to take and pass these examinations. Alfie Kohn has spent a career arguing against this in the K-12 realm, noting that the tests "have a very powerful impact on instruction, almost always for the worse. Teachers feel increasingly pressured to take time away from real learning in order to prepare students to take these dreadful tests."[401] At the graduate level, in a professional school, the temptation is further inducement to seeing students as customers and giving them what they want (rather than what they need).

The primary problem in all this may be the failure of professional schools to explain themselves, their mandate, and the mission of the respective disciplines they serve. Freeman Dyson, reviewing a popular account of theoretical physics, notes, "progress in science is often built on wrong theories that are latter corrected. It is better to be wrong than to be vague."[402] In many professional schools, theories are neglected because there is insecurity in the substance or relevance of these theories. It is a greater problem, however, that the faculty of these schools often have a hard time explaining how theories or the knowledge supporting their discipline mesh with the realities of what the practitioners in the field are about (and what their students will one day be doing). Perhaps the problem is due to the invisibility of the professionals we educate and unleash on the world. As some commentators observe, "Many of the contributions of librarians are invisible to library clients – not by accident, but by design. It is actually part of the professional practice of librarians to protect their clients

---

[401] Alfie Kohn, *What Does It Mean to Be Well Educated? And More Essays on Standards, Grading, and Other Follies* (Boston: Beacon Press, 2004), p. 29.
[402] Freeman Dyson, "The World on a String," *New York Review of Books* 51 (May 11, 2004), p. 16.

from the messy details of their work. As a result, few people have much of an idea of what librarians do."[403]

Is This A Fair Assessment? Once in a while I experience a week in which everything I am engaged in is a reminder that in the modern university the faculty member can be seen simply as a hired laborer, far less significant than the academic administrators and middle managers outnumbering them. Things often do look differently on the inside of an organization than they do from the outside. To the outside, the faculty member appears to hold one of the cushiest jobs in the world, with a minimum number of hours required to be in the classroom, most of his time free for reading and reflection, and immense flexibility to come and go as one pleases. Much of this perception is true, of course, at least in the days and weeks that work well. As the university continues its incorporation, these times seem to occur less often.

Universities have become more businesslike, at least in appearances, and with it the faculty's role seems to have diminished. Many of us have given up on the endless meetings now required for some semblance of faculty governance because we desire the time to do other things, or, and more importantly, because we have become cynical about what we really gain from such uses of our time. University administrators have filled the void and our influence has declined, at least in charting where the university is headed, how it uses its resources, and how it portrays itself to the world. I am certain that many who read what I have written will object, thinking of exceptions to the dire observations I have made about the state of library schools or themselves able to offer proof that they function very differently. My goal is not to castigate anyone, since there are many fine educators and scholars in these schools. My aim is to generate some thinking about the present condition and future of these schools, and, I admit, I am more worried that many will be just as happy to see the complete disappearance of the library school from higher education. I worry because I fear for what this means for libraries, for book publishing, for reading, and for the significance of the word in American culture – all critical public goods.

Those who believe in the value of such schools can fight their battles in the classroom, perhaps the last place faculty have authority. The heart of the university is the classroom, where students assemble to learn and where the only way they can learn is for someone to come there having expertise to share – the faculty member. If this is the heart of the university, and if

---

[403] Nardi and O'Day, *Information Ecologies*, p. 82.

the faculty is the key, then it is the faculty who still retain the power and who shape what the university is and what it will always be. While students are eternally upset with faculty about reading loads, course assignments, and grades, it is also with faculty that whatever joy of learning they will experience will come. As Robert Post argues, "the function of academic freedom is not to liberate individual professors from all forms of institutional regulation, but to ensure that faculty within the university are free to engage in the professionally competent forms of inquiry and teaching that are necessary for the realization of the social purposes of the university."[404] Faculty in professional schools need to determine what this means in their domains. Post notes that academic freedom is not about protecting professors so they can do their own work, but instead it is "designed to create the liberty necessary to facilitate the advancement of knowledge, understood as the unimpeded application of professional norms of inquiry."[405] Given what faculty in library and information science schools are normally engaged in, issues such as access to information and the preservation of the cultural record, one would think that they would have strong and well-defined views of their own academic freedom in the increasingly dangerous corporate university.

Where the Heart Is – The Classroom. Confrontations with university administrators remind us (research and teaching faculty) that we never want to do what they do, despite the bigger offices, higher salaries, and staff assistance. University administrators, removed from the classroom and in the corporate model farther removed than ever, are the targets for gripes about education costs, losing football teams, poor telecommunications networks, and congested campus cafeterias. They will almost never experience the joy of learning and the experience of teaching when the "eureka" moment occurs for both faculty and students.

In the classroom, faculty members are in control (unless they have signed away their rights). And in the university, removing the faculty will end the university (although some academic administrators are increasingly unable to understand this basic truth). The university is still fundamentally about knowledge and the exchange of knowledge is transacted in the classroom, in old-fashioned lectures or seminars that have been the hallmarks of the university for at least a century and a half. University administrators really can't reach us there as effectively as they can in other

---

[404] Robert Post, "The Structure of Academic Freedom," in Beshara Doumani, ed., *Academic Freedom After September 11* (New York: Zone Books, 2006), p. 64.
[405] Post, "The Structure of Academic Freedom," p. 70.

ways. Even if they schedule us to teach different courses, we teach what we want and what we believe needs to be taught. If they remove us from the classroom, students still manage to find us. And if students can't find us, we still write and publish for our professional colleagues and, for a few, even for wider realms of the public. Anyone walking in and around the fringes of a university, by peering into nearby coffee shops and restaurants, will still see faculty conversing with each other and with students. Education is going on. Often the administrators won't be seen in these places.

Focusing on the classroom does not mean that we reject necessarily all information technology. We can be suspicious of the societal and educational implications of technology and still be effective in our use of e-mail, the World Wide Web, and the resources of digital libraries and archives. We can harness information technology for both teaching and scholarship, as Edward Ayers, dean and professor of history, suggests: "Information technology has not made the impact on higher education—or at least on the core missions of higher education—that it has made on many other aspects of society. We've built a great infrastructure that has transformed many social and business aspects of our work and our libraries, but teaching and scholarship have been relatively little touched. I think we're ready for the next stage: building tools that can be carried into the heart of the academic enterprise. For teaching, we need tools that anyone can pick up, that can be customized, that are quick and adaptable, and that are less expensive in money, time, and commitment. For scholarship, we need to craft forms of scholarly presentation that take advantage of the power of the new media we now possess. For both teaching and scholarship, therefore, we need IT people and academic people to work together more closely than ever before."[406] Of course, we need to know what to say to the IT people, and this necessitates that we understand our own objectives and adhere to our own values.

My own situation is a good case in point. I came to a professional school in order to continue my career efforts to strengthen the status of my discipline in society. I have long held to three career objectives, including: strengthening the scholarship supporting the discipline, raising up the next generation of academics to teach in the university, and creating a separate masters degree to support the profession. Teaching, researching and writing, and administering are not always functions that go together very

---

[406] Quoted from the electronic version of Edward L. Ayers, "The Academic Culture and the IT Culture: Their Effect on Teaching and Scholarship," *Educause Review* 39 (November/December 2004): 48-62.

well, especially in professional schools. Most faculty measure their careers by other markers, such as books published, and it is a good thing; the faculty members in professional schools seem quite willing to exist with little discernible results stemming from faculty governance. This is, after all, the essence of the professional school. With its foot in one door of the university and its other in the grimier world of a profession, faculty would be constantly pulled in these and other directions.

Hope and Inspiration. I find hope and inspiration in a book about the publishing industry, written by Andre Schiffren and published in 2000, a personal account of the challenges facing the publishing industry.[407] Schriffen, associated with publishing since 1958, is the former head of Pantheon Books who was pushed out by corporate takeovers of its parent company and who started The New Press in 1990 to offer an alternative to changes within publishing working against quality books, risky authors and subjects, and a focus on anything but the most bottom of bottom-lines.

One concerned with the state of the university or that of professional education will recognize much that is in the book. Schriffen describes how publishers, overtaken by corporate conglomerates, abandoned the old system of publishing a few clear publishing blockbusters in order to underwrite the possibility of publishing less profitable but high quality books to a system where *each* book must be profitable or not published at all. Schriffen recounts how older, often smaller publishing houses, with expert editors working patiently with authors with meaningful things to say, were gobbled up by corporate entities with more accountants than editors, with the former always looking for the next money maker (regardless of quality or long-term importance). Schriffen provides considerable attention to the shift on short-term, immediate profits threatening the publication of works by new authors, controversial volumes, and riskier titles.

Schriffen perceives publishers as playing extremely important social and cultural functions, adding to humanity's knowledge, rather than being only a business. He is interested in quality, making a difference, adding knowledge, facilitating change – all features that also used to be critical components of most universities and where we have witnessed substantial decline. What is most reassuring, and hence most hopeful for us, is that Schriffen takes some bold steps to create a new publishing entity, the New Press, running deliberately against the grain and trends of the corporate model of publishing. Schiffren is entrepreneurial with a belief that quality publishing

---

[407] Andre Schiffren, *The Business of Books: How International Conglomerates Took Over Publishing and Changed the Way We Read* (New York: Verso, 2000).

makes a difference in the world. He finds supporters, takes chances, and ignores the corporate model and in this I think the faculty in professional schools need to emulate him.

I think we need to commit to building a self-sustaining, quality education program reaffirming the historic role of the university as a repository of knowledge and the faculty as critics and change agents. Likewise, we need to work against a business or corporate model and, perhaps, we need a commitment to a new kind of library school. We need to acknowledge that we have an important product to sell, a quality education in an area of critical importance to society, its organizations, and its citizens. We have something we can believe in.

You might have been expecting to read more about technology, given the kind of professional school being discussed here. Honestly, however, these schools also ought to be about records, books, and a cultural approach to understanding society. Without question, technology and its use and understanding will always be important. We cannot afford, if we still want to call ourselves educators, to become a new form of Luddites. We must be able to embrace technology (I am not giving up my Apple laptop), but we need to do so in a way that helps faculty colleagues make adjustments with newer forms and enables us to work with students who do not fully understand the limitations of the technology they have grown up with and often take for granted. There are always challenges to be faced in the generational differences in accepting certain technologies. Poet Dana Gioia writes, "For years many intellectuals and academics have observed these trends with a mixture of disappointment and detachment. While lamenting the sorry state of literacy among the public, they remained confident in the power of print culture among educated Americans. That confidence now seems misplaced. Books, magazines, and newspapers are not disappearing, but their position in the culture has changed significantly over the past few decades, even among the educated. We are now seeing the first generation of young intellectuals who are not willing to immerse themselves in the world of books. They are not against reading, but they see it as only one of the many options for information."[408] Just as we find ourselves explaining to students that not all scholarship and information is found on the World Wide Web, we must also orient them to issues like eroding privacy and government and corporate accountability, the obsolescence of digital information and the potential loss of public and

---

[408] Dana Gioia, *Disappearing Ink: Poetry at the End of Print Culture* (Saint Paul, Minnesota: Graywolf Press, 2004), p. 5.

organizational memory, and the societal values and norms that necessitate the creation of a knowledge to be used for the public good. What has always engaged me in my chosen profession has been a sense of the immense importance of records and the intriguing set of problems and issues that threaten our documentary heritage. It is fun to wrestle with new and continually emerging problems and the challenges of explaining them to others.

Academic Pleasure. Many critics of higher education attack faculty about their research activities, either blasting faculty for not teaching enough or for engaging in research and writing that is incoherent, jargon-laden, and irrelevant to modern life. James Axtell, professor of humanities at William and Mary, focuses on the values of research as a central function of university life and faculty responsibility, with, as the book's title suggests, a keen eye for the joys of being an academic. Axtell considers the dangers of a creeping vocationalism throughout all of higher education, a perspective suggesting some interesting challenges to faculty residing in professional schools, the cradle of vocationalism in the university. Axtell helps the reader, especially one considering an academic life, to consider the forces that pull in or push out someone from heeding the call to be a professor.[409] Aimed at answering what he deems to be the growing chorus of criticism about higher education, Axtell's book is a rare positive perspective about life in the university.

Many of the volumes mentioned in this book relate to the role of the faculty in producing meaningful and useful scholarship. Volumes about the corporate university almost always wrestle with whether the newly emerging model of higher education is enabling students to be taught in a manner equipping them to function as citizens in the modern world or to grapple with the ambiguities of a post-modern culture. William H. Willimon and Thomas H. Naylor examine the excesses of campus life, from substance abuse to the meaninglessness many students feel, and wonder whether this is the natural outcome of problems in higher education. They enumerate concerns leading to the "abandonment by higher education of the moral, character-related aspects of education, the widespread but, we believe, erroneous assumption on the part of administrators that it is possible to have a college or a university without having an opinion of what sort of

---

[409] James Axtell, *The Pleasures of Academe: A Celebration and Defense of Higher Education* (Lincoln: University of Nebraska Press, 1998).

people ought to be produced by that institution."⁴¹⁰ Big questions, and not too many answers, seem to follow in the many explorations of the academy.

Many faculty members reflect on whether their research, writing, and teaching really make any difference in the world, a perspective generated by the sometimes-concentrated energies brought to bear on such functions for the purpose of promotion and tenure or responding to other reward structures within the university. English professor Richard E. Miller suggests that academics ought to be educating people to bring about a better world. While he writes from the vantage of the humanities, noting that the only resources humanities faculty have to achieve this aim are "reading, writing, talking, meditating, speculating, arguing,"⁴¹¹ Miller makes a lot of points anyone in any unit of the university might reflect on, sentiments any academic searching for a higher motive might reconsider, and an objective that too often has been lost in the quest for tenure, research grants, and fame. English professor David Damrosch also has weighed in about the same problems. Examining the "deep structural tensions in the modern university," Damrosch considers the deeply ingrained focus on specialization as being a remnant of the Medieval heritage of the university.⁴¹² Damrsoch aptly describes the monastic, solitary research and writing lives of many faculty, lamenting that faculty don't work well enough together and the increased isolation of many faculty tends to weaken their accountability to the university and society. Damrosch also comments on how the continuing stress on scholarship can weaken teaching, generating incentives to not be in the classroom.

Conclusion: The Academic Heart. Many, from both within and outside of the academy, have lamented about the impenetrability of academic writing. What good to the public, the argument goes, if only a few other experts can understand the reports on research or efforts to convey some knowledge? Frederick Crews has parodied the problem in his fictitious set of proceedings of a Modern Language Association meeting on the meaning of Winnie the Pooh, with essays ranging across radical feminist, cultural studies, and postcolonial perspectives. This is one of the funniest examinations of academic or scholarly writing anyone could read, but it has

---

[410] William H. Willimon and Thomas H. Naylor, *The Abandoned Generation: Rethinking Higher Education* (Grand Rapids, MI: William B. Eerdmans Publishing Co., 1995), p. 15.
[411] Richard E. Miller, *Writing at the End of the World* (Pittsburgh: University of Pittsburgh Press, 2005), p. 4.
[412] David Damrosch, *We Scholars: Changing the Culture of the University* (Cambridge: Harvard University Press, 1995), p. 4.

a very serious purpose – reconsidering whether the university still has an important public or useful role in society.[413]

Other academics have tried to relate other factors, such as their personal religious faith, to their role in the university. Now this may seem odd to comment on since nearly every religion is represented both among faculty and students. One volume includes essays considering how the Christian faith influences notions of academic disciplines, scholarship, vocation, community, and reaction to changing intellectual trends such as postmodernism.[414] Norman Klassen and Jens Zimmerman provide a Christian interpretation about the evolution of the university, issues about how worldviews are both formed and applied, and how personal perspectives affect scholarship.[415] The point here is not to espouse a particular religious belief set, but it is important to understand that one's personal views might help an academic to navigate through the difficulties of comprehending a more important role for their profession both in the university and society.

What these kinds of writings suggest is that both a good sense of humor and a sense of a higher calling can assist any of us to understand the university and our role in it. We don't need the same kind of humor or the same religious beliefs, but we do need the ability to laugh and something bigger to believe in order to make sense of something as complex as the university. We need to have some sense of our own values as we navigate in the corporate university. And whether we hold such values may be the most important issue for us to reflect on.

---

[413] Frederick Crews, *Postmodern Pooh* (New York: North Point Press, 2001).
[414] Douglas V. Henry and Michael D. Beaty, eds., *Christianity and the Soul of the University: Faith as a Foundation for Intellectual Community* (Grand Rapids, MI: BakerAcademic, 2006).
[415] Norman Klassen and Jens Zimmerman, *The Passionate Intellect: Incarnational Humanism and the Future of University Education* (Grand Rapids, MI: BakerAcademic, 2006).

Chapter Six

Archival Studies: A Case Study

Introduction. One way to envision the challenges facing modern professional schools, especially what used to be called library schools and that now some believe have morphed into information schools, is to examine in greater detail what has occurred to one major aspect of these schools. What follows concentrates on the development of graduate archival education, one of the recent manifestations of programmatic tracks in these schools, partly because this area is a good case study but mostly because it is the aspect of these schools I am most familiar with. Also, this area has seen a tremendous growth in student enrollment (both masters and doctoral students) and the hiring of faculty, or, as my then 24 year-old daughter remarked, it is "hot" among her generation.

I have been writing about the education of archivists for two decades, most of this since I joined a library and information science faculty. My earliest writings focused on the efforts to strengthen professional credentials, image, and mission in society (especially in how archivists related to other disciplines).[416] This included an effort to consider the most fundamental aspects of what constitutes a profession, and whether the archival community matches up to these elements (a debate that has not been resolved yet).[417] In the mid-1980s, before I became an academic, I was also involved in drafting new and expanded guidelines for graduate archival education, eventually adopted by the Society of American Archivists in 1988. My role was expanding the description of knowledge covered by such programs so that there was a recognition that these educational programs

---

[416] Richard J. Cox, "Strategies for Archival Action in the 1980s and Beyond: Implementing the SAA Goals and Priorities Task Force Report," *Provenance* 3 (Fall 1985): 22-37 and "Archivists and Public Historians in the United States," *Public Historian* 8 (Summer 1986): 25-41.

[417] Richard J. Cox, "Professionalism and Archivists in the United States," *American Archivist* 49 (Summer 1986): 229-47.

needed to be grown beyond a few courses taught by adjuncts in history or library and information science programs.[418]

After I became responsible for an archives program, my writings about education in this field transformed. On the one hand, it began to reflect my own efforts to design and nurture a graduate program, and on the other it made me think more about the nature and issues confronting professional education. Some old ideas about professional education began to draw my attention. For example, in 1948, Ernest Cadman Colwell, a faculty member and then President of the University of Chicago, noted that the professional school in the university "has as its primary and distinctive obligation... the advancement of knowledge in a particular profession; the education of students to carry these advances still further in the next generation; and, finally, the criticism of its own profession in terms of standards and performance."[419] It was precisely such matters that engaged my own thinking. I began to write about the desirability of separate masters degrees,[420] how to prepare individuals to work with digital archives and recordkeeping systems,[421] the role of continuing education in the field and its relationship to graduate education,[422] how the graduate curriculum addresses archival functions such as advocacy,[423] how specializations such as archives fit into a generalized degree as traditionally the MLIS has been defined,[424] and societal and other factors influencing the development of

---

[418] "Educating Archivists: Speculations on the Past, Present, and Future," *Journal of the American Society for Information Science* 39 (September 1988): 340-43 comments on some of my early notions about education.

[419] Ernest Cadman Colwell, "The Role of the Professional School in the University," *Library Journal* (December 1993): 82, from reprint of 1948 LJ essay.

[420] Richard J. Cox, "The Masters of Archival Studies and American Education Standards: An Argument for the Continued Development of Graduate Archival Education in the United States," *Archivaria* 36 (Autumn 1993): 221-31.

[421] Richard J. Cox, "The Roles of Graduate and Continuing Education in Preparing Archivists for the Information Age," *American Archivist* 56 (Summer 1993): 444-57.

[422] Richard J. Cox, "Continuing Education and Special Collections Professionals: The Need for Rethinking," *Rare Books & Manuscripts Librarianship* 10, no. 2 (1995): 78-96.

[423] Richard J. Cox, "Advocacy in the Graduate Archives Curriculum: A North American Perspective," *Janus* no. 1 (1997): 30-41.

[424] Richard J. Cox and Edie Rasmussen, "Reinventing the Information Professions and the Argument for Specialization in LIS Education: Case Studies in Archives and Information Technology," *Journal of Education for Library and Information Science*, 38 (Fall 1997): 255-267.

graduate education for records professionals.[425] I also engaged, with a small group of collaborators, in a major assessment of the status of archival education programs in library and information science schools.[426]

In this chapter I am placing the status and potential fate of graduate archival education alongside the fate of the main professional schools hosting these programs. This is not a particularly novel way of approaching such concerns. Library educators have long worried about the connection of their schools to the university.[427] My purpose here is to discuss the nature of graduate archival education to demonstrate just how uncertain a foundation library schools may have built within the university. Some might argue that the addition of archival programs might be another indicator of the unwise trend of library schools to strive to do everything. I would argue, instead, that it is a window into the challenges faced by such professional schools as they attempt to satisfy professional groups, employers, university administrators, scholars and other colleagues, and the public and shape a meaningful place for the schools where there is a sufficient quality of life for faculty to pursue their beloved teaching and scholarly ambitions.

Others looking at professional schools and their faculty have detected similar issues and challenges. David Labaree, analyzing education schools, places them in the context of typical problems faced by professional schools in the changing modern university. Labaree notes how professional education is not "unique in being driven by market pressures and by concerns about the useful application of knowledge." This observer also focuses on the tensions of between applied fields and the roles of faculty, suggesting that education school professors can either "embrace" the role of the university professor and turn their back on teaching education or "embrace" the teaching profession and turn their back on the university. Labaree examines the schools' poor reputation, lack of respect, divided

---

[425] Richard J. Cox, "Millennial Thoughts on the Education of Records Professionals," *Records and Information Management Report* 15 (April 1999): 1-16.
[426] Richard J. Cox and Elizabeth Yakel, David Wallace, Jeannette Bastian, and Jennifer Marshall, "Archival Education in North American Library and Information Science Schools," *Library Quarterly* 71 (April 2001): 141-194 and "Educating Archivists in Library and Information Science Schools," *Journal of Education for Library and Information Science* 42 (Summer 2001): 228-240.
[427] See Abraham Bookstein, "Library Education, Yesterday and Today: Library Education in the University Setting," *Library Quarterly* 56, no. 4 (1986): 361 and Evelyn H. Daniel, "The Library/Information School in Context: The Place of Library/Information Science Education Within Higher Education," *Library Trends* (Spring 1986): 630-631.

loyalty between working practitioners and the demands of the research university, mission, and challenges – all relating to issues faced by other professional schools such as in library and information science.[428]

Many faculty in professional schools struggle with their role in a university, torn as they are between professions with their own practical agendas and research and publication building knowledge and theory. Another study of business schools charts a story similar to what Labaree describes with the education schools. Tracking the nature of the business school from the late nineteenth century to the present, Rakesh Khurana of the Harvard Business School chronicles how these schools have been critical to giving legitimacy to management as a profession with a distinct body of knowledge, a sense of expertise, professional autonomy, and an ethos of service (all concepts rooted in the Progressive era of a century ago giving birth to many other disciplines such as library science). Khurana reveals how the past century has witnessed business schools struggling with their identity and mission, buffeted by changes in society, business, and the role and influence of the federal government and major foundations such as the Carnegie and Ford. The author is particularly concerned with the demise of the professionalism model with an emphasis on knowledge generation, codes of conduct, and the ideals of service to a focus on wealth accumulation, competition among the schools for rankings, shifts by the schools to stressing their social capital value (how going to a particular school better positions an individual for career advancement and other success) rather than any notion of a public good, and, ultimately, the loss of a "historical metanarrative of management as a profession."[429]

If faculty members engage in building scholarship, they may be chided by the very professions they supposedly equip individuals to work in, and if they focus on teaching to prepare these practitioners they may be shunned in their own schools for a lack of productivity. This is a challenge needing creative responses. Immersing themselves in the most pressing issues of present practitioners may lead these faculty members to engage in new forms of scholarship that can press the profession to re-examine its own roots, principles, and assumptions. The professional school may be a troubling place for some, but it can also be a place of great energy.

---

[428] David Labaree, *The Trouble with Ed Schools* (New Haven: Yale University Press, 2004), pp. 13, 121.
[429] Rakesh Khurana, *From Higher Aims to Hired Hands: The Social Transformation of American Business Schools and the Unfulfilled Promise of Management as a Profession* (Princeton: Princeton University Press, 2007), p. 368.

CHAPTER SIX

Coming to the Crossroads. After many decades during which various committees of the Society of American Archivists led deliberations concerning the education of archivists, we are now in the interesting position where individual graduate-level educators are leading the discussions. This is a radical change. Graduate archival educators have not been in such a position of leadership for very long. In the mid-1980s, I led the subcommittee of the SAA's Committee on Archival Education and Professional Development drafting of new graduate education guidelines because I was *not* then an educator and would be impartial. Today, I doubt someone would be picked outside of the education community without at least a fuss being made. Educators expect to be leading discussions concerning graduate education.

One's reactions to all this might be different depending on whether you are a working archivist or an educator of future archivists (still, in my opinion, a *working* archivist). Archival practitioners may see this development as troublesome. How will they be assured that what prospective archivists are learning in the classroom will be relevant to the skills and attitudes needed on the job? Archival educators may be equally concerned that the students they are teaching will be unhappy with the positions, responsibilities, and salaries they are obtaining. How do educators teach their students to be as knowledgeable as possible *and* responsive to the situations faced by archivists and archival problems in the real world? Such questions seem endemic to such professions, even when the vast majority of educators bring extensive experience to the classroom. Debates like this have gone on since the days of Melvil Dewey in American librarianship, as well as in nursing, law, and other professions. It is precisely why commentators on higher education often single out professional education as a special problem to be dealt within the university.[430]

While some universities are embracing stronger connections with their local communities, it is not always the case that faculty are offered balanced means between teaching and research by which to gain tenure and promotion. Jo Ann M. Gora, a university president (Ball State), states, with no hesitation: "Universities can no longer afford to be 'ivory towers,' for many reasons. We in higher education are more accountable and responsible to the larger community today than we ever have been, and demands for that accountability and responsibility are only going to increase

---

[430] A good introduction to the tensions and stresses in professional education in the university is Derek Bok, *Higher Learning* (Cambridge: Harvard University Press, 1986), chapter three.

in coming years." She describes how her school provides each student "an immersive learning experience," partly "because it provides important services to people around our state and across the country, demonstrating our accountability and responsibility to others." While faculty in LIS schools, including those that are focused on archival studies, might applaud such concepts as reflecting what they already do, it is important to note that Gora's comments mostly discuss cases connected to business (perhaps another reflection of the corporate university idea). This is particularly troubling now when we see libraries, museums, and archives having their financial guts cut out in the fiscal crisis.[431]

More confused will be those individuals considering becoming archivists and seeking out information on where to obtain the best education and training. If they find the Society of American Archivists education directory they will find information on *"programs"* that range from one course to full-fledged masters degrees, schools with only adjunct faculty to those with clusters of specialized regular faculty, and schools in both history and library and information science. What if the interested individual happens to pick up an education directory from the Association of Records Managers and Administrators? They will find very different information. Worse, what if this person just asks around? Responses could be bewildering.

There have been some amazing changes in graduate archival education in North America, a movement from scattered workshops and miscellaneous graduate courses to masters' degrees and multi-course specializations. The Society of American Archivists, since its inception seventy years ago, has been predicated on serving *all* archivists equally well. Anyone who declares that he or she is an archivist, no matter what education they may or may not have, is to be equally treated and regarded, but the graduate programs have sought to attract the best students to give them the best education in order to place them in the best jobs – hardly the egalitarian mission the Society has been based on. The financial costs, entrance requirements, emphasis on theory and methodology, and often more aggressive visions for what archivists should do mean that not all archivists are created equal.

Graduate Archival Education at the Beginning of the 21st Century. Archivists have seen many different phases in the development of North American

---

[431] Jo Ann M. Gora, "Ivory Towers No More," *University Business*, October 2007, available at http://www.universitybusiness.com/viewarticle.aspx?articleid=907.

graduate education. In the 1930s and 1940s, there were efforts to define a new kind of educational program, when the first courses on archives were offered. Then, over the next few decades, there was the parallel development of graduate courses in library schools and history departments. More recently, we have seen the expansion into specific degrees or, at the least, concentrated clusters of courses supported by multiple faculty members. Some programs are focused on educating individuals to be knowledgeable about records and record-keeping systems and technologies, preparing students for careers across a broad array of organizations and fields. Other programs focus on the cultural dimensions of archives and historical records, with an emphasis on these records as source materials for the historian and other researchers. Still other schools stress very traditional archival skills, orienting their classroom and students to practical experience.[432]

The nature of archival education has been the subject of a long-term debate *within* the profession. That is part of the problem. Archives, with a focus on the nature of records and record-keeping, the technologies supporting all this, and the dual managerial and cultural purposes of archives for evidence and information, is an interdisciplinary field. This is very different from other fields. Carl Schorske argues, for example, "History can only exist in a symbiotic relationship with other disciplines. By virtue of its untheoretical, associative character, it depends on them for its analytic concepts. Nor does history have a particular subject matter of its own. Virtually the only stable center of the historian's armamentarium is the simple calendar that determines what came before something, what came after."[433] While some might argue the same for archival science or archival studies, I believe that the basis of archival knowledge or theory *is* an interdisciplinary one regardless of whether there is a core unifying knowledge or not. The debate about archival theory and education ought to cut *across* many disciplines, precisely what often does not happen as fields professionalize and cluster within specific academic programs. Archival educators could be associated with history, public history, library and information science, public administration, business, or law.

---

[432] A perusal of the current Society of American Archivists education directory reflects the range of different philosophies. The directory is available at the Society's web site, http://www.archivists.org.

[433] Carl Schorske, *Thinking with History: Explorations in the Passage to Modernism* (Princeton: Princeton University Press, 1998), p. 16.

Archival educators have tended to be a conservative lot. Earlier educational guidelines were often drafted to reflect what was already going on, rather than to point to where archival education needed to go. For a while the educational guidelines pointed down the road toward separate degree programs, but there was a weak response. There have been some changes in strengthening curriculum, but whether this is the result of these guidelines is uncertain. This may be the result of the fact that these are guidelines, not standards – that is, voluntary not buttressed by any accreditation or other regulating body (unless one counts ALA's indirect accreditation of graduate archival education in its oversight of MLIS degrees).

There are other factors or obstacles in nurturing archival education. There is little feedback from the employers of archivists about what such graduate programs should be teaching. Then, of course, there is the question of what employers educators should seek input from for the content and structure of education. Should they listen to the small, local historical society who is interested in having someone work with its traditional manuscript collections? Or, should they work with the Fortune 500 corporation needing someone to work as a part of a team in designing a complex electronic records system? Obviously, the advice will be very different from such remarkably different sources. The Society of American Archivists wants to listen to both and respond in positive ways. The graduate educator will only scratch his or her head in disbelief at the prospect of constructing a coherent program that can do both.

Whither Archival Educators? Archival education is not just the result of blindly or mindlessly responding to the cacophony of voices from the field. North American archival educators have usually not been willing to band together. In San Diego in 1996 a few educators who had been discussing some issues of mutual concern put together an invitation-only conference prior to the SAA annual meeting. The invitation-only aspect created ill will, even though it was directed at full-time regular educators and schools already making a strong commitment to the education of archivists and other records professionals. Conspiracy theories, charges of elitism, and angry accusations followed. What began as an effort to push along graduate education was derailed, perhaps because this is still a relatively young aspect of the archival field.

The youthfulness of graduate archival education can be seen in other ways. Some educators believe that they can rely on an annual two-hour meeting of the Archival Education Roundtable at SAA meetings for the exchange of information and other business. Another indication is that educators continue to be in short supply, and there is only now beginning to be any real preparation of future educators in doctoral programs. The long-cherished idea that the future of research rests on the establishment of graduate programs and the employment of regular faculty members seems to be more myth than objective; the number of faculty doing research and programs promoting their students to be engaged in research activities is relatively small.

There are hopeful signs, such as in the creation of multiple-faculty programs allowing more focus on developing a stronger curriculum, team-teaching, administrating the program, and joint advising – all to the benefit of students. Other possibilities emerge as well. There is time for joint-grant writing, collaborative research and writing, sharing of reading lists, and a more focused effort on influencing other courses to reflect archives and records sensibilities. Distance education offers the possibility of enriching curriculum and teaching, and there have been a few experiments in this. Even simpler is the banding together by educators from different schools for informal discussions, leading to special issues of journals, book projects, mutual grant proposals, and conferences (education pre-conferences at SAA meetings between 1995 and 2004 and ultimately the Archival Education and Research Institute beginning in 2009 and operating independently with the aid of an Institute of Museum and Library Services grant).

The emerging independence of the educators is a positive sign of what lies ahead. While this does not seem to be the time to be growing new degrees in higher education, there are many schools (especially in library and information science) recruiting faculty to teach about archives, preservation, and records management (and closely related matters such as cultural heritage management). How the educators define the core purposes of graduate education will influence who gets hired to teach and how extensive the educational programs will be, although they will have to define it far beyond the vision held by the supporters of the certification of archivists.[434] New and more complex record-keeping technologies press the educators by introducing a larger group of competitors for managing records. Many organizations, policymakers, and even records professionals look to technical solutions to many records issues. As educators, we know

---

[434] I have made dramatic shifts in my views about archival certification, having shifted from a supporter to a detractor. I describe my reasons for this change in my chapter on certification in *Archives and Archivists in the Information Age* (New York: Neal-Schuman Publishers, Inc., 2005), chapter 5.

the need of educating individuals both to understand records and record-keeping systems as well as the technologies supporting these systems.

Archival Educators and the Road Ahead. Archival educators must clear a road ahead for where they want graduate education to be going. I believe that fundamentally important to accomplishing this is the need for archival educators to determine how and when they should work together. They can rely on SAA to set the direction for graduate education and work with this association; build an alliance with another professional association with an interest in the education of information professionals or records issues; establish an independent professional association (there are faint steps in that direction with AERI); and create informal working groups with common philosophies and objectives in order to share resources or to work on specific projects. Whatever archival educators do, they must position themselves to meet regularly in order to work on common concerns, collaborate and share research, provide a forum for doctoral students preparing for academic teaching positions, and enable a more intensive and effective consideration of matters relating to graduate archival education.

The future of graduate archival education rests primarily with what graduate educators deem it to be. This future also will be affected by the administrators of higher education who must approve the degrees, certificates, and specializations; by the individuals and institutions hiring graduates; and by professional associations such as the Society of American Archivists. It also rests, it seems, with the fate of library and information science schools.

Are There Really New Directions and Innovations in Archival Education? In the United States just two decades ago, we lacked enough graduate educators to hold a meeting, or even to fill a modest sized restaurant table. A conference in Boston in August 2004, the third meeting since the mid-1990s, was a matter for celebration, as well as some disappointment. I did not hear much about new directions or innovations, and I am concerned why. The 2004 conference presentations reflect some promising change in the development of archival education, but they also suggest a step backward when considered against previous assessments (many essays and reports were published since the 1930s about preparing individuals to practice as archivists). Many of the comments made in 2004 echo some of the educational themes dating to the earliest days of the modern archival community. Over the past thirty years, however, we have had a number of evaluations suggesting that archival knowledge is dependent on the establishment of archival faculties residing in universities.

CHAPTER SIX

What concerns me is a stagnation in the development of graduate archival education after progress over the past quarter of a century. I worry that there is a shift towards "credentialism," with increased discussion about competencies. I also worry about the lack of research in graduate archival education. I am also concerned about what we were *not* discussing in this meeting, some gaps that I believe do not figure well for the future improvements of educating individuals to work as archivists. In all such matters, there is a connection between problems associated with the ongoing evolution of archival education and changes in the library and information science schools hosting the vast majority of the programs.

We may be immature when considering matters related to the higher education of archivists. Terry Eastwood's assertion that there is "little agreement on what the architecture of the archival curriculum should be" is powerful testimony that we are still in the early building stage of such education.[435] Eastwood's concerns about gaps between what is taught and skills sought are telling. Eastwood's depiction of the lack of comfort felt by archival educators when asked about the skills they teach and the skills their students require continues to be a problem for some educators, but I also worry that the shift of higher education to the corporate model – with its focus on students as customers, generating revenue, distance education, and competencies statements – is encouraging a renewal of interest in training and skills, not education.

Archival educators should not be surprised when they receive criticism and disdain for the conceptual or theoretical discourse of the classroom. Many of our leading archival repositories are still struggling with the nature of their mission and how to state this mission, so why should we expect useful answers about what practitioners need to know? When they do answer, they tell us the new archivist should know everything (without the salaries enabling people to stay in school as long as needed to gain such knowledge). Even if the employers gave us the perfect, succinct answers to skills, knowledge, and competencies, I am not sure what we would do with such information. Even many professional schools believe they can hire a single faculty member who has expertise in all areas of archival work and who has mastered every nuance of the knowledge supporting archival work.

Skills and competencies are not what we should be teaching in a university classroom (these are the province of workshops, institutes, or in-

---

[435] Terry Eastwood, "Building Archival Knowledge and Skills," paper presented at the Third SAA Archives Educators Forum, August 2, 2004, Simmons College, Boston, Massachusetts.

service training programs). If one carefully examines entry-level job postings, the most consistent refrains are for experience, verbal and written communication skills, and interpersonal skills.[436] Are these attributes we should be teaching in our classrooms, or, are these qualities we might expect individuals to bring to graduate school? Of course, it is quite difficult to resist such problems when the host schools are so caught up in credentialism, revenue generation, and mass delivery systems.

Change Agents versus Purveyors of Competencies. As professors, archival educators should be change agents, critiquing present practice, gathering information about new approaches to strengthen the archival mission, and engaging with the public and policymakers about the importance of records and recordkeeping. Employers often tend to have a limited view of archival work, stressing arrangement, description, and reference work at the expense of appraisal, policy, or administration. While Frank Burke desired a professoriate to be the theologians of the field, I believe the profession needs scholars interacting with both the nature of documentation and the practices of administering this documentation.[437] It is a call for renewed scholarship that could be appropriately sounded for library and information schools as well.

Terry Eastwood adds good recordkeeping practices to the objectives of the archivist and what is taught in the classroom. The disciplinary split between archivists and records managers has been bad for both, confusing to the organizations hiring records professionals, and bad for society with concerns for a wide range of records roles from accountability to corporate and societal memory. There is another aspect to this. Eastwood describes that "building a recordkeeping system requires careful analysis of business functions, activities, procedures, and needs," skills that could be termed "archival analysis" and are "fundamental to almost all aspects of records and archival work."[438] And here we have it – archivists are experts (scholars) on recordkeeping systems. This may be, of course, one reason why at times it is difficult to communicate about the archival mission within library and information science schools; being authorities on records suggest that we are educating people to be experts on evidence rather than information. And, sometimes, this is a difficult chasm to cross.

---

[436] See my "Employing Records Professionals in the Information Age: A Research Study," *Information Management Journal* 34 (January 2000): 18-33.
[437] Frank Burke, "The Future Course of Archival Theory in the United States," *American Archivist* 44 (Winter 1981): 40-46.
[438] Eastwood, "Building Archival Knowledge and Skills."

CHAPTER SIX 153

It may be necessary to focus on competencies in our era of accountability to assess the knowledge one must possess to be an archival practitioner, but I wonder if the responsibility for this falls on the doorsteps of graduate education programs and their faculty. Thirty years ago, the relationship between competencies and education might have been more pertinent if only for the fact that *all* of the people teaching in the classroom were practitioners, teaching based on experience; yet, those who began to muse about the value and nature of archival education with a real professoriate were longing for something more. Now I wonder if some of the discussion about competencies and distance education is not leading archival educators and the field astray.

We can discern such problems in the attitudes reflected by colleagues building a collaborative distance education program. One of the project architects, in discussing the various audiences for the introductory course, states that one potential audience is history doctoral students who can learn about archives for their own research and as an employment backup if an academic position is not available.[439] The decision by the schools involved in the distance education experiment not to build a curriculum but to offer courses already taught and allow students at the various schools to take them as independent studies might seem practical, but such an approach provides no program coherence or substantial grounding in the field's knowledge; indeed, we have here a credential for sale, something that might appeal to those counting the bottom line. Distance education can allow content to be packaged in digestible bites and training replaces education, relying on textbooks at a time textbooks are unable to capture the complexity of archival knowledge. Thirty years ago, the SAA's Committee on the Seventies put considerable emphasis on the need for textbooks for education, but this was a period when the profession had few textbooks or journals.[440] Times have changed.

Textbooks and Pedagogy. No single textbook now provides adequate coverage of archival knowledge. Textbooks can build a convenient framework for practice, but in the classroom they need to be critiqued and complemented by other scholarship. If archival work is a discipline, it is one that is multi-disciplinary, drawing on other fields ranging from history to

---

[439] Elizabeth Dow, "Harmonizing Archives 101: Collaboration to Support the Collaborative," paper presented at the Third SAA Archives Educators Forum, August 2, 2004, Simmons College, Boston, Massachusetts.

[440] Philip P. Mason, "The Society of American Archivists in the Seventies: Report of the Committee for the 1970's," *American Archivist* 35 (April 1972): 193-217 (the section on education is at pp. 207-210).

the information sciences. If archivists are to be educated as experts in records and recordkeeping systems, then they need to follow the scholarship addressing this topic wherever it might lead. A textbook can provide a general overview or serve as a convenient knowledge or practice benchmark, but it can never substitute for the range of scholarship addressing the complexity of records and records systems. Distance education pressures the instructor to work down from complexity to neatly package a skills program, where PowerPoint bullets and exercises predominate and the scholarship about archives and records can be ignored.

Archival educators are considering new modes of pedagogical delivery, and this can be good. Eastwood argues, for example, that the "debates of former times about its [the education of archivists] viability and proper place in the university have given way to concern on how to give it greater effect or bring it into line with current societal needs."[441] With this I wonder if, in fact, archivists haven't entered the higher education game too late. This is especially relevant as we consider some of the other problems facing graduate archival education. Susan Davis believes that we are still not meeting the "educational needs of the profession," because of the "lack of consistency in archival education curricula, the prevalence of programs within the degree programs of other professional areas, and the overall scarcity of qualified graduate archival educators." Because of the challenges of making graduate education accessible to all geographic areas, she considers the possibilities of distance education but she also reflects on their effectiveness, costs, and how they address different learning styles.[442] The point is whether distance education meets the needs of graduate education in the archival field, an issue likely not to be considered if tuition revenue continues to be the major focus of many professional schools.

Archival educators are still working at a modest level. These educators cannot afford to consider something like distance education apart from what they believe graduate education should be. Is graduate education merely the substitute for the earlier training venues of workshops and institutes? Burke wanted a new kind of faculty member to re-invigorate graduate archival education because what was occurring was "archival training under the guise of archival education."[443] Paul Conway argued

---

[441] Eastwood, "Building Archival Knowledge and Skills."
[442] Susan E. Davis, "Distance Education for Archivists: Panacea or Peril?" paper presented at the Third SAA Archives Educators Forum, August 2, 2004, Simmons College, Boston, Massachusetts.
[443] Burke, "Future Course of Archival Theory," p. 44.

CHAPTER SIX 155

shortly after Burke that graduate faculty would be the innovators, leaders, and researchers in the field,[444] and one wonders how this can happen if the educators primarily reflect what is going on in the field.

Having a presence in the university requires archival educators to emphasize disciplinary scholarship, rigorous teaching, and contributions to public knowledge. While the various SAA graduate education guidelines have stressed that a chief attribute of the faculty member is to have experience, the guidelines also changed to stress that these individuals must possess the attributes to be tenured in the university.[445] It might be too late to transform archival education because of the change to corporate universities with concerns for marketing, credentials, revenue, and customers. Some of the discussion at the conference about competencies and distance education may play well in the new corporate university, but may not help the archival professional mission. On the other hand, the discussion about archival education abroad, where the emphasis is as much on undergraduate studies, ought to cause us to wonder if our graduate programs generate better scholarship or stronger practicing archivists.[446]

What is the Ideal Educational Preparation for Archivists? There are unanswered questions about the advantages or disadvantages of different educational approaches, suggesting that it seems time to determine what is the ideal educational preparation. Karsten Uhde's discussion of archival education in Central Europe may reassure us in North America that our efforts with the array of recording media and waffling definition of archival knowledge as information science or an older historical science are not unique. However, we can find such assessments back to the early twentieth century, when the modern archival profession emerged. Uhde worries, "we will have two kinds of archival education and perhaps two kinds of archivists: those who will be educated to work with older material and those who will be educated to work more or less as a combination of archivist

---

[444] Paul Conway, "Archival Education and the Need for Full-time Faculty," *American Archivist* 51 (Summer 1988): 257.

[445] "Society of American Archivists Guidelines for Graduate Archival Education Programs," *American Archivist* 51 (Summer 1988): 387-388; "Development of a Curriculum for a Masters of Advanced Studies Degree," [1994], now only available through the Internet Archive, and "Guidelines for a Graduate Program in Archival Studies," [2002] available at the SAA's website at www.archivists.org.

[446] Cathrine T. Nengomasha, "Training for the Archival Profession in Namibia," paper presented at the Third SAA Archives Educators Forum, August 2, 2004, Simmons College, Boston, Massachusetts.

and documentalist."[447] In the United States, Samuel Flagg Bemis postulated about the same bifurcated discipline in the 1930s, except that for Bemis the dividing line was not technology but historical scholarship.[448]

What Uhde and Bemis describe is a natural reaction to the changing circumstances of disciplines, and while archival educators must reflect carefully how they respond, they need to reassure themselves that this is nothing new. Likewise, Hans Scheurkogel's speculations about the masters degree needed in Europe includes observations about the "incredible amount of disciplines that someone entering the profession as a master is expected to have knowledge of" or the lack of distinction between "disciplines which are *functionally* related to archival science ... and disciplines which are useful in *interpreting* the archives." He notes how such problems have been resolved within the Netherlands by focusing more on "problem-solving skills, organizing skills, recognition of specific learning necessities," leading to a "reframing of the curriculum from a (academic) discipline-oriented to a competency-oriented curriculum." He also is amused by the persistent efforts by the archival profession to define "what 'body of knowledge' is required to become a 'real' archivist."[449]

Such questions also loom over the American archival community. Elizabeth Yakel and Jeannette Bastian are probing into the question of whether there is a core archival knowledge, how it can be taught, and whether the literature conveys this knowledge.[450] By dissecting the curriculum, there is no question about the contributions their study makes – but there is a lot to debate about their recommendations. Yakel and Bastian want this core knowledge at the center of the graduate programs and endorsed by the profession, but will the profession endorse graduate education given its propensity to seek a lowest common denominator? Is it healthier to have all programs teaching the same core knowledge or

---

[447] Karsten Uhde, "New Education in Old Europe," paper presented at the Third SAA Archives Educators Forum, August 2, 2004, Simmons College, Boston, Massachusetts.

[448] Samuel Flagg Bemis, "The Training of Archivists in the United States," *American Archivist* 2 (July 1939): 154-161.

[449] Hans Scheurkogel, "What master do we want? What master do we need? And ... what master do we deserve?" paper presented at the Third SAA Archives Educators Forum, August 2, 2004, Simmons College, Boston, Massachusetts.

[450] Elizabeth Yakel and Jeannette Bastian, "Is There a Core Archival Knowledge?: Archival Education in North American History Departments and Library Schools," paper presented at the Third SAA Archives Educators Forum, August 2, 2004, Simmons College, Boston, Massachusetts.

different programs taking different angles to this knowledge? What is noteworthy with their work is that they are giving the profession real data to examine, with archival educators actually engaged in research.

What should be taught in a graduate program? Competencies can quickly become skills and skills can be reduced to clerical activities (such as seen in the teaching of records management classes in community colleges). Concerns about technical skills continue to be a challenge in the education of archivists. Helen Tibbo argues, "technology is now an ever present aspect of archival life," and that "all archivists must be technologically savvy and aware of key issues and best practices." Tibbo worries that given the general duration of the typical masters program that "adequate technology education" is not possible. However, given the expansion of interest in archival issues outside of the field, she sees the possibility of some kind of post-masters certificate program in technology education. The idea has merit, although it is as likely that what Tibbo has in mind can be acquired from other sources than graduate education, causing one to ask what is the line between graduate archival education programs and in-service training and experience gained on the job.[451] Introducing students to archival knowledge requires technology, if only because technology and recordkeeping are intertwined. In this sense, educating archivists in library and information science schools would seem to be an excellent idea.

Gaps and Omissions. The 2004 conference presentations ignored some substantial problems and issues. Karen Gracy, for example, notes the teaching of audiovisual archiving is affected by its "paltry" and "difficult to obtain" literature.[452] Here is an entire area of research and scholarship begging to be undertaken, also questioning how well the graduate archival faculty is contributing to scholarship and the discipline's knowledge. Thirty years ago, with the report of the Committee of the Seventies, an astonishing assumption about the field was made; the SAA's lack of endorsement for distinct degrees resulted because it believed that "even if combined with related courses in records management, information sciences, administration of general historical agencies or programs, the result ... would still not constitute a sufficient intellectual discipline to merit a

---

[451] Helen R. Tibbo, "Archival Education Programs in the Information Age," paper presented at the Third SAA Archives Educators Forum, August 2, 2004, Simmons College, Boston, Massachusetts.

[452] Karen Gracy, "Mainstreaming Moving Images and Sound: Educating the Next Generation of Archivists to Value and Care for Audiovisual Archives," paper presented at the Third SAA Archives Educators Forum, August 2, 2004, Simmons College, Boston, Massachusetts.

separate graduate degree."[453] Do archivists and archival educators still believe this? Is a focus on competencies and an emphasis on distance education perhaps not evidence that they do?

There is an expanding and diverse professional literature.[454] Add to this the publications of other professional associations, trade and professional publishers, and scholarly monographs from a wide array of disciplines, and it is no longer easy to keep up with the archival literature. For those relying on Schellenberg's two volumes, Jenkinson's manual, and other manuals, then, a lot is being missed, even if archival faculty members have played a modest role in contributing serious scholarship (considerably different from what Burke and Conway hoped for). One wonders if the academics don't have the time to read, reflect, and research, who will have the time in this professional community? One also might wonder what they teach? The weaknesses and needs of scholarship can easily be forgotten in the embrace of skills and competencies. Archival educators can get mired in the nature and diversity of topics to be offered in their courses, and, given the state of the existing literature, they can likewise spend ample amounts of time building course materials, concocting case studies, and locating practical exercises in fieldwork.

How do these educators balance their energies, identify their priorities, and use their resources? Does being a practice-based profession, as we generally assume ourselves to be and as our graduate education guidelines affirm, mean that only practitioners can write the manuals, contribute to the professional journals, and build a knowledge based exclusively on archival labor? In their zeal to establish comprehensive graduate programs with multiple faculty members and to expand into other teaching venues, such as distance education, archival educators may be using precious resources that should be devoted to building knowledge.[455] Archival educators cannot do everything, even if the mixed signals coming from our university administrators have gotten more frequent and confusing. For archival

---

[453] Mason, "The Society of American Archivists in the Seventies," p. 210.
[454] See my "Forming the Records Professional's Knowledge: North American Archival Publishing in the 20th Century," *Records & Information Management Report* 20 (March 2004): 1-13 for my views on this matter.
[455] There are other dangers as well. As the authors of a manual on archival internships suggest, "Too great an emphasis on internships may reduce archival education to mere training, but with no practical learning at all, students are ill-equipped to enter a workplace that places a high value on experience." Jeannette Bastian and Donna Webber, *Archival Internships: A Guide for Faculty, Supervisors, and Students* (Chicago: Society of American Archivists, 2008), p. 15.

educators, the difficulties of setting priorities is even harder, since the size of the faculty is quite small and we have the professional community to convince as well.

Rethinking Graduate Education Priorities. Graduate archival education has stagnated. The SAA backed off of its endorsement of a separate masters degree, and the profession seems to be uninterested in rallying around this as a need.[456] To complicate matters further, there are not enough individuals qualified to assume full-time, regular tenure stream academic posts; the profession lacks enough both to fill new positions and to replace a corps of faculty who will begin retiring soon.[457]

A considerable portion of the major graduate archives programs is in library and information science (LIS) schools, already possessing small faculties and broad responsibilities. Few seem likely to plunge into a new masters program, so we may be stuck at having a handful of schools with multiple faculty members. The future of LIS education may be uncertain, because it is often at odds with its professional community, is striving to move in other directions stretching already limited resources, and is not building connections to traditional functions of the university (such as scholarship and public knowledge). Finally, higher education is in a major corporate mode, putting its attention on matters like generating revenue, creating new groups of adult learners, and watching the bottom line; students are customers, chairs in classrooms need to be filled, credentials are products to sell, and conveying knowledge via teaching is a commodity. This may not be a good time for very small programs, tracks and specializations within degrees, to argue for expansion.

Is the archival community in the business of real graduate education, or is it in the business of training practitioners as fast and as cheaply as it can? Terry Cook, at the 1999 North American graduate educators meeting, expressed similar concerns, arguing for the primacy of "original research by archivists into the history and contemporary nature of archival records,

---

[456] And there is nothing new here either, as Fred Miller recounted in his "The SAA as Sisyphus: Education Since the 1960s," *American Archivist* 63 (Fall/Winter 2000): 224-236; Miller's essay was originally written in 1983 and published posthumously.

[457] The study by Wendy Duff and her colleagues, noting that students in MLIS programs seem to have no interest in becoming educators in the archives field, may be another indicator of troubles ahead. Wendy Duff, Joan Cherry, and Nalini Singh, "Evaluating Master's Program in Information Studies: A Student Survey," paper presented at the Third SAA Archives Educators Forum, August 2, 2004, Simmons College, Boston, Massachusetts.

records creators, recording media, and recordkeeping systems."[458] Such agendas may be problematic as graduate educators are building a closer relationship with practitioners. One is primarily a producer and conveyor of archival knowledge, and the other mainly a consumer and applier of that knowledge. We can find an example of this in the second edition of David Carmichael's manual on archival arrangement and description, acknowledging that many individuals working with historical materials "will never receive graduate degrees in archival education" and that we should "recognize the contributions of non-professionals and assist them with better tools."[459] My concern is who should be devoting their attention to preparing such materials; is it practitioners like Carmichael or the academics in the field? Educators and practitioners simply look at things differently.

Faculty Roles. Archival faculty must acknowledge a priority for strengthening the knowledge of the field, including being change agents not just reflectors of practice. Of course, much of archival knowledge has a practical origin. Archival academics are the ones with the greatest potential for engaging the public and influencing public policy, because they are the ones who have the resources to explore, meditate on, and formulate new ideas and refresh old ones. They cannot do such these things if they are mostly engaged in teaching basic skills.

Archival academics are both part of and distinct from the majority of the professional community. If they adopt a role as knowledge producers and as disciplinary critics, rather than workshop teachers, archival academics still must balance between the practical and the theoretical. All of this is made more difficult by most of the faculty having once been practitioners, meaning that educators cannot become the radical separatists Richard Niebuhr critiqued, reminding us that anyone who is part of a particular culture can never fully escape it (and its attitudes, precepts, and tools).[460] I am not arguing for such separation, and I am mindful that, for better or worse, all archival educators are immersed in the present professional culture (and it would be foolish to critique something to the

---

[458] Terry Cook, "The Imperative of Challenging Absolutes in Graduate Archival Education Programs: Issues for Educators and the Profession," *American Archivist* 63 (Fall/Winter 2000): 385.
[459] David W. Carmichael, *Organizing Archival Records: A Practical Method of Arrangement and Description for Small Archives*, 2nd ed. (Walnut Creek, CA: AltaMira Press, 2004), p. vii.
[460] H. Richard Niebuhr, *Christ and Culture* (New York: HarperSanFrancisco, 2001; org. pub. 1951), p. 69.

point that it disappears). We labor to make the archival discipline better, and its mission more successful.

Despite many more graduate archival educators and more complex educational offerings, we have not reached a critical mass in the education in this discipline. Nearly forty years ago, H. G. Jones hoped that the National Archives would take a stronger role in graduate education, creating in tandem with a university a masters degree, supporting three adjunct professorial posts – "eminent scholar," a "distinguished archivist," and an "outstanding records management expert." This education program would be overseen by a group consisting of the new faculty members and representatives of various professional, governmental, and scholarly associations.[461] Jones's comments are the product of a particular time and a particular movement, the lobbying for reestablishing the independence of the National Archives, but there is some merit in the broader notion of a national (or comprehensive, dedicated archival) school updated to present circumstances, especially as has been thoroughly documented in American higher education, adjuncts possess little influence, being one of the great laboring under classes of the modern era.[462]

Most of us have been nearly euphoric about the growth in the number of courses and doctoral students. While this certainly does represent progress over what the archival profession thought possible, it is as good a time to ask now whether this is as far as archival education can go. One problem may be the attitudes and objectives of present faculty, as they focus on all forms of training and educating, from remedial workshops to rigorous graduate degrees, dissipating the ability to engage in research and educate doctoral students. Another problem may be the dearth of qualified individuals to fill current faculty slots, replace retiring faculty, or allow any expansion in the concentration of graduate faculty in archival studies. A third problem may be the lack of faculty to discourse with each other within programs, weakening the ability or interest of graduate faculty to engage in scholarly and professional conversation.

The creation of a major school with a real faculty of eight or ten people concentrated in archival studies could resolve some of these matters. Imagine having a faculty with specialists in the history of the profession and records and recordkeeping systems, particular archival functions such as

---

[461] H. G. Jones, *The Records of a Nation: Their Management, Preservation, and Use* (New York: Atheneum, 1969), pp. 218-222 (quotation, p. 219).

[462] For some compelling exploration of this issue, see Benjamin Johnson, Patrick Kavanagh, and Kevin Mattson, eds., *Steal This University: The Rise of the Corporate University and the Academic Labor Movement* (New York: Routledge, 2003).

appraisal and arrangement and description, institutional archives such as government and corporate, electronic media, special media such as moving images and sound, international archival matters, and policy and ethical considerations. This faculty could support comprehensive degrees, mentor the next generation of educators, run research centers for interdisciplinary research on matters of critical importance to the professional community, organizations, and society. In other words, imagine having this faculty do what other university departments and schools have long been doing.

Archival educators also need to reconsider their role in contributing to the knowledge of the field. There is a synergy between teaching and research, but the small number of graduate faculty and limited resources, especially in time, challenges this. Some interesting research about education is going on, but that is only one area for working. What about the remarkably rich potential for research about the history and nature of records and recordkeeping systems, records and information policy, the ethics of records administration, archives as a conveyor of public memory, records and accountability, forging and duplicity in documents, security and access in democratic societies, electronic records systems, and digital and other means of preservation? Archival knowledge is not limited to what archivists practice in their repositories. Even if graduate educators start with the latter, and work from there, I am not convinced that the new faculty posts in archival studies opened in the past twenty years should be engaged in teaching the same courses, the same content, and striving to turn out practitioners for the same kinds of positions. There can be strength in diversity, but I believe that the strength comes from building knowledge that contributes to the public good with graduate archival educators emphasizing the importance of their role in research and scholarship. If archival educators don't take the discipline seriously, who will?

Since graduate faculty members are judged on research, teaching, and service, it is unlikely that archival faculty will neglect any of these. Yet, experience makes us aware that these are not equal, and that individual professors need to sort out what makes the most sense in their school. Whether one might agree with my assessment or not can be debated, but I believe that the most critical responsibility is contributing to disciplinary knowledge and the public good. This gives us both something to teach and a reason for professional and societal service. When I see graduate archival programs offering courses with a single, outdated textbook, I look to see whether the person teaching this has made any contributions to our disciplinary knowledge (and often they have not). Just as someone is not an

CHAPTER SIX

archivist who accepts an archival post with no formal education or relevant experience, so anyone walking into a classroom is not automatically a legitimate educator. The problem with over-stressing credentials and competencies may derive from such weaknesses. And the problems with the stagnated development of our graduate programs may also derive from too heavy a reliance on adjunct instructors who possess experience but who have no inclination for research, theory, and knowledge.

Do graduate archival educators have to possess professional experience? The various SAA education guidelines all say yes,[463] even though experience is never really defined, nor its value – is *all* archival experience sufficient for preparing one to be an educator? These statements reflect a suspicion by archival practitioners about what is going on in the graduate programs, nothing that is new in professional education. However, a sign of maturation in graduate archival education will be seeing individuals entering the academic corps who are attracted to the field because of intriguing intellectual, policy, administrative, and historical questions rather than because they once arranged and described a few records. This is not bad, because we can build into our programs regimented experiences, both by the use of adjuncts who possess working knowledge and through fieldwork (provided that we give the adjuncts and fieldwork supervisors some investment in the education programs). In fact, this is a good development, because it gives both the graduate programs and the profession a greater investment in knowledge building. In the past and even today, many of the educational programs were apprenticeship operations, focusing on practice and experience; most of the fieldwork credits are reserved for archival representation, as if this is all an archivist needs to know. We need to bring the adjunct faculty into the faculty experience (giving them a voice in the program, through an advisory committee or regular faculty meetings – rather than just using them as hired guns) and structuring fieldwork to be educational experiences (where students are required to read about and analyze the relationship between theory and

---

[463] The 1988 guidelines stipulate a director with "an archival background that includes practical experience and administrative responsibility, active professional involvement, and publications"; "Guidelines," p. 388. The 1994 guidelines affirm the same principle, namely, "Tenure-track archival teaching faculty must possess both formal academic education in archives and relevant archival experience"; "Development of a Curriculum," section 3B. Little changed with the 2002 guidelines, calling for faculty who with "archival experience including work within an archival repository," among other things; "Guidelines," section IIIA.

practice, between what goes on in the classroom and the repository – rather than just having students be cheap labor). None of this is easy.

Teaching and Other Faculty Priorities. If the graduate archival programs assume their only responsibility is supplying entry-level archivists, they may squander the progress made in strengthening archival education. Faculty need to emphasize building a base of scholarship, both through their own work and through the support of doctoral programs, and using this knowledge base to educate individuals entering the field beyond entry-level positions, filling specialized or administrative positions. It is clear we have a shortage of potential graduate faculty, and this needs to become a priority. However, it is difficult to imagine building doctoral programs, mentoring doctoral students, and guiding dissertation research if graduate educators have their time consumed by teaching masters students, running workshops, and supporting distance education. There is a synergy that comes from a professor's own research and the attraction of doctoral students; if archival faculty members are not doing research, how will this happen? Doctoral programs are heavy resource users, and it is time that the profession emphasizes this area.

Teaching is a critical matter in graduate archival education, but we have to put it in the perspective of both our place in higher education and our relationship to the professional community. Good teaching requires hard work, expertise of a particular discipline, solid goals, and lots of practice. Ken Bain, in his excellent study analyzing college teaching, argues that the best teachers are master experts in their fields, treat teaching as a serious intellectual exercise or responsibility, engage their students with the disciplinary literature, adopt interdisciplinary approaches to tackle problems and issues, and always know that they are learning about how to teach.[464] Perhaps we should be focusing on teaching, not delivery, methods.

Teaching also brings to the forefront a major issue, the degree to which faculty ought to have been practitioners. Acknowledging that a substantial aspect of archival knowledge is practice-based, should all archival educators have practical experience? This begs the question about what kind of experience. It also ignores that a considerable amount of experience can be learned through visits to archives and observation, consulting, interviews, and research. It may be unrealistic to seek out individuals with considerable professional experience *and* earned doctorates, research, and scholarly interests. Not all experienced archivists can teach, just as not all faculty can

---

[464] Ken Bain, *What the Best College Teachers Do* (Cambridge, MA: Harvard University Press, 2004).

practice – but, perhaps, there is a common ground. Whether this is the examination of competencies is questionable, since discussions about this have equated competencies with a list of skills to be taught and ticked off a checklist. I think archival knowledge and practice are more complex than this, requiring us to re-consider the university's historic role and our place in it. The responsibility of any academic program, especially one on the graduate level, is complex, with many factors and interested parties. We must re-evaluate our own particular development, future directions, and priorities, and chart the best course for strengthening graduate education and the field's knowledge.

Social scientist Michael Walzer, in his writings about the nature of war, breaks military responsibility into three components. There is the *upward* responsibility to the military commanders and, ultimately, the people. There is the *downward* responsibility to the soldiers one commands. And there is the *outward* responsibility to all the people whose lives are affected by a war.[465] In much the same way, graduate archival educators need to reflect on their responsibilities. We have an *upward* responsibility to the university and to people who believe in education as both a public good and as a means to knowledge. We have a *downward* responsibility to the students we teach, offering them the best education we can. And we have an *outward* responsibility to society, including the professional community, affected by the administration of records. It is only when we look at our work in its complex environment that we can best sort out our priorities.

Archival Fieldwork as a Fall Back. One of the anchors, and by this I mean it in two ways – a persistent aspect of graduate education and as a drag on the development of such education – is the continuing stress on fieldwork (whereby practice or practical training is a focus of the educational programs). Some historical context is in order.[466] Prior to 1940, there was

---

[465] Michael Walzer, *Arguing About War* (New Haven, Conn.: Yale University Press, 2004), pp. 23-29.

[466] For the historical background, check the following articles by Richard C. Berner, "Archival Education and Training in the United States, 1937 to Present," *Journal of Education for Librarianship* 22 (Summer/Fall 1981): 3-19; Jacqueline Goggin, "'That We Shall Truly Deserve the Title of Profession': The Training and Education of Archivists, 1930-1960," *American Archivist* 47 (Summer 1984): 243-254; Robert Sidney Martin, "The Development of Professional Education for Librarians and Archivists in the United States: A Comparative Essay," *American Archivist* 57 (Summer 1994): 544-558; Frank B. Evans, "Archival Training in the United States: An Unresolved Problem," *Archives et Bibliotheques de Belgique* 46 (1975): 518-48; and H.

no formal education or training in the United States; in effect, what people learned to become archivists was completely experiential (not a bad approach if one believes that archival work is a craft and apprenticeship the best means to learn a craft). During the twenty years after 1940, isolated graduate courses and institutes were created, providing a kind of archives *appreciation*. Limited in time and resources, these courses and institutes could do little more than skip lightly over all the facets of archival work or provide the basis for building networks for mutual assistance.[467] The individual seeking a career in archives depended on *working* in archives and the practicum, as a component of archival education, was extraordinarily limited.[468]

A reliance on experience has remained intact. In the 1960s and 1970s, there was a simultaneous growth in academic archives, a proliferation of adjunct faculty, and the emergence of the three course sequence with one of these courses being the practicum (the other two courses were an introductory one and an advanced topics or issues course). The three-course sequence was formalized as part of the Society of American Archivists graduate archival guidelines in 1977. Since then, there has been a revolution in graduate archival education, with more programs now supporting multiple, tenure track and tenured faculty. A wide array of

---

G. Jones, "Archival Training in American Universities, 1938-1968," *American Archivist* 31 (April 1968): 135-54.

[467] For the continuing problem with the focus on the institute or workshop mentality, refer to James M. O'Toole, "Curriculum Developments in Archival Education: A Proposal," *American Archivist* 53 (Summer 1990): 460-466; O'Toole, "The Archival Curriculum: Where Are We Now?" *Archival Issues* 22, no. 2 (1997): 103-113; and Timothy L. Ericson, "Professional Associations and Archival Education: A Different Role, or a Different Theater?" *American Archivist* 51 (Summer 1988): 298-311.

[468] In one of the few assessments of the practicum's role in archival education, Frederick Stielow focused on one of the continuing problems with this aspect of archival education -- rigidity in requirements for the student to be exposed to all archival functions within 150 hours. Frederick J. Stielow, "The Practicum and the Changing Face of Archival Education: Observations and Recommendations," *Provenance* 8 (Spring 1990): 1-12. The educational standards for the practicum Stielow was commenting on had been published as "Program Standard for Archival Education: The Practicum," *American Archivist* 43 (Fall 1980): 420-422. Helen R. Tibbo, "A Vision of Archival Education at the Millennium," *Journal of Education for Library and Information Science* 38 (Summer 1997): 221-225, also describes this continuing problem of trying to do too much, now challenged even more by the need to have students who are literate in information technologies.

philosophical orientations to archival education has also developed – some focused on records and record-keeping systems, others on technology, some on cultural sources, and, finally, others on the importance of records for accountability and evidence.[469]

The predominance of experience in archival education is evident by comparing the 1994 graduate archival education guidelines with later Society of American Archivists guidelines. The 1994 guidelines suggest, "Archival science is the core of archival knowledge. It is divided into theory, methodology, and practice." The guidelines then provide a separate statement on the practicum or "experiential learning," also suggesting this is "an opportunity for archivists already working in the field to contribute to archival education." While this statement wisely affirms that the primary function of the practicum is educational, it does not really address the tension between theory and practice, knowledge and application that resides with the continuing use of the practicum.[470] While the SAA's educational guidelines call for this experience to be part of an *educational* process, it is difficult to know whether this is happening. The Society's educational directory provides few clues about this. Some program descriptions include a reference to the practicum but not in sufficient detail to comprehend how it fits in as part of an *educational* process.[471]

Since graduate archival education has traditionally been positioned in either history departments (modestly) or library schools (and their successors), it is possible to examine the issue of the archival practicum and archival graduate education in the context of the continuing concern about and study on the relationship between practical training and theory-based

---

[469] These developments have been captured, to some extent, in the 1988 and 1994 SAA graduate guidelines and the 1996 guidelines on continuing education. I described the impact of the 1988 guidelines in "The Masters of Archival Studies and American Education Standards: An Argument for the Continued Development of Graduate Archival Education in the United States," *Archivaria* 36 (Autumn 1993): 221-31. The current SAA guidelines for the MAS degree and for continuing education can be found at http://www.archivists.org.

[470] For example, Stielow recognizes some of this when he argues that "Students must be recognized for the advanced theoretical knowledge that they can bring to the site. Although relative neophytes on the bench, these are graduate students who have had the leisure to study abstract concepts, which could aid the repository. They should not be exploited as cheap labor ..., but managed to ensure the development of pleasant and effective future colleagues." Stielow, "The Practicum and the Changing Face of Archival Education," p. 11.

[471] The education directory is at http://www.archivists.org/prof-education/edd-index.asp.

education in library and information science. Since the emergence of the first library school, there has been debate about the relationship between theory and practice. From the late nineteenth century to the 1923 Williamson Report on library education, the practicum, internship, or fieldwork was a major element of the education of librarians. Although in the intervening years the practical training of prospective librarians has slipped in its prominence in graduate library education, most schools continue to possibilities for practical training. A continuing appearance of articles and studies on the general issue of theory versus practice reveals that this issue remains an important one for the library and information science field. From the early twentieth century until the present, there has been a steady parade of surveys of ALA-accredited library schools to determine their attitudes and commitments to the practicum, internships, and fieldwork, along with historical reviews on the topic. There also have been other efforts to determine employers' and students' perceptions of the respective values of practical training in the graduate library school context.[472]

---

[472] Some of the writings on the relationship between practice and education include M. Evalyn Clough and Thomas J. Galvin, "Educating Special Librarians: Toward a Meaningful Practitioner-Educator Dialogue," *Special Libraries* 75 (January 1984): 1-8; John O. Hempstead, "Internship and Practical Application in Educating School Library Personnel," *Journal of Education for Librarianship* 12 (Fall 1971): 116-32; Joe Morehead, *Theory and Practice in Library Education: The Teaching-Learning Process* (Littleton, CO: Libraries Unlimited, Inc., 1980); Joe Morehead, "The Theory Practice Problem and Library-Centered Library Education," *Journal of Education for Librarianship* 14 (Fall 1973): 119-28; S. D. Neill, "The Place of Practice in a Graduate Library School," *Libri* 25 (July 1975): 81-97; Esther L. Stallmann, *Library Internships: History, Purpose and a Proposal*, University of Illinois Library School Occassional Papers, no. 37 (Urbana: Library School, 1954); Barbara A. Ward, "A Rationale for Field Experience in Library Education," *Journal of Education for Librarianship* 13 (Spring 1973): 232-37. Research studies include Louis Coburn, *Classroom and Field: The Internship in American Library Education; An Inquiry Into Its Development and Evaluation*, Queens College Studies in Librarianship no. 3 (Flushing: Queens College of the City University of New Work, 1980); Laurel Grotzinger, "The Status of 'Practicum' in Graduate Library Schools," *Journal of Education for Librarianship* 11 (Spring 1971): 332-39; Audrey W. Hall, "Library School Fieldwork Placements: Problems and Practice," *Library Management* 7, no.2, (1986); William J. Martin, *The Practical Element in Library Education: A Survey* (Belfast: Department of Library and Information Studies, Queen's University, 1979); Margaret E. Monroe, *Issues in Field Experience As An Element in the Library School Curriculum: A Background Paper*, 1971 (ERIC Report ED-200 231); Roger C. Palmer, "Internships and Practicums," in *The Administrative Aspects of Education for Librarianship: A Symposium*, ed. Marry B. Cassata and Herman L. Totten (Metuchen, N.J.: Scarecrow Press,

Training or Education? Studies on archival education likewise affirm that the practicum is perceived to be an integral part of the training of prospective archivists, with nearly all affirming the value of practical work. A survey of archival educators three decades ago reveals, "practical work ... looms large in the minds of the instructors."[473] Although a survey of educators today might show some shifting of emphasis away from the practicum, every graduate archival education program in the United States includes the practicum as a fundamental element of the training of archivists. What is fascinating, of course, is what has been ignored about *other* requirements for graduate education. The Society's educational guidelines suggest, "archival education is both academic and professional; therefore, it includes both scholarly and experiential elements" (that is, both a thesis and a practicum). Yet, while every program provides the opportunity for the practicum, the opportunity for scholarly research is severely limited – currently, there are few programs with a thesis requirement.

Practical experience has been one of the driving forces behind graduate archival education, but it has also been a millstone impeding the development of graduate archival education (even the field itself). What

---

1975), pp. 239-53; John Richardson, Jr. and Peter Hernon, "Theory vs. Practice: Student Preferences," *Journal of Education for Librarianship* 21 (Spring 1981): 287-300; Miriam Tees, "Graduate Education for Special Librarians: What Special Librarians Are Looking for in Graduates," *Special Libraries* 77 (Fall 1986): 190-97; Mildred C. Tietjen, *A Study, Comparison and Evaluation of Instructional at ALA Accredited Graduate Library Schools in the United States and Canada, with Special Attention Focused on Practical Experience or Field Work Provided within the Curricula* (Bethesda, Md.: ERIC Document Reproduction Service, ED 126892, 1975); Neil C. Van Deusen, "Field Work in Accredited Library Schools," *College and Research Libraries* 7 (July 1946): 249-55; Brenda White, Associates, *The Impact of Library and Information Studies Education on Subsequent Career Progression* (London: British Library, 1986); Herbert S. White and Marion Paris, "Employer Preferences and the Library Education Curriculum," *Library Quarterly* 55 (January 1985): 1-33; Virginia Witucke, "Library School Policies Toward Preprofessional Work Experience," *Journal of Education for Librarianship* 16 (Winter 1976): 162-72; and Helen T. Ziegler, Lois C. Bailey, and Mildred Clapp, "The Merits and Weaknesses of Library School Training as Seen by Recent Graduates," *Library Journal* 58 (July 1933): 585-89. Twenty years ago over 90 percent of library and information science programs have a practicum; J. Gordon Coleman, Jr., "The Role of the Practicum in Library Schools," *Journal of Education for Library and Information Science* 30 (Summer 1989): 19-27 (and there is little reason to think that this has changed much since then).

[473] Ames Sheldon Bower, "Whence and Whither: A Survey of Archival Education," *Georgia Archive* 5 (Summer 1977): 47.

should a student know? If the recent SAA guidelines are any indication, there can be no debate that everything identified as part of archival knowledge can be dealt with experientially. Even the SAA education guidelines acknowledge this, stating that "no graduate program in any discipline can provide all the scholarly and experiential knowledge needed for its practitioners."[474] It seems unlikely that a student can learn everything from experience, no matter how carefully planned. Are there limitations in the gap between theory or knowledge and practice?[475] While theory is often assailed as being impractical, it does not appear that even carefully coordinated practice could be immune from similar criticism.[476] That is, can practice provide a full and rich experience that educates future archivists for the broadest range of possible problems and challenges that they might face? Is experience crucial or essential for a graduate to get their first position? There is no doubt that experience is heavily featured in all job advertisements, but we do not know whether experience is more important than learning about archives and records management theory and

---

[474] The guidelines are at http://www.archivists.org/education/masguide.html.

[475] The predominant effort to set forth the modern importance of archival theory in the context of education is Luciana Duranti, "The Archival Body of Knowledge: Archival Theory, Method, and Practice," *Journal of Education for Library and Information Science* 34 (Winter 1993): 8-24. While I disagree with the particulars of her definitions, I certainly concur with the importance of a theoretical basis. For a similar statement, refer to Heather MacNeil, "Archival Theory and Practice: Between Two Paradigms," *Archivaria* 37 (Spring 1994): 6-20. The useful aspect of MacNeil's description is her effort to see this as a continuum, where methodology connects practice and theory.

[476] The debate about the relevance of theory in archival work reached its nadir in the writings of John Roberts, but it has been part of a continuing professional discussion extending back twenty years. The debate was started by Frank G. Burke's provocative essay, "The Future Course of Archival Theory in the United States," *American Archivist* 44 (Winter 1981): 40-46. Burke's essay prompted a number of responses, including Lester J. Cappon, "What, Then, Is There to Theorize About?" *American Archivist* 45 (Winter 1982): 19-25; Gregg D. Kimball, "The Burke-Cappon Debate: Some Further Criticisms and Considerations for Archival Theory," *American Archivist* 48 (Fall 1985): 369-76; and John W. Roberts, "Archival Theory: Much Ado About Shelving," *American Archivist* 50 (Winter 1987): 66-74, the latter essentially denying both the existence or importance of theory in this profession. For the most useful discussion about practice and theory refer to John W. Roberts, "Practice Makes Perfect, Theory Makes Theorists," *Archivaria* 37 (Spring 1994): 111-121 and Terry Eastwood, "What is Archival Theory and Why Is It Important?" *Archivaria* 37 (Spring 1994): 122-130.

methodology. We are in a transition stage, as graduate archival education programs are established and the field shifts its job descriptions to accommodate better-educated practitioners.

It is surprising, indeed, that the matter of the relationship of internships to practice and education, despite a vast literature in other professions, has not spurred on much in the way of research or even deeper reflection. What is the ideal knowledge to be taught to archives graduate students?[477] My own sense is that these individuals need to become records experts,[478]

---

[477] There is a vast literature that examines internship and practica in various disciplines, far greater than can be addressed in this research prospectus. Some of the kinds of studies worth looking at are as follows: Robert D. Brown, "Supervising Evaluation Practicum and Intern Students: A Developmental Model," *Educational Evaluation and Policy Analysis* 7 (Summer 1985): 161-67; C. Patricia Freed, "A Study to Identify Student and Faculty Opinions of Graduate Student Learning in Social Work Practicums," Ph.D. dissertation, University of Denver, 1974; Philip A. Hirsch and Gerald L. Stone, "Effects of Gender, Setting, and Research Productivity on Intern and Employment Suitability Ratings," *Journal of Counseling Psychology* 30 (January 1983): 76-82; Judy Kopp, "Changes in Graduate Social Work Students' Use of Interviewing Skills from Training to Practicum," Ph.D. dissertation, Washington University, 1982; Alice K. Murata, "Attitude Differences and Change During a Counseling Practicum in Graduate Students Preparing for Work at Different Educational Levels," Ph.D. dissertation, Northwestern University, 1969; Joan Daniels Pedro, "Induction into the Workplace: The Impact of Internships," *Journal of Vocational Behavior* 25 (August 1984): 80-95; Donald F. Perras, "The Relationship Between Nine Descriptive Variables of Special Education Graduate Students and Tutoring Performance in a Practicum Setting with Emotionally Handicapped Children," Ph.D. dissertation, George Peabody College for Teachers, 1975; Philip John Perry, "A Study of Change in Student-Teacher Attitudes Towards Child-Centered Policies and Practices," Ph.D. dissertation, University of Washington, 1981; Michele A. Sweeney, "Teacher Socialization: The Pre-Practicum Experience with Third-Year Human Movement Majors," Ed.D. dissertation, Boston University, 1984; and Jon Wagner, "Integrating the Traditions of Experiential Learning in Internship Education," *Journal of Experiential Education* 6 (Fall 1983): 7-14.

[478] The return to an emphasis on records and recordkeeping can be seen in two trends. The most pervasive and far-reaching trend may be the work on electronic records management from an archival perspective that, despite many remaining challenges, seeks to establish archivists and records managers in the groups working with the electronic information technologies. See Paul Marsden, "When is the Future? Comparative Notes on the Electronic Record-Keeping Projects of the University of Pittsburgh and the University of British Columbia," *Archivaria* 43 (Spring 1997): 158-173 and Margaret Hedstrom, "Building Record-Keeping

learning about records and record-keeping systems (so that archival functions can be applied). Students must be oriented to the legal, political, social, cultural, economic, administrative, technical, and scholarly aspects of records and recordkeeping. As Terry Eastwood writes, the "first object of archival theory is the nature of archival documents or records"[479]; the question when considering the practicum, then, is how well it can support this and its application?

How Students Learn. How do students best learn about archival work? I posit they learn by a deep immersion into the historical, methodological, and theoretical literature, from many disciplines. This deep immersion requires building a knowledge framework enabling them to evaluate critically the professional literature, ascertaining its strengths and weaknesses. For example, students need to understand that the growth of writing about ethnic, racial, and gender archives is also the result of the influence of social history, the influx of individuals with training in this area, and the growth of public history. The student learns to appreciate each professional essay as an historical document reflecting its own era, understanding that present trends may shift dramatically in the future. Admittedly, this is different from perceiving masters students as adult learners, as some have, where students are older, more practically oriented, and not academic in inclination.[480] Personally, I still cling to the idea that students must have an academic grounding, because it is essential for enabling them to learn and grow in a lifetime of inquiry about the archive, archiving, and recordkeeping.

Field experience does not help to spur on the kind of interdisciplinarity records professionals require. For decades the debate was about *where* graduate archival education should be located. More recently, there has been discussion about the content of such education as it relates to the traditional structures of the archives, records management, library and information science, and history fields. Either way, the practicum is static in its ability to reflect the nuances of archival knowledge.[481] Graduate archival

---

Systems: Archivists Are Not Alone on the Wild Frontier," *Archivaria* 44 (Fall 1997): 44-71.

[479] Eastwood, "What is Archival Theory and Why Is It Important?", p. 125.

[480] Deborah S. Grealy and Sylvia D. Hall-Ellis, *From Research to Practice: The Scholarship of Teaching and Learning in LIS Education* (Westport, Conn.: Libraries Unlimited, 2009).

[481] See, for example, Edwin Bridges, Gregory S. Hunter, Page Putnam Miller, David Thelen, and Gerhard Weinberg, "Toward Better Documenting and Interpreting of the Past: What History Graduate Programs in the Twenty-First

education also can change more quickly and react to external forces more effectively than what actual archival and records programs do or might do. This is, perhaps, another reason why practicum students should be encouraged to reflect on the differences between the classroom and the real world work place – it can serve as a source of balancing theory with practice.

Students learn by directed practical exercises meant to draw them more deeply into various aspects of the ideal knowledge. These practical exercises work because they are embedded in formal evaluation in the classroom of what records professionals know and do. And, these practical exercises should be like the more objective process of writing case studies intended to teach principles and to support critical evaluation skills.[482] How many students in a fieldwork experience obtain such a focus? Many students thrown into fieldwork are not mentored in these experiences. They are *supervised*, and this is very different than what is required in an educational process.

Can Students Learn Everything? Can students learn *everything* they need to know *before* entering into their first professional position? Prior to 1980, the quantity and range of formal coursework was remarkably limited, suggesting that there really was little room for a debate about the relationship of theory to practice because education was focused on practice, in-service training,

---

Century Should Teach About Archival Practices," *American Archivist* 56 (Fall 1993): 730-749; Richard J. Cox and Edie Rasmussen, "Reinventing the Information Professions and the Argument for Specialization in LIS Education: Cases Studies in Archives and Information Technology," *Journal of Education for Library and Information Science* 38 (Fall 1997): 255-267; F. Gerald Ham, Frank Boles, Gregory S. Hunter, and James M. O'Toole. "Is the Past Still Prologue? History and Archival Education," *American Archivist* 56 (Fall 1993): 718-729; Lawrence J. McCrank, "History, Archives and Information Science," *Annual Review of Information Science and Technology* 30 (1995): 281-352; J. Michael Pemberton and Christine R. Nugent, "Information Studies: Emergent Field, Convergent Curriculum," *Journal of Education for Library and Information Science* 36 (Spring 1995): 126-138; and Tyler O. Walters, "Rediscovering the Theoretical Base of Records Management and Its Implications for Graduate Education," *Journal of Education for Library and Information Science* 36 (Spring 1995): 139-154. There is always extreme reactionary views, such as represented by Vernon R. Smith, "Pedagogy and Professionalism: An Evaluation of Trends and Choices Confronting Educators in the Archival Community," *Public Historian* 16 (Summer 1994): 23-43.

[482] See, for example, Richard M. Kesner, "Employing the Case Study Method in the Teaching of Automated Records and Techniques to Archivists," *American Archivist* 56 (Summer 1993): 522-531.

or apprenticeship.[483] Being theoretical meant little more than reading, maybe discussing, the volumes by Jenkinson and Schellenberg, the collected writings of Margaret Cross Norton, and some essays in a limited number of archival journals or pre-assembled readers. Even today, in the more comprehensive education programs, it is unlikely that everything can be taught *or* experienced. When I spend 12 to 15 class sessions on archival appraisal, for example, I hardly ever think that I have done anything but given students a good foundation for approaching this crucial archival function.[484] Archivists, when debating the issue of theory and practice, often tend to lose sight of the fact that neither is monolithic. Even in that most besieged discipline, literary studies, there are those who remind us of how careless we can become in typecasting other viewpoints. Denis Donoghue writes, "it may be prudent to distinguish between Theory as an institution, which comes armed with the coercive force of a capital letter, and theories, which are more modest plays of mind, local notions."[485] Likewise, many of the theories helping archivists are there for forming a perspective that helps one to approach huge and often seemingly hopeless tasks – like appraisal.

Students bring with them an immense range of career objectives. Some want to work in local historical societies with personal manuscripts collections, while others desire to work in larger corporate or government organizations. While there are some *common* principles for *all* records, how can you teach them basic administrative approaches when there may be some who will work nearly by themselves and others who might join a staff of dozens? The answer, of course, is that the educator picks an orientation and tries to factor in other scenarios and issues. A well-designed practicum can help, but if it is poorly designed and offered it detracts from the course work – using up valuable course time and more formal orientation to archival principles and practices. The value of the practicum may also be neutralized because a student could do a fieldwork in one kind of institution and wind up working in a very different environment. The only surety that this would not occur is if both educators and site supervisors of student

---

[483] A good discussion of such issues is Terry Eastwood, "Nurturing Archival Education in the University," *American Archivist* 51 (Summer 1988): 228-251.

[484] I wrote about my experience in teaching this course in the concluding chapter of my *Documenting Localities: A Practical Model for American Archivists and Manuscripts Curators* (Metuchen, New Jersey: Scarecrow Press and Society of American Archivists, 1996).

[485] Denis Donoghue, *The Practice of Reading* (New Haven: Yale University Press, 1998), p. 21.

internships are in tune in focusing on records and record-keeping systems, a somewhat theoretical approach that seems counter to what the archival practicum has traditionally supported.

A similar problem occurs among the educators themselves. Nearly all graduate archival educators bring their *own* interests and experiences to the classroom as well. Although it is not nearly as bad as thirty years ago when all educators were adjuncts, there are nevertheless serious limitations if an educator relies too much on his or her own experience. The point is, *everyone's* limitations are substantial – the only solution is to go beyond practice to theory and methodology and, even more preferable, to go to multiple faculty arrangements to bring in a range of experience, professional practices, and disciplinary orientations. Others have struggled with similar problems. Terrence McDonald laments that historians themselves have provided a "bad example." They "have for the most part refused to put their own practices at risk by much methodological or theoretical writing, preferring instead to know history when they see it and therefore being more proficient at boundary maintenance – identifying what is 'not history' – than at theorized reflection on their own practice."[486] The same problem has occurred when graduate archival education is supported primarily by adjuncts or if the practicum becomes the focal point of such education.

These kinds of issues should get archival educators thinking about the limitations of practice as part of an educational process. Each institution can possess different emphases or even missions (think of the differences between for-profit institutional archives, government archives, and collecting repositories). Missions transform how one approaches appraisal, descriptive services, and access, and if we send a student out into the field, he or she will be exposed to these differences. The student will only be able to understand such differences if educators prepare them for this. The problem gets murkier. In most institutions, arrangement/description and reference/access remain the strongest and most dominant functions. Are these the most important archival functions. Appraisal, with implications for the nature of every other archival function and with a unique role in an era buried in information would seem to be a more crucial function. However, despite a rich debate about appraisal, this function seems to be a neglected one in the field.

Limitations of Practice. We can state similar concerns about administration and public programs. Archivists in for-profit, corporate environments

---

[486] Terrence McDonald, ed., *The Historic Turn in the Human Sciences* (Ann Arbor: University of Michigan Press, 1996), p. 7.

probably should not emphasize arrangement and description, needing to target other critical problems such as designing and implementing electronic information systems supporting archival and records management, ensuring the use of records for accountability and evidence purposes, and contributing to the viability of corporate memory for ongoing work in their organizations. Some of this can be learned on-the-job. It is more likely, however, that such matters will only be learned in the classroom where students obtain a sufficient dose of directed reading in and discussion about organizational management and related research.

The limitations of practice are revealed in other ways. A number of our programs rely on adjunct educators, but how much time can any adjunct put into developing and teaching courses? These individuals reflect their own professional responsibilities, both to be efficient with their time as well as to build on their own knowledge base (based on their practice). Many consider this as the strength adjuncts bring to archival education, but the result may be little more than an unwieldy apprenticeship system, especially as many adjuncts have little interaction in or responsibility for the academic departments in which they teach. Then there are the students. Can they learn by bad experience, relate classroom learning to experience gained in their fieldwork, and relate archival and other records-oriented literature to whatever experience they gain as part of their educational programs? To do all this, we need more comprehensive courses providing opportunities for reflection by both students and faculty. For example, an extensive orientation to the history of records, record-keeping and archives can provide a much-needed context for comprehending current records issues and challenges, but this is not likely to happen if the education programs are severely limited in courses or concentrated on experience.[487]

Finally, there is the experience that the field requires for hiring. Experience is preferred above all other attributes, but how do you assess the quality of experience and the ability of students to relate one experience to a very different one? We are at a transition stage. Experiential requirements are a hangover from the old pre-1980 days when education was thin. Certification, with its reliance on experience, is another tension reflecting the particular professional stage we are at on the eve of a new century. Pre-appointment education, at a more rigorous level, is needed and it is developing. There is the problem of whether this kind of education will

---

[487] I discussed the value of this perspective in my "The History of Primary Sources in Graduate Education: An Archival Perspective," *Special Collections* 4, no. 2 (1990): 39-78.

be available to everyone, given the relatively small number of comprehensive programs. However, we can recognize that all archivists are not the same, and we can compensate for this by offering stronger advanced workshops with more stringent requirements for those who can take them.[488]

Archival educators need to formalize it as *real* graduate education rather than allow it to remain as technical training or a form of remedial education. Some educators have been very careful to make distinctions between the more formalized internship and the less structured practicum: A "practicum is used to refer to programs of briefer scope and duration involving less responsibility for theory formation and more emphasis on skill development." An "internship is defined ... as a full professional experience involving all phases of an assignment from theorization to application."[489] The archival practicum needs to evolve into something like more formal internships if it is to have a key educational role. The practicum might be tied to more formal research, leading in turn to publishable research benefiting both students *and* profession.[490]

There are other options for strengthening this part of our graduate programs. We can build experience into these programs by requiring students to work in part-time archives positions, either paid or as volunteers, while they attend classes. Educators can then develop applications for relating students' work experiences to what is being discussed in class. The important matter is that there be a synergy between the experience and classroom discussion, so that the experience can be critically analyzed in a manner enriching classroom discussions. There could be a formal course focused on helping students relate theory to practice.

---

[488] The need for more rigorous notions of continuing education can be seen in my "Continuing Education and Special Collections Professionals: The Need for Rethinking," *Rare Books and Manuscripts Librarianship*, 10, no. 2 (1995): 78-96. The Society of American Archivists also has issued "Guidelines for the Development of Post-Appointment and Continuing Education and Training Programs," at http://www.archivists.org/PACE97.html.

[489] For such distinctions, refer to John Hempstead, "Internship and Practical Application in Educating School Library Personnel."

[490] Think of the role more research-oriented internships could do for the profession. Since Paul Conway's call for such research -- his "Facts and Frameworks: An Approach to Studying the Users of Archives," *American Archivist* 49 (Fall 1986): 393-407 – we have had a modicum of research responses. Conway provides a template for applied research easily built into a fieldwork experience and providing a useful bridge between student, site supervisor, and educator.

For students to obtain credit for fieldwork, they would be required to attend this class along with fellow students who are also taking the practicum option or meeting the practicum requirement. Students would be asked to read some seminal works on theory and practice and the nature of professional practice and education.[491] Case studies, especially those supplementing or amplifying what students experience in fieldwork, also would help.

The Big R and LIS Fieldwork. We do not have a substantial literature about the practicum in the archives field, but we can learn from research about the practicum in library and information science education. The research studies completed on internships and practica in library and information science education reveal a consensus on the need for a balance between theory and practice, but a lack of agreement about how that balance should be achieved. A large portion of the prospective employers of special librarians surveyed perceived that an internship or practicum was an essential part of their basic education. Additional studies reveal that other prospective employers of librarians as well as students also desire an education that combines theory and practice. Still other studies have struggled with how such internships or practica should be integrated into library education. One study of accredited graduate library schools notes that the main reason for excluding field experience was not "primarily in the question of its value, but in the difficulties of administration, and in its academic priority in an already crowded curriculum."[492] These research studies reveal a number of issues needing further analysis, as Grotzinger concludes: "the crucial question, which this and prior studies have failed to answer is: Would the graduate of the accredited library school be more effective or qualified on the job if he completed a field experience as part of his study?" The same question can

---

[491] For example, students could profitably benefit by reading works such as Andrew Abbott, *The System of Professions: An Essay on the Division of Expert Labor* (Chicago: University of Chicago Press, 1988); Steven Brint, *In an Age of Experts: The Changing Role of Professionals in Politics and Public Life* (Princeton: Princeton University Press, 1994); Howard Gardner, *Creating Minds: An Anatomy of Creativity Seen Through the Lives of Freud, Einstein, Picasso, Stravinsky, Eliot, Graham, and Gandhi* (New York: Basic Books. 1993); Howard Gardner, *Leading Minds: An Anatomy of Leadership* (New York: Basic Books, 1995); and William M. Sullivan, *Work and Integrity: The Crisis and Promise of Professionalism in America* (New York: Harper Business, 1995).

[492] Laurel Grotzinger, "The Status of 'Practicum' in Graduate Library Schools," *Journal of Education for Librarianship* 11 (Spring 1971): 338.

be asked about archivists. Conducting such studies is extremely important.[493]

Thinking Like a Records Professional. Archival educators understand that there is a vast difference between education and training and that their job is to educate students to *think* like archivists. The graduates of our programs must be prepared to handle a rapidly changing world. The practicum, sitting loosely within graduate education as it does (as a fossil of earlier educational programs), possesses many limitations. The practicum is focused on what is going on at present. In most cases, it has little connection to what came before or what might be developing. At the least, the practicum should be diverted away from arrangement and description work *unless* this work is involved in new standards or major evaluative and decision-making processes. Students need to be placed within institutions in order to learn how archivists grapple with crucial challenges, relate to their parent organizations, and serve the needs of researchers.

The practicum is also a potential liability if educators see their role as change-agents in the field. When I teach appraisal, for example, my focus is on orienting students to understand the basic principles, methodologies, *and* problems associated with how appraisal is carried out. In this area, it is almost impossible not to envision oneself as a change agent since appraisal is often ignored in the field. We can certainly see how we need to look similarly at other critical matters such as electronic records management (where there are few programs at all) or public outreach and advocacy (where there is the need for stronger, more effective efforts).

Conclusion: A New Way to Consider Archival Education: Archival Studies in iSchools. American graduate archives programs have been connected to library schools and then library and information science schools for more than a half-century, competing for a while with history departments but emerging as fully embedded in the former by the 1990s. But there is a new kid on the block – iSchools (Information Schools). How are graduate programs in archival studies affected by the transition of many of the traditional library and library and information science (LIS) schools to the newly emerging iSchools?

I won't belabor this point of a new association of archival studies with, perhaps, a new kind of professional school because I have written, in collaboration with one of the pioneers of the iSchool movement, more fully

---

[493] "The Status of 'Practicum,'" pp. 338-39.

about this topic elsewhere.[494] As archival studies programs developed over the past few decades, digital recordkeeping slowly emerged as the most pressing concern in equipping individuals to function as archivists. Christine Borgman matter-of-factly states, "Preservation and management of digital content are probably the most difficult challenges to be addressed in building an advanced information infrastructure for scholarly applications."[495] Archival studies, like library and information science, is interdisciplinary in its examining, critiquing, and exploring the nature of records, recordkeeping, and the archive.

While the emergence of iSchools as a consortium is relatively recent, their origins reflect a more sustained dialogue among faculty and deans of a number of library and information science and related programs around the broader implications of information technologies for their curricula, their institutions, and the information professions. The iSchools also are committed, more so than their predecessors, to creating "an intellectual space where true interdisciplinarity plays out," seeking to "create an environment where issues of information are addressed systematically, regardless of disciplinary heritage or presumed 'ownership'." This requires the schools to be in a "constant state of adaptation within their core competencies, while building necessary bridges among disciplines."[496] Archival studies are clearly a vital participant in this interdisciplinary dialogue. And assuming that the iSchool movement does not lead to the jettisoning of critically important traditional knowledge of the old library school, we should have some promising days ahead.

---

[494] Richard J. Cox and Ronald L. Larsen, "iSchools and Archival Studies," *Archival Science* 8 (2008):307-326.
[495] Christine Borgman, *Scholarship in the Digital Age: Information, Infrastructure, and the Internet* (Cambridge, MA: MIT, 2007), p. 7.
[496] Ronald L. Larsen, "iSchools," *Encyclopedia of Library and Information Sciences*, forthcoming; also available at http://www.ischools.org/site/history/

Chapter Seven

Looking for Our Way (Reading and Writing) in Professional Schools

Introduction: Doom, Gloom, and Full Speed Ahead. Professional schools have had a prominent place in the modern university since the late nineteenth century in the United States. When we consider European versions of professional schools, we can find them dating back to the early nineteenth century and, occasionally, even into the seventeenth century. Despite such a history, surprisingly, there are not as many analyses of the role of the professional school in the university as one might suspect. Some of the ruminations about the university by individuals like Derek Bok provide chapters reflecting on such academic units in the larger context of the university. Some scholars, such as Edward W. Said, have written assessments of the role of the faculty as public intellectuals contrary to the role of practical, professional training.[497] Such efforts are by no means new, although very different in tone from earlier assessments. One of the older analyses of professional education is by Edgar H. Schein, considering many of the issues remaining relevant today: the changing nature of work and society; the definition of a profession and professional education; the changing needs of students; and calling for new kinds of professional education requiring different learning approaches and faculty.[498]

For many, the emergence of professional schools is synonymous with the modern university, while for others these same schools, and the splintering of the university into many different disciplines, represents a subverting of university goals. In the late twentieth century, there began an effort to reunify our approaches to the generation of knowledge and the training of specialists, namely the efforts to establish interdisciplinary

---

[497] Edward W. Said, *Representations of the Intellectual* (New York: Vintage Books, 1996) and *Humanism and Democratic Criticism* (New York: Columbia University Press, 2004).
[498] Edgar H. Schein, *Professional Education: Some New Directions* (New York: McGraw-Hill Book Co., 1972).

programs (even though the success of these efforts is uneven).[499] Now it seems that everyone going to the university, whether in the humanities or in a professional school, is chasing credential(s) to ply a trade.

We can accept that the LIS schools have had an interdisciplinary foundation, at least when we examine the typical backgrounds of their faculty – history, anthropology, cognitive sciences, electrical engineering, computer science, philosophy, political science, and, yes, library and information science. Have these schools been all that successful in building connections across the university? One argument, among many, for the iSchool movement, has been the construction of a more interdisciplinary experience enabling stronger networking with the rest of the university. This implies a lack of success in the past, especially when considering the pile of traditional LIS programs closing in the 1980s into the early 1990s. What aspects of the new movement suggest a better chance for success in the future?

Can't Get No Satisfaction. When reflecting on the role of faculty, whether in professional schools or in some other part of the university, the matter of their satisfaction often becomes a topic of discussion. Faculty members complain as much about their lot in life as students complain about reading loads and writing assignments; such concerns have been part of the university since its inception.[500] In one analysis of a faculty survey, it is reported that "public institutions were regarded as easier places to balance personal and professional obligations. Young professors at public colleges were more likely than those at private institutions to agree that they had support, from their institution and their departmental colleagues, for having

---

[499] Julie Thompson Klein, *Interdisciplinarity: History, Theory, and Practice* (Detroit: Wayne State University Press, 1990) and *Crossing Boundaries: Knowledge, Disciplinarities, and Interdisciplinarities* (Charlottesville: University Press of Virginia, 1996).

[500] Jason M. Breslow describes a report revealing "junior faculty members at public colleges rate their institutions higher than do their counterparts at private colleges," whereas "private institutions get higher marks than public ones in young professors' ratings of job satisfaction over all." The findings come from the "latest in a series of surveys by the Collaborative on Academic Careers in Higher Education, or Coache, which is a unit of the Harvard Graduate School of Education. More than 7,000 full-time, tenure-track faculty members at 77 colleges and universities participated in the online survey, which was conducted from October to the following January in both 2005 and 2006." Jason M. Breslow, "Young Professors at Private Institutions Report Greater Overall Level of Job Satisfaction," *Chronicle of Higher Education*, September 18, 2007, http://chronicle.com/daily/2007/09/2007091808n.htm, accessed September 18, 2007.

CHAPTER SEVEN

and raising children." Apparently "professors at private institutions seem to get more out of 'the nature of their work.' In terms of their teaching duties, for example, faculty members at private institutions get more satisfaction from such areas as the level and number of courses that they teach, the degree of influence they have over courses, and the number and quality of their students." We learn more about such feelings, since "professors at private institutions report feeling better about such areas as the amount of time they have for research, the influence they have over their research, and the amount of external funds they are expected to find."[501] I guess there is nothing too surprising about this.

I haven't seen any recent job satisfaction studies involving library and information science, but it would be interesting to consider just how they see themselves as they balance research, teaching, and service in a more complicated set of challenges. In today's modern university, faculties often receive mixed signals about what is the appropriate balance between these responsibilities. The kind of self-evaluation system put into place in recent years at most professional schools is an effort to be clearer and to enable faculty to sort out such issues. However, on a regular basis, discussion emerges suggesting that this is not all that clear. It may be that people who tend to become faculty, those often with a particular driving mission or a personal sense of responsibility about what they believe is their role in the university, profession, and society, may bring with them the seed of their own satisfaction or dissatisfaction. If one's predisposition is to question, challenge, probe, and speculate what they see as professional or societal assumptions, it is likely in such a quest for change that they might sow their own seeds for being unhappy (always wanting something more and better) in their position in the university. Individuals preparing to be faculty need to sort through such matters, wrestling with their own aims and agendas, so that they can come to terms with what they see as their real missions. In these personal struggles, there is both personal and professional satisfaction to be found.

What Do I Do? I have had a sometimes funny, sometimes disturbing, running conversation with a friend about what I do. At first blush, this is an annoying question because I am a professor and my young friend aspired (now he is one) to be a professor as well. Why, then, would he pose such a question? After all, I have achieved – rising to the uppermost rank of a full

---

[501] The full report, "Tenure-Track Faculty Job Satisfaction Survey: Highlights Report," is available on the Coache site http://gseacademic.harvard.edu/~coache/.

professor with tenure – what anyone who considers an academic career most wants to possess. Given that securing tenure stream university positions, let alone tenure itself, is becoming a more elusive prize in the present university as business, where students are customers, courses and the knowledge of faculty are commodities, and the fiscal bottom line is the focus of both faculty and administrators, why would my young friend ask me such a question. In hindsight, I originally wrote these ideas in a journal I kept a few years ago, but I now see that his (and my) confusion may result from my being in a *professional* school, the venue of the conflicted modern university most buffeted by confused signals between education and training, generating revenue and contributing to scholarship, and doing stuff and just reflecting on the state of the world. No wonder he had *lots* of questions about what I was doing in the university.

The impetus for the posing of his question was his visit to my home library. I have a pleasant study, perhaps the nicest room in my century old working class house in that quintessential working class city, Pittsburgh. The room was a reflection of Michael Pollan's observation about the nature of reading, perceiving it as a "vaguely sensual, slightly indulgent pleasure, and one that had very little to do with the acquisition of information. Rather than a means to an end, the deep piles of words on the page comprised for me a kind of soothing environment, a plush cushion into which sometimes I could barely wait to sink my head. More often than not, I could remember almost nothing the moment I lifted myself out of the newspaper or magazine or paperback in which I'd been immersed. Not that I usually bothered to try. Mostly I just let the print wash over me, as if it were indeed warm water, destined to swirl down the drain of my forgetfulness."[502] Three-quarters of the room is shelved over from floor to ceiling, the remainder of the wall space painted a Martha Stewart color (my wife's idea) appropriately named "bookbinding green" (and yes, I like the color as well). In the center of one wall is a gas-fired fireplace. At one time most of the other available wall space was covered with reproductions of gargoyles or framed prints and photographs of writers at work producing manuscripts. Now, in a losing effort to declutter our lives (losing as I continue to add books and music cds at a ridiculous rate), there is a mirror and two eighteenth century Chippendale prints, one of a library table and the other of a writing table, appropriately mimicking the room's use. The pine floor used to be bare and stained, but as it was generally rough and the

---

[502] Michael Pollan, *A Place of My Own: The Education of an Amateur Builder* (New York: Random House, 1997), p. 54.

CHAPTER SEVEN 185

object of my wife's scorn, we covered the room in a neutral Berber carpet. The furniture used to be a mixture of antique reproductions, cast offs, and Pottery Barn or Bombay Company instant collectibles, but we shed this furniture in favor of a wonderful oak Mission desk made at about the same time the house was built. We found a Mission side chair, and we added a couple of small Mission side tables, an Eastlake chair (subsequently given away), and a wicker chair (both of us have discovered the wonderful, comfortable and utilitarian Mission style of a century ago, leading us to search for additional pieces as we shed other belongings). The study is not a room that should be featured in *Architectural Digest*, but it is a comfortable room for working, reading, writing, and thinking, with a Victorian feel suggesting photographs of the period. Lately, mimicking the Arts and Crafts aesthetic, I have covered a good part of the walls with my own landscape paintings.

The library beckons to all aspiring academics and scholars, but not necessarily for any of the reasons that I have described. What beckons is that the room is filled with books, and it is these books that prompt my young friend's question. Filling a small Mission bookcase are several shelves of books about documents, record systems, and the history of writing. As you move left to the first major bookshelf you find books piled high about the state of American higher education, museums, photographs, lithography and printmaking, maps and cartography, and a host of other subjects. As the eye roams we see large clusters of books on the history of ideas, historiography and historical research methods, public memory, the concept of time, the history of films, the history of books, privacy and security in the modern information age, and the history of religion. These books are the building blocks of my life, at least that part of my life concerned with my career and the academy. Yet, it takes a bit of sleuthing before one can guess just what my academic career is about, as science and the humanities seem to crowd onto each other with no unifying point. Nevertheless, you can learn about who I am by carefully examining the books on the shelves. Alberto Manguel has written that reading is like breathing and that we are what we read.[503] As reading is so essential to life, you can get at a person's inner self by examining what they read.

My Library and What I Do. The library in my home is not a rare book room or special collections, saving that the books are in various ways *special* to me. The books blare out with their mish-mash of colors, bindings, cloth and soft backs; there are few rare or unique items in this room. This is a

---

[503] Alberto Manguel, *A History of Reading* (New York: Viking, 1996), pp. 7, 173.

working library. Nearly any book pulled off of the shelves will produce a book with interlining, annotations, scraps of notepapers, and other indicators that the library is in practical use. Still, the eclectic nature of the titles will make someone, like my friend, wonder just what the practical ends are intended to be. If there is some guiding theory in the selection of the books, it is not obvious in their organization. The only clue seems to be the odd volume with my name on the spine and *archives* or *records* figuring into the title. Indeed, if someone pulled down one of my own books, they could match my library with citations, markings with quotations – and they could begin to see that there was some rationale in the library's contents. In some ways, my reading reflects that of others who have tended to read broadly, even indiscriminately. Jill Kerr Conway remembers, "I was educating myself through reading everything within reach – a topsy-turvey mixture of children's books, my mother's books on current affairs, war correspondents' accounts of the war, my father's books on stock breeding..." "I read omnivorously," Conway continues, "everything that came to hand, and through reading my mother's books I asked questions about politics and history which both parents took for signs of high intelligence."[504] Of course, some mystery would have to continue, since my over-sized university office is also filled with books, journals, off prints, and additional evidence of some kind of academic career. At this other office, the clue to its mystery would be found in examining the syllabi of the courses I teach. In the oddly ugly and now thoroughly dysfunctional building is an office that is the heart and mind of a teacher. Scribblings in many of those books are clues to lectures, meetings with students, and faculty service of one sort or another.

"What do you do?" echoes in this room because the topics of the books in this library do not seem to reflect the needs or interests of a professor who teaches in a school of library and information sciences. Where are the how-to manuals, the professional textbooks, and the professional journals that might seem a better fit for someone teaching in a school concerned with giving individuals credentials to earn a living? My library does not fit the expectations of someone who is on the faculty of a professional school, or, perhaps, it does not match with the stereotype of such a school, a stereotype held both within and without the university. As it turns out, it seems, the *real* question might be, "What's wrong with professional schools?" And this kind of question ties into a larger problem.

---

[504] Jill Kerr Conway, *The Road from Coorain* (New York: Vintage, 1990), pp. 4, 65.

We have lost sight of the fact that reading is "magical"[505] or that "Real books are more than mere repositories for information. They are objects," argues Douglas Rushkoff, "and they are meant to be experienced as such. The function of a dictionary is to provide the meaning of a word. The function of a book is to provide a reading experience. It's more than a transmission of data: It's a transmission of essence."[506] The enchantment of the modern Information Age has withered such notions, no matter how romantic they might seem.

All of this explains my personal library. All of the books have been assembled to support a deeper understanding of records, archives, and the people and institutions creating and collecting them. They can be overwhelming, and remind us that we are deep into a different kind of information era. Maureen Corrigan senses, "I can't imagine living in rooms without books ..., but ... I also think the comfort books offer is qualified. All those voices, all those thoughts, all those reminders of how much there is to read and how little time there is to read it. Mentally and physically, books can be oppressive, even hazardous."[507] Such a deeper comprehension is necessary, for sure, for teaching and researching. But as I have built this collection of books over the years, my reading and scholarly interests seem to have separated me more from the typical faculty found in a professional school focused on library and information sciences. There is, of course, the debate about whether archival studies belongs in the information sciences, but that argument can't proceed too far since records possess a content that is information. In my own work, I have tried to make distinctions between the kind of information found in records and the manner in which information is often viewed in the professional schools where I travel and communicate, but there is little question as to the fact that archival information is an important component of information. Moreover, information scientists and librarians need to be concerned with other matters such as preservation, authenticity, reliability, and accuracy – all hallmarks of the principles supporting the administration and study of archives. The source of the problems I am detecting must reside elsewhere.

Peering Over Your Shoulder. We can see where our priorities rest by walking around and looking at each other's desks in our workplaces and our homes. Besides thinking about working with our new students and having a

---

[505] Lynne Sharon Schwartz, *Ruined by Reading* (Boston: Beacon Press, 1996), p.19.
[506] Douglas Rushkoff in Kevin Smokler, ed., *Bookmark Now: Writing in Unreaderly Times* (New York: Basic Books, 2005), p. 236.
[507] Maureen Corrigan, *Leave Me Alone, I'm Reading: Finding and Losing Myself in Books* (New York: Random House, 2005), p. 56.

fresh start at the beginning of a new academic year, many of us are also glad to start with a clean desk. Perhaps, we should not worry too much about such matters. Desks and their contents have been the subject of literary and other discourse, as we examine their messy desktops, and surprises of old documents, decayed food, various office supplies, and almost anything else imaginable. Some perceive creativity in the clutter. And, for sure, our desks, those of faculty, are often cluttered with the notes, sources, and inspirations we use for teaching. Indeed, we could extend this cluttered desktop to our computers. "For me, reading today," Alberto Manguel ponders, "the notes I take while reading are held in the vicarious memory of my word-processor. Like the Renaissance scholar who could wander at will through the chambers of his memory palace to retrieve a quotation or a name, I blindly enter the electronic maze buzzing behind my screen. With the help of its memory I can remember more accurately (if accuracy is important) and more copiously (if quantity seems valuable) than my illustrious ancestors, but I must still be the one to find an order in the notes and to draw conclusions."[508] We can discover fragments of half-written essays, random notes, partially completed outlines, unsent letters and memorandum all on our computers just as we might once have found them in our desks. As an educator of archivists and records managers, I am particularly sensitive to what sits around on desks, but, at the beginning of any new term, I take more solace that my messy desk might be the source of insight – especially as I go into my first class session and need fresh insights in how to educate these students. Along with an increased commitment to working and communicating with each other, we need a new resolve to make connections between the divergent documentary sources of our respective fields and between the functions of teaching and research.

Over one long weekend I rediscovered why I like certain aspects of the academic lifestyle. Having turned in final grades, I declared that I was done until the next term and headed into the couple of weeks of Christmas holidays. Technically, our holiday would not start for another week, but having fulfilled all my requirements for teaching, I decided I needed a break and shut down for a little bit of extra time away from the school. Doing this is not easy, or not as easy as it seems. As I finished my teaching responsibilities, a succession of emails and telephone calls poured into my office, beckoning me to attend sundry faculty meetings. I declined. It is one of the reasons, maybe the best one, why tenure is worth protecting.

---

[508] Manguel, *History of Reading*, pp. 61-62.

Keeping up public appearances and even a sense of guilt conspire against taking such actions. You create the perception that you are not a team player or that you dislike your colleagues or that somehow you are lazy. Yet over the first three days of my "break," I hosted a party for my students scattering for the holidays, attended a couple of holiday open houses, and read four books. Reading and reflection are what separates the academic from many other professionals. I read in an eclectic fashion, looking for ideas, insights, and inspiration that I can use in my own teaching, research, and writing. But a life of books is not always equated with being a professor, even on the inside of the university. There are different perceptions about such reading, of course. Lynne Schwartz thinks "reading at random – letting desire land – feels like the most faithful kind."[509] Harold Bloom seems to agree, to an extent, when he writes, "We ought to read for many purposes, and to gain copious benefits, but the cultivation of an individual consciousness is certainly a prime purpose, and a major benefit, of deep reading. Zest and insight: these are the attributes of the solitary reader's consciousness that are most enhanced by reading. Social information, whether past or contemporary, seems to me a peripheral gain of reading, and political awareness an even more tenuous dividend."[510] I read for all these reasons – and more.

Do Faculty Read? Two events come to mind. The first occurred at dinner with a speaker of a forum co-sponsored by our school. The convivial dinner, including the speaker and a few other faculty and students, along with the dean of our school, was proceeding nicely. At one point it became obvious that the speaker and myself were prodigious and equally eclectic readers and soon we were swapping book titles and capsule book reviews. I was stimulated. Then the conversation took an odd turn, when it became obvious that the two of us also bought and annotated our books. One of the others, listening quietly for a while, chided us for not using libraries. At once I became aware of what separates a classroom teacher from a university administrator, since I bought and built a library to support my teaching. Books were not props or furniture (as Nicholson Baker once reminded us) nor were they merely crutches to cover my insecurities (as a friend once counseled me), but they were real working tools, my box of hammers and screwdrivers for building courses, constructing and deconstructing theories, and fabricating lectures. What was missing here was a sense of how we transform the books we possess. As Manguel

---

[509] Schwartz, *Ruined*, p. 106.
[510] Harold Bloom, *How to Read and Why* (New York: Scribner, 2000), p. 173.

contends, "And while Gutenberg's printing press, recreating the miracle of the loaves and fishes, multiplied one same text a thousand times, every reader proceeds to individualize his or her copy with scribbles, stains, markings of different sorts, so that no copy, once read, is identical to another."[511] There was something insidious in the dinner comments, however, suggesting that books were really not so important for one teaching in a school of information sciences (one still stubbornly hanging onto libraries as a venue for its graduates). The dangerous aspect of such a commentary was more dramatically played out in another incident.

The other incident is both more humorous but somehow sadder. In the mid-1990s I embarked on teaching one of the common core course requirements for all masters students in our library and information science degree program, wandering outside of the normal area of my own specialization. After I handed out the course syllabus and reviewed the course requirements, many of my students rebelled, upset about what they perceived to be a heavy reading load (the equivalent of a book a week – not at all an onerous reading requirement for a graduate course). I discovered, very quickly, that this was a load that was substantially heavier than what most of the students in the program seemed accustomed to having (this has since changed). The number of students dropped by half in a week, and I discovered that one of my colleagues encouraged students to consider dropping the course. What was the basis for this individual's activity? What was her motive? She openly declared that "library students don't learn by reading books," an assessment that sent me into spasms of laughter. Why were they here, then? Students, even in library school or any other professional school, learn by reading books (and they learn by reading many other publications as well). The irony of all this was, of course, if they did not learn by reading books why would they want to work in a library, a place that still mostly revolved around the printed word?

Even with the competition of e-books and e-journals, and most certainly the challenges posed by the Internet/World Wide Web, students in this kind of professional school need to learn about printed books, the five hundred year information revolution showing little sign of losing its significance. The technology of book publishing and the economics of printing had been transformed, but the mechanism of reading persisted much as it had since Augustine discovered his mentor silently perusing a book. Perhaps my colleague was correct, suggesting that the students

---

[511] Alberto Manguel, *Into the Looking-Glass Wood: Essays on Books, Readings, and the World* (San Diego: Harcourt, Inc., 1998), p. 269.

entering into the school had long ago abandoned the art of reading. Bloom muses, "A childhood largely spent watching television yields to an adolescence with a computer, and the university receives a student unlikely to welcome the suggestion that we must endure our going hence even as our going hither: ripeness is all. Reading falls apart, and much of the self scatters with it."[512] One of our responsibilities must be to transform students' attitudes about reading, as well as to assist them to gain a greater appreciation of the legacy and continuing utility of print.

Perhaps what is being reflected here is the unnecessary bureaucratization of the university, a process that is more likely to have a negative impact on professional schools with their focus on practice, revenue, and anything but scholarship. Higher education has often been criticized for not extending enough administrative control over faculty, but there are reasons for why such controls should be loose or flexible. As Donald Kennedy explains, "there are powerful reasons for the degree of freedom that faculty members enjoy. Creativity does not prosper, nor does entrepreneurial initiative flourish, under firm bureaucratic control."[513] The problem may be that creativity is now being harnessed completely to revenue generating schemes, rather than more traditional functions like teaching or research. Professional schools, often seen as cash cows, have little room for being creative in this sense, unless creativity is defined in more mercenary terms. Professional school faculty, those who are committed to the well being of their field, often suffer because their disciplines are interested in practical applications, the production of practitioners, and basic manual writings. We tend to consign creativity to other activities. Deborah Haynes argues, for example, that "Becoming an artist is not a mysterious process, though it is challenging. An aesthetic education requires intention, concentration, discipline, perseverance, and more than anything else, the will to learn."[514] Yet, writing, even the professional kind, and certainly teaching, are activities requiring a healthy dose of creative expression.

Reading for the Big Picture: An Example. Reading is essential for understanding what any information technology represents. James Dewar's article on the printing press and the Internet looks for historical contexts by

---

[512] Bloom, *How To Read*, p. 23.
[513] Kennedy, *Academic Duty* (Cambridge: Harvard University Press, 1997), p. 139.
[514] Deborah Haynes, *Art Lessons: Meditations on the Creative Life* (Boulder, CO: Westview Press, 2003), p. 16.

which the present era can be effectively understood.[515] Dewar turns to historical explanation because "it is difficult to see where the information age is leading because the technologies fueling it are still being developed and at a furious rate [and] ... because of the breadth of the impact of information technologies to date." Dewar finds Elizabeth Eisenstein's explanation of the impact of the printing press to be uncannily parallel to today, leading to a final argument for an unregulated Internet because the future will be dominated by unintended consequences and take a long time to develop. Dewar believes that "there has been only one comparable event in the records history of communications" to the recent revolution in the information technologies – the printing press. What makes the printing press comparable is the "one-to-many communications capability" since, in his opinion, "it is networked computers that define the information age." Where Dewar goes wrong is his using history to *predict*. He concludes with some discussion about policy implications, primarily arguing that the Internet should be unregulated and that we should be open to experimentation to gain additional understanding about the consequences of the Internet's use.

History is, of course, a messy process. And looking at different eras can also show that human actions, such as networking, too often attributed to the power of new technologies actually represent basic human needs and endeavors.[516] All of this may be even more relevant as we participate in various university meetings. Will we recognize anything that is being said about us, or will we find history being re-invented? Hopefully, this will be a time to discuss ideas for the future with full recognition of both our strengths and weaknesses – precisely the kind of perspective we can gain by looking at our history. But we tend not to want to do this, because history is so complicated. Let's keep things simple, and let's sell our product – credentials for individuals wanting relevant jobs in an era built on the uses and misuses of information technology. It is also the result of our own poor reading, inadequate research, and meager efforts to write for professional colleagues and the broader public. It is also the result of being caught up in the temptations of our present information age rather than being critics or observers of it.

---

[515] James Dewar, "The Information Age and the Printing Press: Looking Backward to See Ahead," *Ubiquity* no. 25 (August 15 - 21, 2000) at http://www.acm.org/ubiquity/views/j_dewar_1.html.
[516] At least, this is what I argued in my response to Dewar -- "The Information Age and History: Looking Backward to See Us," *Ubiquity* (26 September-October 4, 2000), available at http://www.acm.org/ubiquity/.

We might not expect to find such dissension among the ranks of faculty in professional schools such as library and information science. Yet, there is just as much dissension there as elsewhere, although the dissension tends not to make headlines or be reflective of the kinds of debates that became characterized with the moniker of "culture wars." The source of the dissension also may be very different. Dissension with a particular professional school is the result of the faculty members' disparate academic backgrounds and professional orientations. In the typical library and information science school we have individuals with backgrounds in engineering, information science, computer science, telecommunications, library science, the humanities, and the sciences (and as we move to iSchools the range of disciplinary backgrounds expands). All are focused on some dimension of understanding information, but the faculty represents a very wide range of ways to do this.

There are other continuing tensions within such schools. The differences between library and information science can be vast, with one far more committed to people and applications and the other to tools and technologies. One might also argue that library science might be an oxymoron. Given the library field's orientation to people and service, just what is the dimension of such activity that deems itself to be a science? There have been arguments that bibliometrics, the study and measure of the use of sources, or classification, the organization of human knowledge, constitute the essence of such a science, but there are problems here as well. How many working librarians practice bibliometric analysis? And, to boot, the teaching of and research on classification and cataloguing has seemed to be more of a dying topic within schools educating future librarians. Even information scientists can't get off lightly here. There are innumerable definitions of "information," and even where there are individuals who claim to be able to measure and quantify information, there are many competing notions of information itself. The danger here is that the immersion in the world of tools and techniques may diminish any enthusiasm, on the part of faculty and students, for something as basic and essential as reading. This has happened elsewhere. In literature programs the biggest problem was that a "whole generation of professional students of literature have turned away from reading," because of a shift to techniques of deconstructing literature. As Robert Alter reflects, "One need not argue for an attitude of unreserved adulation toward literature, but without some form of passionate engagement in literary works, without a deep sense of deep pleasure in the experience of reading, the whole enterprise of teaching and writing about literature quickly becomes pointless."[517]

Turning Diversity Into Strength. My own sense is that diversity breeds strength (isn't this pretty fundamental to the notion of the modern university?), both for teaching students and for interdisciplinary research, but it may also be the source of internal weaknesses in these schools. We often tend to read very different literatures, work on very different problems, and often hang out in very different professional and scholarly circles. For years, for example, I have spent more time building scholarly connections with others outside my school working on problems similar to my own areas of interest and effort. But other faculty members in my school are also doing this, and this tends to weaken any school's infrastructure, not in the kind of open hostility we see in English departments, but in more subtle ways (if we don't seek ways to unify ourselves). We become fragmented and we stay fragmented, and our school is often the worse for all this (this seems, at the moment, to be rapidly changing in a positive fashion). People who ought to be talking with each other seem to avoid opportunities that would have them doing precisely this. And I do not mean the normal faculty meetings, faculty retreats, and other regular meetings. These meetings never provide the opportunity for sharing ideas or for discussing research and scholarship. They are the venues for politicking and for filling in the blanks in strategic plans and budget requests; while these may be necessary, they are hardly very useful for enhancing the level of discourse one might hope for in a university setting. And the end result is often countless meetings with mixed or uncertain outcomes that take time away from other vital responsibilities, namely research and reading; these latter functions ought to be seen as the fuel that runs not only our teaching but that influence when and why we engage in all the other meetings and bureaucratic tasks.

Bringing a wildly disharmonious faculty into a room to discuss the name of the school, curricular issues, professional objectives and goals, budgets, or any other such matters seems to be doomed from the start (and it often is). But it is not always that way. One glance at that incredible array of writing about information, and it is not difficult to see why such diversity of viewpoint is so important. It is, nevertheless, continuously difficult to come together and to produce or attract academic leadership to resolve such issues, differences of opinion, and help us, as an extra benefit, to chart

---

[517] Robert Alter, *The Pleasures of Reading in an Ideological Age* (New York: W. W. Norton and Co., 1996), p. 11.

the future. Most of the time the difficulties generated by the diversity are good practice for each and every one of us, forcing us to become better and more articulate advocates of our positions. The exercise can be frustrating, and it often makes us look disorganized and unfocused in the academic community. If nothing else, perhaps we ought to practice in our meetings what we preach about in our classrooms – or, and maybe this is a necessity, we ought to make sure that no students ever hear us at our faculty meetings. The real problem may be that we don't share much in the way of common readings or sources among ourselves. As Alberto Manguel suggests, "Most of our societies (by no means all) have assembled around a book and for these the library became an essential symbol of power. Symbolically, the ancient world ends with the destruction of the Library of Alexandria; symbolically, the twentieth century ends with the rebuilding of the library of Sarajevo."[518] The point is, of course, that a common source serves as a symbolic unifying center. Are such centers visible in library and information science programs where information scientists, librarians, archivists, and others operate?

Such challenges can be exaggerated by the most mundane elements and features, such as lack of venues for discussion, particular kinds of meetings and communal meeting places not luring us out of the monastic cells that are our offices. How can we think of ourselves as an academic community? Faculty, sitting in offices within feet of each other, cannot be brought together even by electronic mail. While we can wax romantic about the process of reading, such as Geoffrey O'Brien does when he writes – "The unread book is the life yet to be lived, the promise that there will be new ideas, images never yet glimpsed"[519] – the unread email message is nothing more than a breakdown in communication or the collapse of an opportunity for nurturing various levels of discourse. In our electronic networks most lurk while a few participate.

Even if we used the network in an intense way, this kind of virtual communication has limitations because we can't see each other, it is easy to misinterpret written postings, and it works against more leisurely exploration of topics – something frequently commented on by those examining networked communication. Librarian of Congress James Billington, in an interview, mused: "One of the many steps by which humanity moved from primitive forms of communication to more complex

---

[518] Manguel, *Into the Looking-Glass Wood*, pp. 265-266.
[519] Geoffrey O'Brien, *The Browser's Ecstasy: A Meditation on Reading* (Washington, D.C.: Counterpoint, 2000), p. 94.

forms was the invention of the sentence. In chatrooms, sentences are endangered. The inexactness of the language that is used in chatrooms and quick messaging [like email] creates the potential for misunderstandings. In person, even inarticulate conversation is accompanied by mannerisms and tone and other things that qualify the conversation."[520] At best, electronic mail is only *one* means for sustaining community, and it is only sufficient if it is part of other activities and events in an organization's life. We need to remember that email requires an act of writing as well. If we approach the use of email in this fashion, we can also see the social aspects of its use. As William Zinsser argues, "All writing is a journey, and it begins with an invitation."[521] By sending an email message, we are inviting others to communicate with us or to work together.

Looking for Something to Pull Us Together. A library and information science school can lack something that pulls it together – and surely there are commonalities as we educate even our diverse groups of information professionals – perhaps because of the increasing challenges of educating students to be prepared for working with both analog and digital sources, both legacy materials and the next great information technology, and in a diversity of venues ranging from public to private, cultural to corporate, and modest to large in scale. I have seen electronic weekly newsletters, a printed alumnae newsletter, Web sites, and various organizational structures for planning and communication. All of these seem to not foster developing community, a corporate memory or identity, or vision, factors laboring against both formal and informal working groups. Who knows what might happen if such regular even if informal groups would materialize. Historians have determined, for example, that just sitting around in taverns led to alternative discourse venues contributing to social and political upheaval.[522] So, maybe a little booze might help too at times. One of the things we know happened in those taverns was that there was a communal reading of newspapers, cultivating both a common source of knowledge and a sense of how information was to be conveyed. One thing in common with many humanities professors in the university today is that they teach and do reading. As Mark Edmundson says, "They cultivate attentiveness to written words, careful consideration, thoughtful balancing, coaxing forth of

---

[520] *Yahoo! Internet Life* 6 (September 2000): 80.
[521] William Zinsser, *Writing About Your Life: A Journey into the Past* (New York: Marlowe & Co., 2004), p. 101.
[522] See, for fun, Peter Thompson, *Rum Punch & Revolution: Taverngoing & Public Life in Eighteenth-Century Philadelphia* (Philadelphia: University of Pennsylvania Press, 1999).

disparate meanings, responsiveness to the complexities of sense."[523] It may be, in schools of library and information science, that such communal processes are absent. Focusing on grabbing bits and bites from the Web may not be a satisfactory substitute. Perhaps this is something the new iSchools might improve upon (although it is too early to tell about this)

We have fallen prey to our own prognostications about the Web as the hub of the present information era. Robert Johnson, vice president for information services at Rhodes College in Memphis, Tennessee, criticizes some universities for moving books out of their libraries in favor of computer access terminals for using digital information sources. Johnson, understanding the richness of resources offered by the Web, also believes that "by its very nature the online world is geared to deliver quick facts" discouraging "serious contemplation." " A book, on the other hand, conjures up images of comfort – sitting before a fire, perhaps with a cup of cocoa, maybe sprawled in a porch glider or propped up in bed. Such environments encourage frequent pauses to reread an especially engaging line or contemplate what one has just encountered."[524] This is precisely what library and information science schools need to be sensitive to and the kind of advice they need to heed.

If we need to rethink communal acts like reading, then we also need to reevaluate why and for whom we write, and what we write about. The world has an image of university faculty sitting in their offices and libraries, reading and reflecting about the larger issues in their fields and society. Professional writing is something that may fall far short of any such popular notion.

Professional Writing. For someone who does not know me, I certainly seem like a successful writer. I published my first essay when I was twenty-three, and from that time on I published steadily. From my early twenties until my late thirties, my focus was on producing scholarly essays. Essays were all I had time for, as I worked as an archivist and records manager during the day, a discipline where one's boss often looked askance at someone who was writing and publishing, with suspicion about whether they were doing this on the job when they should have been doing something else. For most in my field, if they wrote at all, it was on their own stolen time and often about matters far removed from administering and preserving historical records; if they wrote, it was as if they did it to

---

[523] Mark Edmundson, *Why Read?* (New York: Bloomsbury Publishing, 2004), p. 36.
[524] Robert Johnson, "Libraries, Please You're your Books," *Christian Science Monitor*, October 7, 2005, available at http://www.csmonitor.com/2005/1007/p09s01-coop.html, accessed October 11, 2005.

escape from the boundaries of their profession or, perhaps, expressing a frustration with their lot in life at not being what they really wanted to be – a writer, a scholar, an academic.

As an academic, my writing was transformed. Prior to joining the university in 1988, I had written a regular stream of essays. After becoming a faculty member, I continued to write essays, but my focus shifted to writing and publishing books as well. I felt so free of my 9-to-5 job that I wrote more than ever before, sometimes even when I should have been doing something else (like going to a faculty meeting – sometimes when at a faculty meeting I scribbled away on something). Starting in 1990, I began publishing books and since then, at the time of writing this, I have written and had published more than a dozen books. I have plans for writing many more books, and the satisfaction in conceiving, constructing, and completing a book continues to motivate me. I must concur with writer Bret Lott's assessment, "And like all genuine truths, the only truths worth knowing, this one is immutable, has no context out of which it can be taken, applies to the published and unpublished alike: writing is its own reward, and why I write."[525]

While I never grow tired of writing, for reasons described below, I have grown weary and somewhat disappointed with my audience. The topics of my writing have been concentrated in the history and nature of archives, and I have written both scholarly works and basic primers in this area. There are decided shifts in my writing aims. When I was a practicing archivist and records manager, many of my essays were about practical concerns I daily dealt with or historical excursions questioning practical aspects of archival work. Even in my days of utilitarian purpose, there were signs that I was laying claim to certain more scholarly aspects of archival knowledge. And it was in this quest that I detected my first sense of audience trouble. As my practical essays became more conceptual, I sensed a tension with my intended audience. Many archivists, manuscripts curators, and records managers, even with substantial academic preparation behind them, scanned the journals and newsletters for nuggets of practical insights for application rather than for epistemological insights about what they were doing. It was even in these reasonably early days, my late twenties and early thirties, that I felt I was cutting across the grain of my audience's interests. Toward the end of this time, a colleague quipped to me that every

---

[525] Bret Lott, *Before We Get Started: A Practical Memoir of the Writer's Life* (New York: Ballantine Books, 2005), p. 43.

time he read one of my essays, he felt that he was witnessing four essays trying to escape. Looking back, I was trying to do too many things.

Almost forty years ago I started a career as an archivist, embarking in this field because of a love of history. My days would be filled with working with letters, diaries, receipts, account books, photographs and the researchers seeking to use such documentation. What I was doing is what still attracts individuals to the archival profession, a desire for immersing oneself in old records. In the midst of these happy, more carefree days, I discovered that I had a greater interest in the essential nature of documents, why and how they were created, maintained, and destroyed or collected, than in the efforts to organize and prepare the records for scholars, genealogists, students, and others to use. This led to the development of a philosophy in educating individuals to become first experts in records and recordkeeping systems. This placed me on a crash course, one that still remains a tension today, between the hows and whys of what an archivist is supposed to do or know. It is the classic conflict between theory (often used pejoratively) and practice (often used as bedrock commonsense). I became intrigued with how a corporate archives, family papers, and individual collections of manuscripts were formed and what they represented as evidence, memory, and information. I was less interested in their practical utility than in the inherent interesting ideas and concepts emerging from reflecting on them. There was more of the academic than might be useful in the daily work of a practitioner. These were the seeds of my later idea that the archivist must be a scholar of records and recordkeeping systems. The old professional tension between theory and practice is being played out in different ways in today's university, as the university slips more and more into a corporate mentality. Eric Gould remarks that we have "commodity knowledge" – "knowledge that has a use for the world of work, professional and preprofessional training, policy development, inventions, and patents" and "symbolic knowledge" – "knowledge that deals with value judgments, ethical, cultural, aesthetic, and philosophical argument, and speculative science."[526] One of our tasks is to determine how both to develop and convey such knowledge.

Writing as a Lifetime Pursuit. My scholarly interests intensified as I moved from being a manuscript curator to a municipal government archivist and records manager to the head of a large administrative unit in a state government archives. Along the way I read what I could about archival

---

[526] Eric Gould, *The University in a Corporate Culture* (New Haven: Yale University Press, 2003), p. 102.

administration and records management, as well as getting the opportunity to meet and interact with many more experienced professionals (finding even a few who shared some of my interests). I found the knowledge of the field to be interesting, but often incomplete and shallow in perspective and aim. After more than a decade in management positions, I joined a research and development project experimenting with the drafting of basic standards for historical manuscripts programs and also with a pioneer archival planning endeavor. Each position elevated my preoccupation with the most fundamental questions about what archivists and other records professionals do. The questions became more complex and intense. From here it was an effortless move into a faculty position, or so I thought at the time.

Moving into the university brought some relief, as well as new challenges. With the advantage of hindsight, I can see two distinct advantages in regards to my writing. First, the university post transformed research and writing from a pastime to a priority. Now, much of my performance was measured by the quality and quantity of scholarship that I produced, although in more recent years the rise of the corporate university model has seemed to make the priority generating revenue (although no one will get promoted or tenured without any mark on scholarship). I had more time to reflect, pose questions, gather evidence, and create more substantive writing; the beginning of my writing books was clearly the most obvious change. Second, in entering the classroom, I had to take my practical knowledge, place it into its context, take it apart and reassemble it, and understand not just how to do something but be able to explain why some function was necessary. In teaching in the first couple of years, I sensed that I learned more about my profession and its practice than I had in nearly sixteen years of working in the real world. There is, of course, as many have acknowledged, a synergy between teaching and research. A. Bartlett Giamatti reflects, "Research, in whatever field, alone or in groups, done late at night or snatched at dawn, in laboratory, library, or at home, pursued for a few hours a day or throughout weekend, during vacation or on leave, is the essential source from which teaching is drawn."[527] I concur.

It is deceptively easy to describe two decades of experience, but, in reality, each year brought personal and professional conflicts, doubts, controversies, questions, some answers, lots of soul-searching, and more questions. Indeed, to be engaged in asking questions, let alone answering

---

[527] A. Bartlett Giamatti, *A Free and Ordered Space: The Real World of the University* (New York: W. W. Norton & Co., 1990), p. 149.

them, that challenge cherished beliefs, traditions, and practices is a sure-fire means to be labeled a troublemaker. I have been called abrasive, elitist, condescending, arrogant, and worse. Apparently, I am not the only one who sees some of this. Gerald Graff muses, "Away from home, I became part of an intellectual community again, as I am when I write and publish, whereas at home I am expected to teach my classes and attend faculty meetings but otherwise to mind my own business and keep my ideas to myself. On the road I am encouraged to assert myself intellectually – that is why I have been invited to give the lecture or attend the conference – whereas asserting my ideas at home would evidently threaten too many others who have their own ideas. Campus culture is governed by a tacit code of democratic silence, whereby we all agree to muzzle ourselves so that no individual or group gets their way."[528] On more than several occasions I resolved to pursue another career, and even now, this kind of reflection is done on a regular basis. Professional schools, it turns out, do not always provide a hospitable environment for asking questions, as they often seem to possess a focus on pat systems of practice designed to reassure tuition paying students that they are gaining basic tools by which to ply a trade. Critics of the encroaching corporate mindset have noted that this trend threatens the idea of the university as a public good or a place where critical inquiry can occur as education becomes equivalent to nothing more than job training;[529] this is even more noticeable in the typical professional school.

Writing Benchmarks. As I look back at that benchmark year, 1988, I see a major shift in my writing, although initially it was just in the quantity of what I wrote that was the primary difference. Some themes – such as historical aspects of archival work and the attributes of the archival community as a profession – continued, in some ways renewed by my reflecting on and building a curriculum to educate individuals to function as archivists and records managers. There were other, not so subtle, changes as I matured as an academic. I had more time and opportunity to probe into very basic elements of the profession, such as the nature of a record or document. More importantly, however, my working on a curriculum for the education of archivists forced me to consider both what are the core elements of archival knowledge and the most essential aspects of archival

---

[528] Gerald Graff, *Clueless in Academe: How Schooling Obscures the Life of the Mind* (New Haven: Yale University Press, 2003), p. 76.
[529] Henry A. Giroux, "Neoliberalism, Corporate Culture, and the Promise of Higher Education: The University as a Democratic Public Sphere," *Harvard Educational Review* 72, no. 4 (2002): 433.

practice. This led to a decided shift in research and writing about the appraisal of records (the identifying and selecting of records with research or continuing value) as the most essential and unique aspect of archival thinking and doing. Later, because of my work on defining the notion of an archival document and identifying what records possess archival value, I also found myself engaged in professional debate about the core importance of records in society; this helped lead to a fundamental reworking of the curriculum to reflect that archives were not only important as historical sources or as repositories of cultural or symbolic value, but because they possessed essential evidence and value for accountability.

Much of my own research and writing about archives for evidence and accountability reflected internal debates within the archival community. Indeed, most of my writing is directed at the archival community. This has been, however, a source of angst for myself, as I have grown older and my own academic career has progressed. Every university professor has faced this question: am I reaching the right audience with my writing? For me, as my primary scholarly interests have morphed into matters of the importance of recordkeeping for accountability and evidence, reflecting particular concerns with issues such as government secrecy and the ethics of recordkeeping in every organization (including the university), the matter of a more public audience has increased in personal importance. The issues that I seem mostly to teach and write about are ones with particular significance to the public and public policy, and yet the records professionals' important insights into such concerns are not visible to the public. The small group of individuals within the archival community who have written about such matters have tended to restrict their essays to professional journals or to professional publishers; you will not find their ideas displayed in journals of broad public opinion, such as the *New York Review of Books* or *Harper's*, or in the major book chains. If I am committed to the notion that records and their administration are critical to society, its organizations, and its citizens, then I must be committed to making my views more broadly known. There are practical reasons, among the many reasons, for doing this. Graff believes that "when academics address outsiders they get practice looking at their field from their big-picture perspective, and that perspective enables them to speak more forcibly to fellow insiders."[530]

Writing and Graduate School or Vocational Training. I continue to learn new things about archives and the records systems producing them. As a teacher

---

[530] Graff, *Clueless*, pp. 144-145.

I learn more than I ever did practicing the trade. The ancient tension between theory and practice is endemic to all professions. It is intensified in professional schools, where many disciplines collide with the demands of the university. In such schools the debate has different twists, materializing, for example, as friction between that of a graduate school and vocational training. And, in considering the increasing corporate influence on the university, one also must understand how the task of asking questions is being eroded. In the university, and especially in the professional school, expressing a love for learning becomes even more difficult as larger classrooms are created that meet the financial analysts' and corporate expectations and that muffles those students who want to learn.[531] While in certain sectors of the university, students resist this model because it leads to a much too "narrow sense of responsibility, agency, and public values because it lacks a vocabulary for providing guidance on matters of justice, equality, fairness, equity, and freedom, values that are crucial to the functioning of a vibrant, democratic culture,"[532] in the professional school such resistance seems more isolated or less prevalent. Even in a school educating future librarians and other information professionals, individuals who will wade into the thick of battles about intellectual property, secrecy, privacy, and other crucial matters, many of the older students come focused on the credential; in other words, they want to get in and out as quickly as possible, and they generally do not want to cause trouble that will impede their acquisition of a professional license. While some, like Gould, remind us of the practical connection of the university to society – "No one can mistake what the modern university stands for: service to society" – no one, I believe, meant it to be so cynical a connection as this.[533]

What I am describing here is a subject that has teased and tormented other academics for generations. Every university professor has dreamed of having a wide readership and influence, whether we are discussing the fourteenth century or the twenty-first. What have moved such concerns to the forefront, of course, are the result of the intensification of specialization in the last century and the emergence of various sciences. The school where I teach is built around a variety of such sciences that emerged at various epochs since the late nineteenth century; library science developed in the earlier period, followed by information science a half century later and still

---

[531] Giroux, "Neoliberalism, Corporate Culture, and the Promise of Higher Education," p. 434.
[532] Giroux, "Neoliberalism, Corporate Culture, and the Promise of Higher Education," p. 454.
[533] Gould, *University in a Corporate Culture*, p. 4.

later archival science (some would argue that the latter developed earlier, but in the American context it only started to be visible in the university in the 1970s). The establishment of these fields in the university has come with pressure on research and the dissemination of research in increasingly specialized journals read only by other specialists. Among all these specializations come a variety of definitions of information and very different orientations to similar issues and problems. The balkanization of the modern university can be seen in a professional school, a microcosm of the larger university, where faculty read very differently, write very differently, direct their work to extremely different audiences, and rarely talk over any of these matters with each other. And, added to such challenges, there is hardly any public presence of any of these fields, even though the immense outpouring of tomes on the modern information age suggests that faculty in professional schools supporting these fields would have some such connections.

My school is not unique in any of this. We can see some of the same tensions in the history profession, evolving from great amateurs, like Francis Parkman and George Bancroft, to historical science (with archives and libraries as their laboratories) in the emerging modern university in the late nineteenth century to wave after wave of new professional historians adopting the methods of social scientists (the latter perhaps lessening the ability of historians to write for a broader audience). Anthropology, literary studies, and other disciplines also have faced such problems, while library and archival science have never really had a public audience to begin with. And that is at the heart of my dilemma, and the crisis in my own writing. How does one measure their success or impact of their own scholarship? Many people in my field look to citation studies as one means (although, ironically, even as bibliometrics is a core aspect of library and information science knowledge the ability to rank faculty research productivity or the journals they publish in is compromised).[534] All academics look to tenure and promotion as another measure. But if one is committed to a professional mission such as mine, contending that records are absolutely crucial to society and its governance, are such measures adequate? Can one, considering such matters, merely focus on contributing to a highly specialized and, some would say, arcane knowledge without considering the matter of adding to or supporting the public good? This led me to wrestling

---

[534] See, as one example, Lokman I. Meho and Kristina M. Spurgin, "Ranking the Research Productivity of Library and Information Science Faculty and Schools: An Evaluation of Data Sources and Research Methods," *Journal of the American Society for Information Science and Technology* 56, no. 12 (2005): 1314-1331.

through with the notion of writing, and the prospects of reaching out into a more public scholarship.

Writing, whether it is fiction or creative non-fiction or the most mundane professional sort, is a tough and complex task. Bret Lott, for example, sees little difference between writing fiction and non-fiction, when he notes that "Without the consciousness of the artist – without the unique being seeing the human condition we all of us see each and every day of our lives through the singular window behind which we stand – there can be no art, whether of the fictive form or factual, and the unfortunate and blessed truth of this is that there can be no teaching to you any technique for being the unique being you are. To believe in technique is to pretend there is only a certain size and shape window that will allow us to see, and to pretend there is only one watcher behind them all. To pretend there is a technique or even a compendium of techniques that will give you you, is to pretend there is only one essay, one story, and one poem."[535] Amen.

The Challenges of Writing. Many successful writers discourse about the solitary, tedious existence that writing can be. Norman Mailer, successful at both fiction and non-fiction, describes writing as characterized by its "meanness" and the "very monotony of the process." Mailer laments, "There's nothing so very attractive about going into a room by yourself each day to look at a blank piece of paper (or monitor) and make calligraphic marks."[536] Nonetheless, academics might say that it is better than sitting through the monotony of a faculty meeting.

Other well-known writers have similar views about writing. Joyce Carol Oates bluntly states that "writing is the most solitary of arts," feeling strongly enough about this that she starts her reflection on writing this way.[537] Nadime Gordimer suggests that writing is the "most solitary of occupations," similar to being a "keeper of a lighthouse."[538] Stanley Karnow likens writing to the "loneliest of occupations, akin to long-distance running" and E. L. Doctorow says that writing is work, "hard and slow" where "you live enslaved in the book's language, its diction, its universe of

---

[535] Lott, *Before We Get Started*, p. 107.
[536] Norman Mailer, *The Spooky Art: Thoughts on Writing* (New York: Random House, 2004), p. 127.
[537] Joyce Carol Oates, *The Faith of a Writer: Life, Craft, Art* (New York: HarperCollins Publishers, Inc., 2003), p. xi.
[538] Nadine Gordimer in Marie Arana, ed., *The Writing Life: Writers on How They Think and Work: A Collection from the Washington Post Book World* (New York: Public Affairs, 2003), p. 60.

imagery, and there is no way out except through the last sentence."[539] These and other writers emphasize how difficult it is to write, at least successfully. Annie Dillard, in her excellent book on writing, suggests that the writer often does not have control of his or her task, when "part of a book simply gets up and walks away," when "it wanders off to die."[540] Bonnie Friedman argues that writing can be such a hateful experience that the writer wants to be distracted, fearful that left alone they will produce something lousy.[541] She writes, "I wanted to get everything in that room just right before my writing began. I was afraid that just as a good idea was about to come to me, about to leap the synapse and appear full-blown, a fly would appear, and jar me, and the idea would fall in the gap and be lost forever, something impossible to recall because it was never really *known*."[542] Friedman adds, "We are afraid of writing, even those of us who love it. And there are parts of it we hate. The necessary mess, the loss of control, its ability to betray us, as well as the possibility that what we write might be lousy, it might just stink... ."[543] I know I go back and forth in hating what I write, and I never am satisfied – I just let it go.

Given the legendary aspects of higher education, attracting (so they say) misfits and individuals who don't want to interact with or work for others, it may be possible that some of these characteristics of writing are what attracts someone to the academy. The move of the university to be corporate-like – focused on generating revenue, marketing credentials, and allying research with business goals – has been met with animosity by many faculty. A humanist in a professional school, such as what I represent, can often be stressed out, as my orientation is for long, solitary hours in the library or archives, gathering evidence to be used in another solitary venture, crafting an essay or constructing a book. Still, there has to be a goal beyond residing in self-imposed solitude. Richard Rhodes believes that in "writing, we make our way out of our isolation onto the commons that we share."[544] Of course, we can't come out of that isolation, if we have no

---

[539] Stanley Karnow and E.L. Doctorow in Arana, *Writing Life*, pp. 159, 209.
[540] Dillard also ruminates about the difficulty of committing a vision to a page, suggesting that the "page is jealous and tyrannical; the page is made of time and matter; the page always wins"; Annie Dillard, *The Writing Life* (New York: HarperPerennial, 1990; org. pub. 1989), pp. 16, 57.
[541] Bonnie Friedman, *Writing Past Dark: Envy, Fear, Distraction, and Other Dilemmas in the Writer's Life* (New York: HarperPerennial, 1994; org. pub. 1993), pp. 10-11, 15.
[542] Friedman, *Writing Past Dark*, pp. 10-11.
[543] Friedman, *Writing Past Dark*, p. 15.
[544] Richard Rhodes, *How to Write: Advice and Reflections* (New York: Quill, 1995), p. 2.

audience. More importantly, the emerging corporate university may be making it harder to consider doing this. Jennifer Washburn describes what has happened to the knowledge commons: "Historically, of course, one of the central missions of the university was to nurture and protect the knowledge commons, the pool of knowledge and ideas unencumbered by ownership claims that is freely available to researchers and the public at large. Like our national parks, timber, and water resources, this pool of knowledge – much of it funded by U.S. taxpayers – is a crucial part of the public domain. Unfortunately, in recent years, despite the revolution in information technology, the size of the knowledge commons has diminished, as more and more ideas, subject to restrictive patents and licenses, get cordoned off behind high proprietary fences."[545]

Many writers, when they reflect on their craft, liken their occupation to construction, and as any amateur home maintenance nut knows, constructing something will only be harder if one has no plan for what he or she is building. Annie Dillard makes some insightful analogies about writing as constructing, noting, "The line of words is a hammer. You hammer against the walls of your house. You tap the walls, lightly, everywhere. After giving many years' attention to these things, you know what to listen for." As everyone knows who has done construction, you have to possess the right tools and appropriate building materials. Dillard recounts, "How fondly I recall thinking, in the old days, that to write you needed paper, pen, and a lap. How appalled I was to discover that in order to write so much as a sonnet, you need a warehouse." Envisioning the writing project takes plenty of space: "You can easily get so confused writing a thirty-page chapter that in order to make an outline for the second draft, you have to rent a hall. I have often written with the mechanical aid of a twenty-foot conference table. You lay your pages along the table's edge and pace out the work. You walk along the rows, you weed bits, move bits, and dig out bits, bent over the rows with full hands like a gardener. After a couple of hours, you have taken an exceedingly dull nine-mile hike. You go

---

[545] Jennifer Washburn, *University, Inc.: The Corporate Corruption of American Higher Education* (New York: Basic Books, 2005), p. 146. Washburn discusses the demise of openness in scientific research, mostly fueled by the commercialization of the research; increasing challenges to intellectual property and the ownership of ideas; biases built into the research by corporate sponsors; growing use of ghostwriters, where a prominent name in research is invited to put their name on an essay; corporations suppressing negative research; and the disappearing knowledge commons – the commons being part of the historic mission of the university.

home and soak your feet."[546] Richard Rhodes forthrightly states, "Writing is a craft," perhaps best summing up the notion of writing as construction.[547]

Academic Storytellers. Academics must seem to be in the best position to undertake a major construction project of preparing a book, although few want to be seen as being engaged in a craft. After all, they often have student research assistants and a warehouse of tools and supplies in their major academic libraries. Yet, it is often the very same academics who believe they have lost their audience, as they undertake research in order to do what is necessary to get tenure or to acquire research funds. The faculty members often write for each other, losing either sight of or interest in any other audience other than like-minded specialists. They worry less about clear exposition and more about peer review, less about relevant scholarship and more about mimicking the arcane language of their field. Peter Turchi's delightful book equating writing to cartography provides a valuable insight into this academic mess: "So the world of a story is a thing we create or summon into being, but which the reader participates in creating and understanding. A story or novel is a kind of map because, like a map, it is not a world, but it evokes one (or at least one), for each reader."[548] If academics stay confined within their own specialized arena, they lose their voice and their way, their power to communicate beyond a handful of other like-minded souls.

Turchi's analogy is relevant to the problem faculty in library and information science schools face. As he considers how we are filling in the blanks on maps, the problems with maps being accurate, the trouble with words representing reality and ideas, and the nature of imposing order when we write, he goes farther in characterizing the relationship between author and writer. Do we, LIS faculty, have a well-defined map for our guidance? Can we agree even where the map should be directing us? Are iSchools doing any better at this early stage of the movement?

The challenges academics face in writing for the public is more complicated than the arcane qualities of disciplinary expertise. At the least, we need to understand that the co-opting of corporate language in the academy can lead to confusion and, ultimately, misplaced priorities and poor decisions. We have seen this in other sectors of our society. The thoughtful curmudgeon, Lewis Lapham, long-time editor of *Harper's*, discusses this in relation to the Bush administration's Iraq quagmire: "The

---

[546] Dillard, *Writing Life*, pp. 4, 46.
[547] Rhodes, *How to Write*, p. 15.
[548] Peter Turchi, *Maps of the Imagination: The Writer as Cartographer* (San Antonio, Texas: Trinity University Press, 2004), p. 166.

senior managers of the Bush Administration came to Washington knowing how to manufacture disinformation in commercial quantity: appreciative of the uses of advanced technology and familiar with the idioms of opaque abstraction ('contingency planning process,' 'polycentric multi-polar paradigm,'") acquired during their years of experience in the country's corporate boardrooms and reactionary policy institutes."[549] Basically the same thing has happened within universities, although the potential for confusion is even greater. Academics have long used arcane jargon isolated to their own disciplines, and the multitude of disciplines within in a university can produce a cacophony of dialects and languages making the Tower of Babel story appear as a goal to improve matters. It may seem amazing, to outsiders at least, that many schools have turned their back away from libraries, institutions widely known by the public (if not always completely understood). Gerald Graff, in his assessment about what has occurred within the university in recent years, may be close to the source also affecting library schools. Graf states that the subject of his book is "cluelessness, the bafflement, usually accompanied by shame and resentment, felt by students, the general public, and even many academics in the face of the impenetrability of the academic world." It is a place where we "perpetuate the misconception that the life of the mind is a secret society for which only an elite few qualify." He believes that we make our "ideas, problems, and ways of thinking *look* more opaque, narrowly specialized, and beyond normal capabilities than they are or need to be."[550]

Academics have been creative, and they have generally both borrowed from and learned the jargons from other fields. For a long time, however, the one arena, the one most critical to the running of the university that was protected from all this, was where university administrators and faculty and staff talked to each other – that is, in the governance of the university. Faculty members were the administrators at one time, but that seems to have gradually changed as the corporate model has become more prevalent. Instead of faculty and administrators conversing with each other in plain language, now we increasingly witness the use of business- or government-speak that often seems more to obscure the real business we are in, education and knowledge generation. We can discern such problems in the denseness of so many of the statements issued by universities to the faculty, staff, and public. Gould muses, for example, "Few administrators actually

---

[549] Lewis Lapham, "Notebook: That's Why the Lady is a Tramp," *Harper's* 308 (June 2004): 11-12.
[550] Graf, *Clueless*, p. 1.

believe that civic duty replaces intellectual activity, but having it all ways at once is precisely what mission statements and administrative reports and memos mean to do. It is the ambivalence of the university's relation to society, itself a mixed metaphor, which indicates the cultural contradictions in academic culture."[551] This has been particularly hard on professional schools, where their faculties already have to speak a different language to the practitioners of their field and where often their mission has been seen as extremely tenuous by others in the university who see less research productivity and a lower level knowledge tied to fairly pedestrian looking work. For these schools the results can be disastrous.

Writing Under Strategic Planning in the Academy. The corporate mindset in universities may be best seen in strategic planning processes. Every academic unit or department submits an annual plan setting goals and evaluating progress. As anyone knows who has been involved in strategic planning, such an exercise can either be immensely useful or a complete waste of time, with the latter usually occurring if not everyone in the organization buys into the process. The planning process can become a humorous academic shell game, where, months after a plan is submitted it is pronounced as inadequate but where the specifics of its inadequacy are not fully revealed (seeming to be a deliberate process intended to exercise control). The faculty is blamed for being slow, cumbersome in approach, and too pre-occupied with themselves. This tension between faculty and administrators is fairly typical in the modern university. "Today, it is fashionable to criticize academic culture for its inefficiency and failure to move ideas more rapidly from the laboratory to the marketplace," argues Washburn. "What's forgotten is how effective this same culture has been in furnishing society with valuable public goods that markets do a poor job of producing on their own: a reliable and ever-expanding body of scientific and technological knowledge; a well-trained cadre of students and workers; a richly endowed public information commons; and an educated citizenry."[552] Whatever the utilitarian problems associated with this game, it is clear that faculty engaged in learning to write such strategic planning documents probably tarnish their writing and its ability to communicate to a broader readership.

The way we approach the kinds of questions generated by planning efforts must be framed by the historic, long-standing roles of universities, and more specifically, professional schools within universities. There are no

---

[551] Gould, *University in a Corporate Culture*, p. 88.
[552] Washburn, *University, Inc.*, p. 195.

easy answers, and, in fact, there are answers that are sometimes very complex. The strengths of a professional school can reside in the diversity of faculty, disciplines they represent, research interests they pursue, teaching approaches they use, and general perspectives they possess about the information professions and the present Information Age. Even if we honestly engage the questions involved in planning, the end results become obvious over time. A somewhat disjointed, clumsy vision statement – striving to appeal to everyone – may be written. More and more time will be spent in meetings discussing what we should be doing, rather than actually doing anything (a meeting is a process and an activity, but it does not always lead to results). More faculty will give up on the process, ceasing to go to planning meetings. And, rather than bringing faculty together, the planning process eventually leads to a schism between faculty supporting the school's administration and those who do not (the latter usually by just ignoring the meetings rather than by any vocalization of their concerns). A normal result of strategic planning is intended to be the investing of all people in the organization in both the process and the final goals and objectives. Writing anything meaningful under such circumstances is quite difficult. This kind of exercise works against the very principles or practices that generally support good wiring. As William Zinsser argues, "Given a choice between two projects – one that you feel you ought to write and one that sounds like fun – go for the one you'll enjoy working on. It will show in your writing. The reader should always think that the writer is feeling good."[553] It is no fun striving to answer questions or meet expectations that are never fully defined or made clear.

Can We Have Vision in the Corporate University? One of the reasons so many professors, in different fields, have written about the problems of their research is because they often feel betrayed or feel that they have betrayed themselves. They have lost their inner vision that originally called them to the academy and scholarship. Psychology professor Gail Hornstein, contemplating the dense academic writing so often taken for granted these days, concludes, "Beyond the aesthetic and intellectual rewards of writing for a broader public, there are practical advantages as well. We're living at a time when academics are increasingly being called upon to explain and justify our work. Aren't we playing right into the hands of our critics when abstruseness makes us seem irrelevant?"[554] Good point.

---

[553] William Zinsser, *Writing About Your Life: A Journey Into the Past* (New York: Marlowe & Co., 2004), p. 48.
[554] Gail A. Hornstein, "Prune That Prose: Learning to Write for Readers Beyond Academe," *Chronicle Review*, September 7, 2009,

Non-academic writers ought to inspire us. Writers advise writing about what interests you, the "ideal" scenario according to Norman Mailer.[555] Anne Lamott argues that the writer must believe in what they are doing, "or nothing will be driving your work. If you don't believe in what you are saying, there is no point in your saying it. You might as well call it a day and go bowling."[556] Some academics become excellent bowlers after they secure tenure, partly because they cease caring about their own field. Bonnie Friedman argues, "Write what you care about. Don't write one more word you don't care about. Don't waste any more of your life on what does not matter to you. Write only what matters to you – those scenes, those dialogues. Get messy. Before you get neat, get very, very messy. Write until you are more alive than you have ever been before."[557] One most often sees this problem in academe with doctoral students, who become so focused on meeting expectations, getting the dissertation done, that they often cease caring about their subject or forget why they became interested in doing a doctoral program in the first place.

It is difficult to imagine being free to be a writer in the new corporate university. The modern university, with a constant eye on the financial bottom-line, is in danger of losing its moorings. We can start reading all the new books coming out focused on this very real concern, but we do not need to be so energetic. Any book with some emphasis on knowledge and education will contain a standard description of the university that shows what we might be losing. Lewis Pyenson and Susan Sheets-Pyenson in their book on science provide an example. "Universities do not make society," they write. "They teach what people want to learn, and they give voice to what people prefer to learn." We should pause and note that "people" does not mean the government or the corporation. They continue: "But because they are keepers of tradition and accumulated wisdom, their response time is slow. This allows universities to become authorities for what we know." We can sense the tensions being created. The business success books all preach speed, receptivity to change, and risk management. And, it is hard to distinguish between the business and the government manual books. Nothing should be slow and tradition, like bureaucracy, is evil. The Pyensons then argue that, "Relative isolation from prosaic concerns

---

http://chronicle.com/article/Prune-That-Prose/48273/, accessed October 9, 2009. I am indebted to Leigh Star for reminding me of this essay.
[555] Mailer, *Spooky Art*, p. 49.
[556] Anne Lamott, *Bird by Bird: Some Instructions on Writing and Life* (New York: Anchor Books, 1995; org. pub. 1994), p. 106.
[557] Friedman, *Writing Past Dark*, p. 60.

provides a unique environment for encouraging new knowledge about the world."[558] However, it is now nearly impossible to tell any difference between the world and the university. Profits are necessary, students are customers, faculty members are staff.

To be a successful writer, one must possess a passion and feed that passion. This is evident when one writes about what they think is important, not what will make them successful. William Zinsser advises, "Write about things that are important to you, not about what you think readers will want to read, or editors will want to publish or agents will want to sell. Readers and editors and agents don't know what they want to read until they read it. If it's important to you, it will be important to other people."[559] Likewise, James Carroll believes that a "writer's final authority has, finally, to be his or her own conscience and imagination. You can't worry about what other people are going to make of what you write. And you can't be trying to get permission from somebody."[560]

This is, of course, an area where academics may suffer, as so much of their careers are spent trying to win approval by doing the things they need to obtain tenure and promotion, working their way through peer review processes everywhere they turn, and building citation counts of their work. Nevertheless, most academics start out with a passion for their area of expertise, and a passion that usually extends beyond the small circle of other like-minded academics that they may be most often in communication with; indeed, the passion remains, even if it is a memory, and it is often the source of professors' dissatisfaction with their own writing. If you believe that what you are teaching and writing about somehow connects to a greater public good, then you will always desire to acquire and influence an audience extending far beyond a small group scattered around in universities. For myself, my belief that records are essential to society dictates my desire to get this message out into the public. In this sense, professors can be viewed as kinds of artists. Joyce Carol Oates provides a glimpse of what I mean when she says, "To write is to invade another's space, if only to memorialize it; to write is to invite angry censure from those who don't write, or who don't write in quite the way you do, for whom you may seem a threat. Art by its nature is a

---

[558] Lewis Pyenson and Susan Sheets-Pyenson, *Servants of Nature: A History of Scientific Institutions, Enterprises and Sensibilities* (New York: W. W. Norton and Co., 1999), p. 47.
[559] Zinsser, *Writing About Your Life*, p. 202.
[560] James Carroll in Diane Osen, ed., *The Book That Changed My Life: Interviews with National Book Award Winners and Finalists* (New York: Modern Library, 2002), p .9.

transgressive act, and artists must accept being punished. The more original and unsettling their art, the more devastating the punishment."[561] Academics want this kind of treatment, if for no other reason than that such criticism suggests that at least someone is reading their work and taking it seriously enough to be angry.

Have We Lost Our Passion? Academics can become so immersed in their own reward system that they lose their enthusiasm for writing (at least writing in a way that might stand a chance of being read outside of the academy). Anne Lamott provides a sense of this, even outside of the university: "Perfectionism is the voice of the oppressor, the enemy of the people. It will keep you cramped and insane your whole life, and it is the main obstacle between you and a shitty first draft."[562] Academic perfectionism is a bit different than what she has in mind, where the professor is constantly fixated in publishing in the leading journal or in the one providing the highest profile for their tenure and promotion. Such an emphasis can kill one's writing, bending and twisting it into a form and style that is indecipherable except to the initiated. Joyce Carol Oates substantiates such a process, asserting, "Never be ashamed of your subject, and of your passion for your subject." Oates continues, suggesting that she "never thought of writing as the mere arrangement of words on the page but the attempted embodiment of a vision; a complex of emotions; raw experience."[563] The academic life often inhibits passion and weakens vision, suggesting why so much of academic writing is lifeless or impenetrable.

This loss of focus is something we need to fight against, and it is a major battleground in the professional school where technique and technology often seem to rule the day. Dinesh D'Souza, among many, is troubled to see "more and more of our educational institutions move away from the liberal arts and focus on 'high-tech education.' Courses in computing and programming are replacing courses in literature, political science, and history. The goal is to educate young people to function better in a technological society. But it is a terribly shortsighted strategy. The reason is that knowing about computers is going to become less important in the near future." The love affair with the computer is at an all time high, either in our base affection with the device or in our desperation to ensure that every living soul is literate in its use. D'Souza continues, "As some of the most insightful members of the tech world recognize, we are in a

---

[561] Joyce Carol Oates, *The Faith of a Writer: Life, Craft, Art* (New York: HarperCollins Publishers, Inc., 2003), p. 33.
[562] Lamott, *Bird by Bird*, p. 28.
[563] Oates, *The Faith of a Writer*, pp. 22, 35.

transitional phase in which computer literacy seems of paramount importance; that phase will soon pass." He sees "content" as becoming "supreme." "By content I don't mean just 'information'; rather, I mean knowledge, understanding, and wisdom."[564] Mark Edmundson concurs with such assessments. On the one hand, he acknowledges that "Now that computers are everywhere, each area of inquiry in the humanities is more and more defined by the computer's resources. Computers are splendid research tools."[565] But he also sees a dark side to this situation: "Instead of spending class time wondering what the poem means, and what application it has to present-day experience, students compile information about it." "By putting a world of facts at the end of a key-stroke," Edmundson continues, "computers have made facts, their command, their manipulation, their ordering, central to what now can qualify as humanistic education. The result is to suspend reflection about the differences among wisdom, knowledge, and information."[566]

Perhaps the strongest connection between writing and the academic life is the mutual emphasis on learning a craft, mentioned earlier and important enough to be mentioned again. Nearly every writer reflecting on how they became a writer stresses this aspect of the occupation. Norman Mailer states casually that he "learned to write by writing."[567] Anne Lamott emphasizes the painful process of having first to endure "terrible first efforts."[568] She reflects, "I came to believe that I might be able to put a pencil in my hand and make something magical happen ... . Then I wrote some terrible, terrible stories."[569] Or, as only someone who has taught writing can say, "Successful writers are not the ones who write the best sentences. They are the ones who keep writing." Bonnie Friedman continues, "They are the ones who discover what is more important and strongest and most pleasurable in themselves, and keep believing in the value of their work, despite the difficulties."[570] William Zinsser compares writing to hitting a baseball: "*Writing* is a negative game. Very few sentences come right the first time, or even the second or third time. Even the best writers are initially .300 hitters, struggling against heavy odds to say what

---

[564] Dinesh D'Souza, *The Virtue of Prosperity: Finding Values in an Age of Techno-Affluence* (New York: Free Press, 2000), p. 246.
[565] Edmundson, *Why Read?*, p. 14.
[566] Edmundson, *Why Read?*, p. 15.
[567] Mailer, *Spooky Art*, p. 14.
[568] Lamott, *Bird by Bird*, pp. xx, 25.
[569] Lamott, *Bird by Bird*, p. xx.
[570] Friedman, *Writing Past Dark*, p. xiii.

they want to say."⁵⁷¹ Academics also must learn the craft of their own scholarly writing, mastering citation styles, accepted jargon peculiar to their own disciplines, the conventions of presenting research methodologies and data, and the variations in the array of journals they might publish in, as well as the great differences between trade, university, and professional presses.

Public Audiences. What is involved in such assessments concerns learning about the larger world of scholarship, and there are similarities between what writers and university professors face. Annie Dillard reflects that "writing sentences is difficult whatever their subject. It is no less difficult to write sentences in a recipe than sentences in *Moby-Dick*. So you might as well write *Moby-Dick*."⁵⁷² I must admit that I think Dillard's notion is both brilliant and sobering (and it is my personal favorite assessment about writing). It is likely to make any academic, especially those who have spent careers and considerable time writing for a narrow scholarly or professional audience, panic and speculate about wasted life and time. What Dilliard is getting at is close to the heart of one of the major academic crises of the last half-century, the loss of a public audience. Admittedly, the university administrator or faculty member states the problem in less elegant form. We can understand the problems academics face with their writing because of the increasing misunderstanding of the university by the general public. Donald Kennedy believes, "The university and its faculty, with their contemporary focus on knowledge production, seem inclined to limit their responsibility to a domain that is strictly academic. But the public almost surely expects more."⁵⁷³ The public certainly expects university faculty to weigh in on issues of public policy. But, as Kennedy explains, "In the first two-thirds of the twentieth century, university faculty members played a dominant role among the nation's 'public intellectuals.' Today there is growing doubt that academic scholars enjoy that level of prominence or have that much influence in the shaping of public awareness."⁵⁷⁴ All this is not because academics are not working hard, building knowledge, or laboring over those sentences. They have just lost their way. This may be especially true for professional schools and other academic units that have professionalized their activities.

Academics are likely to cast their mission in different words, but they are not far away from what writers pine over in their own efforts to find a

---

⁵⁷¹ Zinsser, *Writing About Your Life*, p. 113.
⁵⁷² Dillard, *Writing Life*, p. 71.
⁵⁷³ Donald Kennedy, *Academic Duty* (Cambridge: Harvard University Press, 1997).
⁵⁷⁴ Kennedy, *Academic Duty*, p. 278.

voice, carve out a story, get published, and gain a readership. All writers, whether university-based or freelancers, realize that the chance of being financially or worldly successful is a fleeting quest. Anne Lamott concludes, "Publication is not going to change your life or solve your problems. Publication will not make you more confident or more beautiful, and it will probably not make you any richer."[575] Academic writers, most I am willing to bet, would not trade a broader readership base for a bigger royalty check. All of this relates to the "central paradox" that goes both with writing and being a member of a faculty. Bonnie Friedman suggests, "On the one hand, we must write for ourselves. On the other, we must not forget the world."[576] Similarly, the individual first attracted to being a professor usually gets into the business because of a particular love for the subject, involving both research and teaching, then finds that one must write in a certain way, read particular writing, and construct and deliver teaching in a way that compromises their own love of the subject. Again, this relates to the larger mission of writing, what Joyce Carol Oates describes as the aspect of writing that is art, seeking personal redemption.[577] It is a good analogy, because every form of writing – fiction or non-fiction, memoir or arcane social science research, storytelling or philosophy – has some connection to this quest.

Writing is about meeting basic human needs, whether one describes this in purely personal terms or as some dimension of a larger social good. William Zinsser believes that "writing about one's life is a powerful human need,"[578] and we could expand on this to assert that writing is an intense human impulse. Days that go by where I don't write just a little bit seem somehow empty or incomplete; writing is as necessary as eating, sleeping, and defecating (and sometimes the latter result is close to the end product of writing). E. L. Doctorow connects writing to storytelling, and he sees the latter as an inherent human trait and need. Doctorow argues that even though "we live in an age that is scientifically oriented, even as we hold to the values of empiricism, demanding of our propositions that they be tested and of our legal case that they rest on demonstrable evidence, our modern minds are still structured for storytelling. Facts may change, evolve, they do so all the time, but stories find their way to the unchanging core of

---

[575] Lamott, *Bird by Bird*, p. 185.
[576] Friedman, *Writing Past Dark*, p. 67.
[577] Oates, *The Faith of a Writer*, pp. 39-41.
[578] Zinsser, *Writing About Your Life*, p. 6.

things."[579] One might add that writing grant proposals, strategic plans, and memoranda don't substitute for this kind of writing, unless, perhaps, that is all you have. Denis Donoghue, in one of those laments about what has happened to the teaching of literature in the university, reflects such concerns: "I don't recall feeling the need of a theory to get me started in reading literature or listening to music. In those days one learned a few rudimentary skills by practice or, as in my case, by apprenticing oneself to a master or several masters."[580] Donoghue thinks that the "purpose of reading literature is to exercise or incite one's imagination; specifically, one's ability to imagine being different."[581] One could argue that at least some of the purpose of library and information science schools is to embrace the notion of the book and the purpose of libraries.

Fact or Fiction. There are many questions that could be asked about my commentary. For one, is professional or academic writing the same or possess similar characteristics to creative writing and what has been termed public scholarship? Richard Rhodes, who has written both, perhaps provides the clearest insight into this: "Considered as a craft, technically, the writing of fiction and the writing of verity are identical processes but for one significant difference: we expect to conform to verifiable external references, while the information conveyed in fiction need be only internally consistent."[582] Of course, in our postmodern age, a worldview many claim is waning, we have seen the blending or blurring of fiction and non-fiction writing leading to public controversies concerning the work of scholars. Robert Fulford even believes that postmodernism subverts the primary mission of the university when he writes, "Having become securely lodged in the universities, postmodernism seems at times to reverse what many imagined was the university's function. Where once we might have asked professors to make difficult writers easy for us, now they make easy writers difficult, turning them into puzzles, muffling them in layers of aggressively impenetrable jargon and priestly theory. There is no work of literature that cannot be made more obscure by postmodern critics. What starts out as storytelling becomes, in their hands, a kind of elaborate cultural

---

[579] E. L. Doctorow, *Reporting the Universe, The William E. Massey Sr. Lectures in the History of American Civilization* (Cambridge, MA: Harvard University Press, 2003), p. 25.

[580] Denis Donoghue, *The Practice of Reading* (New Haven: Yale University Press, 1998), pp. 4-5.

[581] Donoghue, *The Practice of Reading*, p. 56.

[582] Rhodes, *How to Write*, p. 57.

dance whose choreography can be understood only by critics and teachers."583

Cases of plagiarism, sometimes defended in odd if not creative fashion, have plagued scholars in a number of disciplines, but so has the fabrication of data or evidence. Historians Michael Bellisiles and Joseph Ellis are the most recent, high profile cases of such infractions, where Bellisiles misused archival evidence and Ellis concoted lies about his personal life, undermining their general scholarly contributions. One interesting interpretation offered about these two (and other similar) cases, is that these scholars were engaged in what could be called creative non-fiction (what some have termed public scholarship). There is speculation that by building popular audiences, using literary agents, working with trade publishers lacking the normal scholarly review process of a university press, and aiming at much enhanced fiscal return for their work, there were added pressures and fewer safeguards contributing to the scholarly infractions.584

Absent the problems, the quest by historians like Ambrose, Bellesiles, Ellis, and Goodwin to gain a broader audience is a noble and important one. Besides from whatever personal motivations were involved, these and other scholars have become increasingly aware that they have been writing for other specialists and losing their broader audience, and certainly that of the general public. A historian, or any other scholar, engaged in research that they believe will make a difference to society can do nothing else but lament the loss of readership. In my own field, my conviction of the importance of records and historical evidence for every aspect of life comes with the sense that archivists have never possessed a broad audience, and the pressing and constantly unfolding controversies and events regarding the growing government secrecy, restricted access to information, increasing control of publishing by just a few international conglomerates, and other matters makes this lack of a voice more galling. In some ways, this is even more poignant for those identifying themselves as information scientists or professionals. Working within the midst of the hyped up modern information age, most of the debate about the nature and use of

---

[583] Robert Fulford, *The Triumph of Narrative: Storytelling in the Age of Mass Culture* (New York: Broadway Books, 1999), p. 113.

[584] See, especially, Jon Wiener, *Historians in Trouble: Plagiarism, Fraud, and Politics in the Ivory Tower* (New York: The New Press, 2005); Peter Charles Hoffer, *Past Imperfect: Facts, Fictions, Fraud – American History from Bancroft and Parkman to Ambrose, Bellesiles, Ellis, and Goodwin* (New York: Public Affairs, 2004); and Ron Robin, *Scandals and Scoundrels: Seven Cases That Shook the Academy* (Berkeley: University of California Press, 2004).

information and information technologies has been framed by journalists and freelance writers.

One might surmise that it is easy to be captivated by the lure of publishing advances, fat royalty checks, book tours, and autograph signings. We are entrepreneurs willing and able to parlay our expertise into projects of interest to us. The interest may be generated because of the possibility of extra financial gain, of pursuing intellectually engaging projects, or of reaching new groups with the particular message we believe is important to society. Consulting is one form of functioning as entrepreneurs, but the more common expression is writing articles and books (some directed at small groups of similar expertise, some aimed at wider audiences). While some of this work is motivated by the possibility of additional financial gain to support ourselves and our families, mostly we engage in such work as a means of staying connected with the real world, the practitioners in our fields, and to acquire additional materials for case studies to enrich our teaching. Or maybe we just write because we have to, as many writers, such as Zinsser contend: "Whether your memoir ever gets published isn't finally the point. There are many good reasons for writing that have nothing to do with getting published. One is the personal satisfaction of coming to terms with your life narrative – getting your story sorted out and preserved on paper. Another is the archival satisfaction of leaving to your local library or historical society your memories of your community as you knew it when you were younger. This is priceless information for scholars and social historians. It doesn't have to take the form of a published book to give those scholars the facts they need. You can print your memoir handsomely on your computer and have it duplicated and bound by your local copy shop. The shelves of town and college libraries are rich in these homemade gems of recollection."[585]

We are contributors to the university's historic function as a repository of human knowledge. Through our research, publications, teaching, and service to our professional colleagues and other constituents we strive to add new knowledge for the betterment of humanity and our professional communities. While some of this work may be measurable, much of it is not as it accumulates over decades and longer periods of time. Because of the nature of the disciplines we represent, we also have a uniquely important role to play in the creation, maintenance, preservation, design, and use of the university library and the broader digital library that is at the heart of the repository function. The main problem is that as faculty needed

---

[585] Zinsser, *Writing About Your Life*, p. 7.

to focus on their own teaching, research, scholarship, and professional service – because that is what faculty do – administration and planning pushed aside these activities and responsibilities unless they brought with them revenue of some sort. Some faculty simply turned to their own work and their own students, ignoring faculty and other meetings, and weakening faculty governance.

Conclusion: Planning, For What? Many academics are trying to reach out to broader audiences (the public, or at least that portion that reads books), not just because they want to make extra money or to become famous (although some perhaps sought this as well), but because they thought they could reach someone (get someone to listen to a new idea or engage someone in dialogue about an important issue) who was not just interested in theories, arcane discussions, or endless footnotes. But the world really isn't receptive to this. Richard Posner's book on the decline of the public intellectual in America,[586] one of many on this topic, lays the blame directly at the feet of the academic who, according to Posner, was writing about things he or she did not know anything about, making ludicrous predications and pontificating with authority when the authority was not deserved. In other words, the academic should retreat back into the cloister. Although Posner does not specifically address the professional school, it is not hard to imagine that he would be critical of the faculty there. Most write only for their narrowly defined professional circles, and few venture into public policy or the town square.

Academics, in professional schools or elsewhere within the university, are trying to influence public knowledge. By this, we mean that knowledge that is in the public domain via publication in major public opinion and literary magazines, publishing in readily accessible e-journals, the design and publication of Web sites, public lectures, interviews with journalists and other media representatives, and other channels reaching a wider segment of the public. We intend to utilize our expertise for support of public policy and debate, legislation bettering societal information services and access, and the use of information systems in all aspects of society, from public education to government and other institutions providing public benefits.

We can take some solace in the successful transition of some academics into public scholars, such as Neil Postman, Henry Petroski, and Witold Rybinzinki. There are many more to choose from than one might guess, although they still represent a very small percentage of the community of

---

[586] Richard Posner, *Public Intellectuals: A Study of Decline* (Cambridge, MA: Harvard University Press, 2001).

academic scholars. These three academics are as much public intellectuals as experts in their own discipline, with long careers producing books that can be found in both the university bookshop and the big chain stores. Neil Postman (to focus on just one), the late chair of the Department of Culture and Communications at New York University who died in 2003 at age 72, was a prolific author (20 books and more than 200 articles over forty years) of accessible books about education, the media, information technology, and culture. He started with a degree in English Education from Columbia Teachers' College and spent his entire academic career at New York University. Postman's books had a consistent feel to them, usually running two hundred or so pages, featuring very clear writing, teasing the reading with interesting comparisons across history and cultures, and often offering devastating and sweeping conclusions that goaded the reader into either being infuriated or wanting to know more. As Lance Strate reflects, Postman's "contributions, as a scholar, teacher, and public intellectual, enriched many different fields of study, including semantics, linguistics, communication, media studies, journalism, education, psychology, English, cultural studies, philosophy, history, sociology, political science, religious studies, technology studies, etc."[587] Much of his earliest writing was about English education, but Postman eventually expanded his scholarly scope to media and technology, pioneering the idea of "media ecology," a term he concocted in 1968, combining the "study of symbols, symbol systems, and symbolic form with the study of media and technology."[588]

Postman's most critical book about technology, *Technopoly*, was a sobering read: "One way of defining Technopoly, then," wrote Postman, "is to say it is what happens to society when the defenses against information glut have broken down. It is what happens when institutional life becomes inadequate to cope with too much information. It is what happens when a culture, overcome by information generated by technology, tries to employ technology itself as a means of providing clear direction and humane purpose. The effort is mostly doomed to failure. Though it is sometimes possible to use a disease as a cure for itself, this occurs only when we are fully aware of the processes by which disease is normally held in check."[589] Postman's best-known work, *Amusing Ourselves to Death*, was published two decades ago but it is still as fresh as the day it was written.

---

[587] Lance Strate, "Neil Postman, Defender of the Word," *ETC* (Winter 2003-04): 341.
[588] Strate, "Neil Postman, Defender of the Word," p. 344.
[589] Neil Postman, *Technopoly: The Surrender of Culture to Technology* (New York: Vintage Books, 1992), pp. 71-72.

Some lament that Postman was not as well known as others who wrote about technology, the media, and the society, such as Marshall McLuhan, but he was far better known than most university based scholars.

One might wonder just what impact the Internet has had on the quality of writing academics engage in and produce. We are members of disciplines connected to informal groups, networks, formally organized associations often with stronger alliances to these bodies than to our departments, the school, or the university. The existence of the Internet makes it possible for developing virtual academies whereby we read each other's research, recommend readings, plan courses, and chart future directions for our own segment of the information professions. We may be too quick to blame digital communication for poor writing, but many point past that and develop other explanations. "The real reason writing is so bad in cyberspace is that people simply don't write well anymore, online or off," explain O'Conner and Kellerman in their book about online writing.[590] I have long believed that the real source of attracting students to a professional school like the one I reside in is by the faculty developing some profile as scholars. And scholars are developed from a lifetime of reading and reflecting. The Goldstones speculate, "If you start your children off with books that are well-written, whose plots demand attention, with characters drawn with depth and wit, that is the type of reading they will come to enjoy. On the other hand, kids who are exposed to nothing but pop fiction or joke books or superficial biographies of sports heroes will become used to those and unlikely to move to anything more challenging."[591] Denis Donoghue worries that such concerns may be too late, arguing "There has been a shift of interest, especially among young people, from the written word to film and TV and tape. Reading a book is not a social or communal act, it is a private matter. There is also a widespread belief that books are a going or a gone medium; the future is the World Wide Web. Certainly it is hard to imagine a time when enthusiasm for books will be as vigorous as it was forty or fifty years ago."[592] So, one of the many questions may be just how professional programs, such as library and information schools, find these people or nurture them when they are discovered. And, more importantly, what the faculty has to teach about in such schools.

---

[590] Patricia T. O'Conner and Stewart Kellerman, *You Send Me: Getting It Right When You Write Online* (Orlando: Harvest Book, Harcourt, Inc., 2002), p. 4.
[591] Lawrence and Nancy Goldstone, *Deconstructing Penguins: Parents, Kids, and the Bond of Reading* (New York: Ballantine Books, 2005), p. 190.
[592] Donoghue, *The Practice of Reading*, p. 17.

Chapter Eight

Teaching in the Professional School in the Changing University

Introduction: Heat About Teaching. Teaching is drawing considerable heat both within and outside the university. Critics on the outside of the university persistently complain about how little many faculty members teach, lament the fact that many faculty reaching a certain star level in their fields are often recruited for major positions seemingly attractive because of light teaching loads, or bemoan the lack of attention placed on evaluating teaching. Many of the same complaints are sounded on the inside of the university. Like the never-ending debate within professions about the balance between theory and practice, the debate about the connection of teaching to other responsibilities of faculty, mostly research and publication, also never seems to abate. I view teaching as critical for reclaiming the worth of professional schools, and, as I have hinted throughout its pages, I think it only works if it is linked to research or scholarship that keeps a faculty member current with his or her field, and excited about it as well.

Some argue that teaching and research should not be viewed as two separate tasks. I do not disagree. Some distinguish between them because the prevailing dialogue in higher education for the past couple of generations has been to separate them. I remain concerned that there is both substantial tradition and scholarship suggesting that these various matters (such as research/teaching or education/business planning) are, indeed, significant challenges endemic to modern higher education. The large quantity of writings about higher education (and not by people on the outside, but by those within like Derek Bok) feel compelled to address such dichotomies. Within the library and information science fields, for example, the matter of formal education versus apprenticeship and theory versus practice have been consistent topics of discussion, writing, research, and hand-wringing for decades, spanning in some cases more than a century. These issues or tensions often come up within the ranks of the practitioners we hope to send our graduates into, requiring us to be able to think these matters through.

Teaching is an activity that often does not gain the same degree of attention as other activities of faculty. In one of the best books about teaching, James Banner and Harold Cannon strongly argue that teaching is a calling, not a nuisance impinging on other faculty interests. They also comment that teachers, at all levels of education, spend too little time reflecting about what teaching entails, how it should be evaluated, and how it is developed. Banner and Cannon also suggest why teaching may be neglected, arguing that teachers convey knowledge not information, a confusion that has emerged amidst all the hype in the modern information era.[593] The development of the Internet and the emergence of the World Wide Web with its rich resources has also prompted many schools to develop distance education programs pouring out data and often disparaging traditional teaching techniques (such as the lecture and the seminar) regardless of whether they seem to have worked or not as educational venues. In our time, it seems more hip and trendy to focus on the technologies of teaching rather than its substance. And as one might suspect, this is particularly a temptation for schools of library and information science wanting to be on the cutting edge of our new knowledge age.

Our obligation to students is to teach them something. A syllabus serves as a contract between student and teacher. We come to class prepared to present new information to students that will enable them to learn. We assign them readings and work in order to support the educational function. Yet, in the learning process, the student might *never* be right, except in their expectation of learning something from us. Moreover, since we are in the business of educating students, we are preparing them for the long-term. Many of us have experienced some sort of reassurance when we hear back from a former student three or more years from when they took classes with us, suggesting that now they were beginning to understand what and why we taught what we did. The only service contract we can offer them is a foundation of knowledge they can build off of in learning on the job or in taking more specialized continuing education courses updating their knowledge and skills.

Teaching Disparities. There is an interesting disparity in the attention given teaching by faculty who are in the classroom and administrators counting the pennies for putting them there. Clearly, distance education is part of the larger movement by the university to refashion itself into a revenue generating corporate entity. This creates a conflict between the faculty member's last bastion of academic freedom, the classroom, and the

---

[593] James M. Banner, Jr. and Harold C. Cannon, *The Elements of Teaching* (New Haven: Yale University Press, 1997), pp. ix, 4, 9.

control of that classroom in the name of increased efficiency and economy. There is, of course, a fine line between ensuring accountability and instilling excessive control. Surprisingly, at least to me, some of the more poignant examples of the easily unbalanced state of affairs are now in the university, the supposed cradle of free speech, thinking, and inquiry. David Noble, in his acerbic analysis of distance education, provides a sense of this. Noble writes, "once faculty and courses go online, administrators gain much greater direct control over faculty performance and course content than ever before and the potential for administrative scrutiny, supervision, regimentation, discipline and even censorship increase dramatically." Administrators likely would argue that this system will enable them to make faculty more accountable to the university and to the students (and parents) paying the bills. We now have a similar problem with research. As Noble argues, the "commercialization of academic research brought universities and industry into close partnership; it made some people very rich and no doubt resulted in the development of some new technologies. But it also ushered in a brash new regime of proprietary control, secrecy, fraud, theft, and commercial motives and preoccupations."[594] The latter suggests the need for systems of accountability, but one wonders how far we should go. It also suggests how teaching is being re-invented, not always in very positive ways, by the use of new educational technologies.

Teaching is also the activity most likely to create tensions and conflicts for individuals newly entering the academic ranks. Assistant professors find themselves in the position of needing to tread carefully so as to not offend the senior faculty who will ultimately determine their professional fates. The newer colleagues are also the ones most conscious of the need to compile stellar records of publishing and grantsmanship, even while they often have courses poured on them requiring the development and testing of new syllabi. The conflicting messages sent to these individuals sometimes lead them to become intensely self-reflective about their lives and careers and, in the worst case, to leave academe altogether. James Lang chronicled his first year, in a very public fashion, concluding that "The most complex relationship I find myself having to negotiate in my continued development as a teacher, then, is the one between my past and present selves."[595] Written in a biting, self-deprecating fashion, Lang's account is, nevertheless, a poignant tale about the often mysterious status of teaching in the

---

[594] David Noble, *Digital Diploma Mills: The Automation of Higher Education* (New York: Monthly Review Press, 2001), pp. 32, 38.
[595] James Lang, *Life on the Tenure Track: Lessons from the First Year* (Baltimore: Johns Hopkins University Press, 2005), p. 128.

university, one even more complex in professional schools where pressure is placed on faculty from the fields they represent to teach certain skills in particular ways.

The tension between teaching and other functions in a professional school in the corporate university is especially intense. Many commentators on the new corporate university stress the changes seeming to erode more traditional emphases on functions such as teaching. Gould sees how the market economy is challenging liberal arts disciplines and development of knowledge. He doubts that liberal education for its own sake is something that will be revived again, but Gould does not mean we can't or shouldn't rethink the idea of a liberal education, problems facing it, how we define it, and how it had previously worked to make the American university the most influential in the world.[596] Others disagree. Wendell Berry is particularly bleak, arguing that "The complexity of our present trouble suggests as never before that we need to change our present concept of education. Education is not properly an industry, and its proper use is not to serve industries, either by job-training or by industry-subsidized research. Its proper use is to enable citizens to live lives that are economically, politically, socially, and culturally responsible. This cannot be done by gathering or 'accessing' what we now call 'information' – which is to say facts without context and therefore without priority. A proper education enables young people to put their lives in order, which means knowing what things are more important than other things; it means putting first things first."[597] Some might find fault with Berry's outside perspective, but many insiders have stated much the same. Giamatti, for example, bluntly comments, "Basic research – that is, investigation that seeks new knowledge and understanding rather than solutions to immediate problems – is the essential nature of research on the part of all scholars."[598]

Professional schools have long operated with a focus on the practical because of the faculty's attention to their respective field's practice. If faculty members drift too far off from the common perspective on professional practice, they may be deemed to be irrelevant by the field and suffer in both reputation and recruitment. If on the other hand, faculty members become too wedded to mundane practice and service to the

---

[596] Eric Gould, *The University in a Corporate Culture* (New Haven: Yale University Press, 2003).
[597] Wendell Berry, *In the Presence of Fear: Three Essays for a Changed World* (Great Barrington, MA: The Orion Society, 2001), p. 9.
[598] A. Bartlett Giamatti, *A Free and Ordered Space: The Real World of the University* (New York: W. W. Norton and Co., 1990), p. 247.

profession, they may harm their own ability to build the scholarly research record they need to ply their trade within the university. Piling on top of them is the new reality of the cost-conscious university, where teaching is a salable product. Gould believes that the university must be a "highly diversified corporate entity, serving a vast clientele and most often supplementing its traditional revenue sources from teaching and research with other enterprises. In recent years, the character of the university has changed quite dramatically, from an institution in which learning is a competitive right to one in which it is a purchasable commodity in a consumerist culture."[599] Gould does not believe that the older liberal tradition should be jettisoned or that a crass market mentality should replace such ideals; rather he merely wants the university to be more responsible in how it meets its mission.[600] Developing a teaching philosophy in such an environment can be a challenge. Some, myself included, desire small class sizes where there is a more intimate relationship instructor and student, all the while knowing that the university administrators are counting heads and figuring your cost-effectiveness. This makes it hard to create the desirable synergy between teaching and research we all really want.

Teaching as Business. There are other realities in the corporate university creating havoc with our teaching. Jennifer Washburn wisely points out that only a small portion of universities have potential for profits, maybe no more than two dozen, and even these at most will barely break even: "The more universities try to sell politicians on the idea that they can serve as engines of economic growth," she speculates, "the more they are setting themselves up for failure and undermining the basis for their public support."[601] The Bayh-Dole Act established the possibility of closer collaboration between universities and corporations, but it has happened in a way often protecting corporations and their proprietary information first and foremost.[602] Washburn adds an interesting insight here about the nature

---

[599] Gould, *University in a Corporate Culture*, p. 72.
[600] Gould writes, "The intellectual ideals of liberal education that sustained it for so long – its concern for the nature of knowledge, its passion for defining reason and truth, its need to fit together an analytic, ethical, aesthetic, and ideological making of a worldview, its insistence on the importance of rhetoric and argument – cannot be effectively replaced simply by a theory of market responsiveness within the professionalized disciplines"; *University in a Corporate Culture*, p. 176.
[601] Jennifer Washburn, *University, Inc.: The Corporate Corruption of American Higher Education* (New York: Basic Books, 2005), p. xii.
[602] Washburn, *University, Inc.*, p. 17.

of public criticism of universities, with concerns about liberal political and social agendas, except for the potential "corrupting influence of another interest group: big business."[603] What this suggests is that faculty in professional schools, like library and information science, interested in research may be pushed to chase after corporate and government funding programs at the expense of other responsibilities. Indeed, this seems, from my vantage, to have occurred, reflected in two ways. First, these professional schools seem to be competing with each other to announce who has gotten the bigger grants. This consumes more and more of the discussion on listservs and at conferences. Second, all research seems to be defined in terms of the revenue it generates. What is lost here is a real commitment to scholarship; in truth, much of the research and writing needed has little need for funding, except for modest travel grants and similar types of support. The corporate model whacks everything out of proportion.

Some faculty in professional schools may look the other way when they chase research dollars, justifying their courses being offered as an after thought or by someone else supported by their funding (given many students' primary concern for credentials). Gould, for example, observes that "The contemporary university may not enjoy quite the same power for legislating cultural legitimacy that it once did, but it can still provide very strong constructions of social reality by appearing – as our elite schools do – to link the intellectual and the economic value of a degree as a credential."[604] Gould argues, "Of all late-capitalist markets, American higher education is indeed extraordinarily successful because it is highly diversified, flexible, and based on an endless consumer need for degrees in order to enter the general or professional workplace."[605] Others consider another model, something very different than a vocational one. Washburn says, "one could argue that in a knowledge-driven economy it is all the more important that undergraduates are provided not with narrow vocational training but with a broad-based foundation in reading, writing, arithmetic, and science – an education that sharpens the students' intellectual faculties, their curiosity about the world, and their ability to think critically and creatively. Because technology and the state of knowledge in nearly every discipline are changing so rapidly, the most valuable skill universities could impart is the capacity to learn and grow intellectually throughout one's

---

[603] Washburn, *University, Inc.*, p. 71.
[604] Gould, *University in a Corporate Culture*, p. 24.
[605] Gould, *University in a Corporate Culture*, p. 30.

lifetime."[606] How a faculty member determines what path to follow is a troublesome matter. They may hear conflicting messages every day, and they may wonder if whatever choice they make will be the right one, as the priorities of the corporate university changes daily as it follows a highly volatile market.

There is another challenge when it comes to teaching, and that is balancing a love of learning with the aspects necessary for pursuing a profession.[607] But what does a love of learning mean these days? A faculty member ought to be motivated by this, more so than by a love of money. This ought to translate into a love of teaching, the kind growing into an interest in careful preparation for class sessions and mentoring of students. Unfortunately, this love seems to have disappeared in many quarters; indeed, some could argue that it is difficult to try to love something that your employer doesn't value. Lucinda Roy, in her disturbing and moving account of the April 16, 2007 shootings at Virginia Tech, reflects that research universities are far less interested in teaching than in research dollars or any other means to generate revenue: "With the pressure to generate income more pronounced than it has ever been it is unlikely that teaching will retain the level of recognition it deserves any time soon."[608] And, in this, we may ultimately see the virus that kills the professional school (and other parts of the university).

Students First? It is not difficult to relate teaching to reading, research, and writing. Obviously, good teachers continually immerse themselves in the current knowledge of the field, both to prepare for lectures and to develop challenging and relevant reading lists for their courses. There is another dimension to the teaching process, interaction with students, which adds an interesting and varied dimension to the faculty member's world. Every educator has experienced that moment when a new insight develops

---

[606] Washburn, *University, Inc.*, p. xii.
[607] Giamatti, *A Free and Ordered Space*, p. 120.
[608] Lucinda Roy, *No Right to Remain Silent: The Tragedy at Virginia Tech* (New York: Harmony Books, 2009), p. 178. Roy even places the problem with teaching assessment as one of the factors of the school's inability to deal with troubled students. She provides an interesting assessment of teaching evaluations, asserting that the student evaluations of teaching have evolved from something intended to assist faculty to a means to judge faculty, creating a process causing teachers to be "less adventurous" and "making some teachers think twice before they offend or provoke a student, and making professors and instructors less willing to report troubled students, especially if the teacher knows he or she could receive a blistering evaluation from the student in response" (p. 188).

in the midst of a dialogue with students; students, coming to a field fresh will see things that the veteran hand has not. Writers, discussing their craft, often consider such possibilities in their work. Norman Mailer reflects, "I prefer doing a book that is not too carefully prepared. Some of my best ideas come because I haven't fixed my novel's future in concrete. Once you know your end, it's disastrous to get a new idea."[609] Charles Johnson equates the "process of writing" to "an adventure; you never know how things are going to configure themselves ... . If a writer isn't surprised and he doesn't feel suspense, then the reader won't."[610] In this way, writing and teaching are similar – full of uncertainties and potential discoveries.

A portion of one's time in the classroom and in advising also requires the mentoring of students in their writing. Scott Crider has given us an excellent window into the nature of teaching about the academic essay where logos – or being logical – is the central feature of academic writing, and where determining a thesis and learning how to generate testimony as authority is the order of the day.[611] As others have suggested, knowing how to compose an academic argument is a good skill to possess. Frank Cioffi believes that the "academic argument ... forms the central and most important kind of nonfiction writing that you should master, even if you don't get a chance to use it after graduating from college. It's important not only because it draws on elements of all the other forms of nonfiction writing and hence will allow you to move to any of those forms relatively easily. It also replicates the method by which ideas are created. It teaches you to think."[612] The classroom might be the crucible where such arguments are formed, or, perhaps, the force driving one into a quiet room to reflect and write away from the boisterous and sometimes rancorous discussions by students in the classroom (real and virtual).

Working with students, grading student papers, and developing the means of inspiring students about how to express themselves in written form can't hurt anyone's progress in writing. It is far more than merely correcting student papers for proper grammar. Richard Rhodes provides a fair criticism of such a simplistic perspective: "Most books that purport to

---

[609] Norman Mailer, *The Spooky Art: Thoughts on Writing* (New York: Random House, 2003), p. 91.
[610] Quoted in Diane Osen, ed., *The Book That Changed My Life: Interviews with National Book Award Winners and Finalists* (New York: The Modern Library, 2002), p. 40.
[611] Scott Crider, *The Office of Assertion: An Art of Rhetoric for the Academic Essay* (Wilmington, DE: ISI Books, 2005).
[612] Frank Cioffi, *The Imaginative Argument: A Practical Manifesto for Writers* (Princeton: Princeton University Press, 2005), p. 1.

teach writing advise you to write as simply as possible. You may be constrained by a formal requirement, as students usually are in papers, in which case it's wise to comply. But good standard English isn't more virtuous than any other style. Different voices, different styles, suit different purposes. The more of them you learn to command, the more resources you bring to writing."[613] Our work with students should be a reminder about how hard it is to write effectively (and how difficult it can be to teach anything in an effective fashion). As Frank Cioffi reflects, along with nearly everyone who has written about writing, "Writing is hard work, and good writing, while it occasionally springs magically or bewilderingly from your frontal lobes, will more often be the result of revision, reflection, and many hours' anguished labor. Labor is the right word, for indeed writing does resemble giving birth to something new."[614] Bret Lott sees it this way: "Because the longer I write – and this is the one sure thing I know about writing – the harder it gets, and the more I hold close the truth that I know nothing."[615] Even those who consider other sources for molding writing, such as creativity and inspiration, still note the need for hard labor. Alice Flaherty examines the role of emotions, brain structures, writing pleasures and pains, and creativity. She says "writing regularly, inspiration or no, is not a bad way to eventually get into an inspired mood; the plane has to bump along the runway for a while before it finally takes off."[616] Ellen Gilchrist advises that writing is something achieved through doing it and being willing to take criticism.[617] So, no matter what we think we are doing,

---

[613] Richard Rhodes, *How to Write: Advice and Reflections* (New York: HarperCollins Publishers, 1995), p. 41.
[614] Cioffi, *The Imaginative Argument*, p. 44. Susan Minot mulls it over in this way: "I am very fortunate to make my living by writing, though I feel I got to this point through no more design than having followed an often bewildered instinct and by simply always writing. I believe that what an artist needs most, more than inspiration or financial consolation or encouragement or talent or love or luck, is endurance;" Susan Minot in Marie Arana, ed., *The Writing Life: Writers on How They Think and Work: A Collection from the Washington Post Book World* [New York: Public Affairs, 2003], p. 51.
[615] Bret Lott, *Before We Get Started: A Practical Memoir of the Writer's Life* (New York: Ballatine Books, 2005), pp. 12-13.
[616] Alice W. Flaherty, *The Midnight Disease: The Drive to Write, Writer's Block, and the Creative Brain* (Boston: Houghton Mifflin Co., 2004), p. 86.
[617] In her interesting *The Writing Life* (Jackson: University Press of Mississippi, 2005) is some sage advice: "Write what you know. Show, don't tell. Writing is rewriting – All of those things are probably true most of the time for every writer. A writer who is writing at white heat with the muse at his shoulder doesn't need any rules.

as faculty members, even in professional schools, we will be cajoling, prompting, begging, and, sometimes, even inspiring students (and ourselves) to write better (and to do all things better).

Other Kinds of Literacy. Those of us teaching in library and information science programs should feel a special burden to work with our students in improving their writing and other skills. As O'Conner and Kellerman candidly state, "In the age of the computer, anybody who can't write can't connect."[618] In our schools we spend countless time and effort worrying about an ever elusive computer literacy, when we ought to be stressing out about a more basic literacy. We also fret about getting our students to learn how to master the seeking of information, when we ought, just as frequently, get them to learn how to organize and communicate information.[619] Immersing students into reading is a great means of forcing them to understand how important basic writing skills will be for their future careers and lives. Ben Yagoda considers that any writing style is like a "fingerprint."[620] According to Yagoda, style is critical: "Every time we write

---

All he needs to do is be a good typist" (p. 71). Gilchrist won't use a computer, but instead she writes and edits by hand and on a typewriter, saving every draft (p. 41). She adds: "Writing is rewriting. Write what you know. The reward has to be within yourself. Tell the truth about what you know and what you feel. Find out things. Read great literature. Then write. It's only typing. Stop talking about it and do it, or else admit you only want this master's degree so you can teach" (p. 79). Finally, "A writer is a person who writes, who continues to create, who believes he can create and that the world is full of material that if we all wrote all the time we would never begin to use it up" (p. 113).

[618] Patricia T. O'Connor and Stewart Kellerman, *You Send Me: Getting It Right When You Write Online* (Orlando: Harvest Book, Harcourt, Inc., 2002), p. 91.

[619] Jill Kerr Conway, describing her discovering history and English as her subject in college, provides an idea about the difference between information and learning: "Better still was my inner feeling that I had found something I could do well, and my new awareness that university study was about learning and reflection, not the cramming of texts and information"; *The Road from Coorain* (New York: Vintage Books, 1990), p. 168. Robert Alter, likewise, shows how literature can fail us: "This means that as readers we will sometimes run the risk of inventing a connection in the text where there is only a gap. For the most part, however, the dangers of overreading are far outweighed by the dangers of underreading, a habit to which modern culture, with its popular journalism and its rapid electronic messages, predisposes us"; *The Pleasures of Reading in an Ideological Age* (New York: W. W. Norton and Co., 1996), p. 47.

[620] Ben Yagoda, *The Sound on the Page: Style and Voice in Writing* (New York: HarperResource, 2004), p. xvii.

a word, a phrase, a sentence, we have to choose from what seems like an infinite number of acceptable candidates. Then, just as significantly, we choose how to link the sentences together into paragraphs. Together, these decisions constitute a style."[621] You master an acceptable style for your purposes, and then you develop your own.[622]

Teaching writing requires faculty in library and information science schools to develop different approaches than what we are accustomed to preaching about – the smooth, efficient, and foolproof acquisition of information. Derrick Jensen promotes a somewhat laborious process: "When I was teaching myself how to write I'd hand copy (longhand) entire pages from books I liked, forcing myself to slow down and pass the words through my body – from my eyes to brain into my bloodstream and through my guts and heart and lungs before I settled on which passage to copy, then moving again through eyes and brain and down my arms to come out my fingertips – thus learning how the words felt in every part of me. From this I learned what a good beginning feels like, a good ending, a good description. I learned how great writers move someone across a room, show pain, show love."[623] Yagoda also supports the idea of copying passages from others' works, a process that is a form of careful reading intended to "train the ear to pick up the strains of other writers' styles."[624] E. L. Doctorow describes the process as looking for the right "voice," revealing how important it is to remember how challenging writing can be and how important it is to teach: "A book begins as an image, a sound in the ear, the haunting of something you don't want to remember, or perhaps a great endowing anger. But it is not until you find a voice for whatever is going on inside you that you can begin to make a coherent composition. The language you find precedes your intention or, if not, is sure to transform it."[625] We might be a bit intimidated to try to get our students to write effectively by mimicking what they regularly encounter in the

---

[621] Yagoda, *Sound on the Page*, p. 29.
[622] "Early in a career, in order to get published, or hired, it is often important for a writer to master a middle style – to learn to do things the way everyone else is doing them. At that point, he or she can start becoming different"; Yagoda, *Sound on the Page*, p. 118.
[623] Derrick Jensen, *Walking on Water: Reading, Writing, and Revolution* (White River Junction, Vermont: Chelsea Green Publishing Co., 2004), p. 116.
[624] Yagoda, *Sound on the Page*, p. 228.
[625] E. L. Doctorow, *Reporting the Universe*, The William E. Massey Sr. Lectures in the History of American Civilization (Cambridge, MA: Harvard University Press, 2003), p. 59.

professional literature, but we need to teach them how to evaluate this literature (and this evaluation ought not to cease with the content or argument but also include the effectiveness of the writing).

What is it that we are seeking to accomplish in such teaching? We are seeking to introduce students to work that will transform their careers, if not their lives, and, as well, that might inspire them to write a meaningful essay or book of their own. Barry Lopez says, "If you do become a working writer, and if your creative life continues to develop, there are going to be points throughout when you are reading a book that will alter the direction of your work."[626] Edmundson adds, "The text of a book lies in its power to map or transform a life."[627] Of course, the way we often try to get students to pick through books, as if they are performing Google searches on the Web, won't assist us in getting them to slow down and reflect on such matters. Schwarz sees that it is not technology but us that may be killing the spirit of reading and reflection in the modern information age.[628] We want to engage our students in understanding the importance of reading and writing, how these are very human functions persisting through endless generations. Although Alberto Manguel can confidently state that "A book becomes a different book every time we read it,"[629] in fact the acts of reading and writing have not changed as much as what the technocrats and information age pundits would have us believe. Critic Harold Bloom suggests, "The way we read now, when we are alone with ourselves, retains considerable continuity with the past, however it is performed in the academies,"[630] pushing us to remember that we in library and information science schools need to be cognizant of the potentially perverse damage we can do if we mess around too much in deconstructing these very basic human impulses.

Dialoguing with Students. Our students need us to teach them the rudiments of writing, of developing a critical spirit to examine not merely information but evidence and knowledge. It is interesting that writers themselves want advice. The irrepressible Anne Lamott asserts, "But by all means let someone else take a look at your work. It's too hard always to

---

[626] Quoted in Osen, p. 88.
[627] Mark Edmundson, *Why Read?* (New York: Bloomsbury, 2004), p. 129.
[628] "If those of us who live by language become superfluous in years to come, it will not be because of the advance of technology, but the loss of coherent discourse"; Lynne Sharon Schwartz, *Ruined by Reading: A Life in Books* (Boston: Beacon Press, 1996), p. 24.
[629] Alberto Manguel, *A History of Reading* (New York: Viking, 1996), p. 10.
[630] Harold Bloom, *How to Read and Why* (New York: Scribner, 2000). p. 21.

have to be the executioner."[631] William Zinsser extends the point even farther: "The best teachers of an art or a craft are their own best textbook. Students who take courses from those teachers – writers, painters, musicians, dancers, gardeners, cooks – really want to know how their teachers do what they do."[632] Are we ready to function in that way? Even in my own field, archival studies, we can reflect about this. Zinsser says, the "most important principle for writing the story of your life: mere facts aren't enough. No matter how many details you diligently collect about the people and places and events in your past, they won't add up to a memoir. You must make a narrative arrangement."[633] And this is the case even if all the best and most dramatic archival and other sources magically present themselves to you.[634] It is something I ask of myself quite regularly, and I worry because so often the dialogue between me and my students seems to be to urge them to develop better writing skills and to cease whining about what they perceive to be heavy and unfair reading loads.

Instead people who associate themselves with our contemporary information age seem to be ones who seek to intimidate people about their lot in this era. Wendy Lesser, in her fine book about the pleasures of reading, angrily notes, "Like everyone else who endured the closing months of 1999, I recall being bombarded over the airwaves by spurious novelties and momentous opportunities of every kind; and when I was assured that the bulk of this onslaught would be over on January 1, I was irritable enough to ask, 'After the millennium, will they stop running the dot-com commercials, too?' Those two transformations – the meaningless click of the calendar, and the huge technological change that has altered our work lives, our social lives, our financial lives, our intellectual and artistic lives – seemed merged into one. At the age of forty-seven I felt distinctly left

---

[631] Anne Lamott, *Bird by Bird: Some Instructions on Writing and Life* (New York: Anchor Books, 1995), p. 57.
[632] William Zinsser, *Writing About Your Life: A Journey into the Past* (New York: Marlowe & Co., 2004), p. 137.
[633] Zinsser, *Writing About Your Life*, p. 162.
[634] Zinsser wonders, "How should you begin? As always, that's the horrible problem. You're found that old trunk with all the letters and postcards and photographs and diaries, the school and college textbooks, the football programs and ticket stubs, the wedding announcements and baby shower invitations. Your life is there waiting for you in scraps of paper and scraps of memory. Now all you have to do is to put it together" (*Writing About Your Life*, p. 164).

behind, a remnant of the book-reading past."⁶³⁵ She shouldn't feel too bad. After all there are some who still believe in the power of books, even ones in traditional print, even in places like schools of library and information science, places that often seem more like the camps of the enemy of such basic human activities as reading. Recognizing this might just be the salvation of these schools, if there is to be any hope for them at all.

Teaching Who We Are. We can answer the question of who we are by putting ourselves (and our schools) into the historic context of the university, recognizing that our schools are a microcosm of the entire university, a conglomeration of academic groups loosely configured about the broad, almost non-definable, sense of the information professions. This is critical since library and information science schools or iSchools are a community without a common history (or not much of one). The concept of an Information Age has been advanced as a rationale, but this is more mythical than based in reality (every era was dependent on information and a consumer of information). We need to create opportunities to identify commonalities among the faculty, such as understanding that society (all individuals, all organizations) operates about information "documents."⁶³⁶

As we are teachers, preparing future information professionals (at the bachelors and masters levels) and future educators of information professionals and leaders in their fields (at the doctoral level), it is important that we identify and develop a story. Being teachers is an extremely labor-intensive responsibility, requiring great effort to stay current with the research and scholarship of our fields and needing extreme sensitivity to and deliberate counseling of our students. Teaching is not about selling products or reaching customers; it is about educating individuals to see the big picture of societal conditions, understand the details of the challenges of technology, and the needs of individuals and organizations of all sorts. In fact, as I have commented on a number of times in this volume, we seek to be innovators and change agents in our own disciplines, aiming to strengthen professional knowledge and practice.

In this teaching, we are convinced of the importance of information to improve the performance and quality of society, the life of its citizens, and its institutions. While we have many different perspectives about how

---

⁶³⁵ Wendy Lesser, *Nothing Remains the Same: Rereading and Remembering* (New York: Houghton Mifflin Co., 2003), p. 67.
⁶³⁶ For the concept of information documents see John Seely Brown and Paul Duguid, *The Social Life of Information* (Boston: Harvard Business School Press, 2000) or David M. Levy, *Scrolling Forward: Making Sense of Documents in the Digital Age* (New York: Arcade Publishing, 2001).

information is defined or focus on different elements of information (the archival studies program focuses, for example, on evidence and the value of evidence for accountability and societal and organizational memory), we share a commitment that information is critical to life, as well as a common sense that information needs to be managed, preserved, accessible, protected, and processed in practical forms.

How prominent is discussion about teaching in university planning processes? Often, this planning is more a corporate process, where a more simplified aim such as profits or revenue is targeted (disguised, of course, by some academic platitudes). Professional schools are particularly susceptible to such thinking, because they need to justify, in an expeditious manner, their worth to the larger university.

Can Teaching Support Business? Anyone who has served on a tenure committee knows the story. An individual under consideration builds a solid record of inquiry into practical computer applications. The review process, resulting in a positive recommendation, still seems curious. We shift through external review letters in which the commentators write in glowing fashion about the research but always with a slightly guilty edge. There were comments about how the research was not theoretical enough or that somehow it was too concerned with solving real world problems. While we could certainly argue that pursuing theory for the sake of learning is at the heart of the university, so is serving society's needs. Somehow, we are struggling with the kind of balance needed between learning, teaching, thinking, and building practical tools. I am sure that the university has been grappling with this for a thousand years, but one wonders whether the university will exist for an equal distance of time in the future if such pressures for unhealthy change continue. One also wonders if perhaps either the professional school will prove to be a short-lived phenomenon or, if the *entire* university will become nothing more than a professional school.

Professional schools constantly face new mandates for entrepreneurial activities. I always wonder if we are willing to take up these challenges? As we labor at public relations, we rob ourselves of the ability to be innovative. Here are some thoughts from Gary Hamel, a management expert, on the factors that enable organizations to become innovative.[637] Hamel believes that for an organization to be a "perpetual and radical innovator," it must

---

[637] These comments are excerpted from an interview with Hamel in the e-journal *Ubiquity: A Web-based publication of the ACM* (Volume 1, Number 32, Week of October 9, 2000), available at http://www.acm.org/ubiquity/interviews/g_hamel_1.html.

have "individual competence." "We now have to give people the new thinking tools that will allow them as individuals to imagine and edit and improve and champion rule-breaking ideas." One would imagine that instilling thinking within an organization would not be very difficult for a university unit, but, it seems, it is just as hard an achievement as in any other organization. Hamel continues, "The second thing that's required is not competence but connection. The speed and the amount and the quality of innovation depend on the number of connections among individuals and their ideas... . So to get more innovation in the company, I need to be able to connect the individuals in that company in new and interesting ways. What we've been working on is developing a way for people to make those connections in the cause of innovation." In some schools, people do not want to connect. They resist sharing ideas, as if someone would rob them. Hamel is not done. "The final thing that's required is climate. And that's just a broad catchall saying that we have organizations, for the most part today, that were built for the Industrial Age. They were built for an age in which scale, efficiency, replication, dual hierarchy, and control were things that caused you to win. And in fact, most of our management, processes and systems look at variety as a bad thing... . So we're going to have to create new climates in organizations that reflect these new realities – that yes, diligence and scale and quality are all very important but now we need self-organization, imagination, adhocracy. Those things have to be valued and seen as legitimate and not seen as simply strange deviances from our otherwise perfect alignment and unending pursuit of efficiency." As everyone knows who studies corporate culture, transforming such culture in any way is an extremely difficult thing to do. It requires hard work, commitment, and trust. In the university we need a radical re-structuring of the monthly faculty meetings, more individual initiative and less focus on elaborate process and a search for the elusive (and often imaginary) consensus, stronger faculty governance, and a more active planning process with better information and a stronger governance (as opposed to advisory) role.

New Academic Years. At the beginning of each new academic year, I spend most of the first week meeting with new students, listening to their concerns, answering their questions, and advising them about what courses they should take through the next year. It is a typical experience, with most of the students being focused on requirements and worried about workloads in the graduate courses. Occasionally, I have a welcome encounter with a new student, when one expresses concerns about what they need to learn and ask questions about the knowledge they need to build. As I talk with such students, I privately worry about how well they might do in a professional school or, indeed, any graduate program.

I worry about the general state of higher education and the possible lowering of expectations we have for students. Samuel Hazo, the MaAnulty Distinguished Professor Emeritus at Duquesne University, complains, the "current collegiate goal is not the beginning of wisdom but proficiency (in marketable skills), not breadth of knowledge but adjustment, not cultural understanding but social (upward) mobility. In brief, the goal of graduating free men and women (intellectually free) has been replaced by giving degrees to instantly employable trainees." Hazo argues that the "primary result, except in all too few instances, is that college graduates are essentially programmers and planners, not thinkers."[638]

Every year we have a chance to start afresh – just as we have in redesigning our courses and cleaning up our desks and offices – and to fix such problems. The first week of every academic year we have our first faculty meetings. Perhaps we can use these meetings to focus first on educating students, building an environment in which we reflect how we contribute to knowledge as part of a university, and then consider other matters such as enrollment and revenue. Perhaps if we emphasized these other aspects of our work, the more mundane issues might take care of themselves. As we consider faculty agenda topics perhaps we can consider each matter for how it affects education, knowledge, research, and the preparation of well-rounded graduates before we worry about financial gain and other similar concerns.

Once, in a pique about what was and was not happening in my school, I plunged into an interview with another school in the same field, indulging in the old academic shell game, where, when dissatisfied with your present lot, you make the appearance of considering another offer, all in the hopes of getting your own school to improve your salary, status, teaching load, or something. But I was only half committed to the game since I was never really contemplating a move. It was like starting a new academic year. Doing something like this can lead to some odd incidents, and a portion of this interview remains in my mind as one of those kinds of events. The school I was being interviewed by was renowned for its emphasis on the theoretical dimensions of the information professions. I was asked very early in the interview about what my theoretical orientation was in my own

---

[638] Samuel Hazo, "The Selling Out of Higher Education," *Pittsburgh Post-Gazette*, September 3, 2000, available at http://www.post-gazette.com/forum/20000903edhazo6.asp.

work. Well, my work is educating students to work as archivists and records managers. Was I an adherent to some aspect of postmodernism, structuralism, post-structuralism, or the like, all "isms" floating about the fringes of my field. While I had read into these various mindsets, most seemed greatly flawed in some way. As I sat there ruminating on this question, I realized I had nowhere to go with this question that would please my interrogators. Finally, I simply answered them that my theoretical orientation was that "records were and are important to society, its organizations, and its people." This received the response of awkward silence. Given how often records were dismissed as bureaucratic obstacles, I am sure the people interviewing me thought I had lost my mind. I knew, of course, that for all practical purposes, the interview was over, but as academics do, we sparred for a while more.

In hindsight, I realized that this was a good answer. For one thing, many archivists and records managers had come to assume that society accorded them and their field respect as well as understanding. As a result, they had long since come to lose sight of what it was that they were doing that really was important. Obviously, it was critical for me to inculcate this into my students and into my classroom discussions, but it hardly seemed to be the kind of comment likely to endear you to anyone in a university. Universities are notoriously bad record keepers. Some have argued that universities are the most over-documented of all American institutions, and this is true if you take into account the large number of archival programs supported by them. Merely counting the number of institutional archives is by no means a good gauge, however. The majority of these academic archives accept records reactively, as they are transmitted pell-mell from various segments of the university. The vast majority of universities lack substantial archives programs, In my nearly two decades at a university, I have never once received a single directive indicating anything about the maintenance of my personal papers or records related to grants or even the students I advise.

Can We Teach Ourselves? One week a new printed marketing tool suddenly appeared for the faculty to use with corporate audiences, only not all of the faculty could use it, since the library and information science was described in two sentences – and there was avoidance of the word "librarians" as if corporations won't be interested in them. What makes all of this so particularly galling is the realization that marketing requires at least some ability to make forecasts about economic conditions and employment trends. The development of this corporate marketing sheet occurred during the height of the dot.com boom. A few short years later, and the burst of the high technology industry reveals that we were not doing a very good job in assessing potential directions in the economy and society more broadly. Yet, there have been more books published and more print churned out in making great promises for the grand future of society and its uses of information technology. Indeed, one can declare that the entire World Wide Web is one grand advertising scheme for the promises of the technologies. We can be merely cynical and assume that this is the result of merely believing our own hype. However, if one looks at the history of the library community, one sees that librarians have often tended to be more skeptical and more cautious about the promises of information technology. Given the presence of these individuals in the school, one would have expected, especially since we are in the university, that more dialogue would have occurred and more balance achieved in how the school planned its programs and its future. A kind of technological determinism rode roughshod over all deliberations. Some of the very matters some of us were advising our students to be careful about were not being given their due in faculty deliberations. We are a lot better about such issues today.

My own school reorganized and tore down departmental barriers that often contributed to such problems. It has also made itself part of the iSchool movement, an effort by many former library science programs to develop broader interdisciplinary approaches to the role of information in society. However, for nearly all of the schools that have dropped the word library and taken up the information banner, the majority of the students enrolled in these programs are interested in very traditional aspects of employment, such as school and public librarians, archivists and preservation administrators. Each of us in such schools hope for and aspire to new kinds of intellectual vitality, but we have a long way to go before we demonstrate true interdisciplinary approaches or a stronger presence in the research universities where we reside.

Running the Classroom. Universities inform faculty that they do not control classrooms (even though we have more control there than anywhere else). We are sent, weekly it seems, messages about what we can say, what we cannot say, about how to deal with students with disabilities (and everything seems to be a disability), about how to observe religious holidays, about how to present research – and the list of reminders goes on and on (but most of us have little confidence that we would do any better than what Virginia Tech did a couple of years in its shootings). A glance at the typical university Web site will find much more about staff and faculty requirements than about academic programs, and most of us, because of the sheer impracticality of trying to absorb even a small portion of this, ignore it and try to deal with other activities that improve what we do in the classroom. Working on our own research or reading a book in a reflective manner that might stimulate a new lecture are much preferred than waiting for the next missive from the university administration. And, fortunately, publishing (both print and digital) is another means of teaching, extending us outside of the classroom.

I have been told that I "intimidate" students, perhaps because I am not always sympathetic to student complaints about heavy reading loads and writing assignments. There is failure within the professional schools in our system of higher education because we tend to coddle our students (at least some, but too many, of them). We tell them we will teach them skills to do a real job, providing them a credential so that they will be hired. Sometimes we boil everything down to simplistic elements that do not challenge students, and transform them into customers. We want to counsel them, befriend them, guide them, and, along the way, take their money. This is, of course, just another manifestation of the corporate takeover of the university, the turning of higher education into just another business. If in the real world we wouldn't challenge customers, why would we do it in the university? In order to keep the students happy and them (or someone) paying the bills, we need to entertain rather than educate them, spoon feed rather than press them. Educational standards suffer, as must the quality of professional practice ultimately offered by the graduates of such programs.

Some of these problems I attribute to the nature of professional schools, where they work so hard to explain that they are reflecting professional practice in their classrooms. Since many of our students come to us either with some experience or with some strong sense of the nature of the profession, when we question or analyze current professional practice some of the students become unnerved. Even when I try to explain to these students that our school and its classrooms and computer laboratories ought to be a safe place to think differently, to experiment, and, consequently, to learn, some of the students have a difficult time accepting any of this. They did not want to question, they mainly wanted the tools to practice – not realizing that they need to be able to think in a bigger way in order to utilize the tools.

Our students are graduate students. Supposedly, they had already been the recipient of a college education, but some students are not prepared to think critically or to be challenged. Perhaps this is the kind of student that professional schools attract, or, and more scary, perhaps this is what happens to these individuals when they cross the portal into a professional school. This is, of course, the failure of the modern university, which now sees itself as not being responsible for challenging students but to run them as customers through their diploma mills. And in the professional schools, these mills may be operating much more efficiently and effectively than in any other part of the university.

Teaching and Researching. Frustrated and restless with my own academic position, I had interviewed at another professional school. It was a lark, of course, as these things tend to be, but it was necessary for my own mental health and resulted in a formal offer. It had been another of those soul-searching times for determining what I want to do with the rest of my life. The issue is not an unusual one for an academic like me, a full professor with tenure, concerning whether I want to emphasize teaching along with research and publishing versus more administrative concerns, an issue accentuated by my residing in a professional school. The usual tension, at least the one most often discussed in books about higher education, seems to be the space separating teaching and research. That dichotomy (the way it is often characterized) also exists in a professional school as well, but professional schools also have added matters such as connections with professional associations, a heavier stress on fieldwork and practical applications, and more concern with practice than with theory or knowledge. The space separating these two functions seems to be no greater than that represented by the university office one occupies.

The building my school functions in, or tries to function in, is one of those odd structures of the early 1960s with spaces discouraging working, teaching, and meeting (although many in it have carved out usable places in it – I love my office). I have seen worse buildings, but this provides little solace on a daily, practical basis. The building, built as a think-tank or research center and later acquired by the university, apparently was acclaimed for its architecture. All this convinces me about, however, is that architecture celebrated soon after its creation does not always stand the test of time. Truly great and functional architecture attains status over time, and because it provides hospitable space for the people who work in it. All of the publicity and recruiting photographs of my building carefully disguise the structure, showing a few people gathered about its front steps, not showing what lies beyond the steps, a jumbled pile of concrete slabs and blocks. The building reminds you of one of those World War Two-era bomb shelters or gun emplacements.

The university keeps providing small quantities of funds for some patchwork renovations, and we have seen some improvements (although with every improvement we seem to end up with another quirky space). I witnessed a cluster of offices with real improved space, but ending – almost in a nightmarish planning mishap of the kind that a Donald Norman or Jane Jacobs writes about – with a ridiculous misshapen room that could not be used effectively for conferences, seminars, or other classes or meetings; it was finally appropriated as a collaboratory space, but anyone walking into the room cannot help but notice how much space is wasted. In the process of the renovations, I got an expanded and quite generous office – but that was not the success of the story (even I misestimated how the knocking down the wall between my existing office and a supply closet would turn out). The success came in working out a deal to paint my office a color (a dark steely gray named "Antique Pewter") different than the beige color running throughout our school and other university offices, hallways, and restrooms.

The success in this was not a more attractive office, but in my expressing myself. I felt better about myself. I felt more about being part of an academic community, in that I advertised something about me (rather than about university requirements). Students seemed more relaxed in the office. And faculty and staff wandered down the hallway to peer in, cautiously expressing that a variation in the color scheme made a positive difference. While it was a minor act, simple to execute and costing me about forty dollars, it was a deeply satisfying act of rebellion, one, I believe, in keeping with the historic sense and role of the university. Despite the pressures on the university to become more "corporate," faculty have always been nonconformists, nailing stuff to walls, critiquing society, and dialoguing with the public leaders, about what ails us. Having an office with different colored walls seemed the right thing to do. And when a university photographer remarked to me when he was in my office completing an assignment that I had one of the nicest offices in the university, it was merely an extra bonus (later, a photograph of the office appeared on a new recruiting and marketing brochure).

Big office or no, the challenge of figuring out the balance between teaching and researching is ever present. Nearly every faculty member who has written some sort of reflection about the academic life, has commented on this issue. David H. Porter captures something of the difference between teaching and research and publishing when he writes about his experiences in working briefly at a major research university: "I must confess that not until I taught a term at Princeton in 1986 did I myself fully recognize just how distinctive are the small colleges I'd known all my life... . What I heard at Princeton all day, every day, in office after office, was the whine and whirr of ink-jet printers, testimony to the scholarly energy of my colleagues, who were turning out books and articles at a rate both impressive and inspiring. In contrast, the sounds I was used to hearing in the halls at Carleton were those of students talking with each other, of undergraduates stopping at an office for a quick chat with a faculty member, of conversations continuing as a student left a more formal conference in one of those offices.... . It was simply that I felt in my bones as never before the profound differences in institutional mission: Princeton's central mission is to advance learning through cutting-edge research, Carleton's to offer a superb undergraduate education. Both institutions were fulfilling their missions admirably – but these missions were as different as the sounds they evoked."[639] The challenge is to find where professional schools fit in all this (as well as where we, personally, think we fit into the schools).

Do We Listen to Ourselves? Even in a school of information sciences, it sometimes seems that only a few use effectively electronic mail (or other such digital communication systems), and of those that do seem uncomfortable with it, producing responses that are awkward, unclear, or, too late in responding. Why can electronic mail in a school of information sciences be used poorly? Does the problem of the use of such technologies have more to do with the culture of professional schools? One must picture what a school of information sciences is about in our modern era, often with a focus on various programs in library and information sciences. There are probably many ways to characterize these distinct programs, but the most straightforward way is to note that some are more attuned to people needs and activities than others. We also can say that one is much more oriented to technology and its applications than the others, although the faculty might disagree with such an assessment. What all this really means is that the diversity of the faculty is one of its chief assets, building on the many disciplines represented, even though this prompts struggles with the meaning of the diversity. The multitude of faculty backgrounds generates very different world perspectives, and this makes it difficult to agree on a common vision or annual priorities. Yet, the most critical barrier to developing common ground has been a culture working against both communication and consensus.

My experience suggests that faculty members are not willing to use email for anything but the most mundane matters (announcing a lecture,

---

[639] David H. Porter, "A Story Untold and Questions Unasked," in *Liberal Arts Colleges in American Higher Education: Challenges and Opportunities* (New York: American Council of Learned Societies, Occasional Paper no. 59, 2005), pp. 206-207.

reminding us about a meeting and forwarding the agenda, or sending out news of a death, birth, marriage or other such event). One reason for the lack of use may be the unwillingness of faculty to put in writing their particular viewpoints on any matter, afraid that it might eventually be used against them. This is akin to academic speech codes and the corporate mindset affecting faculty governance and freedom. Faculty are made to be overly sensitive to the possibility that they might give offense, and this can weaken their ability to engage in open discourse not only in the classroom but in faculty meetings.

Using email and using password protected Web sites can greatly facilitate cooperative work. A few years before I had worked with faculty colleagues scattered in several universities to co-author a lengthy research article. After a face to face meeting where we decided how to divide up the research, nearly all the remainder of the deliberations were conducted via email and the use of a password accessible Web site where we could write up reports, comment on drafts, and amend drafts of the essay – all with clear indicators of who was contributing what. The work proceeded smoothly and quite expeditiously, all serving as a reminder of what could be achieved within a single academic unit utilizing the same, fairly simple, technologies. This does not always happen in faculty units, the lack of use of information technologies seeming very counter to a library and information science school's purpose for existing. Is the lack of use of email by faculty simply another lapse in accountability? Someday a student may arrive at my office door and refuse to hand in the required paper, decrying the lack of accountability because we now live in the visual age where writing is not as important or where any form of grading is unfair. In order to teach others, we usually have to teach ourselves.

Teaching Others. Early in 1999 the *U.S. News and World Report* ranked archivists as part of its "hot" professions, predicting that it would "grow dramatically for years to come as government at all levels, corporations, libraries and museums put their records into an electronic format." The magazine continued to specify the importance of archivists, noting that they "typically get training in the field of library and information science, where they learn how to evaluate the importance of documents and decide in which formats it is most suitable to store them."[640] As always, good news

---

[640] The *U.S. News and World Report* story was picked up by others. In *Business First of Buffalo*, 8 February 1999, a story was published entitled "Archiving May Be Bringing Some New Jobs to an Old Field."

for marketing purposes, even if unreliable by any means of data gathering and analysis.

Other older segments of the information professions have been included in such employment assessments. As the Information Age proceeds, especially in the aftermath of the development of the World Wide Web, there appears to be a renewed appreciation for traditional skills, such as cataloguing and retrieving, possessed by librarians. Paul Gilster, wrestling with what it is the average person needs to know about information technology, notes the frustrations many have with the "lack of standardization" of Internet search engines. "Consider the outcome if every public library in the world used its own cataloging scheme to shelve its books," Gilster writes. "Each time you entered a different library, you would have to study its cataloguing system in order to determine how to find a particular book or magazine. This is where we are on the Internet today." Gilster calls for librarians to take a more active role in how the World Wide Web is developed.[641]

Given that news magazines and freelance writers are declaring the need for archivists and librarians, one might surmise that we would hear more from the fifty-plus schools of library and information science in North America. After all, the past decade has seen great, protracted discussions about the "information highway," the emergence of the World Wide Web, the use of information technology in schools, knowledge about computer technology, growing concerns about personal privacy and government secrecy, the apparent or inevitable demise of the printed book, widening gaps between "information haves and have-nots," the commercialization of information, and the dwindling number of publishers of books and journals. Look at these topics. Aren't these precisely what one would expect students in library and information science schools to be learning about? If that is the case, and it most certainly is, then we would expect the faculty at these schools to be heavily engaged in the wide-ranging and important public debates about the roles of information and information technology in modern society.

Others have argued that such faculties have an important, broader public role to play. A decade ago, in an article published in the primary journal for library and information science education, Karen Sy asked whether such educators were "ready to participate in information policy

---

[641] Paul Gilster, *Digital Literacy* (New York: John Wiley and Sons, Inc., 1997), p. 173. Others have made similar statements, most notably Clifford Stoll, *Silicon Snake Oil: Second Thoughts on the Information Highway* (New York: Anchor Books, 1995).

advising." Their skills and interests certainly supported such a role, Sy argued, even as there were weaknesses, such as the lack of research on information policy matters.[642] More recently, a few library and information science schools have become homes for the newly termed field of "social informatics," the study of the impact of information technology on society.[643] Even in schools without such a focus, one can find courses designed to help students understand the broader social implications of information, information technology, and the information professions. Looked at in this way, our teaching should extend far beyond our classrooms, students, and host universities.

This is especially true for those faculty teaching future archivists and records managers. There has been a decided shift to a clearer mission emphasizing records for accountability coupled with a greater sensitivity for more active advocacy.[644] As the challenges of electronic records emerged and even threatened to overwhelm this discipline, advocacy changed to accountability.[645] Now, as graduate archival education curriculum expands, especially in library and information science programs, we are beginning to see more courses on issues like accountability and advocacy.[646] Even if we are in a very early stage of such developments, these are good signs.

With the hindsight of a decade or more when library and information science faculty were called to be activists, one might be prone to consider

---

[642] Karen J. Sy, "Are Library and Information Science Faculty Ready to Participate in Information Policy Advising?" *Journal of Education for Library and Information Science* 30 (Spring 1990): 298-314.

[643] Rob Kling, "What is Social Informatics and Why Does it Matter?" *D-Lib Magazine* 5 (January 1999) at http://www.dlib.org/dlib/january99/kling/01kling.html.

[644] For background on this, refer to Elsie Freeman Finch, ed., *Advocating Archives: An Introduction to Public Relations for Archivists* (Metuchen, N.J.: The Society of American Archivists and Scarecrow Press, Inc., 1994).

[645] This transition has been reflected most directly in the writings of Australian archivists and records professionals, and these writings have had a decided impact on North American records sensibilities. See Margaret Hedstrom and David Wallace, "And the Last Shall Be First: Recordkeeping Policies and the NII," *Journal of the American Society for Information Science* 50, no. 4 (1999): 331-339.

[646] The University of Pittsburgh School of Information Sciences created a new course entitled Archival Access and Advocacy, offered for the first time in the summer 1999 term. The Pittsburgh program has had a decided orientation to such matters, and other archival education programs seem to be offering similar courses as their curriculum expands. See Richard J. Cox, "Advocacy in the Graduate Archives Curriculum: A North American Perspective," *Janus* no. 1 (1997): 30-41.

just whether such faculty have been involved in policy making or, at the least, influencing the parameters by which debate about such policy should occur. There are at least three ways to measure this – literal participation in information policy deliberations (such as what occurred with the old National Information Initiative), research about information policy, and participation in the broader public debates as reflected in publication in journals playing an important role in such debates.

LIS and Public Scholarship. It is a good time to be an information professional like a librarian or an archivist. By "public scholarship" I mean those "intellectuals, writers and thinkers who address a general and educated audience," to borrow from one of Russell Jacoby's tirades against academe,[647] acknowledging that faculty in schools such as library and information science have opportunities for engaging in such scholarship. Jacoby, critiquing higher education, laments that faculty have shifted away from public scholarship: "Campuses are their homes; colleagues their audience; monographs and specialized journals their media. Unlike past intellectuals they situate themselves within fields and disciplines – for good reason. Their jobs, advancement, and salaries depend on the evaluation of specialists, and this dependence affects the issues broached and the language employed."[648] At the heart of this is that being advocates for matters like accountability or ethical issues requires not only teaching future practitioners, but also having faculty who can write effectively about such matters in a broad public forum.

This description of public versus academic scholarship is telling for library and information science education. While the American Library Association and related archives and information professional associations have been extremely active about a whole host of social and ethical information issues, the faculty of the schools have followed academic norms by publishing in specialized journals or writing specialized monographs. They have missed other opportunities. Records are in the news every day, enhancing the public understanding of their value for accountability, evidence, and societal memory. The continuing stories about the assets of Holocaust victims and the contentious debate about the exhibition of the Enola Gay, the plane used to drop the atomic bomb on Hiroshima, have both advanced the significance of archives for societal memory and accountability. Likewise, the rapid development of the World

---

[647] Russell Jacoby, *The Last Intellectuals: American Culture in the Age of Academe* (New York: The Noonday Press, 1987), p. 5.
[648] Jacoby, *The Last Intellectuals*, p. 6.

Wide Web has prompted numerous publications on the nature of electronic information and the general societal value of computers. Both implicit and explicit in such writings, which have coalesced into a virtual industry in its own right, is the appropriate and potential role of information professionals.

As a faculty member, it is nice to have such an array of popular, controversial, and stimulating writings about the use of information and evidence for students to read, contemplate, and discuss. In my teaching experience, I have found it easier to engage students in thinking about critical issues facing information professionals if they have to deal with conflicting or controversial viewpoints (although many students are not always happy about having to do this).[649] These writings and discussions generally bring the societal relevance of the information professional to the fore, except for one major problem. Faculty of library and information science schools are generally invisible in these published discussions, prompting many questions from students and causing one to reflect on why these opportunities are being missed. Other kinds of academic units have been engaged in public scholarship for quite a while. Patricia Nelson Limerick, a historian at the University of Colorado at Boulder, has provided an interesting gloss on this from the humanities perspective: "The Center of the American West is one indication of the beginning of a shift in academe toward more acceptance of applied work, and it's certainly not the only example. I have met professors on my own campus and elsewhere who are at work in all sorts of applied ways, serving as expert witnesses in litigation on behalf of Indian tribes, working with schoolteachers, consulting with elected and appointed officials, and guiding governmental agencies and advocacy groups."[650] Given the nature of what we are involved in, I have always thought that we ought to be publishing for broader audiences, as some of our colleagues – David Levy, Paul Duguid, John Seely Brown, and Matthew Battles – have done.

Library and information science education has been connected to the university for over a century. If, as Neil Postman argues, "universities have a sacred responsibility to define for their society what is worthwhile

---

[649] See my "Unpleasant Things: Teaching Advocacy in Archival Education Programs." *InterActions: UCLA Journal of Education and Information Studies* 5, Issue 1, Article 8 (2009), available at http://repositories.cdlib.org/gseis/interactions/vol5/iss1/art8, for some discussion of this.

[650] Patricia Nelson Limerick, "Tales of Western Adventure," *Chronicle of Higher Education*, 54 (May 9, 2008), http://chronicle.com/weekly/v54/i35/35c00101.htm.

knowledge," then we can question why the faculty responsible for educating future information professionals in the era self-described as the Information Age are not seeking broader public forums for issues important to them and to society.[651] In fact, the rise of disciplines a century ago was intimately connected with just such a public mission. Historian Thomas Bender, examining the establishment of new graduate schools in the Progressive period (the era when both librarianship and archivy were established), writes that these early academics "were not contained by the service ideal of expertise; they strove for direct contact, open communication, with the educated public" and their early graduate schools were founded "to reform our public life, our civic life, our politics." Perhaps, something has been lost over the past century. Indeed, Bender states that "Today, the public is at once increasingly representative, and more fragmented, making it harder to find, to reach, and to define."[652]

But this is the Information Age! There are not only numerous issues, but there are numerous mechanisms by which many elements of the public and policymakers can be reached. A review of the most influential print outlets on public policymakers reveals a remarkable interest in information technology and related issues. Steven Brint, using a survey of American "writers, thinkers, and editors," identified the most "influential" periodicals and supplemented these publications with a "representative sample" of "periodicals of the right and left."[653] I have used this group of periodicals to try and determine first the range and frequency of articles appearing about Information Age issues and second who are the authors of these essays. I have not worried about the particular viewpoints being expressed in these articles, assuming that they would reflect the full spectrum of perspectives we see reflected in books, newspapers, and even the World Wide Web itself. The journals Brint selected have decided points of view, from one end of the political spectrum to the other.

The initial impression one develops in examining these "influential" journals is that they are publishing a substantial quantity of material on issues directly concerning the Information Age and intimately connected to the kinds of matters faculty at library and information science schools

---

[651] Neil Postman, *Conscientious Objections: Stirring Up Trouble About Language, Technology, and Education* (New York: Vintage Books, 1988), p. 3.
[652] Thomas Bender, *Intellect and Public Life: Essays on the Social History of Academic Intellectuals in the United States* (Baltimore: Johns Hopkins University Press, 1993), pp. 67, 130.
[653] Steven Brint, *In an Age of Experts: The Changing Role of Professionals in Politics and Public Life* (Princeton: Princeton University Press, 1994), pp. 155-156.

would be interested in. Through the 1990s, these nineteen periodicals published slightly over seven hundred articles on Information Age issues. Stories about information technology issues – from new developments to fears and implications of the uses of the technology – are the most common topics for such publications. These stories reflect the array of books covering the full spectrum of viewpoints on these topics. A predominant emphasis of articles is on the complicated and constantly changing matters of privacy, access, copyright, and intellectual property. Issues of censorship and free speech, many concerning the implications of computers and the Internet, are also a regular part of the diet of articles provided by these journals.

It is not only information technology providing the mainstay of Information Age oriented articles in these journals. There is a healthy array of writings on reading, books, and literacy. Some of this writing is in direct reaction to the challenge by computers and the World Wide Web, such as articles on the future of the printed book, but much of it is just a reflection of the interest of these journals and their readers in such matters. One can also discover a good quantity of articles on libraries and their place in society as well as on archives and records issues. Looked at in this way, it seems that a library and information science faculty member could build an entire course based on the popular writings found in these journals. Looked at in another fashion, it is clear that individuals regularly reading such periodicals are being normally exposed to the critical issues we face in the Information Age and about which library and information science faculty would be expected to teach and research. Even if one were to read these periodicals with a stress on the ones concentrated on politics (such as *The American Spectator*), literary topics (such as *Harper's*), or of a more academic persuasion (such as *Daedalus*), it seems evident that one would have continuing exposure to writings on archives, information technology, censorship, books, libraries, and access.

A closer examination of the essays published in these journals reveals their affinity to what library and information science faculty are interested in. The end of the Cold War and the sudden opening of Iron Curtain records brought a remarkable rise in writing about archives and records issues, with espionage a favorite topic.[654] But there have also been stories about more complicated matters, such as the continuing issue of access to

---

[654] Those interested can find citations to specific examples of such articles in my "Accountability, Public Scholarship, and Library, Information, and Archival Science Educators," *Journal of Education for Library and Information Science* 41 (Spring 2000): 94-105.

the Nixon Watergate tape recordings and recordkeeping and Holocaust victims' assets. Reflecting the Culture Wars has been an intensity of writing – from all perspectives – about school textbook censorship and censorship in general. Also figuring prominently, of course, were articles on the contested notion of a literary canon and the purpose and nature of reading. Not unexpectedly there has been a vast amount of writing about the idea of an information "highway," access, security, and personal privacy. The negative or positive aspects of computers on all elements of society has been a consistent topic, including the impact on the economy, the future of publishing, copyright and the ownership of ideas, and education. Finally, writings about libraries have included some remarkably interesting essays, demonstrating the continuing resilience of books, print, and, of course, libraries. The regular appearance of these articles also suggests their continuing importance to readers of these publications. A subscriber to all these journals would be fed a steady diet of articles on archives and records, information technology, censorship and free speech, reading and books, privacy and access, copyright and intellectual property, and libraries.

LIS Faculty in the Public's Eye. Given the affinity of these journals for publishing such articles, one would expect to see submissions from the faculty or graduates of schools of library and information science. Given the number of these schools, supporting over two thousand faculty and hundreds of research agendas related to the topics of the articles being published in these journals, this is a logical conclusion. However, we find a dramatically different result. There are virtually no faculty published from these schools and precious few working in libraries or archives. While over a quarter of the articles published in these periodicals come from academics, not a single author had a current affiliation with a school of library and information science. One conclusion might be that these journals are more open to established writers or support free-lance writers, editors, and journalists accustomed to writing in the appropriate manner and on timely topics for these publications. However, a good quarter of the authors are academics, suggesting that these journals would be open to publishing by faculty from library and information science schools, assuming they can write well on current issues with an absence of professional jargon.

What can we make of this absence of library and information science faculty? Besides the obvious one that perhaps these individuals are simply not interested in publishing in such venues as *Atlantic* or the *New Yorker*, we need to look elsewhere for an explanation. It is very possible that publishing in such journals has proved not to be worth the effort. Publishing in

Harper's or *Commentary* would certainly count little if at all for tenure or even promotion for these faculty, yet other faculty from other disciplines publish successfully in these journals and in the trade press, reaching into the public forum to contend with controversial issues. There is also the effort involved. Moving from an academic venue to a more popular one requires more than just recasting lecture notes or revising research data. You have to write differently, if not considerably better. Historian John Rennie Short provides a glimpse into this dilemma: "Academics have both an advantage and a disadvantage. The advantage is that academics can tell stories for a living. They give lectures and write articles and books. They have access to the cultural means of reproduction. The disadvantage is that they have the freedom to write without being read. Academic articles and books are more often cited than read. Literacy and intelligibility are declining virtues as the conventions of our genres make us more and more unintelligible to the nonspecialist. Perhaps we gain focus, but at the cost of connection. Our audience becomes more sophisticated as it shrinks in size. We need to ask the question, who is our audience? What is the community of tellers and listeners?"[655]

Library and information science faculty, while writing on many of the same topics in these journals, also seem inclined to write only for fellow specialists and with the freedom of writing without the worry of whether they are read. We must lament the lost opportunities to do many things, ranging from presenting important views in broader forums to building a stronger profile for the important roles of information professionals. Is it any wonder that library and information science schools are sometimes deemed unworthy of being in a university? Or, that the public often seems unaware of professionals like librarians and archivists?

It is possible that most library and information science faculty are uninterested in such public scholarship because of other priorities or because they see certain advantages in remaining detached. Historian Theodore S. Hamerow captures many of the problems maintaining some semblance of a relationship with the public in any area of scholarship. He laments that the increasing specialization, more science-like approaches, and professional jargon have built barriers between academic historians and public: "The wall separating the campus from the surrounding community is not without its intellectual advantages. It enables scholars to view their society with greater detachment than would otherwise be possible. They

---

[655] John Rennie Short, *New Worlds, New Geographies* (Syracuse: Syracuse University Press, 1998), p. 108.

become more perceptive critics of its dominant attitudes; they can see more clearly through the veil of rhetoric and piety which obscures established institutions. But their isolation can also lead to the social order which sustains higher education. Academics tend to see themselves as a small company of the righteous defying the hosts of Philistinism."[656] Given that the largest group of academics publishing in the "influential" journals described here are from history, one might give pause to Hamerow's concerns. At least in the case of library and information science faculty the already established interest of these journals on Information Age topics seems like nothing so much as an invitation.

Teaching the Public. Library and information science faculty need to turn to the public interest journals if they want to influence public policy. Given the profusion of courses on topics like information policy, ethics, censorship and privacy, information "haves" and "have-nots," recordkeeping and accountability, and the social and cultural memory roles of libraries and archives, it is hard not to imagine publishing in such venues. Eric Alterman called for renewed interest by academics in public interest journals: "They [journals like *Dissent, The American Prospect, Partisan Review,* and *The Public Interest*] can help shape not only public policy but also the political and intellectual discussions that shape that policy." Alterman also notes, "While many critics bemoan what they see as academe's self-imposed political irrelevance, policy journals offer scholars an opportunity to apply their research to real-life problems."[657] This seems like relevant advice for library and information science faculty.

Faculty who teach in archival studies need to be more public-oriented or, at the least, encourage their students to do so. Court cases bring up the challenges posed to organizations and government in managing records, especially electronic records. It goes beyond court cases, of course. Repeated discoveries of government or corporate improprieties, such as the infamous Tuskegee syphilis experiment or the South African Truth and Reconciliation Commission, provide a sense of the importance of records for accountability. To date, most of the efforts to bring a broader public focus have been the province of freelance writers or academics in other fields.[658] While these authors have made substantial contributions, especially

---

[656] Theodore S. Hamerow, *Reflections on History and Historians* (Madison: University of Wisconsin Press, 1987), p. 87.
[657] Eric Alterman, "Tiny Circulations, Big Idea: 'General Interest' Journals and the Shaping of Public Policy," *Chronicle of Higher Education,* 5 June 1998, p. B6.
[658] One thinks of Janet Malcolm's articles about the management of the Sigmund Freud archives (published in book form as *In the Freud Archives* [New York: Alfred

in providing materials for teaching about such concerns, they generally do not provide the sensitivity or depth of understanding regarding records and information as a public concern. It is up to the faculty of library and information science schools to change this.

Teaching Ethics, Teaching Ethically. Archival and information issues, embedded in university activities, also include ethical concerns. Daniel Greenberg opens a window into such problems when he addresses corporate-sponsored research: "Temptations for ethical lapses are abetted by institutional factors that are untamed. The academic arms race giddily accelerates. In Ponzi-scheme fashion, it inflames the pursuit of money for constructing research facilities needed to attract high-salaried scientific superstars who can win government grants to perform research that will bring glory and more money to the university. Academe's pernicious enthrallment by the rating system of U.S. News & World Report is a disgrace of modern higher education."[659] We can detect how pervasive and deep such issues are by looking into college and university units possessing foundations far different from those of professional schools, where we would expect the race for research money to be a high priority. One commentator on Christian liberal arts education, for example, complains that even there that the administrators have turned students into customers and search for a marketable brand, despite the fact that the "task of a distinctively Christian liberal arts education is to create a community of people formed to resist and challenge the reductionism of a market-driven culture."[660]

We also can see what is happening in the humanities departments within universities. Patricia Cohen reminds us that over the generations there has been the idea that a "traditional liberal arts education is, by definition, not intended to prepare students for a specific vocation. Rather, the critical thinking, civic and historical knowledge and ethical reasoning

---

A. Knopf, 1984], Nicholson Baker's ruminations on the demise of the library card catalog as a form of historical record (included in his *The Size of Thoughts: Essays and Other Lumber* (New York: Vintage Books, 1997), or the collection of essays on records and secrecy published as Athan G. Theoharis, ed., *A Culture of Secrecy: The Government Versus the People's Right to Know* (Lawrence: University Press of Kansas, 1998).

[659] Daniel S. Greenberg, *Science for Sale: The Perils, Rewards, and Delusions of Campus Capitalism* (Chicago: University of Chicago, 2007), p. 276.

[660] James K. A. Smith, *The Devil Reads Derrida and Other Essays on the University, the Church, Politics, and the Arts* (Grand Rapids, MI: William B. Eerdmans Publishing Co., 2009), p. 45.

that the humanities develop have a different purpose: They are prerequisites for personal growth and participation in a free democracy, regardless of career choice." Cohen then focuses on the notion that many are now arguing that the current economic situation challenges such a belief. Cohen points to recent surveys, news about the cancellation of faculty searches in areas like religion and philosophy, and the need for the humanities "to justify their existence to administrators, policy makers, students and parents. Technology executives, researchers and business leaders argue that producing enough trained engineers and scientists is essential to America's economic vitality, national defense and health care. Some of the staunchest humanities advocates, however, admit that they have failed to make their case effectively." She cites individuals who are trying to emphasize the practical value of the humanities.[661]

Library and information science schools, with strong interests in information technology and a focus on professions such as librarianship and archives, are in a good position to demonstrate a link between the humanities and the information professions. Many archives students (as well as other library and information science students) continue to arrive with a background in the humanities, and it is a necessary background for understanding the history and evolution of archives and recordkeeping systems. We need to consider how to capitalize on this relationship, partly to demonstrate why humanities backgrounds are still vitally important in our present technocratic era. We also must become more persuasive in writing our cases, and there is increasing evidence that academics realize this. In one recent writing primer we read that the "underlying structure of effective academic writing – and of responsible public discourse – resides not just in stating our own ideas, but in listening closely to others around us, summarizing their views in a way that they will recognize, and responding with our own ideas in kind. Broadly speaking, academic writing is argumentative writing, and we believe that to argue well you need to do

---

[661] Patricia Cohen, "In Tough Times, the Humanities Must Justify Their Worth," *New York Times*, February 24, 2009, available at http://www.nytimes.com/2009/02/25/books/25human.html?_r=1, accessed February 24, 2009. Some tension has developed due to efforts at some universities to professionalize their liberal arts programs; see Andy Guess, "Professionalizing Liberal Arts, and Vice Versa," *Inside Higher Education*, January 25, 2008, http://insidehighered.com/news/2008/01/25/aacu.

more than assert your own ideas."⁶⁶² Those of us in library and information science need to start the arguing.

Building a New Constituency in a New World. We need to remind ourselves, that we are now operating in a new world of openness and transparency, where students and prospective students, practicing professionals who were former students, and other scholarly and professional colleagues expect to have ready access to what we think, what we teach, and the research we do. In early 2009, for example, the Massachusetts Institute of Technology moved beyond its earlier groundbreaking move to provide course materials online to place its research products online as well and, again, for free (this action was based on a decision taken the previous year by Harvard University's Faculty of Arts and Sciences).⁶⁶³ We know that the world we are preparing librarians and archivists for is changing rapidly. An article in the *New York Times* describes the "growing cadre of 21st-century multimedia specialists who help guide students through the digital ocean of information that confronts them on a daily basis. These new librarians believe that literacy includes, but also exceeds, books."⁶⁶⁴ Maybe someone had just done some good marketing, but, regardless, such media coverage provides opportunities for our schools to connect to the public square in ways we have not accomplished before.

We are very accustomed to hearing or reading the self-congratulating messages that we presently live in *the* Information Age. Ian F. McNeely and Lisa Wolverton provide an easy to read historical analysis of that claim identifying the library, monastery, university, Republic of Letters, disciplines, and the laboratory as the major means for generating and using new knowledge. While the authors focus on the Western tradition, they also trace the influence of that tradition in non-Western cultures, suggesting that doing this kind of analysis corrects our view of new digital information systems: "We risk committing a serious error by thinking that cheap information made universally available through electronic media fulfills the requirements of a democratic society for organized knowledge. Past generations had to win knowledge by using their wits, and never took what they knew for granted. Recalling their labor and travail is, if anything, more important than ever if we are to distinguish what is truly novel about the

---

[662] Gerald Graff and Cathy Birkenstein, *They Say/I Say: The Moves That Matter in Persuasive Writing* (New York: W.W. Norton and Co., 2008), p. 3.

[663] Jeffrey R. Young, "MIT Professors Approve Campuswide Policy to Publish Scholarly Articles Free Online," *Chronicle of Higher Education*, 23 March 2009.

[664] Motoko Rich, "The Future of Reading: In Web Age, Library Job Gets Update," *New York Times*, February 16, 2009.

'information age' from what is transient hype."[665] Towards the end of the book, McNeely and Wolverton firmly state that "Promoters of the vaunted 'information age' often forget that knowledge has always been about connecting people, not collecting information."[666] And if one walks away from reading the book with nothing other than this idea, the time will have been well spent.

McNeely and Wolverton place the university in the interesting historical context of the efforts to produce knowledge. Here is an instance in the chapter on the Republic of Letters: "We now call a question 'academic' when it bears no relation to the real world. But ... early modern academicians, even when pedantry got the better of them, always aimed to captivate people of stature and influence, to educate and entertain them at the same time."[667] Later when considering the early disciplines, the authors observe that "However faint its echo in today's dry academic writing, the frontier spirit lives on in the institution of the academic discipline. To add to the encyclopedia of knowledge requires more than the industry and calculation of Adam Smith's earnest businessman. It requires the passion born of a missionary impulse and transferred to the calling of specialized research."[668] Of course, these astute observers do not miss the changing nature of the university, where "corporations and universities are in some ways trading places" in the creation and marketing of knowledge.[669] And the concept of the laboratory provides a kind of commentary on the university and its future: "Producers of disciplinary knowledge might take their cues from the laboratory's engagement with public needs instead of tailoring their ideas, inventions, publications, and pedagogy to enclosed, self-sustaining communities of subspecialists."[670] It is McNeely and Wolverton's conclusion about the continuing importance of the laboratory that might surprise some; most would have bet on either the university or the Internet as being named as the critical player in generating knowledge in the future.

The older notion of the Republic of Letters suggests what we now refer to as public intellectuals, individuals who engage in scholarship in a manner that captures the public's attention and opens debate and discussion in a

---

[665] Ian F. McNeely with Lisa Wolverton, *Reinventing Knowledge: From Alexandria to the Internet* (New York: W. W. Norton & Co., 2008), p. xx.
[666] McNeely and Wolverton, *Reinventing Knowledge*, p. 271.
[667] McNeely and Wolverton, *Reinventing Knowledge*, p. 153.
[668] McNeely and Wolverton, *Reinventing Knowledge*, p. 202.
[669] McNeely and Wolverton, *Reinventing Knowledge*, p. 265.
[670] McNeely and Wolverton, *Reinventing Knowledge*, p. 274.

way that illuminates both scholars and the public. One would think that faculty residing in schools focused on books, archives, reading, information, and information technology – all issues permeating our society's media – would be involved in such public dialogue. That has not been the case. The problem may have less to do with the nature of these schools and more to do with what has happened to the notion of public intellectuals. Writer Russell Banks hints at the problem: "By and large, our so-called public intellectuals nowadays operate out of think tanks and universities and hold to ideologically determined agendas, financed largely by the military-industrial complex of multinational corporations. They are sociologists and historians, scientists and bureaucrats, scholars and out-of-work journalists and policy wonks, paid to produce papers, articles, and books that will further the political ambitions of one or the other of our two political parties and the financial interests of corporate America. From time to time, one or another of them is invited to come up to the Big House and help run the plantation – think Paul Wolfowitz, Condoleezza Rice, Elliott Abrams. Mostly, they are lobbyists in sheep's clothing. They are certainly not poets, novelists, playwrights, or artists of any sort."[671] While LIS faculty members are not artists, or apparently very good lobbyists, there is no reason to think we can't transform this and gain a greater voice.

Conclusion: Preparing the Next Generation of Faculty. Like most academic units, LIS and iSchools are facing the prospects of future faculty shortages. New studies on doctoral programs suggest that there has long been the need for speeding up the normal time range for doctoral study, shortening it less than the six or seven years it now requires. A study on social science doctorates completed by the University of Washington's Center for Innovation and Research in Graduate Education (considering the fields of anthropology, communications, geography, history, political science and sociology) presents a number of reasons for the reducing of the time needed as well as suggesting that such programs need to expand their focus from mostly research to also considering how to assist their students prepare for academic careers.[672] The need is no less in the space once occupied by the old library school (in fact, the need may be more pronounced because of the greater diversity of faculty needed in iSchools to

---

[671] Russell Banks, "Notes on Literature and Engagement," in Toni Morrison, ed., *Burn This Book: PEN Writers Speak Out on the Power of the Word* (New York: HarperCollins, 2009), p. 63.
[672] Scott Jaschik, "The Impact of 'Time to Degree,'" *Inside Higher Education*, January 30, 2009, available http://insidehighered.com/news/2009/01/30/tdd.

cover both traditional and essential library functions and to offer courses and programs in new and emerging information management areas).

Quality of life issues are also emerging as more serious factors in what young academics are envisioning as their career paths. A survey of over eight thousand doctoral students in the University of California system reveals a growing interest in finding positions on "family friendly" campuses, not research universities with the prospects of limitless work hours. This report makes a number of suggestions, including transforming academic timelines to allow greater personal flexibility, relaxing the pressure to move through academic ranks quickly and placing emphasis on the importance and quality of research, and building better support for families.[673] Can they find quality of life in the LIS schools or the new iSchools? Despite many of my concerns about such schools in the changing university, I think this is still possible.

There are other reasons for paying attention to what is happening in the universities and their professional schools. As we play and experiment with new information technologies, we do run the risk of losing any sense of rational perspective on what these technologies will allow us to do, including how they contribute to or detract from the quality of life. In late 2008, scientists and business leaders met at the NASA-Ames Research Center to design a university taught completely by computers, based on the notions promoted by individuals such as Ray Kurzweil that computers will become smarter than people. While such ideas have been limited to using computers to perform more like graduate assistants do today, there is no reason to believe that the idea is not to replace professors altogether.[674]

Some have even predicted the end of faculty. Lots of individuals writing about the economics of higher education and the notion of the corporate university have seemed to approach their topic as if the university is a victim of external, uncontrollable factors. Marc Bousquet places the responsibility directly on decisions being made by university administrators. Bousquet tracks the shift from regular full-time faculty to part-time adjunct faculty, the growth of administrators, from a non-profit to profit-seeking agenda, and to virtual, faculty-less classrooms. Most importantly, perhaps, Bousquet contends we are "witnessing the disappearance of the

---

[673] Scott Jaschik, "Rejecting the Academic Fast Track," *Inside Higher Education*, January 15, 2009, http://insidehighered.com/news/2009/01/15/family.
[674] Jeffrey R. Young, "Will Electric Professors Dream of Virtual Tenure?" *Chronicle of Higher Education*, 55, issue 14, November 28, 2008, p. A13.

professorate,"[675] and, if for no other reason than this, this is a book worth reading. With the end of faculty comes, I think, the end of professional schools such as once occupied by the old library school. However, I do not believe that this could be the result of a faceless set of technological innovations or even bleak economic and societal factors, but, if it happens, it will be the result of what the faculty in such schools allowed to happen. And, as well, it will be the result of an abandonment of important traditional values once espoused by library schools, schools of library and information science, and lost in the new iSchools through neglect or design. That doesn't have to happen, of course.

---

[675] Marc Bousquet, *How the University Works: Higher Education and the Low-Wage Nation* (New York: New York University Press, 2008), p. 71.

Epilogue

Introduction. Library schools, library and information science schools, or iSchools – whatever we choose to call them today or in the future – ought to be in the midst of the intellectual life of the modern university. Numerous commentators, many cited in this volume, assume that the university library was the intellectual heart of colleges and universities, and it should not be that much of a step to connect likewise to the professional schools producing the individuals staffing the library. For some, however, it is a big gap to step over, since there often has been little recognition of these professional schools in the university. Why, then, should these schools be accorded a higher profile? Much of the shaping of the corporate university is, after all, the result of its use or potential (sometimes, really, imagined) use of a vast array of digital information technologies. Yet, there are conflicting and confusing signs about what this might mean, and it is here that I turn to some concluding thoughts.

Donald Norman, the guru of logical and practical design, provides a clue to the possibilities in the use and management of information technologies. Norman believes that "as machines start to take over more and more, ... they need to be socialized; they need to improve the way they communicate and interact and to recognize their limitations. Only then can they become truly useful."[676] He is dealing, of course, with the "limitations" of machines – "they do not sense the world in the same way as people, they lack higher order goals, and they have no way of understanding the goals and motives of the people with whom they must interact."[677] One of the more interesting points Norman makes, at least a point that is interesting for library and information science schools, is the interdisciplinary nature of design: "Design cuts across all disciplines, be it the arts or sciences, humanities or engineering, law or business. In universities, the practical is often judged less valuable than the abstract and theoretical. Universities, moreover, put each discipline into separate schools and departments, where people mainly talk to others within their own narrowly defined categories. This compartmentalization is optional for developing specialists who understand their narrow area in great depth. It is not well suited for the

---

[676] Donald Norman, *The Design of Future Things* (New York: Basic Books, 2007), p. 9.
[677] Norman, *The Design of Future Things*, p. 14.

development of generalists whose work cuts across disciplines. Even when the university tries to overcome this deficit by establishing new, multidisciplinary programs, the new program soon becomes its own discipline and grows more and more specialized each year."[678] Does it not seem rational that a school of information sciences, as well as both its predecessor and successor, ought to be able to break such barriers down and become a cosmopolitan center for the trade or creation of new ideas?

Norman's assessment seems awfully close to the nature of the challenges we face in our professional schools. Norman argues that we need a "science of design."[679] "We need a new approach," he argues, "one that combines the precision and rigor of business and engineering, the understanding of social interactions, and the aesthetics of the arts"[680] – and even here we can hear echoes of our schools' discussions about technology, people, and society at professional conferences, faculty meetings, and in our classrooms. Perhaps what this means for us at this point in our historical juncture is to embrace something that seems completely new, or at least substantially refreshed, that is, the iSchools.

All of this requires mastering a discipline (or some would argue a metadiscipline), and all too often we in library and information science act as if we don't represent a discipline (with a foundational knowledge) but a craft (with a set of skills to be taught quickly, giving the students their money's worth). Howard Gardner, the prolific Harvard cognitive scientist, addresses the new ways we need to prepare for the future in education, business, and the professions. He identifies and discourses on five cognitive abilities that we need to develop and nurture – the disciplinary mind, synthesizing mind, creating mind, respectful mind, and the ethical mind. His comments on the disciplinary mind provide a window into his thinking as represented in the book. He argues that it takes a decade to master a discipline, and that education, seen as a lifelong activity, is a key into enabling such mastery. Gardner lays out the steps for achieving the disciplined mind. He argues that "an individual is disciplined to the extent that she has acquired the habits that allow her to make steady and essentially unending progress in the mastery of a skill, craft, or body of knowledge."[681] There is a lot in this volume providing food for thought for how and what we teach in our schools. For example, Gardner at one point notes that the "ability to knit

---

[678] Norman, *The Design of Future Things*, pp. 171-172.
[679] Norman, *The Design of Future Things*, p. 172.
[680] Norman, *The Design of Future Things*, p. 173.
[681] Howard Gardner, *Five Minds for the Future* (Boston: Harvard Business School Press, 2006), p. 40.

together information from disparate sources into a coherent whole is vital today,"[682] a statement nearly all of us will acknowledge without trouble but then one that we will counter by our own resistance to cooperate across disciplinary, professional, and political boundaries within our own schools and between our schools and other units within the host universities.

Some of the challenges LIS schools face may be, at least partly, the result of attitudes and approaches the faculty members of these schools carry with them. Mary Burgan, once general secretary of the American Association of University Professors, hints at some of these in a book about the changing nature of the modern professoriate. She contends that there is a "devaluation of intellectual work in general. Our culture tends to think that the only work worth paying for is work that produces some tangible, often short-term profit."[683] Burgan contends that those preparing various kinds of professionals may be immune from this a certain degree, but this may explain why some library and information science faculty members teach practically, focus on the ties with the professional community, and shun theoretical and research responsibilities. It may suggest that substantial change in some programs may only occur when there is a generational shift in individuals holding faculty posts.

Burgan also worries about the value of distance education, because she believes it diminishes a certain kind of social and intellectual community and is easily subverted to economic and marketing efforts breaking knowledge down into small bites and turning education more into a factory process (true enough, but it may also create new kinds of communities). Library and information schools have, in recent years, embraced distance education as a way of reaching individuals who might not have the opportunity to get such an education and as a tactic to provide a supply of librarians and other information professionals where there are shortages. However, this is also a means both to burdening faculty in ways that weaken their opportunity to engage intellectually with the field and to become dependent on the use of adjuncts in ways that diminish faculty governance and the quality of the education their schools offer. Getting to the point, distance education programs are not the sole or pre-eminent solution to all the issues faced by library and information science schools;

---

[682] Gardner, *Five Minds for the Future*, p. 82.
[683] Interview by Scott Jaschik with Mary Burgan, "What Ever Happened to the Faculty?", November 20, 2006, *Inside Higher Education*, available at http://insidehighered.com/news/2006/11/20/burgan. Her book is *What Ever Happened to the Faculty? Drift and Decision in Higher Education* (Baltimore: Johns Hopkins University Press, 2006).

what we face is more complicated (and the predications, often glibly offered, about the possibility that all education will be offered remotely are likely more fantasy than reality; if anything, educational technologies will supplement how we teach and who are in our classrooms).

Whatever else library and information science schools may be wrestling with (and there is a lot on their plate), it probably won't include concerns about enrollments (unless the economy completely collapses and most professional jobs disappear – and maybe that will happen, since I originally wrote this optimistic statement *before* the demise of the financial industry and other sectors of the economy). Nevertheless, we are dealing now with what some refer to as the "encore" generation, healthy baby boomers retiring and then returning to the workforce to look for new ways of making contributions to society. We are encountering many baby boomers who are facing 30 years of retirement, many dissatisfied with their former careers and looking for a way to do new and more positive things, especially as predictions of labor shortages of 9 million in 2010 and 18.1 million in 2020 loom ahead of us. Since many of these baby boomers are fairly sophisticated in their knowledge and use of information technology, there may be a new market for new and different students for schools like ours. Many articles are appearing suggesting that librarians are cool, such as one oft-quoted essay appearing in the *New York Times*: "With so much of the job involving technology and with a focus now on finding and sharing information beyond just what is available in books, a new type of librarian is emerging — the kind that, according to the Web site Librarian Avengers, is 'looking to put the "hep cat" in cataloguing.'"[684] While there continues to be efforts to engage digital natives with the value of the library and its services,[685] the older generation grew up with libraries, books, and the value

---

[684] See Kara Jesella, "A Hipper Crowd of Shusters," *New York Times*, July 8, 2007, Section 9, p. 1, 2, http://www.nytimes.com/2007/07/08/fashion/08librarian.html?_r=1&ref=style&oref=slogin.

[685] A report of a session at the annual meeting of the American Library Association concerns getting students who grew up with video games to apply their knowledge in the library. According to Scott Jaschik, "Speakers said that gaming skills are in many ways representative of a broader cultural divide between today's college students and the librarians who hope to teach them." Scott Jaschik, "When 'Digital Natives' Go to the Library," *Inside Higher Education*, June 25, 2007, http://insidehighered.com/news/2007/06/25/games.

of both in our society. Yet all this may depend on whether higher education itself is able to ride out these more recent economic woes.[686]

Some have worried that those more in the library portion of the library and information science paradigm have not embraced a broader interdisciplinary foundation for their work (in fact, some have suggested that this is a fundamental reason for the emergence of the iSchool movement). Stephen Bell believes we need more "rigorous discourse" and that "we need to look at how other disciplines stimulate and support discourse." Bell argues, "Library educators should begin to integrate into the curriculum more opportunities for verbal and written discourse, as well as present students with case studies that serve as good examples of discourse and how it advances professional knowledge." He gives as examples the topics the "values of face-to-face interaction versus the immediacy of delivering services virtually" and the "qualifications required of academic librarians."[687] Such self-questioning is at the heart of the academic mindset.

A profound problem with how these professional schools operate may be that they are always dancing around the latest information technologies. David Levy writes, "I will argue that our more–faster–better attitude, which is intimately connected with the striving for technological advance, is driving out slower practices that are essential to our ability to govern ourselves with maturity. Without adequate time to think and reflect, time to listen, and time to cultivate our humanity, and without spaces that are protected from the constant intrusion of information and noise, I do not see how we can respond to the innumerable social and political challenges of the new millennium with the quality of attention they deserve. In order to rectify this state of affairs, I will suggest that we take steps to design spaces and times for reflection and contemplation. Much as the modern-day environmental movement has worked to cultivate and preserve certain natural habitats, such as wetlands and old growth forests, for the health of the planet, so too should we now begin to cultivate and preserve certain

---

[686] Tad Friend, "Protest Studies: The State is Broke, and Berkeley Is In Revolt," *The New Yorker*, January 4, 2010, pp 22-28, a grim assessment of the prospects of the University of California system.
[687] Steven J. Bell, "Good at Reviewing Books But Not Each Other," *Inside Higher Education*, April 27, 2007, available at http://insidehighered.com/views/2007/04/27/bell.

human habitats for the sake of our own well–being."[688] I can think of few faculty in these schools who might describe their homes as places for reflection; most of us have to fight to find times and places for such activity. It is difficult to do this when we focus exclusively on teaching tools, worrying that we are always behind the latest curve of these information tools.

The foundations of our library and information schools may be a bit unstable, a characteristic we can see in three ways. First, the continuing emphasis on the accreditation of MLIS degree programs may be a drag on allowing change and experimentation to occur, essential to being healthy. Second, the recent debates between educators and practitioners does not provide much help in empowering library and information science schools to evolve in a fashion that will strengthen their present and future position within the new corporate university. And, third, the nascent iSchool movement appears promising, but it is certainly too soon to tell what impact this movement might have on this form of professional school.

ALA Accreditation. As the accreditation of the MLIS degree by the American Library Association has evolved, it has proved to be a weathervane for debates between practitioners and educators about just what should be taught in library schools and their latter versions – a debate intensifying as we move farther from library and deeper into other information places. There have been arguments about the composition of the Committee on Accreditation,[689] about whether there is any hope of reconciling the values of practitioners and educators in terms of defining the knowledge to be taught,[690] dropping "library" out of the name of schools,[691] and every other matter under the sun. There is no sign that these debates will disappear; rather, there is a kind of sickening feeling that we will see the same issues emerge with cyclic regularity.

The argument in favor of accrediting the MLIS degree is simple and seemingly convincing, since as Prudence Dalrymple states, "Accreditation

---

[688] David M. Levy, "More, Faster, Better: Governance in an Age of Overload, Busyness, and Speed," *First Monday*, special issue number 7 (September 2006), http://firstmonday.org/issues/special11_9/levy/index.html

[689] William R. Eshelman, "The Erosion of Library Education," *Library Journal* 108, no. 13 (1983): 1309-1312.

[690] David B. Walch, "A Perspective of Academic Librarianship: The Practitioner's Needs and the Educator's Product," *Journal of Library Administration* 11, no. 3 (1990): 87-96, summarizing two decades of such debates.

[691] Bill Crowley, "The Control and Direction of Professional Education," *Journal of the American Society for Information Science* 50, no. 12 (1999): 1127-35.

offers the profession the opportunity – indeed the obligation – to set the standards for entry-level practitioners. High-quality education is a shared responsibility of both the LIS schools and the profession itself."[692] Some library leaders, such as Michael Gorman, have been outspoken advocates for enforcing specific national standards that do not allow individual schools to have flexibility for setting their own vision or mission.[693] Some of the tone of the education debates may have to do with the fact that the library community has relied on the ALA-sanctioned accreditation as a mean of legitimizing professional status.[694] There is insecurity and hypersensitivity on both sides, perhaps reflecting fears that the library profession may be endangered or marginalized and concerns in our professional schools that their status is weak and future uncertain for their university homes.

While the arguments and disagreements seem to have progressed only slightly over the past few decades, there have been occasional critical moments when crises have erupted adding new wrinkles to the discussion (such as the closing of library schools in the 1980s, slipping enrollments in the 1990s, and other such problems).[695] In the wake of these closings, some library and information science faculty have argued that what is needed are stronger accreditation standards that favor schools with a focus more on research and knowledge building than basic practice and skills.[696] Others look past this and worry that a new focus on interdisciplinary research and knowledge may weaken their ability to attract students whose sights are set

---

[692] P. W. Dalrymple, "The State of the Schools," *American Libraries* 28, no. 1 (January 1997): 31.

[693] Michael Gorman, "Whither Library Education?" *New Library World* 105, no. 9/10 (2004): 376-80. Andrew Dillon and A. Norris, "Crying Wolf: An Examination and Reconsideration of the Perception of Crisis in LIS Education," *Journal of Education for Library and Information Science* 46, no. 4 (Fall 2005): 280-298 is a response to Gorman's assessment of the education crisis, trying to present data challenging his assertions. The response clearly reflects how contested and emotional the professional debate about library and information science education is and that it is likely to remain this way.

[694] Kathleen M. Burnett and Laurie J. Bonnici, "Contested Terrain: Accreditation and the Future Profession of Librarianship," *Library Quarterly* 76 (April 2006): 193-219. They contrast this with computer science's interest in accreditation for validating its knowledge.

[695] See, for example, June Lester, "Education for Librarianship: A Report Card," *American Libraries* 21, no. 6 (June 1990): 580, 582, 584, 586.

[696] Bert R. Boyce, "The Death of Library Education," *American Libraries* 25, no. 3 (March 1994): 257-259.

on being practitioners, not theorists or scholars.[697] From my vantage, anyone working in a serious way as a librarian or information professional, must have a scholarly bent; this does not mean that they have to write obscure scholarly monographs or generate a lengthy list of jargon-laden research articles in specialized journals, but that they have to possess an intellectual curiosity enabling them to understand the context of what they do and what they work with.

Some segments of the information professional community, such as the Special Libraries Association, have built on the ALA COA guidelines to develop accreditation standards specific to their own area and needs.[698] A decade ago there was a substantial effort to bring together eight professional associations in librarianship, archival studies, records management, and other information specializations to expand accreditation of library and information science schools and their various specializations.[699] Nothing of any significance came of that effort, but it indicates how the increasing specialization in information work, a natural byproduct of our drifting deeper into the world of cyberspace, is complicating old strategies, identities, and agendas. It becomes more difficult for schools to invest so heavily in the accreditation of the MLIS degree when that degree may only support a portion of the information professions such schools are educating; that the advocates for the MLIS degree are seeking to expand the professional parameters or purposes of the accreditation guidelines is one thing, but the growing tension between the American Library Association membership and faculty in library and information science schools over the education of librarians and the focus on libraries suggest how difficult this may be to resolve.

One of the persistent concerns in the discussion about accreditation is whether this effort enables excellence or just sets a lowest common

---

[697] B. P. Lynch, "Library Education: Its Past, Its Present, Its Future," *Library Trends* 56, no. 4 (Spring 2008): 931-953.

[698] Vivian J. Arterbery, "Accreditation: A Blueprint for Action." *Special Libraries* 77, no. 4 (Fall 1986): 230-234 is an early article arguing for the separate SLA guidelines. Ultimately, such guidelines were developed; see *Competencies for Information Professionals of the 21st Century*. Revised edition, June 2003, Special Libraries Association, available at http://www.sla.org/content/learn/members/competencies/index.cfm.

[699] Susan K. Martin, "A New Vision for Library and Information Studies Accreditation," *Portal: Libraries and the Academy* 2, no. 3 (2002): 481-483.

denominator.[700] Indeed, the library school deans have often spoken out that they worry about a generally monolithic evaluation process and its impact on the increasing diversity among these schools, while also worrying about the implications of abandoning the accreditation imprimatur in a profession that has grown used to having it.[701] Even those who strongly support accreditation and see as essential the involvement of practitioners in the process worry about it "stifling innovation."[702] The need for or interest in innovation in education programs may be restricted to the faculty in these professional schools persistently needing to justify their place in the university, a matter practitioners in the field don't really consider very much (except, perhaps, when they see these schools closed or threatened with closure).

There have been proposals for action intended to resolve some of the disparities between educators and practitioners. One interesting proposal is to equip for and engage practitioners in research.[703] However, there continues to be very little or very general research really testing out the impact of accreditation on library education.[704] And, in fact, looking back over these debates for some decades, we see considerable heated dialogue but little offering any substantive improvements or serious alternatives. It always seems as if no one is really willing to abandon accreditation for the MLIS degree, expand accreditation to other degrees, or to strengthen it in any noticeable way. Given the intensity of discussion about accreditation and the status of library and information science education, we should be surprised about the lack of research or proposals for alternatives.

Recent Heated Debates. The politically entrenched but seemingly conceptually weak (that is, weak in its acceptance by many faculty and a

---

[700] Herbert S. White, "The Education and Selection of Librarians: A Sequence of Happenstances," *Library Journal* 115, no. 17 (October 15, 1990): 61-62.

[701] "Dean's List: 10 School Heads Debate the Future of Library Education," *Library Journal* 119, no. 6 (April 01, 1994): 60-64. See also Blaise Cronin, "Accreditation: Retool It or Kill It," *Library Journal* 125, no. 11 (2000): 54.

[702] P. W. Dalrymple, "Understanding Accreditation: The Librarian's Role in Educational Evaluation," *Portal* 1, no. 1 (2001): 25.

[703] D. Haddow and E. Klobas., "Communication of Research to Practice in Library and Information Science: Closing the Gap," *Library and Information Science Research* 26 (2004): 29-43.

[704] Michael Mounce, "The Effects of ALA Accreditation Standards on Library Education Programs Accredited by the American Library Association." *LIBRES* 15, no. 1 (2005), available at http://libres.curtin.edu.au/libres15n1/Mounce%20-%20Final.htm.

good portion of the information professions) MLIS accreditation system became evident in just the past few years. The 2009 release of the final report of the Library Education Task Force led to a lengthy, interesting, and sometimes acrimonious debate on the JESSE listserv from late May to mid-June 2009. Comments both positive and negative were made in regards to the value of accreditation for library and information science education; opinions were expressed about the positions of professional associations other than ALA, the nature of librarianship in the more broadly defined information professions, the differences between LIS and iSchools, the varying usefulness of individual certification as compared to programmatic accreditation, and ideas about extending accreditation beyond MLIS degree programs to encompass doctoral and other certificate degrees. This task force had been established in 2006.

Towards the end of the 1990s, there was increasing concern about the relevance of the 1992 accreditation standards. In 1999 a congress was held on library education[705] partly leading to new accreditation standards adopted in 2008.[706] The new accreditation standards are not a radical departure in either purpose or content. The guidelines define the purpose of accreditation, reaffirming their long-held historic purpose: "The American Library Association through the Committee on Accreditation protects the public interest and provides guidance for educators. Prospective students, employers recruiting professional staff, and the general public concerned about the quality of library and information services have the right to know whether a given program of education is of good standing. By identifying those programs meeting recognized standards, the Committee offers a means of quality control in the professional staffing of library and information services."[707] Nothing new in this.

A few changes in the new accreditation standards are interesting. For example, they expand the scope of what is being assessed: "The first section of the Standards describes the field of professional practice and its associated areas of study and research. It defines the phrases 'library and

---

[705] 1st Congress: Steering Committee's Final Report, American Library Association. Final Report of the Steering Committee on the Congress for Professional Education, June, 1999, available at http://www.ala.org/ala/educationcareers/education/1stcongressonpro/1stcongresssteeringcommittees.cfm.

[706] The 2008 Accreditation Standards can be found at http://www.lita.org/ala/educationcareers/education/accreditedprograms/standards/index.cfm.

[707] ALA, Standards for Accreditation, p. 4.

EPILOGUE

information studies' and 'school of library and information studies.' These definitions are intended to allow a school to bring forward for the purposes of accreditation any master's degree program (one or more than one) that addresses the field's areas of interest regardless of a degree's name, including for example, degrees entitled Master of Information Science, Master of Librarianship, Master of Arts in Library Science, Master of Information Resource Management, or other similar titles."[708] The 2008 standards are clearly intended to reflect the substantial changes occurring during the previous decade and a half, summarized in this way: "The most important issues at the time of the revision included: diversity, systematic planning, student learning outcomes, definition of the field, interaction with other fields of study and other campus units, distance education, globalization, management, multiple degree programs, values, and ethics."[709] However, this seems a little like trying to balance too many balls in the air at once, with expanding the purpose of these standards while so many in the field really see them being used in much more limited terms.

There were also two other documents emerging from the ALA Presidential Task Force on Library Education. This group presented a report on "Core Competencies of Librarianship" to the ALA Executive Board, ultimately approved by the association's Council on January 27, 2009, an effort to define the "basic knowledge to be possessed by all persons graduating from an ALA-accredited master's program in library and information studies," a reflection of the preceding decade of debate where a vocal portion of library practitioners argued that the schools offering these programs were moving farther and farther away from what librarians needed or valued.[710] The competencies document, reflecting a growing trend in what a variety of professional associations have been engaged in, receded into the background as controversy erupted over the main report of the Presidential Task Force on Library Education.

This task force report recommended that the core competencies be adopted, incorporating them into the accreditation standards, and made a number of sweeping statements that the accreditation standards be composed of "prescriptives," that is, that the standards be both more precise, mandated, and refocused on learning outcomes. If these recommendations had stopped, they may have been greeted with mild

---

[708] ALA, Standards for Accreditation, p. 13.
[709] ALA, Standards for Accreditation, p. 14.
[710] The "ALA's Core Competencies of Librarianship," January 27, 2009 can be found at http://www.ala.org/ala/educationcareers/careers/corecomp/corecompetences/index.cfm

acceptance. But they did not stop there. There were recommendations that the "majority of the permanent full-time faculty teaching in the program" be "grounded in librarianship by virtue of their educational background, professional experience and/or record of research and publication" and that there be a new task force established to evaluate "continuing education, doctoral education" and a variety of other educational programs.[711] Criticism of these proposals emerged quickly, as did defenses of the work of the task force. Even defining what it meant to be grounded in librarianship is complicated; although possessing a doctoral degree in library and information science and with more than two decades of service in a library and information science school I am not sure I qualify (since my focus has been on archival studies).

It is not my intention to offer any in-depth assessment of this debate, especially since it is still ongoing and uncertain just what its meaning may be for professional education. As I finish this manuscript on the eve of the 2010 meeting of the Association for Library and Information Science Education and the ALA Mid-Winter meeting, it is hard not to see or feel the wounds of this debate. An announcement was distributed by the ALA Committee on Education for a forum on the learning outcomes in LIS education and "how the professional community views LIS graduates."[712] A few responses appeared very quickly, reflecting the depth of feelings about these endless discussions between practitioners and educators, with the potential of another avalanche of commentary. Australian Sue Myburgh captures some of my concerns quite well, writing, "It is the task of educators (and I refer here to academics or faculty whose goal is to 'educate' – please look up this word if you do not know what it means) to introduce neophyte information professionals to the DISCIPLINE of 'LIS' (or whatever else you want to call it." She continues, "Employers should get over this – unless they want clerks and administrators, and not professionals who serve a social purpose and assume (quite serious) social responsibilities (which can even involve life and death). It is quite ridiculous for university-based educational programs to attempt to focus on work-related 'competencies,' which they cannot do very well anyway without being in a real-life setting. This is something that employers must assume – as all for-profit businesses assume as well (just look at how new accountants, doctors, lawyers, architects, nurses and so forth are treated and

---

[711] Various versions of this report can be found on the American Library Association website.
[712] Patricia Antrim to JESSE, January 7, 2010.

trained in the first year or two on the job, after university." And she concludes, "But this brings me to a wider discussion about how universities should stop thinking they are money-making training enterprises, and should rather be phrontisteries that encourage creativity and innovation in society."[713] And here we are back, once again, to the challenges for professional schools in the modern corporate university.

iSchools. Some have observed that while library and information science education will survive, this does not mean that it will be in library schools as it has been for generations. As Blaise Cronin posits, library education is only one of many streams within these schools and while he was writing just before the emergence of the iSchool movement this may well be one primary explanation for what these new schools may offer.[714] iSchools are a recent phenomenon in the information professions, perhaps too soon to try to characterize in any in-depth fashion. However, Ron Larsen's history of the movement provides some evidence of the essential characteristics of these schools, noting "An iSchool provides the venue that enables scholars from a variety of contributing disciplines to leverage their individual insights, perspectives, and interests, informed by a rich, 'trans-disciplinary' community." Larsen then offers this definition:

> So what is an iSchool in the 21st century? Informed by decades of debate and responding to exceptionally rapid changes in technology and uncertainty in public policy, iSchools foster the development of an intellectual space where true interdisciplinarity plays out. In so doing, they introduce a range of challenges to traditional university structures and practices regarding organizational boundaries, promotion and tenure policies, doctoral education, research legitimacy, etc., as they create an environment where issues of information are addressed systematically, regardless of disciplinary heritage or presumed 'ownership'. In this way, iSchools respond to the salient issues of the time by stressing the production of strong results. They are in a constant state of adaptation within their core competencies, while building necessary bridges among disciplines. The iSchools recognize that the near-term future will be shaped largely by industry, so their applied research agenda is strongly influenced by these emerging needs and directions. But the iSchools lead industry and government in the study of timeless, recurring, theoretical questions, and educate the next

---

[713] Sue Myburgh to JESSE, January 8, 2010. Phrontisteries are establishments for education, including universities; now you know – I had to look it up.
[714] Blaise Cronin, "Holding the Center while Prospecting at the Periphery: Domain Identity and Coherence in North American Information Studies Education," *Education for Information*, 20 (2002): 3–10.

generation of information professionals who will shape the future of a global information society."[715]

The differences between this vision and that of the vision of the MLIS accreditation are probably obvious (and disturbing to some).

Not surprisingly, the iSchool deans criticized the library education task force's recommendations, arguing that the prescriptive requirements are problematic in a period of "rapid change" and works against the "curricular flexibility" needed in short-term masters programs. These deans called for "empirical research leading to a genuine understanding of the profession and to consider how these needs are, or are not, being met by programs such as ours."[716] We have had very little research about ALA accreditation over the past half-century about its effectiveness, probably suggesting that it is a process more geared for professional status and visibility than something intended for educational quality. Many probably disagree with this latter assessment, but it is difficult to look over the educational debates and not see mostly political debates, tinged by emotions, fears, and angst about the future.

Conclusion. Are iSchools the next best new thing on the horizon? Maybe, although there is a lot to evaluate and think about when we consider the future education of the next generation of information professionals. Do librarians and other information professionals have a future, especially when so many of the technological innovations have seemed to contribute both to negative attitudes about professional barriers and the creation of new disciplines? I have no doubt. Will the schools where these professionals will be educated be different than anything we imagined or had before, something like the present iSchool? Most likely. Will these schools be grounding the next generation of librarian, archivist, and other information professional in many of the ethical and other values long represented in the old library school, especially as the corporate university model continues to become entrenched? This is what worries me. Arthur Clarke, in his science fiction classic *Childhood's End*, states, "Fifty years is ample time in which to change a world and its people almost beyond recognition. All that is required for the task are a sound knowledge of social

---

[715] Ronald L. Larsen, "iSchools," *Encyclopedia of Library and Information Sciences*, forthcoming; also available at http://www.ischools.org/site/history/.

[716] John Unsworth, iCaucus Coordinator, to Office for Accreditation, American Library Association, undated; the full letter is available at http://nora.lis.uiuc.edu/images/pdfs/alaresponse.pdf.

engineering, a clear sight of the intended goal – and power."[717] We have had about the same length of time to fuss about the education of librarians and other information professionals circling around the accreditation of a particular degree, and we have seen our professional and scholarly world change with less, certainly a lot less, power held by us to deal with the changes. I wonder if we still have common goals in sight. And, I wonder if the iSchool movement is also up to the task.

---

[717] Arthur C. Clarke, *Childhood's End* (New York: Ballantine Books, 1990; org. published 1953), p. 62.

List of Works Cited

Note: All electronic sources cited here were available at the time this book went to press.

Abbott, Andrew. *The System of Professions: An Essay on the Division of Expert Labor* (Chicago: University of Chicago Press, 1988).

Adams, Hazard. *The Academic Tribes*, 2nd ed (Urbana: University of Illinois, 1988).

Adkins, Denice. "Latino Librarians on Becoming LIS Educators: An Exploratory Investigation of the Barriers in Recruiting Latino Faculty," *Journal of Education for Library and Information Science* 45 (Spring 2004): 149-161.

Allitt, Patrick. *I'm the Teacher, You're the Student: A Semester in the University Classroom* (Philadelphia: University of Pennsylvania Press, 2005).

Alter, Robert. *The Pleasures of Reading in an Ideological Age* (New York: W. W. Norton and Co., 1996).

American Library Association, *Standards for Accreditation of Master's Programs in Library and Information Studies, Adopted by the Council of the American Library Association, January 15, 2008.*

American Library Association, The "ALA's Core Competencies of Librarianship," January 27, 2009 available at http://www.ala.org/ala/educationcareers/careers/corecomp/corecompetences/index.cfm.

Amis, Kingsley. *Lucky Jim* (New York: Penguin Books, 1992; org. published 1954).

Anderson, Chris. *Teaching as Believing: Faith in the University* (Waco, Texas: Baylor University Press, 2004).

Arana, Marie, ed. *The Writing Life: Writers on How They Think and Work: A Collection from the Washington Post Book World* (New York: Public Affairs, 2003).

Aronowitz, Stanley. *The Knowledge Factory: Dismantling the Corporate University and Creating True Higher Learning* (Boston: Beacon Press, 2000).

Atlas, James. *Battle of the Books: The Curriculum Debate in America* (New York: W.W. Norton and Co., 1992).

Arterbery, Vivian J. "Accreditation: A Blueprint for Action," *Special Libraries* 77, no. 4 (Fall 1986): 230-234.

Alterman, Eric. "Tiny Circulations, Big Idea: 'General Interest' Journals and the Shaping of Public Policy," *Chronicle of Higher Education*, 5 June 1998, p. B6.

Atwood, Margaret. *Negotiating with the Dead: A Writer on Writing* (Cambridge: Cambridge University Press, 2002).

Auld, Lawrence W.S. "Seven Imperatives for Library Education," *Library Journal* 115 (May 1990): 55-59.

Axtell, James. *The Pleasures of Academe: A Celebration and Defense of Higher Education* (Lincoln: University of Nebraska Press, 1998).

Ayers, Edward L. "The Academic Culture and the IT Culture: Their Effect on Teaching and Scholarship," *Educause Review* 39 (November/December 2004): 48-62.

Báez, Fernando. *A Universal History of the Destruction of Books: From Ancient Sumer to Modern Iraq*, translated by Alfred MacAdam (New York: Atlas and Co., 2008).

Baker, Nicholson. *The Size of Thoughts: Essays and Other Lumber* (New York: Vintage Books, 1997).

Baker, Nicholson. *Double Fold: Libraries and the Assault on Paper* (New York: Random House, 2001).

Bain, Ken. *What the Best College Teachers Do* (Cambridge: Harvard University Press, 2004).

Banner, James M., Jr., and Harold C. Cannon. *The Elements of Teaching* (New Haven: Yale University Press, 1997).

Barber, Benjamin R. *An Aristocracy of Everyone: The Politics of Education and the Future of America* (New York: Ballantine Books, 1992).

Baron, Dennis. *A Better Pencil: Readers, Writers, and the Digital Revolution* (New York: Oxford University Press, 2009).

Barron, D.D. "Distance Education and the Closing of the American Library School," *Library Quarterly* 61 (July 1991): 273-282.

Barzun, Jacques. *The House of Intellect* (New York: Perennial Classics, 2002; org. pub. 1959).

Barzun, Jacques. *The American University: How It Runs, Where It Is Going*, 2nd. Ed. (Chicago: University of Chicago Press, 1999; org. pub., 1968).

Barzun, Jacques. *Simple and Direct: A Rhetoric for Writers*, rev.ed. (Chicago: University of Chicago Press, 1985).

Barzun, Jacques. *Begin Here: The Forgotten Conditions of Teaching and Learning* (Chicago: University of Chicago Press, 1992).

Barzun, Jacques. *A Jacques Barzun Reader: Selections from His Works*, ed. Michael Murray (New York: HarperCollins, 2002).

Basbanes, Nicholas A. *A Splendor of Letters: The Permanence of Books in an Impermanent World* (New York: HarperCollins, 2003).

Basbanes, Nicholas A. *Every Book Its Reader: The Power of the Printed Word to Stir the World* (New York: Harper Collins, 2005).

Basbanes, Nicholas A. *A World of Letters: Yale University Press, 1908-2008* (New Haven: Yale University Press, 2008).

Bastian, Jeannette and Donna Webber, *Archival Internships: A Guide for Faculty, Supervisors, and Students* (Chicago: Society of American Archivists, 2008).

Battles, Matthew. "In Defense of the Kindle," *Atlantic*, March 5, 2009, http://www.theatlantic.com/doc/200903u/amazon-kindle-2.

Bell, Steven J. "Good at Reviewing Books But Not Each Other," *Inside Higher Education*, April 27, 2007, available at http://insidehighered.com/views/2007/04/27/bell.

Bemis, Samuel Flagg. "The Training of Archivists in the United States," *American Archivist* 2 (July 1939): 154-161.

Bender, Thomas. *Intellect and Public Life: Essays on the Social History of Academic Intellectuals in the United States* (Baltimore: Johns Hopkins University Press, 1993).

Bender, Thomas and Carl E. Schorske, eds. *American Academic Culture in Transformation: Fifty Years, Four Disciplines* (Princeton, NJ: Princeton University Press, 1997).

Berner, Richard C. "Archival Education and Training in the United States, 1937 to Present," *Journal of Education for Librarianship* 22 (Summer/Fall 1981): 3-19.

Bernstein, Charles. "A Blow Is Like an Instrument," *Daedalus* 126 (Fall 1997): 177-200.

Berry, Wendell. *In the Presence of Fear: Three Essays for a Changed World* (Great Barrington, MA: The Orion Society, 2001).

Bérubé, Michael. *What's Liberal About the Liberal Arts? Classroom Politics and 'Bias' in Higher Education* (New York: W. W. Norton and Co., 2006).

Bérubé, Michael. "Freedom to Teach," *Inside Higher Education* (September 11, 2007), http://insidehighered.com/views/2007/09/11/berube, accessed September 11, 2007.

Billington, James (interview). *Yahoo! Internet Life* 6 (September 2000): 80.

Birkerts, Sven. *The Gutenberg Elegies: The Fate of Reading in an Electronic Age* (Boston: Faber and Faber, 1994).

Birkerts, Sven. *Reading Life: Books for the Ages* (Saint Paul, Minnesota: Graywolf Press, 2007).

Birkerts, Sven. "Resisting the Kindle," *Atlantic Online* (March 2, 2009), http://www.theatlantic.com/doc/200903u/amazon-kindle, accessed March 2, 2009.

Bloch, R. Howard and Carla Hesse, eds., *Future Libraries* (Berkeley: University of California Press, 1995).

Bloom, Harold. *How to Read and Why* (New York: Scribner, 2000).

Blum, Susan D. *My Word! Plagiarism and College Culture* (Ithaca: Cornell University Press, 2009).

Bohannen, A. "Library Education: Struggling to Meet the Needs of the Profession," *Journal of Academic Librarianship* 17, no. 4 (1991): 216-219.

Bok, Derek. *Beyond the Ivory Tower: Social Responsibilities of the Modern University* (Cambridge: Harvard University Press, 1982).

Bok, Derek. *Higher Learning* (Cambridge: Harvard University Press, 1986).

Bok, Derek. *Universities in the Marketplace: The Commercialization of Higher Education* (Princeton: Princeton University Press, 2003).

Bok, Derek. *Our Underachieving Colleges: A Candid Look at How Students Learn and Why They Should Be Learning More* (Princeton: Princeton University Press, 2006).

Bolker, Joan. *Writing Your Dissertation in Fifteen Minutes a Day: A Guide to Starting, Revising, and Finishing Your Doctoral Thesis* (New York: Henry Holt and Co., 1998).

Bonk, Curtis J. *The World Is Open: How Web Technology Is Revolutionizing Education* (San Francisco: Jossey-Bass, 2009).

Bookstein, Abraham. "Library Education, Yesterday, and Today: Library Education in the University Setting," *Library Quarterly* 56 (October 1986): 360-369.

Booth, Wayne C., Gregory G. Colomb, and Joseph M. Williams, *The Craft of Research*, second ed. (Chicago: University of Chicago Press, 2003).

Borchert, Don. *Free for All: Oddballs, Geeks, and Gangstas in the Public Library* (New York: Virgin Books, 2007).

Borgman, Christine. *Scholarship in the Digital Age: Information, Infrastructure, and the Internet* (Cambridge, MA: MIT Press, 2007).

Bousquet, Mark. *How the University Works: Higher Education and the Low-Wage Nation* (New York: New York University Press, 2008).

Bower, Ames Sheldon. "Whence and Whither: A Survey of Archival Education," *Georgia Archive* 5 (Summer 1977): 44-61.

Boyce, Bert R. "The Death of Library Education," *American Libraries* 25, no. 3 (March 1994): 257-259.

Bradbury, Ray. *Zen in the Art of Writing* (Santa Barbara, Calif.: Joshua Odell Editions, 1996).

Breslow, Jason M. "Young Professors at Private Institutions Report Greater Overall Level of Job Satisfaction," *Chronicle of Higher Education*, September 18, 2007, http://chronicle.com/daily/2007/09/2007091808n.htm.

Bridges, Edwin, Gregory S. Hunter, Page Putnam Miller, David Thelen, and Gerhard Weinberg. "Toward Better Documenting and Interpreting of the Past: What History Graduate Programs in the Twenty-First Century Should Teach About Archival Practices," *American Archivist* 56 (Fall 1993): 730-749.

Brint, Steven. *In an Age of Experts: The Changing Role of Professionals in Politics and Public Life* (Princeton: Princeton University Press, 1994).

Brint, Steven, ed. *The Future of the City of Intellect: The Changing American University* (Stanford, CA: Stanford University Press, 2002).

Brown, John Seely and Paul Duguid, *The Social Life of Information* (Boston: Harvard Business School Press, 2000).

Brown, Robert D. "Supervising Evaluation Practicum and Intern Students: A Developmental Model," *Educational Evaluation and Policy Analysis* 7 (Summer 1985): 161-67.

Budd, R. W. "A New Library School of Thought," *Library Journal* 117 (May 1, 1992): 44-48.

Bunge, Nancy. *Master Class: Lessons from Leading Writers* (Iowa City: University of Iowa Press, 2005).

Burke, Frank. "The Future Course of Archival Theory in the United States," *American Archivist* 44 (Winter 1981): 40-46.

Burnett, Kathleen M. and Laurie J. Bonnici. "Contested Terrain: Accreditation and the Future Profession of Librarianship," *Library Quarterly* 76 (April 2006): 193-219.

Campbell-Kelly, Martin and William Aspray, *Computer: A History of the Information Machine* (New York: Basic Books, 1996).

Cappon, Lester J. "What, Then, Is There to Theorize About?" *American Archivist* 45 (Winter 1982): 19-25.

Carmichael, David W. *Organizing Archival Records: A Practical Method of Arrangement and Description for Small Archives*, 2nd ed. (Walnut Creek, CA: AltaMira Press, 2004).

Carmichael, J.V. and Shontz, M.L. "A 'Despised' 'Semi-Profession': Perceptions of Curricular Content Relating to Gender and Social Issues Among

1993 MLIS/MLS Graduates," *Journal of Education for Library and Information Science* 38(2) Spring 1997: 98-115.

Carr, Nicholas. "Is Google Making Us Stupid?" *Atlantic* 302 (July/August 2008):56-58, 60, 62-63.

Chace, William M. *100 Semesters: My Adventures As Student, Professor, and University President, And What I Learned Along the Way* (Princeton: Princeton University Press, 2006).

Chace, William M. "The Decline of the English Department," *American Scholar* 78 (Autumn 2009): 32-42.

Cheng, L-M. "Uncovering Some Problems in the Library and Information Science Education by Following the Footstep of History," *Journal of Educational Media & Library Sciences* 31, no. 2 (1994): 195-217.

Chepesiuk, R. "Learning Without Walls," *American Libraries* 29 (October 1998): 63-67.

Clarke, Arthur C. *Childhood's End* (New York: Ballantine Books, 1990; org. published 1953).

Cioffi, Frank. *The Imaginative Argument: A Practical Manifesto for Writers* (Princeton: Princeton University Press, 2005).

Coburn, Louis. *Classroom and Field: The Internship in American Library Education; An Inquiry Into Its Development and Evaluation*, Queens College Studies in Librarianship no. 3 (Flushing: Queens College of the City University of New Work, 1980).

Cohen, Patricia. "In Tough Times, the Humanities Must Justify Their Worth," *New York Times*, February 24, 2009, available at http://www.nytimes.com/2009/02/25/books/25human.html?_r=1.

Colman, J. Gordon, Jr. "The Role of the Practicum in Library Schools," *Journal of Education for Library and Information Science* 30 (Summer 1989): 19-27.

Clark, Roy Peter. *Writing Tools: 50 Essential Strategies for Every Writer* (New York: Little, Brown and Co., 2006).

Clark, William. *Academic Charisma and the Origins of the Research University* (Chicago: University of Chicago Press, 2006).

Clee, Nicholas. "The Decline and Fall of Books," *Times Online*, May 7, 2009.

Clough, M. Evalyn and Thomas J. Galvin. "Educating Special Librarians: Toward a Meaningful Practitioner-Educator Dialogue," *Special Libraries* 75 (January 1984): 1-8.

Colwell, Ernest Cadman. "The Role of the Professional School in the University," *Library Journal* 118 (December 1993): S1-3, S6-8, S10, S12.

Conway, Jill Ker. *The Road from Coorain* (New York: Vintage Books, 1990).

Conway, Jill Ker. *True North: A Memoir* (New York: Alfred A. Knopf, 1994).

Conway, Jill Ker. *A Woman's Education: The Road from Coorain Leads to Smith College* (New York: Vintage Books, 2001).

Conway, Paul. "Facts and Frameworks: An Approach to Studying the Users of Archives," *American Archivist* 49 (Fall 1986): 393-407.

Conway, Paul. "Archival Education and the Need for Full-time Faculty," *American Archivist* 51 (Summer 1988): 254-265.

Cook, Terry. "The Imperative of Challenging Absolutes in Graduate Archival Education Programs: Issues for Educators and the Profession," *American Archivist* 63 (Fall/Winter 2000): 380-391.

Corrigan, Maureen. *Leave Me Alone, I'm Reading: Finding and Losing Myself in Books* (New York: Random House, 2005).

Coser, Lewis A. *Men of Ideas: A Sociologist's View* (New York: Simon and Schuster, 1997).

Cox, Richard J. "Strategies for Archival Action in the 1980s and Beyond: Implementing the SAA Goals and Priorities Task Force Report," *Provenance* 3 (Fall 1985): 22-37.

Cox, Richard J. "Archivists and Public Historians in the United States," *Public Historian* 8 (Summer 1986): 25-41.

Cox, Richard J. "Professionalism and Archivists in the United States," *American Archivist* 49 (Summer 1986): 229-47.

Cox, Richard J. "Educating Archivists: Speculations on the Past, Present, and Future," *Journal of the American Society for Information Science* 39 (September 1988): 340-43.

Cox, Richard J. "The History of Primary Sources in Graduate Education: An Archival Perspective," *Special Collections* 4, no. 2 (1990): 39-78.

Cox, Richard J. "The Masters of Archival Studies and American Education Standards: An Argument for the Continued Development of Graduate Archival Education in the United States," *Archivaria* 36 (Autumn 1993): 221-31.

Cox, Richard J. "Continuing Education and Special Collections Professionals: The Need for Rethinking," *Rare Books & Manuscripts Librarianship* 10, no. 2 (1995): 78-96.

Cox, Richard J. *Documenting Localities: A Practical Model for American Archivists and Manuscripts Curators* (Metuchen, New Jersey: Scarecrow Press and Society of American Archivists, 1996).

Cox, Richard J. "Debating the Future of the Book," *American Libraries* 28 (February 1997): 52-55.

Cox, Richard J. and Edie Rasmussen, "Reinventing the Information Professions and the Argument for Specialization in LIS Education: Case Studies in Archives and Information Technology," *Journal of Education for Library and Information Science*, 38 (Fall 1997): 255-267.

Cox, Richard J. "Millennial Thoughts on the Education of Records Professionals," *Records and Information Management Report* 15 (April 1999): 1-16.

Cox, Richard J. "Employing Records Professionals in the Information Age: A Research Study," *Information Management Journal* 34 (January 2000): 18-33.

Cox, Richard J. "Accountability, Public Scholarship, and Library, Information, and Archival Science Educators," *Journal of Education for Library and Information Science* 41 (Spring 2000): 94-105.

Cox, Richard J. "The Information Age and History: Looking Backward to See Us," *Ubiquity* (26 September-October 4, 2000), available at http://www.acm.org/ubiquity/.

Cox, Richard J., Elizabeth Yakel, David Wallace, Jeannette Bastian, and Jennifer Marshall, "Archival Education in North American Library and Information Science Schools," *Library Quarterly* 71 (April 2001): 141-194.

Cox, Richard J., Elizabeth Yakel, David Wallace, Jeannette Bastian, and Jennifer Marshall, "Educating Archivists in Library and Information Science

Schools," *Journal of Education for Library and Information Science* 42 (Summer 2001): 228-240.

Cox, Richard J. "Forming the Records Professional's Knowledge: North American Archival Publishing in the 20th Century," *Records & Information Management Report* 20 (March 2004): 1-13.

Cox, Richard J. *Archives and Archivists in the Information Age* (New York: Neal-Schuman Publishers, Inc., 2005).

Cox, Richard J. "Why Survival Is Not Enough," *American Libraries*, June/July 2006, pp. 42-45.

Cox, Richard J. and Ronald L. Larsen, "iSchools and Archival Studies," *Archival Science* 8 (2008): 307-326.

Cox, Richard J. "Unpleasant Things: Teaching Advocacy in Archival Education Programs," *InterActions: UCLA Journal of Education and Information Studies* 5, Issue 1, Article 8 (2009). http://repositories.cdlib.org/gseis/interactions/vol5/iss1/art8.

Crawford, Michael B. *Shop Class as Soulcraft: An Inquiry into the Value of Work* (New York: Penguin Press, 2009).

Crews, Frederick. *Postmodern Pooh* (New York: North Point Press, 2001).

Crider, Scott F. *The Office of Assertion: An Art of Rhetoric for the Academic Essay* (Wilmington, Del.: ISI Books, 2005).

Cronin, Blaise. "Accreditation: Retool It or Kill It," *Library Journal* 125, no. 11 (2000): 54.

Cronin, Blaise. "Holding the Center while Prospecting at the Periphery: Domain Identity and Coherence in North American Information Studies Education," *Education for Information*, 20 (2002): 3–10.

Crowley, Bill. "The Control and Direction of Professional Education," *Journal of the American Society for Information Science* 50, no. 12 (1999): 1127-35.

Csikszentmihalyi, Mihaly. *Good Business: Leadership, Flow, and the Making of Meaning* (New York: Viking, 2003).

Cuban, Larry. *The Blackboard and the Bottom Line: Why Schools Can't Be Businesses* (Cambridge: Harvard University Press, 2004).

Culler, Jonathan and Kevin Lamb, eds. *Just Being Difficult? Academic Writing in the Public Arena* (Stanford, CA: Stanford University Press, 2003).

Dalrymple, P. W. "The State of the Schools." *American Libraries* 28, no. 1 (January 1997): 31-34.

Dalrymple, P. W. "Understanding Accreditation: The Librarian's Role in Educational Evaluation," *Portal* 1, no. 1 (2001): 23-32.

Damrosch, David. *We Scholars: Changing the Culture of the University* (Cambridge: Harvard University Press, 1995).

Damrosch, David. *Meetings of the Mind* (Princeton: Princeton University Press, 2000).

Daniel, Evelyn H. "The Library/Information School in Context: The Place of Library/Information Science Education Within Higher Education," *Library Trends* (Spring 1986): 623-643.

Darnton, Robert. "Google and the Future of Books," *The New York Review of Books* 56, no. 2 (February 12, 2009): 9-11.

Davis, Donald G., Jr. "Ebla to the Electronic Dream: The Role of Historical Perspectives in Professional Education," *Journal of Education for Library and Information Science* 39, no.3 (Summer 1998): 228-235.

Davis, Susan E. "Distance Education for Archivists: Panacea or Peril?" paper presented at the Third SAA Archives Educators Forum, August 2, 2004, Simmons College, Boston, Massachusetts.

"Dean's List: 10 School Heads Debate the Future of Library Education," *Library Journal* 119, no. 6 (April 01, 1994): 60-64.

De Botton, Alain. *The Pleasures and Sorrows of Work* (New York: Pantheon Books, 2009).

Deegan, Marilyn and Simon Tanner, eds. *Digital Preservation* (London: Facet Publishing, 2006).

De La Pena-McCook, K. and J. Lester. "Keeping the Library in Library Education," *American Libraries* 29 (March 1998): 59, 61, 63.

Delbanco, Andrew. *Required Reading: Why Our American Classics Matter Now* (New York: Farrar, Straus, and Giroux, 1997).

DeNeef, A. Leigh and Craufurd D. Goodwin, eds. *The Academic's Handbook*, 2nd ed. (Durham: Duke University Press, 1995).

Dewar, James. "The Information Age and the Printing Press: Looking Backward to See Ahead," *Ubiquity* no. 25 [August 15 – 21, 2000] at http://www.acm.org/ubiquity/views/j_dewar_1.html.

Dillard, Annie. *The Writing Life* (New York: HarperPerennial, 1990).

Dillon, Andrew and April Norris. "Crying Wolf: An Examination and Reconsideration of the Perception of Crisis in LIS Education," *Journal of Education for Library and Information Science* 46, no. 4 (2005): 280-298.

Dimunation, Mark. "Red Wine and White Carpets: What We Didn't Learn in Library School, or When the Dog and Pony Goes Bad," *RBM: A Journal of Rare Books, Manuscripts, and Cultural Heritage*, vol. 7, no. 1 (2006): 73-84.

Dirda, Michael. *An Open Book: Coming of Age in the Heartland* (New York: W. W. Norton and Co., 2003).

Dirda, Michael. *Book by Book: Notes on Reading and Life* (New York: Henry Holt and Co., 2005).

Dirda, Michael. *Readings: Essays and Literary Entertainments* (Bloomington: Indiana University Press, 2000).

Doctorow, E. L. *Reporting the Universe*, The William E. Massey Sr. Lectures in the History of American Civilization (Cambridge, MA: Harvard University Press, 2003).

Donoghue, Denis. *The Practice of Reading* (New Haven: Yale University Press, 1998).

Donoghue, Frank. *The Last Professors: The Corporate University and the Fate of the Humanities* (New York: Fordham University Press, 2008).

Dougherty, Peter J. "A Manifesto for Scholarly Publishing," *The Chronicle Review*, 55, June 12, 2009, p. B10, http://chronicle.com/weekly/v55/i39/39b01001.htm.

Douglas, Scott. *Quiet, Please: Dispatches from a Public Librarian* (Philadelphia: Da Capo Press, 2008).

Doumani, Beshara, ed. *Academic Freedom After September 11* (New York: Zone Books, 2006).

Dow, Elizabeth. "Harmonizing Archives 101: Collaboration to support the Collaborative," paper presented at the Third SAA Archives Educators Forum, August 2, 2004, Simmons College, Boston, Massachusetts.

Downing, David B. *The Knowledge Contract: Politics and Paradigms in the Academic Workplace* (Lincoln: University of Nebraska Press, 2005).

Downs, Donald Alexander. *Restoring Free Speech and Liberty on Campus* (Oakland, CA: The Independent Institute and Cambridge University Press, 2005).

D'Souza, Dinesh. *The Virtue of Prosperity: Finding Values in an Age of Techno-Affluence* (New York: Free Press, 2000).

Duff, Wendy, Joan Cherry, and Nalini Singh. "Evaluating Master's Program in Information Studies: A Student Survey," paper presented at the Third SAA Archives Educators Forum, August 2, 2004, Simmons College, Boston, Massachusetts.

Duranti, Luciana. "The Archival Body of Knowledge: Archival Theory, Method, and Practice," *Journal of Education for Library and Information Science* 34 (Winter 1993): 8-24.

Dyson, Freeman. "The World on a String," *New York Review of Books* 51 (May 11, 2004).

Eastwood, Terry. "Nurturing Archival Education in the University," *American Archivist* 51 (Summer 1988): 228-251.

Eastwood, Terry. "What is Archival Theory and Why Is It Important?" *Archivaria* 37 (Spring 1994): 122-130.

Eastwood, Terry. "Building Archival Knowledge and Skills," paper presented at the Third SAA Archives Educators Forum, August 2, 2004, Simmons College, Boston, Massachusetts.

Edmundson, Mark. *Why Read?* (New York: Bloomsbury, 2004).

Edwards, Paul N. *The Closed World: Computers and the Politics of Discourse in Cold War America* (Cambridge: MIT Press, 1996).

Eisenstein, Elizabeth L. *The Printing Press as an Agent of Change: Communications and Cultural Transformations in Early-Modern Europe* (New York: Cambridge University Press, 1979).

Eisenstein, Elizabeth L. *The Printing Press in Early-Modern Europe* (Cambridge: Cambridge University Press, 1993).

Eisenstein, Elizabeth L. "An Unacknowledged Revolution Revisited," *American Historical Review* 107 (February 2002): 87-105.

Ellis, John M. *Literature Lost: Social Agendas and the Corruption of the Humanities* (New Haven: Yale University Press, 1997).

Engell, James and Anthony Dangerfield. *Saving Higher Education in the Age of Money* (Charlottesville: University of Virginia Press, 2005).

Epstein, Jason. "The Coming Revolution," *The New York Review of Books* 47 (November 2, 2000): 4-5.

Epstein, Jason. *Book Business: Publishing Past Present and Future* (New York: W. W. Norton, 2002).

Ericson, Timothy L. "Professional Associations and Archival Education: A Different Role, or a Different Theater?" *American Archivist* 51 (Summer 1988): 298-311.

Eshelman, William R. "The Erosion of Library Education," *Library Journal* 108 (July 1983): 1309-1312.

Evans, David. "Redefining Faculty Roles," *Chronicle of Higher Education*, September 14, 2009, available at http://chronicle.com/blogPost/Redefining-Faculty-Roles/8016/?sid=at&utm_source=at&utm_medium=en.

Evans, Frank B. "Archival Training in the United States: An Unresolved Problem," *Archives et Bibliotheques de Belgigue* 46 (1975): 518-48.

Fadiman, Anne. *Ex Libris: Confessions of a Common Reader* (New York: Farrar, Straus, and Giroux, 1998).

Fadiman, Anne. *Rereadings: Seventeen Writers Revisit Books They Love* (New York: Farrar, Straus and Giroux, 2005).

Filene, Peter. *The Joy of Teaching: A Practical Guide for New College Instructors* (Chapel Hill: University of North Carolina Press, 2005).

Finch, Elsie Freeman, ed. *Advocating Archives: An Introduction to Public Relations for Archivists* (Metuchen, N.J.: The Society of American Archivists and Scarecrow Press, Inc., 1994).

Finkin, Matthew W. and Robert C. Post, *For the Common Good: Principles of American Academic Freedom* (New Haven: Yale University Press, 2009).

First Congress: Steering Committee's Final Report, American Library Association. *Final Report of the Steering Committee on the Congress for Professional Education, June, 1999*, available at http://www.ala.org/ala/educationcareers/education/1stcongressonpro/1stcongresssteeringcommittees.cfm.

Fish, Stanley. *Professional Correctness: Literary Studies and Political Change* (Oxford: Clarendon Press, 1995).

Fish, Stanley. "The Last Professor," *New York Times*, January 18, 2009.

Flaherty, Alice W. *The Midnight Disease: The Desire to Write, Writer's Block, and the Creative Brain* (Boston: Houghton Mifflin Co., 2004).

Foerstel, Herbert N. *Refuge of a Scoundrel: The Patriot Act in Libraries* (Westport, Conn.: Libraries Unlimited, 2004).

Fogg, Piper. "When Your In Box Is Always Full," *Chronicle of Higher Education*, June 6, 2008, available at http://chronicle.com/weekly/v54/i39/39b01901.htm

Foster, William and Jeffrey Bradach. "Should Nonprofits Seek Profits?" *Harvard Business Review* 83 (February 2005): 92-100.

Franklin, Cynthia G. *Academic Lives, Cultural Theory, and the University Today* (Athens: University of Georgia Press, 2009).

Franzen, Jonathan. "I Just Called to Say I Love You," *Technology Review* 111 (September/October 2008): 88-95, also available at http://www.technologyreview.com/Infotech/21173/page1/.

Frechette, Julie. "Crossing the (Digital) Line," *Inside Higher Education*, May 16, 2008, available at http://insidehighered.com/views/2008/05/16/frechette.

Freed, C. Patricia. "A Study to Identify Student and Faculty Opinions of Graduate Student Learning in Social Work Practicums," Ph.D. dissertation, University of Denver, 1974.

Friedman, Bonnie. *Writing Past Dark: Envy, Fear, Distractions and Other Dilemmas in the Writer's Life* (New York: HarperPerennial, 1993).

Friedman, David D. *Future Imperfect: Technology and Freedom in an Uncertain World* (New York: Cambridge University Press, 2008).

Friend, Tad. "Protest Studies: The State is Broke, and Berkeley Is In Revolt," *The New Yorker*, January 4, 2010, pp 22-28.

Fulford, Robert. *The Triumph of Narrative: Storytelling in the Age of Mass Culture* (New York: Broadway Books, 1999).

Garber, Marjorie. *Academic Instincts* (Princeton: Princeton University Press, 2003).

Gardner, Howard. *Creating Minds: An Anatomy of Creativity Seen Through the Lives of Freud, Einstein, Picasso, Stravinsky, Eliot, Graham, and Gandhi* (New York: Basic Books. 1993).

Gardner, Howard. *Leading Minds: An Anatomy of Leadership* (New York: Basic Books, 1995).

Gardner, Howard. *Changing Minds: The Art and Science of Changing Our Own and Other People's Minds* (Boston: Harvard Business School Press, 2004).

Gardner, Howard. *Five Minds for the Future* (Boston: Harvard Business School Press, 2006).

Garland, James C. *Saving Alma Mater: A Rescue Plan for America's Public Universities* (Chicago: University of Chicago Press, 2009).

Gates, Henry Louis, Jr. *Loose Canons: Notes on the Culture Wars* (New York: Oxford University Press, 1992).

Geiger, Roger L. *Knowledge and Money: Research Universities and the Paradox of the Marketplace* (Stanford: Stanford University Press, 2004).

Germano, William. *Getting It Published: A Guide for Scholars and Anyone Else Serious About Serious Books* (Chicago: University of Chicago Press, 2001).

Germano, William. *From Dissertation to Book* (Chicago: University of Chicago Press, 2005).

Giametti, A. Bartlett. *A Free and Ordered Space: The Real World of the University* (New York: W. W. Norton and Co., 1990).

Gilchrist, Ellen. *The Writing Life* (Jackson, Miss.: University Press of Mississippi, 2005).

Gilmore, William J. *Reading Becomes a Necessity of Life: Material and Cultural Life in Rural New England, 1780-1835* (Knoxville: University of Tennessee Press, 1989).

Gilster, Paul. *Digital Literacy* (New York: John Wiley and Sons, Inc., 1997).

Gioia, Dana. *Disappearing Ink: Poetry at the End of Print Culture* (Saint Paul, Minnesota: Graywolf Press, 2004).

Giroux, Henry. "Neoliberalism, Corporate Culture, and the Promise of Higher Education: The University as a Public Sphere," *Harvard Educational Review* 72 (Winter 2002): 425-464.

Giroux, Henry A. and Susan Searls Giroux. *Take Back Higher Education: Race, Youth, and the Crisis of Democracy in the Post-Civil Rights Era* (New York: Palgrave Macmillan, 2004).

Glasser, Ronald J. "We Are Not Immune: Influenza, SARS, and the Collapse of Public Health," *Harper's* 309 (July 2004): 35-42.

Glazer, Nathan. *We Are All Multiculturalists Now* (Cambridge: Harvard University Press, 1997).

Goggin, Jacqueline. "'That We Shall Truly Deserve the Title of Profession': The Training and Education of Archivists, 1930-1960," *American Archivist* 47 (Summer 1984): 243-254.

Goldstone, Lawrence and Nancy. *Deconstructing Penguins: Parents, Kids, and the Bond of Reading* (New York: Ballantine Books, 2005).

Gollop, Claudia J. "Library and Information Science Education: Preparing Librarians for a Multicultural Society," *College and Research Libraries* 60, no. 4 (1999): 385-395.

Gomez, Jeff. *Print is Dead: Books in Our Digital Age* (New York: MacMillan, 2008).

Gora, Jo Ann M. "Ivory Towers No More," *University Business*, October 2007, available at http://www.universitybusiness.com/viewarticle.aspx?articleid=907.

Gorman, Michael. "What Ails Library Education?" *The Journal of Academic Librarianship*, 30 (March 2004): 99-101.

Gorman, Michael. "Whither Library Education?" *New Library World* 105, nos. 9/10 (2004): 376–380.

Gould, Eric. *The University in a Corporate Culture* (New Haven: Yale University Press, 2003).

Gracy, Karen. "Mainstreaming Moving Images and Sound Educating the Next Generation of Archivists to Value and Care for Audiovisual Archives," paper presented at the Third SAA Archives Educators Forum, August 2, 2004, Simmons College, Boston, Massachusetts.

Graff, Gerald. *Beyond the Culture Wars: How Teaching the Conflicts Can Revitalize American Education* (New York: W.W. Norton and Co., 1992).

Graff, Gerald. *Clueless in Academia: How Schooling Obscures the Life of the Mind* (New Haven: Yale University Press, 2003).

Graff, Gerald and Cathy Birkenstein. *They Say/I Say: The Moves That Matter in Persuasive Writing* (New York: W.W. Norton and Co., 2008).

Grafton, Anthony. *The Footnote: A Curious History* (Cambridge: Harvard University Press, 1997).

Grafton, Anthony. *Worlds Made by Words: Scholarship and Community in the Modern West* (Cambridge: Harvard University Press, 2009).

Grealy, Deborah S. and Sylvia D. Hall-Ellis. *From Research to Practice: The Scholarship of Teaching and Learning in LIS Education* (Westport, Conn.: Libraries Unlimited, 2009).

Greenberg, Daniel S. *Science for Sale: The Perils, Rewards, and Delusions of Campus Capitalism* (Chicago: University of Chicago, 2007).

Grotzinger, Laurel. "The Status of 'Practicum' in Graduate Library Schools," *Journal of Education for Librarianship* 11 (Spring 1971): 332-39.

Grubb, W. Norton and Marvin Lazerson. "Vocationalism in Higher Education: The Triumph of the Education Gospel," *The Journal of Higher Education* 76 (January-February 2005): 1-25.

Guess, Andy. "Office Hours: Coming to a Computer Near You," *Inside Higher Education*, September 18, 2007, http://insidehighered.com/news/2007/09/18/officehours.

Guess, Andy. "Looking Back on 60 Years in Academe," *Insider Higher Education*, October 3, 2007, available at http://insidehighered.com/news/2007/10/03/weingartner.

Guess, Andy. "Professionalizing Liberal Arts, and Vice Versa," *Inside Higher Education*, January 25, 2008, http://insidehighered.com/news/2008/01/25/aacu.

Guess, Andy. "Research Methods 'Beyond Google," *Inside Higher Education*, 17 June 2008, http://insidehighered.com/news/2008/06/17/institute.

Guess, Andy. "Post-Microsoft, Libraries Mull Digitization," *Inside Higher Education*, May 30, 2008, http://insidehighered.com/news/2008/05/30/299icrosoft.

Guess, Andy. "Understanding Students Who Were 'Born Digital,'" *Inside Higher Education*, October 2, 2008, http://insidehighered.com/news/2008/10/02/digital.

Haddow, D. and E. Klobas. "Communication of Research to Practice in Library and Information Science: Closing the Gap," *Library and Information Science Research* 26 (2004): 29-43.

Hall, Audrey W., ed. "Library School Fieldwork Placements: Problems and Practice," *Library Management* 7, no.2, 1986.

Hall, David D. *Cultures of Print: Essays in the History of the Book* (Amherst: University of Massachusetts Press, 1996).

Ham, F. Gerald, Frank Boles, Gregory S. Hunter, and James M. O'Toole. "Is the Past Still Prologue? History and Archival Education," *American Archivist* 56 (Fall 1993): 718-729.

Hamel, Gary, interview. *Ubiquity: A Web-based publication of the ACM* (Volume 1, Number 32, Week of October 9, 2000), available at http://www.acm.org/ubiquity/interviews/g_hamel_1.html.

Hamerow, Theodore S. *Reflections on History and Historians* (Madison: University of Wisconsin Press, 1987).

Hart, Jeffrey. *Smiling Through the Cultural Catastrophe: Toward the Revival of Higher Education* (New Haven: Yale University Press, 2001).

Hatch, Thomas. *Into the Classroom: Developing the Scholarship of Teaching and Learning* (San Francisco: Jossey-Bass, 2006).

Hawkins, Hugh. *Pioneer: A History of the Johns Hopkins University, 1874-1889* (Ithaca, NY: Cornell University Press, 1960).

Haynes, Deborah. *Art Lessons: Meditations on the Creative Life* (Boulder, CO: Westview Press, 2003).

Hayes, Kevin J. *The Mind of a Patriot: Patrick Henry and the World of Ideas* (Charlottesville: University of Virginia Press, 2008).

Hazo, Samuel. "The Selling Out of Higher Education," *Pittsburgh Post-Gazette*, September 3, 2000, available at http://www.post-gazette.com/forum/20000903edhazo6.asp.

Healy, James S. "Distance Library Education," *Library Trends* 39, no. 4 (Spring 1991): 424-440.

Hedges, Chris. *Empire of Illusion: The End of Literacy and the Triumph of Spectacle* (New York: Nation Books, 2009).

Hedstrom, Margaret. "Building Record-Keeping Systems: Archivists Are Not Alone on the Wild Frontier," *Archivaria* 44 (Fall 1997): 44-71.

Hedstrom, Margaret and David Wallace. "And the Last Shall Be First: Recordkeeping Policies and the NII," *Journal of the American Society for Information Science* 50, no. 4 (1999): 331-339.

Hempstead, John O. "Internship and Practical Application in Educating School Library Personnel," *Journal of Education for Librarianship* 12 (Fall 1971): 116-32.

Henry, Douglas V. and Michael D. Beaty, eds. *Christianity and the Soul of the University: Faith as a Foundation for Intellectual Community* (Grand Rapids, MI: BakerAcademic, 2006).

Henry, Neil. *American Carnival: Journalism Under Siege in an Age of New Media* (Berkeley: University of California Press, 2007).

LIST OF WORKS CITED

Hernon, Peter, and Candy Schwartz. "Regaining 'the Foundation of Understanding': the Role of LIS Education." *Library & Information Science Research* 17, no. 1 (1995): 1-3.

Hernon, Peter, and Candy Schwartz. "The Desire is Present, but is the Expertise?" *Library and Information Science Research* 23, no. 3 (Autumn 2001): 209.

Herring, Mark Y. *Fool's Gold: Why the Internet Is No Substitute for a Library* (Jefferson, North Carolina: McFarland & Co., Inc., 2007).

Hersh, Richard H. and John Merrow, eds. *Declining by Degrees: Higher Education and Risk* (New York: Palgrave Macmillan, 2005).

Hess, Charlotte and Elinor Ostrom. *Understanding Knowledge as a Commons: From Theory to Practice* (Cambridge, MA: MIT Press, 2007).

Hexter, Ralph. "The Economic Collapse and Educational Values," *Inside Higher Education*, December 18, 2008, http://www.insidehighered.com/views/2008/12/18/hexter.

Hildenbrand, Suzanne. "The Information Age Versus Gender Equity?: Technology and Values in Education for Library and Information Science," *Library Trends* 47, no. 4 (1999): 669-685.

Hill, Janet Swan. "What Else Do You Need to Know? Practical Skills for Catalogers and Managers," *Cataloging and Classification Quarterly* 34 (2002): 245-261.

Hirsch, Philip A. and Gerald L. Stone. "Effects of Gender, Setting, and Research Productivity on Intern and Employment Suitability Ratings," *Journal of Counseling Psychology* 30 (January 1983): 76-82.

Hoffer, Peter Charles. *Past Imperfect: Facts, Fictions, Fraud – American History from Bancroft and Parkman to Ambrose, Bellesiles, Ellis, and Goodwin* (New York: Public Affairs, 2004).

Holley, R.P. "The Ivory Tower as Preparation for the Trenches," *College and Research Libraries News* 64, no. 3 (March 2003): 172-175.

Hollinger, David A. *Postethnic America: Beyond Multiculturalism* (New York: Basic Books, 1995).

Hooks, bell. *Remembered Rapture: The Writer at Work* (New York: Henry Holt and Co., 1999).

Hoover, Eric. "Letter Circulating Among College Presidents Asks Them Not to Participate in Rankings Survey," *Chronicle of Higher Education*, April 9, 2007, http://chronicle.com/daily/2007/04/2007040902n.htm.

Hornstein, Gail A. "Prune That Prose: Learning to Write for Readers Beyond Academe," *Chronicle Review*, September 7, 2009, http://chronicle.com/article/Prune-That-Prose/48273/, accessed October 9, 2009.

Howard, Jennifer. "Changes and Challenges in Publishing World Dominate Talk at University-Press Association's Meeting," *Chronicle of Higher Education*, June 18, 2007.

Howard, Jennifer. "Scholars' View of Libraries as Portals Shows Marked Decline," *Chronicle of Higher Education*, August 26, 2008, http://chronicle.com/daily/2008/08/4351n.htm.

Hughes, Richard T. *Myths America Lives By* (Urbana: University of Illinois Press, 2004).

Hunter, James Davison. *Culture Wars: The Struggle to Define America* (New York: Basic Books, 1991).

Huston, Therese. *Teaching What You Don't Know* (Cambridge, MA: Harvard University Press, 2009).

"Ideas to Shake Up Publishing," *Inside Higher Education*, July 26, 2007, available at http://insidehighered.com/news/2007/07/26/ithaka.

Inchausti, Robert, ed. *Echoing Silence: Thomas Merton on the Vocation of Writing* (Boston: New Seeds, 2007).

Jackson, H. J. *Marginalia: Readers Writing in Books* (New Haven: Yale University Press, 2001).

Jacobs, Jane. *Dark Age Ahead* (New York: Random House, 2004).

Jacoby, Russell. *The Last Intellectuals: American Culture in the Age of Academe* (New York: Farrar, Straus and Giroux, 1987).

Jacoby, Russell. *Dogmatic Wisdom: How the Culture Wars Divert Education and Distract America* (New York: Anchor Books, 1994).

Jaschik, Scott. "The Evolving (Eroding?) Faculty Job," *Inside Higher Education*, May 1, 2006 at http://insidehighered.com/news/2006/05/01/faculty.

Jaschik, Scott, interview with Mary Burgan "What Ever Happened to the Faculty?", November 20, 2006, *Inside Higher Education*, available at http://insidehighered.com/news/2006/11/20/burgan.

Jaschik, Scott. "When 'Digital Natives' Go to the Library," *Inside Higher Education*, June 25, 2007, http://insidehighered.com/news/2007/06/25/games.

Jaschik, Scott. "Reframing the Debate About What Professors Say," *Inside Higher Education*, September 11, 2007, http://insidehighered.com/news/2007/09/11/aaup, accessed September 11, 2007.

Jaschik, Scott. "University Presses Start to Sell Via Kindle," *Inside Higher Education*, June 24, 2008, http://insidehighered.com/news/2008/06/24/kindle.

Jaschik, Scott. "Rejecting the Academic Fast Track," *Inside Higher Education*, January 15, 2009, http://insidehighered.com/news/2009/01/15/family.

Jaschik, Scott. "The Impact of 'Time to Degree,'" *Inside Higher Education*, January 30, 2009, available http://insidehighered.com/news/2009/01/30/tdd.

Jaschik, Scott. "Farewell to the Printed Monograph," *Inside Higher Education*, March 23 2009, http://www.insidehighered.com/news/2009/03/23/michigan, accessed March 23, 2009.

Jay, Gregory S. *American Literature and the Culture Wars* (Ithaca: Cornell University Press, 1997).

Jeanneney, Jean-Noël. *Google and the Myth of Universal Knowledge: A View from Europe*, trans. Teresa Lavender Fagan (Chicago: University of Chicago Press, 2007).

Jenkins, C. "Far Out Learning," *School Library Journal* 46 (February 2000): 46-49.

Jensen, Derrick. *Walking on Water: Reading, Writing, and Revolution* (White River Junction, Vermont: Chelsea Green Publishing Co., 2004).

Jesella, Kara. "A Hipper Crowd of Shusters," *New York Times*, July 8, 2007, Section 9, p. 1, 2, http://www.nytimes.com/2007/07/08/fashion/08librarian.html?_r=1&ref=style&oref=slogin.

Johns, Adrian. *The Nature of the Book: Print and Knowledge in the Making* (Chicago: University of Chicago Press, 1998).

Johns, Adrian. "How to Acknowledge a Revolution," *American Historical Review* 107 (February 2002): 106-125.

Johnson, Benjamin, Patrick Kavanagh, and Kevin Mattson, eds. *Steal This University: The Rise of the Corporate University and the Academic Labor Movement* (New York: Routledge, 2003).

Johnson, Robert. "Libraries, Please You're your Books," *Christian Science Monitor*, October 7, 2005, available at http://www.csmonitor.com/2005/1007/p09s01-coop.html, accessed October 11, 2005.

Johnson, W. Brad and Carol A. Mullen, *Write to the Top! How to Become a Prolific Academic* (New York: Palgrave Macmillan, 2007).

Jones, H. G. "Archival Training in American Universities, 1938-1968," *American Archivist* 31 (April 1968): 135-54.

Jones, H. G. *The Records of a Nation: Their Management, Preservation, and Use* (New York: Atheneum, 1969).

Kay, Matthew. "Putting Technology in Its Place," *New York Times*, October 11, 2008, available at http://lessonplans.blogs.nytimes.com/2008/10/11/putting-technology-in-its-place/?th&emc=th.

Kennedy, Donald. *Academic Duty* (Cambridge: Harvard University Press, 1997).

Kerr, Clark. *The Uses of the University* (Cambridge: Harvard University Press, 1963).

Kesner, Richard M. "Employing the Case Study Method in the Teaching of Automated Records and Techniques to Archivists," *American Archivist* 56 (Summer 1993): 522-531.

Khurana, Rakesh. *From Higher Aims to Hired Hands: The Social Transformation of American Business Schools and the Unfulfilled Promise of Management as a Profession* (Princeton: Princeton University Press, 2007).

Kilgour, Frederick G. *The Evolution of the Book* (New York: Oxford University Press, 1998).

Kimball, Gregg D. "The Burke-Cappon Debate: Some Further Criticisms and Considerations for Archival Theory," *American Archivist* 48 (Fall 1985): 369-76.

King, Stephen. *On Writing: A Memoir of the Craft* (New York: Pocket Books, 2000).

King, William Davies. *Collections of Nothing* (Chicago: University of Chicago Press, 2008).

Kirp, David. *Shakespeare, Einstein, and the Bottom Line: The Marketing of Higher Education* (Cambridge: Harvard University Press, 2003).

Klassen, Norman and Jens Zimmerman. *The Passionate Intellect: Incarnational Humanism and the Future of University Education* (Grand Rapids, MI: BakerAcademic, 2006).

Klein, Julie Thompson. *Interdisciplinarity: History, Theory, and Practice* (Detroit: Wayne State University Press, 1990)

Klein, Julie Thompson. *Crossing Boundaries: Knowledge, Disciplinarities, and Interdisciplinarities* (Charlottesville: University Press of Virginia, 1996).

Kling, Rob. "What is Social Informatics and Why Does it Matter?" *D-Lib Magazine* 5 (January 1999) at http://www.dlib.org/dlib/january99/kling/01kling.html.

Knuth, Rebecca. *Libricide: The Regime-Sponsored Destruction of Books and Libraries in the Twentieth Century* (Westport, Conn.: Praeger, 2003).

Kohn, Alfie. *What Does It Mean to Be Well Educated? And More Essays on Standards, Grading, and Other Follies* (Boston: Beacon Press, 2004).

Kolowich, Steve. "Bookless Libraries?" *Inside Higher Education*, November 6, 2009, available at http://www.insidehighered.com/news/2009/11/06/library.

Kopp, Judy. "Changes in Graduate Social Work Students' Use of Interviewing Skills from Training to Practicum," Ph.D. dissertation, Washington University, 1982.

Kramer, Mark and Wendy Call, eds. *Telling True Stories: A Nonfiction Writers' Guide from the Nieman Foundation at Harvard University* (New York: Plume, 2007).

Kreuter, Gretchen von Loewe. *Forgotten Promise: Race and Gender Wars on a Small College Campus* (New York: Alfred A. Knopf, 1996).

Kurzweil, Edith and William Phillips, eds. *Our Country, Our Culture: The Politics of Political Correctness* (Boston: Partisan Review Press, 1994).

Labaree, David. *The Trouble with Ed Schools* (New Haven: Yale University Press, 2004).

Lamont, Michèle. *How Professors Think: Inside the Curious World of Academic Judgment* (Cambridge: Harvard University Press, 2009).

Lamott, Anne. *Bird by Bird: Some Instructions on Writing and Life* (New York: Anchor Books, 1995; org. pub. 1994).

Lancaster, F.W. "Implications for Library and Information Science Education," *Library Trends* 32 (Winter 1984): 337-348.

Lang, James. *Life on the Tenure Track: Lessons from the First Year* (Baltimore: Johns Hopkins University Press, 2005).

Lanham, Richard. *The Economics of Attention: Style and Substance in the Age of Information* (Chicago: University of Chicago Press, 2006).

Lapham, Lewis. "Crowd Control," *Harper's* 309 (October 2004): 9-11.

Lapham, Lewis. "Notebook: That' Why the Lady is a Tramp," *Harper's* 308 (June 2004): 11-12.

Larsen, Ronald L. "iSchools," *Encyclopedia of Library and Information Sciences*, forthcoming; also available at http://www.ischools.org/site/history/

Lefkowitz, Mary. *Not Out of Africa: How Afrocentrism Became an Excuse to Teach Myth as History* (New York: New Republic Book, Basic Basic Books, 1996).

Lerer, Seth. "Histories of Reading," *Raritan* 20, 1 (Summer 2007): 108-127.

Lesser, Wendy. *The Amateur: An Independent Life of Letters* (New York: Vintage Books, 1999).

Lesser, Wendy. *Nothing Remains the Same: Rereading and Remembering* ((Boston: Houghton Mifflin, 2002).

Lester, June, "Education for Librarianship: A Report Card," *American Libraries* 21, no. 6 (June 1990): 580, 582, 584, 586.

Lester, June, and Connie Van Fleet. "Use of Professional Competencies and Standards Documents for Curriculum Planning in Schools of Library and Information Studies Education," *Journal of Education for Library and Information Science.* 49 (2008): 43-69.

Levine, Lawrence. *The Opening of the American Mind: Canons, Culture, and History* (Boston: Beacon Press, 1996).

Levy, David M. *Scrolling Forward: Making Sense of Documents in the Digital Age* (New York: Arcade Publishing, 2001).

Levy, David M. "More, Faster, Better: Governance in an Age of Overload, Busyness, and Speed," *First Monday*, special issue number 7 (September 2006), http://firstmonday.org/issues/special11_9/levy/index.html.

Levy, Stephen, interview. *Ubiquity*, Volume 8, Issue 39 (October 2, 2007 – October 8, 2007, http://www.acm.org/ubiquity/interviews/v8i39_levy.html.

Lewis, Harry R. *Excellence Without a Soul: How a Great University Forgot Education* (New York: Public Affairs, 2006).

Lillard, Linda L. and Wales, Barbara A. "Strengthening the Profession: Educator and Practitioner Collaboration," *Journal of Academic Librarianship* 29 (September 2003): 316-339.

Limerick, Patricia Nelson. "Tales of Western Adventure," *Chronicle of Higher Education* 54 (May 9, 2008) http://chronicle.com/weekly/v54/i35/35c00101.htm.

Lipson, Charles. *Cite Right: A Quick Guide to Citation Styles – MLA, APA, Chicago, the Sciences, Professions, and More* (Chicago: University of Chicago Press, 2006).

Littau, Karin. *Theories of Reading: Books, Bodies, and Bibliomania* (Cambridge: Polity Press, 2006).

Lodge, David. *The British Museum Is Falling Down* (New York: Holt Rinehart and Winston, 1965).

Lodge, David. *Changing Places: A Tale of Two Campuses* (New York: Penguin Books, 1978).

Lodge, David. *Nice Work* (New York: Penguin Books, 1990).

Lott, Bret. *Before We Get Started: A Practical Memoir of the Writer's Life* (New York: Ballatine Books, 2005).

Lott, Eric. *The Disappearing Liberal Intellectual* (New York: Basic Books, 2006).

Lucas, Christopher J. *Crisis in the Academy: Rethinking Higher Education in America* (New York: St. Martin's Press, 1996).

Luey, Beth, ed. *Revising Your Dissertation: Advice from Leading Editors* (Berkeley, CA: University of California Press, 2004).

Lukeman, Noah. *The First Five Pages: A Writer's Guide to Staying Out of the Rejection Pile* (New York: Fireside Book, Simon & Schuster, 2000).

Lynch, B. P. "Library Education: Its Past, Its Present, Its Future," *Library Trends* 56, no. 4 (Spring 2008): 931-953.

McCrank, Lawrence J. "History, Archives and Information Science," *Annual Review of Information Science and Technology* 30 (1995): 281-352.

McDonald, Terrence, ed. *The Historic Turn in the Human Sciences* (Ann Arbor: University of Michigan Press, 1996).

McKitterick, David. *Print, Manuscript and the Search for Order 1450-1830* (New York: Cambridge University Press, 2003).

Mailer, Norman. *The Spooky Art: Thoughts on Writing* (New York: Random House, 2003).

Malcolm, Janet. *In the Freud Archives* (New York: Alfred A. Knopf, 1984).

Manguel, Alberto. *A History of Reading* (New York: Viking, 1996).

Manguel, Alberto. *Into the Looking-Glass Wood: Essays on Books, Reading, and the World* (San Diego: Harcourt, Inc, 1998).

Manguel, Alberto. *Reading Pictures: A History of Love and Hate* (New York: Bloomsbury, 2001).

Manguel, Alberto, *A Reading Diary: A Passionate Reader's Reflections on a Year of Books* (New York: Farrar, Strauss, and Giroux, 2004).

Manguel, Alberto. *Stevenson Under the Palm Trees* (Canongate, 2004).

Manguel, Alberto. *With Borges* (London: Telegram Books, 2006).

Manguel, Alberto. *Homer's The Iliad and The Odyssey: A Biography* (New York: Atlantic Monthly, 2007).

Manguel, Alberto. *The City of Words* (Toronto: House of Anansi Press, Inc., 2007).

Manguel, Alberto. *The Library at Night* (New Haven: Yale University Press, 2008).

McLemee, Scott. "After the Last Intellectual," *BookForum* 14 (September/October/November 2007): 15, 17, 59.

McLemee, Scott. "Print or Byte?" *Inside Higher Education*, April 6, 2009, available at http://www.insidehighered.com/layout/set/print/views/mclemee/mclemee237.

McMurty, Larry. *Books: A Memoir* (New York: Simon and Schuster, 2008).

MacNeil, Heather. "Archival Theory and Practice: Between Two Paradigms," *Archivaria* 37 (Spring 1994): 6-20.

McNeely, Ian F. with Lisa Wolverton, *Reinventing Knowledge: From Alexandria to the Internet* (New York: W. W. Norton & Co., 2008).

McSherry, Corynne. *Who Owns Academic Work? Battling for Control of Intellectual Property* (Cambridge: Harvard University Press, 2001).

Marsden, George. *The Soul of the American University: From Protestant Establishment to Established Nonbelief* (New York: Oxford University Press, 1994).

Marsden, Paul. "When is the Future? Comparative Notes on the Electronic Record-Keeping Projects of the University of Pittsburgh and the University of British Columbia," *Archivaria* 43 (Spring 1997): 158-173.

Martin, Robert Sidney. "The Development of Professional Education for Librarians and Archivists in the United States: A Comparative Essay," *American Archivist* 57 (Summer 1994): 544-558.

Martin, Susan K. "A New Vision for Library and Information Studies Accreditation," *Portal: Libraries and the Academy* 2, no. 3 (2002): 481-483.

Martin, William J. *The Practical Element in Library Education: A Survey* (Belfast: Department of Library and Information Studies, Queen's University, 1979).

Mason, Philip P. "The Society of American Archivists in the Seventies: Report of the Committee for the 1970's," *American Archivist* 35 (April 1972): 193-217.

Meho, Lokman I. and Kristina M. Spurgin. "Ranking the Research Productivity of Library and Information Science Faculty and Schools: An Evaluation of Data Sources and Research Methods," *Journal of the American Society for Information Science and Technology* 56, no. 12 (2005): 1314-1331.

Miller, Fredric. "The SAA as Sisyphus: Education Since the 1960s," *American Archivist* 63 (Fall/Winter 2000): 224-236.

Miller, Jane E. *The Chicago Guide to Writing About Numbers* (Chicago: University of Chicago Press, 2004).

Miller, Laura. *Reluctant Capitalists: Bookselling and the Culture of Consumption* (Chicago: University of Chicago Press, 2006).

Miller, Richard E. *Writing at the End of the World* (Pittsburgh: University of Pittsburgh Press, 2005).

Mitchell, Richard. *The Leaning Tower of Babel and Other Affronts by the Underground Grammarian* (New York: Simon and Schuster, 1984).

Molz, Redmond Kathleen and Phyllis Dain. *Civic Space/Cyberspace: The American Public Library in the Information Age* (Cambridge: MIT Press, 1999).

Monroe, Margaret E. *Issues in Field Experience As An Element in the Library School Curriculum: A Background Paper*, 1971 (ERIC Report ED-200 231).

Montague, Rae-Ann and Marina Pluzhenskaia. "Web-based Information Science Education (WISE): Collaboration to Explore and Expand Quality in LIS Online Education," *Journal of Education for Library and Information Science* 48, no. 1 (2007): 36-51.

Morehead, Joe. "The Theory Practice Problem and Library-Centered Library Education," *Journal of Education for Librarianship* 14 (Fall 1973): 119-28.

Morehead, Joe. *Theory and Practice in Library Education: The Teaching-Learning Process* (Littleton, CO: Libraries Unlimited, Inc., 1980).

Morrison, Toni, ed. *Burn This Book: PEN Writers Speak Out on the Power of the Word* (New York: HarperCollins, 2009).

Morton, David. *Off the Record: The Technology and Culture of Sound Recording in America* (New Brunswick, N.J.: Rutgers University Press, 2000).

Mounce, Michael. "The Effects of ALA Accreditation Standards on Library Education Programs Accredited by the American Library Association." *LIBRES* 15, no. 1 (2005). Available at http://libres.curtin.edu.au/libres15n1/Mounce%20-%20Final.htm.

Muddiman, Dave. "Towards a Postmodern Context for Information and Library Education," *Education for Information* 17, no.1 (March 1999): 1-19.

Mummert, Roger. "Handle This Book! Curators Put Rare Texts in 18-Year-Old Hands," *New York Times*, November 2, 2008, in the special education supplement, p. 30.

Murata, Alice K. "Attitude Differences and Change During a Counseling Practicum in Graduate Students Preparing for Work at Different Educational Levels," Ph.D. dissertation, Northwestern University, 1969.

Muscatine, Charles. *Fixing College Education: A New Curriculum for the Twenty-first Century* (Charlottesville: University of Virginia Press, 2009).

Musto, Ronald G. "Google Books Mutilates the Printed Past," *The Chronicle Review*, 55, June 12, 2009, p. B4, http://chronicle.com/weekly/v55/i39/39b00401.htm.

Nardi, Bonnie A. and Vicki L. O'Day, *Information Ecologies: Using Technology with Heart* (MIT Press, 1999).

Nash, Gary B., Charlotte Crabtree, and Ross E. Dunn. *History on Trial: Culture Wars and the Teaching of the Past* (New York: Alfred A. Knopf, 1997).

Neill, S. D. "The Place of Practice in a Graduate Library School," *Libri* 25 (July 1975): 81-97.

Nelson, Cary and Stephen Watt. *Academic Keywords: A Devil's Dictionary for Higher Education* (New York: Routledge, 1999).

Nengomasha, Cathrine T. "Training for the Archival Profession in Namibia," paper presented at the Third SAA Archives Educators Forum, August 2, 2004, Simmons College, Boston, Massachusetts.

Newman, Frank, Laura Courturier, and Jamie Scurry. *The Future of Higher Education: Rhetoric, Reality, and the Risks of the Market* (San Francisco, CA: Jossey-Bass, 2004).

Niebuhr, H. Richard. *Christ and Culture* (New York: HarperSanFrancisco, 2001; org. pub. 1951).

Noble, David F. *Digital Diploma Mills: The Automation of Higher Education* (New York: Monthly Review Press, 2001).

Nolan, James L., Jr., ed. *The American Culture Wars: Current Contests and Future Prospects* (Charlottesville: University Press of Virginia, 1996).

Norman, Donald. *The Design of Future Things* (New York: Basic Books, 2007).

Nunberg, Geoffrey, ed. *The Future of the Book* (Berkeley: University of California Press, 1996).

Nussbaum, Martha C. *Cultivating Humanity: A Classical Defense of Reform in Liberal Education* (Cambridge: Harvard University Press, 1997).

Oates, Joyce Carol. *The Faith of a Writer: Life, Craft, Art* (New York: HarperCollins, 2003).

O'Brien, Geoffrey. *The Browser's Ecstasy: A Meditation on Reading* (Washington, D.C.: Counterpoint, 2000).

O'Brien, George Dennis. *All the Essential Half-Truths About Higher Education* (Chicago: University of Chicago Press, 2000).

O'Connor, Patricia T. and Stewart Kellerman. *You Send Me: Getting It Right When You Write Online* (Orlando: Harvest Book, Harcourt, Inc., 2002).

O'Donnell, James J. *Avatars of the Word: From Papyrus to Cyberspace* (Cambridge, MA: Harvard University Press, 1998).

O'Neil, Robert M. *Free Speech in the College Community* (Bloomington: Indiana University Press, 1997).

O'Toole, James M. "Curriculum Developments in Archival Education: A Proposal," *American Archivist* 53 (Summer 1990): 460-466.

O'Toole, James M. "The Archival Curriculum: Where Are We Now?" *Archival Issues* 22, no. 2 (1997): 103-113.

Oder, N. "LIS Distance Ed Moves Ahead," *Library Journal* 126 (1 October 2001): 54-56.

Olson, Gary M. and Jonathan Grudin. "The Information School Phenomenon," *Interactions* 16 (March/April 2009): 15-19.

Osen, Diane, ed. *The Book That Changed My Life: Interviews with National Book Award Winners and Finalists* (New York: The Modern Library, 2002).

Ostler, L. and Dahlin, T. "Old Wine into New Bottles: Responses to New Approaches in Library Education," *Library Acquisitions: Practice and Theory* 22 (Spring 1998): 41-43.

Palmer, Roger C. "Internships and Practicums," in *The Administrative Aspects of Education for Librarianship: A Symposium*, ed. Marry B. Cassata and Herman L. Totten (Metuchen, N.J.: Scarecrow Press, 1975), pp. 239-53.

Paretsky, Sara. *Writing in an Age of Silence* (New York: Verso, 2007).

Parini, Jay. *The Art of Teaching* (New York: Oxford University Press, 2005).

Paris, Marion. *Library School Closings: Four Case Studies* (Metuchen, NJ: Scarecrow Press, 1988).

Paris, Marion. "Why Library Schools Fail," *Library Journal* (October 1, 1990): pp 38-42.

Pawley, Christine. "History in the Library and Information Science Curriculum: Outline of a Debate," *Libraries & Culture* 40, no. 3 (Summer 2005): 223-238.

Pawley, Christine. "Unequal Legacies: Race and Multiculturalism in the LIS Curriculum" *Library Quarterly* 76 (April 2006): 149-168.

Pearl, Nancy. *Booklust: Recommended Reading for Every Mood, Moment, and Reason* (Seattle, WA: Sasquatch Books, 2003).

Pedro, Joan Daniels. "Induction into the Workplace: The Impact of Internships," *Journal of Vocational Behavior* 25 (August 1984): 80-95.

Pelikan, Jaroslav. *The Idea of the University: A Reexamination* (New Haven: Yale University Press, 1992).

Pemberton, J. Michael and Christine R. Nugent. "Information Studies: Emergent Field, Convergent Curriculum," *Journal of Education for Library and Information Science* 36 (Spring 1995): 126-138.

Perlmutter, David. "Do You Really Not Have the Time?," *Chronicle of Higher Education*, August 22, 2008, available at http://chronicle.com/jobs/news/2008/08/2008082201c.htm.

Perras, Donald F. "The Relationship Between Nine Descriptive Variables of Special Education Graduate Students and Tutoring Performance in a Practicum Setting with Emotionally Handicapped Children," Ph.D. dissertation, George Peabody College for Teachers, 1975.

Perry, Philip John. "A Study of Change in Student-Teacher Attitudes Towards Child-Centered Policies and Practices," Ph.D. dissertation, University of Washington, 1981.

Peters, Tom. "The Future of Reading," *Library Journal*, November 1, 2009, available at http://www.libraryjournal.com/article/CA6703852.html.

Pickering, Sam. *Letters to a Teacher* (New York: Grove Press, 2004).

Pochoda, Paul. "University Press 2.0," University of Michigan Press Blog, May 27, 2009, http://www.typepad.com/services/trackback/6a00e552560e8d8834011570a9a24a9.

Pollan, Michael. *A Place of My Own: The Education of an Amateur Builder* (New York: Random House, 1997).

Pope, Loren. *Colleges That Change Lives: 40 Schools That Will Change the Way You Think About Colleges* (New York: Penguin Books, 2006; rev. ed.).

Porter, David H. "A Story Untold and Questions Unasked," in *Liberal Arts Colleges in American Higher Education: Challenges and Opportunities* (New York: American Council of Learned Societies, Occasional Paper no. 59, 2005).

Posner, Richard A. *Public Intellectuals: A Study of Decline* (Cambridge: Harvard University Press, 2001).

Postman, Neil, with Charles Weingartner. *Teaching as a Subversive Activity* (New York: Dell Publishing Co., Inc., 1969).

Postman, Neil. *Teaching as a Conserving Activity* (New York: Dell Publishing Co., Inc., 1979).

Postman, Neil. *Conscientious Objections: Stirring Up Trouble About Language, Technology, and Education* (New York: Vintage Books, 1988).

Postman, Neil. *Technopoly: The Surrender of Culture to Technology* (New York: Vintage Books, 1992).

Postman, Neil. *The End of Education: Redefining the Value of School* (New York: Alfred A. Knopf, 1995).

Powell, Walter W. *Getting into Print: The Decision-Making Process in Scholarly Publishing* (Chicago: University of Chicago Press, 1985).

Professor X. "In the Basement of the Ivory Tower," *Atlantic*, June 2008, available at http://www.theatlantic.com/doc/200806/college.

Prose, Francine. *Reading Like a Writer: A Guide for People Who Love Books and for Those Who Want to Write Them* (New York: HarperCollins, 2006).

Pyenson, Lewis and Susan Sheets-Pyenson. *Servants of Nature: A History of Scientific Institutions, Enterprises and Sensibilities* (New York: W. W. Norton and Co., 1999).

Raven, James, ed. *Lost Libraries: The Destruction of Great Book Collections since Antiquity* (New York: Palgrave Macmillan, 2004).

Readings, Bill. *The University in Ruins* (Cambridge: Harvard University Press, 1996).

Reuben, Julie A. *The Making of the Modern University: Intellectual Transformation and the Marginalization of Morality* (Chicago: University of Chicago Press, 1996).

Rhode, Deborah. *In Pursuit of Knowledge: Scholars, Status, and Academic Culture* (Stanford, CA: Stanford Law and Politics, Stanford University Press, 2006).

Rhodes, Frank H. T. *The Creation of the Future: The Role of the American University* (Ithaca: Cornell University Press, 2001).

Rhodes, Richard. *How to Write: Advice and Reflections* (New York: HarperCollins Publishers, 1995).

Rich, Motoko. "The Future of Reading: In Web Age, Library Job Gets Update," *New York Times*, February 16, 2009.

Rich, Motoko. "Book Fair Buzz Is Not Contained Between 2 Covers," *New York Times*, June 1, 2009.

Richardson, John, Jr. and Peter Hernon. "Theory vs. Practice: Student Preferences," *Journal of Education for Librarianship* 21 (Spring 1981): 287-300.

Roberts, John W. "Archival Theory: Much Ado About Shelving," *American Archivist* 50 (Winter 1987): 66-74.

Roberts, John W. "Practice Makes Perfect, Theory Makes Theorists," *Archivaria* 37 (Spring 1994): 111-121.

Roberts, Ted. "The "New" Liberal Arts," *Pittsburgh Post-Gazette*, June 24, 2008, http://www.post-gazette.com/pg/08176/892059-28.stm.

Robin, Ron. *Scandals and Scoundrels: Seven Cases That Shook the Academy* (Berkeley: University of California Press, 2004).

Rose, Jonathan, ed. *The Holocaust and the Book: Destruction and Preservation* (Amherst: University of Massachusetts Press, 2001).

Rose, Phyllis. "The Coming of the French: My Life as an English Professor," *American Scholar* 74 (Winter 2005): 59-68.

Rosen, Jeffrey. *The Unwanted Gaze: The Destruction of Privacy in America* (New York: Random House, 2000).

Rothstein, Samuel. "Why People Really Hate Library Schools: The 97-Year-Old Mystery Solved at Last." *Library Journal* 110, no. 6 (April 1985): 41-48.

Roy, Lucinda. *No Right to Remain Silent: The Tragedy at Virginia Tech* (New York: Harmony Books, 2009).

Royal, Robert, ed. *Reinventing the American People: Unity and Diversity Today* (Washington, D.C.: Ethics and Public Policy Center, published by William B. Eerdmans Pub Co., 1995).

Ruch, Richard S. *Higher Ed, Inc.: The Rise of the For-Profit University* (Baltimore: Johns Hopkins University Press, 2001).

Russo, Richard. *Straight Man* (New York: Vintage Books, 1998).

Said, Edward W. *Representations of the Intellectual* (New York: Vintage Books, 1996).

Said, Edward W. *Humanism and Democratic Criticism* (New York: Columbia University Press, 2004).

Sayers, Frances Clarke. *Summoned by Books: Essays and Speeches*, compiled by Marjeanne Jensen Blinn (New York: Viking Press, 1965).

Scheurkogel, Hans. "What master do we want? What master do we need? And ... what master do we deserve?" paper presented at the Third SAA Archives Educators Forum, August 2, 2004, Simmons College, Boston, Massachusetts.

Schein, Edgar H. *Professional Education: Some New Directions* (New York: McGraw-Hill Book Co., 1972).

Schlesinger, Arthur M., Jr. *The Disuniting of America: Reflections on a Multicultural Society* (New York: W. W. Norton & Co., 1992).

Scholes, Robert. *The Rise and Fall of English: Reconstructing English as a Discipline* (New Haven: Yale University Press, 1998).

Schorske, Carl. *Thinking with History: Explorations in the Passage to Modernism* (Princeton: Princeton University Press, 1998).

Schriffen, André. The *Business of Books: How International Conglomerates Took Over Publishing and Changed the Way We Read* (New York: Verso, 2000).

Schwarz, Daniel R. *In Defense of Reading: Teaching Literature in the Twenty-First Century* (West Sussex, UK: Wiley-Blackwell, 2008).

Schwartz, Lynne Sharon. *Ruined by Reading: A Life in Books* (Boston: Beacon Press, 1996).

Shapin, Stephen. *The Scientific Life: A Moral History of a Late Modern Vocation* (Chicago: University of Chicago Press, 2008).

Shapiro, Harold T. *A Larger Sense of Purpose: Higher Education and Society* (Princeton: Princeton University Press, 2005).

Shieh, David. "Professors Regard Online Instruction as Less Effective Than Classroom Learning," *Chronicle of Higher Education*, February 10, 2009, available at http://chronicle.com/free/2009/02/11232n.htm.

Shillingsburg, Peter L. *From Gutenberg to Google: Electronic Representations of Literary Texts* (Cambridge: Cambridge University Press, 2006).

Shirky, Clay. *Here Comes Everybody: The Power of Organizing Without Organizations* (New York: Penguin Press, 2008).

Short, John Rennie. *New Worlds, New Geographies* (Syracuse: Syracuse University Press, 1998).

Showalter, Elaine. *Faculty Towers: The Academic Novel and Its Discontents* (Philadelphia: University of Pennsylvania Press, 2005).

Silverman, Franklin H. *Authoring Books and Materials for Students, Academics, and Professionals* (Westport, Conn.: Praeger, 1998).

Silverman, Franklin H. *Publishing for Tenure and Beyond* (Westport, Conn.: Praeger, 1999).

Silvia, Paul J. *How to Write a Lot: A Practical Guide to Productive Academic Writing* (Washington, D.C.: American Psychological Association, 2007).

Slaughter, Sheila and Larry Leslie. *Academic Capitalism: Politics, Policies, and the Entrepreneurial University* (Baltimore: Johns Hopkins University, 1997).

Small, Ruth V. "A Comparison of the Resident and Distance Learning Experience in Library and Information Science," *Journal of Education for Library and Information Science* 40, no. 1 (1999): 27-47.

Smiley, Jane. *Moo* (New York: Fawcett Columbine, 1995).

Smith, Alexander McCall. *Portuguese Irregular Verbs* (New York: Anchor Books, 2003).

Smith, Alexander McCall. *The Finer Points of Sausage Dogs* (New York: Anchor Books, 2003).

Smith, Alexander McCall. *At the Villa of Reduced Circumstances* (New York: Anchor Books, 2003).

Smith, James K. A. *The Devil Reads Derrida and Other Essays on the University, the Church, Politics, and the Arts* (Grand Rapids, MI: William B. Eerdmans Publishing Co., 2009).

Smith, Vernon R. "Pedagogy and Professionalism: An Evaluation of Trends and Choices Confronting Educators in the Archival Community," *Public Historian* 16 (Summer 1994): 23-43.

Smokler, Kevin, ed. *Bookmark Now: Writing in Unreaderly Times* (New York: Basic Books, 2005).

LIST OF WORKS CITED

Snyder, Don J. *The Cliff Walk: A Memoir of a Job Lost and a Life Found* (Boston: Little Brown and Co., 1997).

Society of American Archivists. "Society of American Archivists Guidelines for Graduate Archival Education Programs," *American Archivist* 51 (Summer 1988): 387-388.

Society of American Archivists. "Development of a Curriculum for a Masters of Advanced Studies Degree," (1994), now only available through the Internet Archive.

Society of American Archivists. "Guidelines for a Graduate Program in Archival Studies," (2002) available at the SAA's website at www.archivists.org.

Society of American Archivists. "Program Standard for Archival Education: The Practicum," *American Archivist* 43 (Fall 1980): 420-422.

Society of American Archivists, "Guidelines for the Development of Post-Appointment and Continuing Education and Training Programs," at http://www.archivists.org/PACE97.html.

Stallman, Esther L. *Library Internships: History, Purpose and a Proposal*, University of Illinois Library School Occasional Papers, no. 37 (Urbana: Library School, 1954).

Stearns, Peter N. *Meaning Over Memory: Recasting the Teaching of Culture and History* (Chapel Hill: University of North Carolina Press, 1993).

Stein, Donald G., ed. *Buying In or Selling Out? The Commercialism of the American Research University* (New Brunswick, NJ: Rutgers University Press, 2004).

Steinhauer, Jennifer. "In His Own Words," *New York Times*, 20 January 2009, available at http://www.nytimes.com/2009/06/20/us/20ventura.html?_r=1&th&emc=th.

Stielow, Frederick J. "The Practicum and the Changing Face of Archival Education: Observations and Recommendations," *Provenance* 8 (Spring 1990): 1-12.

Stoll, Clifford. *Silicon Snake Oil: Second Thoughts on the Information Highway* (New York: Anchor Books, 1995).

Stoll, Clifford. *High-Tech Heretic: Reflections of a Computer Contrarian* (New York: Anchor, 2000).

Strate, Lance. "Neil Postman, Defender of the Word," *ETC* 60 (Winter 2003-04): 341-350.

Sullivan, William M. *Work and Integrity: The Crisis and Promise of Professionalism in America* (New York: Harper Business, 1995).

Sweeney, Michele A. "Teacher Socialization: The Pre-Practicum Experience with Third-Year Human Movement Majors," Ed.D. dissertation, Boston University, 1984.

Sy, Karen J. "Are Library and Information Science Faculty Ready to Participate in Information Policy Advising?" *Journal of Education for Library and Information Science* 30 (Spring 1990): 298-314.

Tees, Miriam. "Graduate Education for Special Librarians: What Special Librarians Are Looking for in Graduates," *Special Libraries* 77 (Fall 1986): 190-97.

Tenner, Edward. "The Prestigious Inconvenience of Print," *Chronicle of Higher Education*, December 15, 2006, http://chronicle.com/weekly/v53/i27/27b00701.htm.

"Tenure-Track Faculty Job Satisfaction Survey: Highlights Report," available at http://gseacademic.harvard.edu/~coache/.

Thelin, John R. *A History of American Higher Education* (Baltimore: Johns Hopkins University Press, 2004).

Theoharis, Athan G., ed. *A Culture of Secrecy: The Government Versus the People's Right to Know* (Lawrence: University Press of Kansas, 1998).

Thompson, Clive. "The Future of Reading," *WIRED* June 2009 p. 50 http://www.wired.com/techbiz/people/magazine/17-06/st_thompson.

Thompson, Peter. *Rum Punch & Revolution: Taverngoing & Public Life in Eighteenth-Century Philadelphia* (Philadelphia: University of Pennsylvania Press, 1999).

Tibbo, Helen R. "Archival Education Programs in the Information Age," paper presented at the Third SAA Archives Educators Forum, August 2, 2004, Simmons College, Boston, Massachusetts.

Tietjen, Mildred C. *A Study, Comparison and Evaluation of Instructional at ALA Accredited Graduate Library Schools in the United States and Canada, with Special Attention Focused on Practical Experience or Field Work Provided within the Curricula* (Bethesda, Md.: ERIC Document Reproduction Service, ED 126892, 1975).

Tibbo, Helen R. "A Vision of Archival Education at the Millennium," *Journal of Education for Library and Information Science* 38 (Summer 1997): 221-225.

Tompkins, Jane. *A Life in School: What the Teacher Learned* (Cambridge, MA: Perseus Books, 1996).

Tuchman, Gaye. *Wannabe U: Inside the Corporate University* (Chicago: University of Chicago Press, 2009).

Tufte, Edward R. *The Cognitive Power of PowerPoint* (Cheshire, Conn.: Graphics Press, September 2003).

Turchi, Peter. *Maps of the Imagination: The Writer as Cartographer* (San Antonio, Texas: Trinity University Press, 2004).

Turner, Frank M., ed., John Henry Newman, *The Idea of the University* (New Haven: Yale University Press, 1996).

Twitchell, James B. *Branded Nation: The Marketing of Megachurch, College, Inc., and Museumworld* (New York: Simon & Schuster, 2004).

Uhde, Karsten. "New Education in Old Europe," paper presented at the Third SAA Archives Educators Forum, August 2, 2004, Simmons College, Boston, Massachusetts.

Vanderkam, Laura. "Books from, and for. The People," *USA Today*, March 12, 2009, p. 9A.

Van Der Werf, Martin. "Researcher Offers Unusually Candid Description of University's Efforts to Rise in Rankings," *Chronicle of Higher Education*, June 3, 2009, http://chronicle.com/daily/2009/06/19270n.htm.

Van Deusen, Neil C. "Field Work in Accredited Library Schools," *College and Research Libraries* 7 (July 1946): 249-55.

Viguers, Ruth Hill. *Margin for Surprise: About Books, Children, and Librarians* (Boston: Little, Brown, and Co., 1964).

Wagner, Jon. "Integrating the Traditions of Experiental Learning in Internship Education," *Journal of Experiential Education* 6 (Fall 1983): 7-14.

Walch, David. B. "A Perspective of Academic Librarianship: The Practitioner's Needs and the Educator's Product," *Journal of Library Administration* 11, no. 3 (1990): 87-96.

Walters, Tyler O. "Rediscovering the Theoretical Base of Records Management and Its Implications for Graduate Education," *Journal of Education for Library and Information Science* 36 (Spring 1995): 139-154.

Walzer, Michael. *Arguing About War* (New Haven, Conn.: Yale University Press, 2004).

Ward, Barbara A. "A Rationale for Field Experience in Library Education," *Journal of Education for Librarianship* 13 (Spring 1973): 232-37.

Washburn, Jennifer. *University, Inc.: The Corporate Corruption of American Higher Education* (New York: Basic Books, 2005).

Waters, Lindsay. *Enemies of Promise: Publishing, Perishing, and the Eclipse of Scholarship* (Chicago: Prickly Paradigm Press, 2004).

Weingartner, Rudolph H. "On the Practicality of a Liberal Education," *Liberal Education* (Summer 2007).

West, Cornell. *Democracy Matters: Winning the Fight Against Imperialism* (New York: Penguin Press, 2004).

White, Brenda, Associates. *The Impact of Library and Information Studies Education on Subsequent Career Progression* (London: British Library, 1986).

White, Herbert S. "Education vs. Training: A Problem of Definition," *Journal of Academic Librarianship* 10, no. 4 (1984): 198-199.

White, Herbert S. "The Education and Selection of Librarians: A Sequence of Happenstances," *Library Journal* 115, no. 17 (October 15, 1990): 61-62.

White, Herbert S. and Marion Paris. "Employer Preferences and the Library Education Curriculum," *Library Quarterly* 55 (January 1985): 1-33.

Wiegand, Wayne A. "Out of Sight, Out of Mind: Why Don't We Have Any Schools of Library and Reading Studies?" *Journal of Education for Library and Information Science* 38 (Fall 1997): 314-326.

Wiegand, Wayne A. "Tunnel Vision and Blind Spots: What the Past Tells Us About the Present; Reflections on the Twentieth-Century History of American Librarianship," *The Library Quarterly* 69, no.1 (January 1999): 1-32.

Wiegand, Wayne A. "Critiquing the Curriculum: The Entrenched LIS Agenda Needs to Change to Reflect the Most Critical Functions of the Library," *American Libraries* (January 2005): 58, 60-61.

Wiener, Jon. *Historians in Trouble: Plagiarism, Fraud, and Politics in the Ivory Tower* (New York: The New Press, 2005).

Williams, Jeffrey, ed. *PC Wars: Politics and Theory in the Academy* (New York: Routledge, 1995).

Willimon, William H. and Thomas H. Naylor. *The Abandoned Generation: Rethinking Higher Education* (Grand Rapids, MI: William B. Eerdmans Publishing Co., 1995).

Wills, Garry. *Mr. Jefferson's University* (Washington, D.C.: National Geographic, 2002).

Wilson, Mark. "Professors Should Embrace Wikipedia," *Inside Higher Education*, April 1, 2008, at http://insidehighered.com/views/2008/04/01/wilson.

Witucke, Virginia. "Library School Policies Toward Preprofessional Work Experience," *Journal of Education for Librarianship* 16 (Winter 1976): 162-72.

Wood, Peter. "Truths R Us," *Inside Higher Education*, September 21, 2007, available at http://insidehighered.com/views/2007/09/21/wood.

Yagoda, Ben. *The Sound on the Page: Style and Voice in Writing* (New York: HarperResource, 2004).

Yakel, Elizabeth and Jeannette Bastian. "Is There a Core Archival Knowledge?: Archival Education in North American History Departments and Library Schools," paper presented at the Third SAA Archives Educators Forum, August 2, 2004, Simmons College, Boston, Massachusetts.

Young, Jeffrey R. "Film School: To Spice Up Course Work, Professors Make Their Own Videos," *Chronicle of Higher Education*, 54 (May 2, 2008), p. A13,, available at http://chronicle.com/free/v54/i34/34a01301.htm?utm_source=at&utm_medium=en.

Young, Jeffrey R. "MIT Professors Approve Campuswide Policy to Publish Scholarly Articles Free Online," *Chronicle of Higher Education*, 23 March 2009.

Young, Jeffrey R. "Will Electric Professors Dream of Virtual Tenure?" *Chronicle of Higher Education*, 55, issue 14, November 28, 2008, p. A13.

Zane, J. Peder, ed. *Remarkable Reads: 34 Writers and Their Adventures in Reading* (New York: W. W. Norton, 2004).

Zboray, Ronald J. *A Fictive People: Antebellum Economic Development and the American Reading Public* (New York: Oxford University Press, 1993).

Zemsky, Robert, Gregory R. Wegner, and William F. Massy. *Remaking the American University: Market-Smart and Mission-Centered* (New Brunswick, N.J.: Rutgers University Press, 2005).

Zerubavel, Eviatar. *The Clockwork Muse: A Practical Guide to Writing Theses, Dissertations, and Books* (Cambridge: Harvard University Press, 1999).

Ziegler, Helen T., Lois C. Bailey, and Mildred Clapp. "The Merits and Weaknesses of Library School Training as Seen by Recent Graduates," *Library Journal* 58 (July 1933): 585-89.

Zinsser, William, ed. *Inventing the Truth: The Art and Craft of Memoir*, rev. ed. (Boston: Houghton Mifflin Co., 1998).

Zinnser, William. *Writing About Your Life: A Journey into the Past* (New York: Marlowe & Co., 2004)

Index

A

AAUP. *See* American Association of University Professors.
Academia, fictional accounts of, 16-17
Academic Bill of Rights, 19
academic essay, writing of, 44-45
academic freedom
    American Association of University Professors' statements on, 42
    and university professors, 41-42, 134, 248
    debates on, 81-84
academics
    and time, 51
    as storytellers, 208
    as teachers, 40
    as writers, 44, 48, 215-17, 221-22, 259
    communicating with the public, 43
    specialization of, 43, 139, 203
    transition to public scholars, 221-22
    vs. public intellectuals, 18
access, to information, viii, xiv, 64, 207
accreditation
    of library schools, xviii,
    of MLIS degree, 270, 278
    shift towards, 151
    standards, 11, 272, 274
    See also American Library Association Committee on Accreditation (ALA COA)
adjunct faculty, 40, 93, 101
administrators, 13, 133, 189, 263. *See also* universities and colleges, presidents and deans of.
African-American studies, 85

ALA. *See* American Library Association.
ALA COA. *See* American Library Association Committee on Accreditation (ALA COA).
American Association of University Professors (AAUP)
    critique of, 41
    general secretary of, 267
    statements on academic freedom, 19, 42
American Library Association (ALA), xvii, 2, 9, 11, 123, 268, 270, 275, 276, 278
American Library Association Committee on Accreditation (ALA COA), xviii, 272, 274
Apple Macintosh products, 118
archival practices
    guidelines, 141, 148, 155, 163, 167
    literature on, 157-58
archival studies
    and I-schools, 179-80
    educators, 145, 148, 150, 154, 160-65, 175, 177, 257
    fieldwork, 165-66, 172-74, 178
    graduate education, 146-50, 159, 167-68
    innovations in, 151
    state of, 141-180
archives, learning about, 172-75
archivists, education of, xiii, 141, 248-50, 259
Association of Records Managers and Administrators, 146
Association of American University Presses, 62
Atwood, Margaret
    on fiction writers, 47
authors, scholars, 50, 52

Auster, Paul
    on stories, 73-74

B

Báez, Fernando
    on book destruction, 66
Barzun, Jacques
    on challenges of teaching, 34-35
    on intellectual matters, 13
    on scholarship, 103-04
    on university, 6-7, 122
Baker, Nicholson, 27, 59, 125, 189
Battles, Mathew
    on the history of the book, 75
Bernstein, Charles
    on role of academic faculty, 12
Birkerts, Sven
    on e-book readers, 63-64
    on reading, 26
Billington, James,
    on communication, 195-96
Blum, Susan
    on plagarism, 111
    on evaluation of teaching, 124
Bok, Derek
    on academics, 40
    on the purpose of the university, 7-8
    on complaints against the university, 39-40
    on corporate university, 122
book collecting, 70, 71
books
    future of, 74-75
    history of, 75
    as objects, 60, 67, 69, 187, 197
    as social capital, 67
    by librarians, 56
    destruction of, 60, 66
    digitization of, vii, 64, 72, 73
    electronic, xiii, 61, 65, 68, 75-76, 137, 190
    purpose of, 73
    printed, 67
    printing, xii
    textbooks, on archiving, 153
books, publishing of. *See* publishing.
Bookselling, 70
bookstores, 29
Borgman, Christine
    on preserving research, 69, 180
    on printed books, 70
Bradbury, Ray
    on the internet, 74
branding, of education, 100
Burgan, Mary
    on education, 267
business schools, 144

C

campus design, and Thomas Jefferson, 5
campus culture, 138, 201
Carnegie, Andrew, 96
Catholic University of Ireland, 5
certification, viii, 132, 149, 176
Chase, William
    on deterioration of English departments, xvii
Cioffi, Frank
    on quality of writing, 43
    on academic argument, 232
classes, sizes of, xx, xxi, 108, 229
classrooms,
    as heart of the university, 133, 134-35
    censorship in, 19-21
    dynamics in, 34
    re-imagining of, 36
    running, 243-44
    time spent in, 232
collecting, 71-71
commercialization, 72
communication, electronic, 42
controversy, 86
copyright issues, Google digitization, 72
corporate model of publishing, 136

INDEX

corporate university, xiv, 93, 94-114, 211-14, 261
corporate university model
    and administrators, 209
    affects on students, 111
    commentaries on, iv-x, 206
    influences on the modern university, 122
    strategic planning processes, 210
    students as customers in, 109
Coser, Lewis A.
    on public vs. academic intellectual, 18-19
courses
    on history of books, 61, 124
    online, xvi
credentials, 108-09
culture wars 82, 85, 87, 255
    and African-American studies, 85

D

Darnton, Robert
    on Google digitization, 72-73
Dewey, Melvil, 12, 90, 145, 193
digital preservation, 68
digital publishing, 77
digital readers. *See* e-book readers
digital resources
    increased interest in, 75
    scholars' dependence on, 67
digitization
    by university presses and libraries, 62
    by Google, vii, 64, 72, 73
    for preservation, 68
    topic in education, viii
dissertations, moving beyond, 51. *See also* PhDs.
Distance education
    and corporate university, 104
    and library schools, 90-91
    approaches to, 36

courses, online, xvi
    delivery of, 89
    economics of, 38-39
    enriching curriculum, 149
    teaching, online, 90
    masters degree, 91
    ownership of materials, 82
    value of, 267
diversification, viii, 194-96
doctoral programs, 13. *See also* PhDs.
Doctoral students, in Library and Information Science, xi

E

e-book readers, xiii, 63, 75
e-books
    in historical context, 65
    increase in, 61, 76
    influence of, xiii
    vs. print book, 65, 68
    See also e-book readers.
Economics,
    of library school, 92
    of online education, 38-39
education
    finances of, 99, 107, 114
    love of, 231
educational institutions
    Library Science vs. iSchools, 55
    ranking of, 10
Eisenhower, Dwight, on free universities, x
Electronic resources. *See* digital resources.
Email, as forma of communication, 195-96, 247-48
English departments
    accounts of, 34
    deterioration of, xvii, 131
    in fiction, 17
Enlightenment, 6, 72-73
Entrepreneurial, 131
ephemera, preservation of, 68
Epstein, Jason

account of publishing, 29
    on the internet, 121
essay writing, 44
ethics,
    in the classroom, 34
    teaching, 258-260

F
Facebook, xix, 98. *See also* social networking.
Faculty
    adjunct, 93, 101
    and academic freedom, 42
    as readers, 189
    disharmonious, 131, 194
    freedom of, 191
    of Library Information schools, public perception of, 255-57
    of library schools, 88, 182, 262
    of professional schools, 144, 230
    research of, 138
    salaries, 13
    See also faculty meetings.
Faculty meetings
    and adjunct faculty, 163
    bureaucratic nature of, 194
    fictional accounts of, 92
    not attending, 133, 188,
    re-structuring of, 240, 241
faith issues, and teaching, 34
farewell address, of President Dwight Eisenhower, x
fieldwork, archival, 165-66, 172-74, 178. *See also* archival studies.
Finkin, Matthew W. and Robert C. Post
    on academic freedom, 42
Fish, Stanley
    on political agendas, 83-84
    on the value of humanities, 96
Flaherty, Alice W.
    on writing and emotion, 48, 234
Franklin, Cynthia
    on academic memoir, xxi
Franzen, Jonathan
    on writing, 74
Frechette, Julie
    on use of technology in teaching, 37

G
Gardner, Howard
    on addressing audiences, 127
    on the disciplinary mind, 266-67
Germano, William
    on scholarly works and publication, 50, 52
    on the marketplace, 50
Giroux, Henry
    on adjunct faculty, 93
    on financing education, 114
    and Susan Searls, on implications of the corporate university, 97-98
Google
    commentary on business aims of, 64-65
    Google digital book project, vii, 64, 72, 73
    Google Scholar, 67
    lawsuit against, 73
    search engine, 236
Gorman, Michael, 2, 271
Gould, Eric
    on the corporate university, 90, 98, 203, 228-29, 230
    on knowledge, 199
Graff, Gerald
    on academic perspective, 202
    on Campus culture, 201
    on changing condition of the university, 86, 209
    on teaching and the culture wars, 38
Guess, Peter
    on virtual office hours, 106
    on modern students, 109-10

INDEX 329

Gutenberg, 31, 75, 77, 190

H
Hallman, Tom
    on storytelling, 48
Henry, Neil
    on journalism school, 14-15
Higher education
    commentaries on, xii
    marketing of, 89
    purpose of, xiv, 11
historiography, 87, 251-52
history of the book
    courses on, 61, 124
    shifting technologies, 75
hooks, bell
    on the academic and writing, 47

I
information
    retrieval, 28
    access to, xix, 64, 207
    schools. *See* iSchool.
Information Age
    xix, 120, 253-54, 260
    and decline of teaching, 41
information technology
    xiv, 19,
    analyzation of, xv
    as source of concern, vii
intellectual property, viii, 82
Internet
    as research source, 71, 110
    teaching of, 65
    perceptions of, 74
    use in classroom, 25, 37
iSchools
    and archival studies, 179-80
    and books, 27
    curriculum of, xv, 44, 73
    definition of, x, 1
    faculty, 262-64
    future of, 277-79
    mission of, xii, 28, 60
    movement, xx, 12, 269, 270
    place in the university, 265-66
    shifting of, xi, xiv, 13, 31, 70
    teaching in, 238
    vs. Library and Information Science (LIS) schools, 55, 274
    See also library schools; Library and Information Science (LIS) schools
information schools. *See* iSchools.
Information Technology (IT)
    courses, 96
    professionals, 135

J
Jacoby, Russell
    on audience of academic writing, 43-44
    on public scholarship, 251
Jeanneney, Noël
    on Google, 64
JESSE listserv
    debate on library and information science schools vs. iSchools, 55-56, 274
Johnson, Charles
    on writing, 232
Johnson, Robert
    on removal of books from libraries, 197

K
Kennedy, Donald
    on freedom of faculty members, 191
    on morality of faculty, 102
    on misunderstanding of the university's mission, 107, 216
Kerr, Clark
    on evolution of the institution, 6
keywords, academic, 14
Kindles, xiii, 62, 63, 64, 75, 76. *See also* e-book readers.

King, William Davies
   on collecting, 71-71
Kirp, David
   on marketing of higher education, 89
Kohn, Alfie
   on being educated, 39
   on corporate model, 95-96
   on education, 92
   on standardized tests, 132

L

Labaree, David
   on education schools, 143-44
Lamott, Anne
   on enthusiasm for writing, 214
   on practical aspects of writing, 45
   on publishing, 217
   on writing, 212, 215
Lanham, Richard
   on online education, economics of, 38-39
Lapham, Lewis
   on strategic planning, 113
   on Bush administration and Iraq, 208-09
learning, love of, 231
Levy, Steven
   on the future of the book, 74-75
Lewis, Harry R.,
   on purpose of higher education, 11
   on struggles of Harvard, 82
liberal education, 20
Librarian of Congress, 27, 59, 125, 189
librarians
   as authors, 56, 125
   building respect for, 56
   role of, 56
   the production of, 22-23
libraries
   and removal of books, 197
   as place, 69, 184-86,
   as social space, 59
Library of Alexandria, 59
library schools
   curriculum of, xv
   closings of, 2
   definition of, 1
   disappearing of, 133
   history of, xviii
   shifting focus of, xiv, 31, 113
   traditional value of, 115-
   vs. iSchools, 55
   See also iSchools; Library and Information Science (LIS) schools.
Library and Information Science (LIS) schools
   critical issues facing, xi
   definition of, 11
   shifting of, 13
   See also iSchools; library schools
literacy
   information, 234
   of public, 137
Lott, Brett
   on difficulty of writing, 233
   on truth, 198
   on writing creative nonfiction, 46-47
   on writing fiction vs. nonfiction, 205
Lukeman, Noah
   on craft of writing, 48

M

McMurty, Larry
   on book collecting and bookselling, 70
   on love of books, 61, 71
Macintosh products, 118
Mailer, Norman
   on writing, 205, 212, 215, 232
Manguel, Alberto
   A History of Reading, 57

INDEX   331

and education of librarians, 61
books of, 57-59
on books, 27, 188-89
on libraries, 59
on reading, 60, 185, 188, 236
Master's degrees, 88,
   and distance learning students, 91
master's degree in library science, 124
memoirs
   academic, xxi, 8
   of a public librarian, 125
   on publishing, 136-37
   value of, 46-47
minorities, 81, 85
multiculturalism, 84, 85, 87
Muscatine, Charles
   on undergraduate education, xx

N
National Archives (United States), 161
Newman, John Henry
   The Idea of the University, 5
Nussbaum, Martha C.
   on citizenship, 81, 130

O
Oates, Joyce Carol
   on writing, 46, 205-06, 213, 214, 217
office hours, virtual, 106
Online education. *See* distance education.
Open Source, 20

P
Paretsky, Sara
   on libraries, 69
   on writing, 50
Pastan, Linda
   on master's degree in library science, 125

Patriot Act, 20
Pawley, Christine
   on history in LIS scholarship, ix
pedagogical approaches
peer review, 29, 208, 213
personal narratives, of teaching, 8-13
PhD
   bell hooks' thoughts on, 47
   desire for, 124
   dissertations, 51
   doctoral programs, 13
plagiarism, 14, 111-12, 219
Pochoda, Phil
   on digital publishing, 77
Pope, Loren, guide to colleges, 9
Posner, Richard
   on academics as writers, 44, 221
Post, Robert C.
   on academic freedom, 134
   and Matthew W. Finkin, on academic freedom, 42
Postman, Neil
   on technology, 222
   transition to public scholar, 221-22
   on universities, 252-53
preservation
   and research material, 162
   arts of, 121
   of books, 64,
   of digital surrogates, 68,
   digital, 64, 68, 180
Presidents, U.S.
   Bush, George W., 208-09
   Eisenhower, Dwight, x
   Jefferson, Thomas, 5
presses, university, 62, 77-78
print culture, 138
printing, innovations in, 30
privacy, 42
professional schools
   faculty, 144, 230
   teaching in, 225-29, 263
professional writing, 197-99

professionalism, and decline of the university, 119, 127-28
public intellectual, vs. academic intellectual, 18
public scholarship
    definition of, 251
    LIS faculty contributions to, 53
publishing
    academic pressure, 50
    accounts of, 29, 136
    and the field of Library Science, 53
    as an industry, 136
    corporate model of, 136
    digital, 77
    history of, 28, 32, 136
    scholarly writing, 50, 52

R
ranking of educational institutes, 9-10, 128
reading
    as communal act, 197
    importance for children, 56
    joy of, 25, 27-29, 55-56
Readings, Bill
    on the corporate university, 97, 127, 130
    on the decline of the modern university, 103
recordkeeping, 153
reflective reading, xiv
research
    and digital resources, 67
    faculty, 138
    methodology, 109
    and the free university, x
Roy, Lucinda
    on Virgina Tech, xx
    on research universities and revenue, 231
Russo, Richard, 92

S
SAA. *See* Society of American Archivists.
Salaries, of faculty members, 13
Sayers, Frances Clarke
    on role of librarians, 56
schools of Library and Information Science, critical issues facing, xi
schools, information. *See* iSchools.
Schools, library. *See* library schools.
Scholars
    as authors, 50, 52
    dependence on digital resources, 67
Schriffen, Andre
    account of publishing, 136-37
September 11th, 20, 81-82, 108
social networking, xix, 20, 37
Society of American Archivists (SAA)
    organization, 141, 145, 146, 148, 149, 150, 159
    guidelines, 141, 155, 163, 167
speech codes, 81
standardized testing, 101, 132
storytelling
    and academics, 49, 208
    importance of, 73-74
    and postmodernism, 218
    and writing, 217
strategic planning, 210-11
students
    as citizens, 81
    as customers, 109-10, 130, 244
    as "digital natives", 109-10
    doctoral, xi
    mentoring and teaching, 231-34, 236
    middle schoolers, 41

T
time, as commodity, xxi, 51
Thompson, Clive
    on printed books, 67
Turchi, Peter

INDEX 333

on writing as cartography, 46-47, 208
teachers, role of, 35, 238
teaching
    and business, 239
    and faith issues, 34
    and technology, 38, 41
    as art form, 33, 40
    as business, 229-30
    critical approaches, xvi
    evaluation of, 112
    first hand accounts, 34
    holistic approach, 36
    importance of, 33-34
    online, 90
technology
    and decline of teaching, 41
    as teaching tool, 37-38
    critiques of, 117, 222
    in the classroom, 86, 105
    suspicion of, 135
    histories of, 120
    shifts in, 75, 116, 137
    teaching of, 37-38, 119
"technopoly", definition of, 222
textbooks, on archiving, 153
theory vs. practice, 95
Tompkins, Jane
    self-assessment, of teaching, 36

U
underachieving, 39
undergraduate educations
    recommendations for change, xx
universities
    decline of, 127
    evolution of, 6
    free, x
    and society, 129
    as professional schools, 129
    history of, 5, 251
    purpose of, 7, 140

University of Pittsburgh, xix, xx, 20
University of Virginia, 5
universities and colleges, presidents and deans of
    Bok, Derek (Harvard University), 7-8
    Colwell, Ernest Cadman (University of Chicago), 142
    Conway, Jill Ker (Smith College), 8
    Gora, Jo Ann M. (Ball State), 145-46
    Hexter, Ralph (Hampshire College), 109
    Lewis, Harry R. (Harvard University), 82
    Shapiro, Harold T. (University of Michigan and Princeton University), 126-27
    von Loewe Kreuter, Gretchen, 8
    Weingartner, Rudolph H. (University of Pittsburgh), 20-21, 107
    See also administrators.
University of Michigan Press, 62, 77
University of Pittsburgh, xix, xx, 20
University of Virginia, 5
university presses
    and digital publishing, 62, 77-78
    decline of, 29, 52
    University of Michigan Press, 62, 77
university presses, directors of
    Dougherty, Peter J. (Princeton University Press), 78
    Pochoda, Phil (University of Michigan Press), 77
U.S. News and World Report, 9, 248, 258

V

Viguers, Ruth Hill
   on building respect for librarians, 56
Virginia Tech, shooting at, xx, 231, 243
virtual libraries, 73
vocationalism, 40, 126, 138

W

Waters, Lindsay
   on decline of university presses, 29, 52
   on professionalism, 119
Weingartner, Rudolph H.
   on liberal education, 20-21, 107
   on cost of education, 107
Wills, Garry
   on Thomas Jefferson and campus design, 5
Wikipedia, 64, 73, 109, 110
World Wide Web. *See* Internet.
Writers
   as contributors to history, 220
   of fiction, 47
writing
   and audience, 44
   and cartography, 46-47, 208
   and emotion, 48, 234
   and the corporate university, 210-14
   and storytelling, 217
   art of, 45, 48, 200-02
   as vocation, 202-05
   challenges of, 205, 233
   craft of, 48
   fiction vs. non-fiction, 205
   formation of academic argument, 232
   practical aspects of, 45
   scholarly articles, 50, 52
   styles of, 47-48, 234
   the academic essay, 44-45
   teaching, 43, 234-36
   technologies, 116-17

Y

Yagoda, Ben
   on writing styles, 47-48, 234-35

Z

Zinsser, William
   on writing, 196, 211, 213, 215-16, 217, 237
   on being published, 22

About the Author

Richard J. Cox is Professor, Archival Studies, University of Pittsburgh School of Information Sciences. He has worked as both an archivist and records manager in a private historical society and in state and local government. Dr. Cox is the author of fifteen books on archives and library and information science topics. He is the only three-time winner of the Waldo G. Leland Award given by the Society of American Archivists for the best book on archives in a given year. He is also a Fellow of the Society.

www.ingramcontent.com/pod-product-compliance
Lightning Source LLC
Chambersburg PA
CBHW021932290426
44108CB00012B/812